# Catalogue of the Collection of American Art at Randolph-Macon Woman's College

## A Selection of Paintings, Drawings, and Prints

Second Edition

# Catalogue of the Collection of American Art at Randolph-Macon Woman's College

## A Selection of Paintings, Drawings, and Prints

Mary Frances Williams

University Press of Virginia
Charlottesville

Supported by a grant from the National Endowment for the Arts in Washington, D.C., a Federal Agency

THE UNIVERSITY PRESS OF VIRGINIA


*Second edition 1977*

Printed in the United States of America

*Library of Congress Cataloging in Publication Data*

Williams, Mary Frances
Catalogue of the collection of American art at Randolph-Macon Woman's College.

First ed. (1965) issued by Randolph-Macon Woman's College under title: Catalogue of the collection of American painting at Randolph-Macon Woman's College.
Bibliography : p.
Includes index.
1. Art, American—Catalogs. 2. Art—Virginia—Lynchburg—Catalogs. 3. Randolph-Macon Woman's College, Lynchburg, Va. I. Randolph-Macon Woman's College, Lynchburg, Va. II. Randolph-Macon Woman's College, Lynchburg, Va. Catalogue of the collection of American art at Randolph-Macon Woman's College. III. Title.

N6505.W53 1977 760'.0973'0740155671 76-51281
ISBN 0-8139-0591-5

# Contents

# Illustrations Preceding Those in the Catalogue

# Foreword to the Second Edition

This second edition includes up-dated exhibition records and literary references for the works catalogued in the edition of 1965. It publishes acquisitions by purchase or gift since 1964. There are many more statements by living artists.

Two new sections have been introduced. The short one on drawings includes nearly all the examples of this medium that the College owns. The section on prints, however, can offer only a sampling of a rather large group.

This edition presents the first full listing of Randolph-Macon's works by Arthur B. Davies in all media: oil, watercolor, drawing, and graphics. More complete descriptions can be made when the works are released from storage, where they are currently placed during alterations in the Art Gallery on Quinlan Street.

The history of the Collection has been extended to the present. Because this is a Bicentennial project, one part calls attention to the cooperation in the arts that the College has always enjoyed with Lynchburg, the Commonwealth of Virginia, and Washington, D.C.

The matching grant from the National Endowment for the Arts is greatly appreciated, and thanks are extended not only to that agency but also to Mrs. Julia M. Jacobsen for her assistance in preparing the grant application.

Special thanks are tendered to President William F. Quillian, Jr., and to Dorothy S. Vickery for their invaluable editorial advice, also to Elliott R. Twery and Robert S. Fuller, both in the art department, and to Louise A. Blunt of Lynchburg for reading the historical sections. The editor thanks M. Gweneth Humphreys and Carl Stern for help with the metric system, Mary Virginia Kagey for proofreading, and Mrs. Harvey K. Hoyt for preparation of the manuscript.

The College continues to owe a debt of gratitude to several persons who have died since the foreword of 1965 was written: Mrs. Beatrice von Keller and Dr. Herbert C. Lipscomb, who were chiefly responsible for the growth of the Collection; and also Ruth H. Blunt and Mrs. John M. Gilchrist.

MARY F. WILLIAMS
Professor of Art and Curator
of the Collection, emeritus

*December 1976*

# Foreword to the First Edition

The purpose of this book is to celebrate the seventy-fifth anniversary of Randolph-Macon Woman's College in 1965–66 by making known its collection of American paintings. For alumnae this is a handbook of the paintings they remember and the new ones they may see. Hopefully, all Randolph-Macon students who read what the artists say and what the records tell will find the paintings more meaningful. As a catalogue this book offers the documentation needed by scholars and curators. The book should also offer assurance to potential donors that their gifts of works of art or gifts for art acquisitions will be well placed at Randolph-Macon Woman's College.

A history of the Collection precedes the catalogue proper. The first and largest section presents paintings by artists too well known to require biographies; the section on works by faculty members and alumnae includes biographies. Every painting catalogued is reproduced. In addition there are reproductions of several drawings and paintings not in the Collection and not hitherto published with the paintings to which they are related.

The author gratefully acknowledges the most valuable assistance of Mrs. Beatrice von Keller, Dr. Herbert C. Lipscomb, and Miss Harriet Fitzgerald, the three persons most responsible for selecting the paintings. Without their help in matters of fact and emphasis this book could not have been begun or finished. The aid of Dr. Gillie A. Larew, dean emeritus, Dr. Roberta D. Cornelius, professor of English, emeritus, and College archivist; and the late Dr. Theodore H. Jack, president emeritus, was also invaluable. Heartfelt thanks are expressed to these persons for sharing so generously their personal experiences. Thanks are given to Dr. William F. Quillian, Jr., president of Randolph-Macon Woman's College, for his encouragement and advice and for College grants for research in the summers of 1958 and 1964.

The collaboration of the artists who laid aside their paint brushes to write the comments now being published is deeply appreciated.

I am grateful to A. McLaren Young, curator of Fine Art Collections, University of Glasgow, for photographs related to "Tanagra" by James McNeill Whistler and for permission to reproduce them; also to the Smithsonian Institution's Freer Gallery of Art for a photograph of its related Whistler drawing; and to Durand-Ruel and Company, Paris, for two photographs related to the painting by Mary Cassatt. Thanks are extended to the directors of the Herron Art Museum of the Art Institute of Indianapolis and of the Davenport (Iowa) Municipal Art Gallery, and to Hirschl and Adler Galleries, New York, for permission to publish photographs of paintings related to ones in the College Collection.

For permission to quote unpublished letters in their possession, the author expresses her appreciation to Mrs. Beatrice von Keller, Mrs. Robert A. Scott, and Dr. Herbert C. Lipscomb. The cooperation of Mrs. Paul A. Rinden '51 in research on Thomas Cole is appreciated.

Mrs. William H. Howell, Jr., and her staff at the Frick Art Reference Library are gratefully thanked for prompt answers cheerfully given and for permission to quote the diaries of Theodore Robinson.

Misses Ruth and Louise Blunt, Mrs. John Marshall Ribble, and Miss Mary Virginia Kagey deserve special mention for reading the history of the Collection in manuscript as does Mrs. John M. Gilchrist for research in New York.

May this book present the paintings of the College Collection in a clearer light so that they may give more instruction and keener delight. Thus they, too, will celebrate the founding of Randolph-Macon Woman's College on March 12, 1891.

M.F.W.

*Lynchburg, Virginia*
*February 1, 1965*

# The Collection of American Art at Randolph-Macon Woman's College

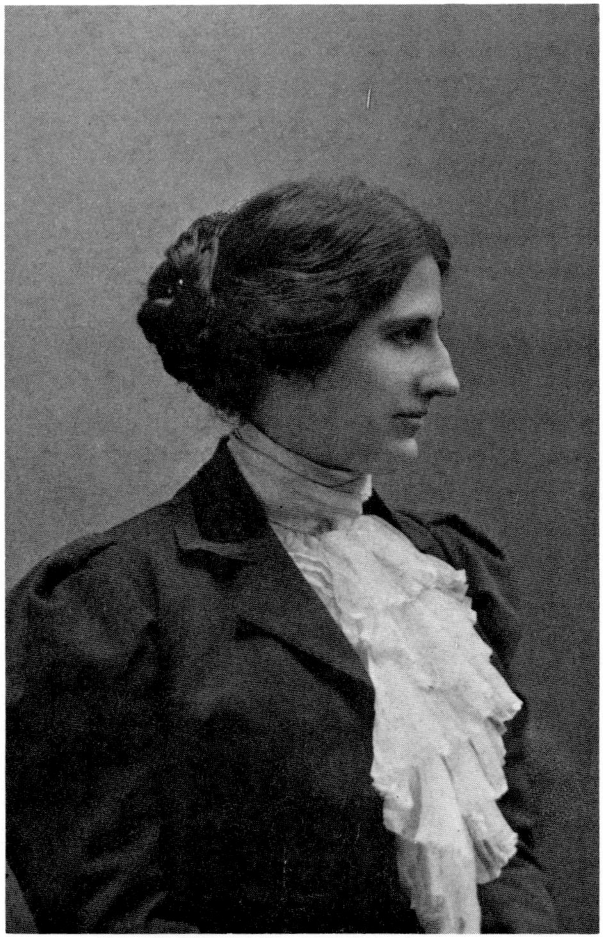

Figure 1. Louise Jordan Smith in a photograph of unknown date.

# History of the Collection

## The First Period: 1893–1928

### *Louise Jordan Smith* (1868–1928)

When Randolph-Macon Woman's College, founded in 1891, opened its doors to students in 1893, the young ladies were taught drawing and painting by Louise Jordan Smith, then twenty-five years of age. (See figure 1.) She was a painter, a Virginian, and a cousin of the founder and first president, William Waugh Smith. She taught French also and took a leave of absence from 1895 to 1898 to polish both her French and her art by studying at the Académie Julian in Paris. Miss Smith's "Self-Portrait" (#158 in this catalogue) depicts a gentle lady. Actually, she was strong-minded and became, by the later 1920s, a rather eccentric professor.

The stories of Miss Louise's personality (transmitted orally for the most part) and records of her activities reveal how lively and even adventurous those early years of Randolph-Macon were, how filled with consciousness of growth. Alumnae of the turn of the century remember vividly how exciting it was to have a role to play in the experiment of collegiate education for women south of the Potomac. Art was to be important in fulfilling the aims that the founders expressed in these words:

> We wish to establish in Virginia a college where our young women may obtain an education equal to that given in our best colleges for young men, and under environments in harmony with the highest ideals of womanhood; where the dignity and strength of fully-developed faculties and the charm of the highest literary culture may be acquired by our daughters without loss to woman's crowning glory—her gentleness and grace.

Louise Jordan Smith played a triple role. She was artist, professor, and organizer. She understood how the handling of a brush and the study of originals could open the eyes of the young. (See figure 2.) She planned exhibitions, created an art association, brought visiting artists on campus, and started the College Collection.[1]

During the years between Miss Smith's return to Virginia from Paris in 1898 and the formal start of the Collection in 1920 she must have cherished the hope that Randolph-Macon might be able to provide for its students an environment of culture. The contrast between what Paris had given her and what the bare walls of the new college offered her art students must have stirred her to action. Her almost systematic expansion of artistic activities in the early years of the College makes it seem that she planned from the start to have a collection, although the word "collection" hardly appears in printed records before 1920.

### *The First Painting*

When the Class of 1907 decided to have a portrait of President William Waugh Smith painted (#21), it was at the repeated insistence of his cousin, Miss Louise, that the commission was given to William Merritt Chase. At that time Chase was the outstanding portrait painter and art teacher in New York. This selection of a nationally, even internationally, recognized painter for the very first academic portrait owned by the College set a pattern. Subsequent commissions for portraits

1. Elizabeth Nottingham, "Silhouette of Miss Louise," *Alumnae Bulletin* 32 (November 1938):3–7.

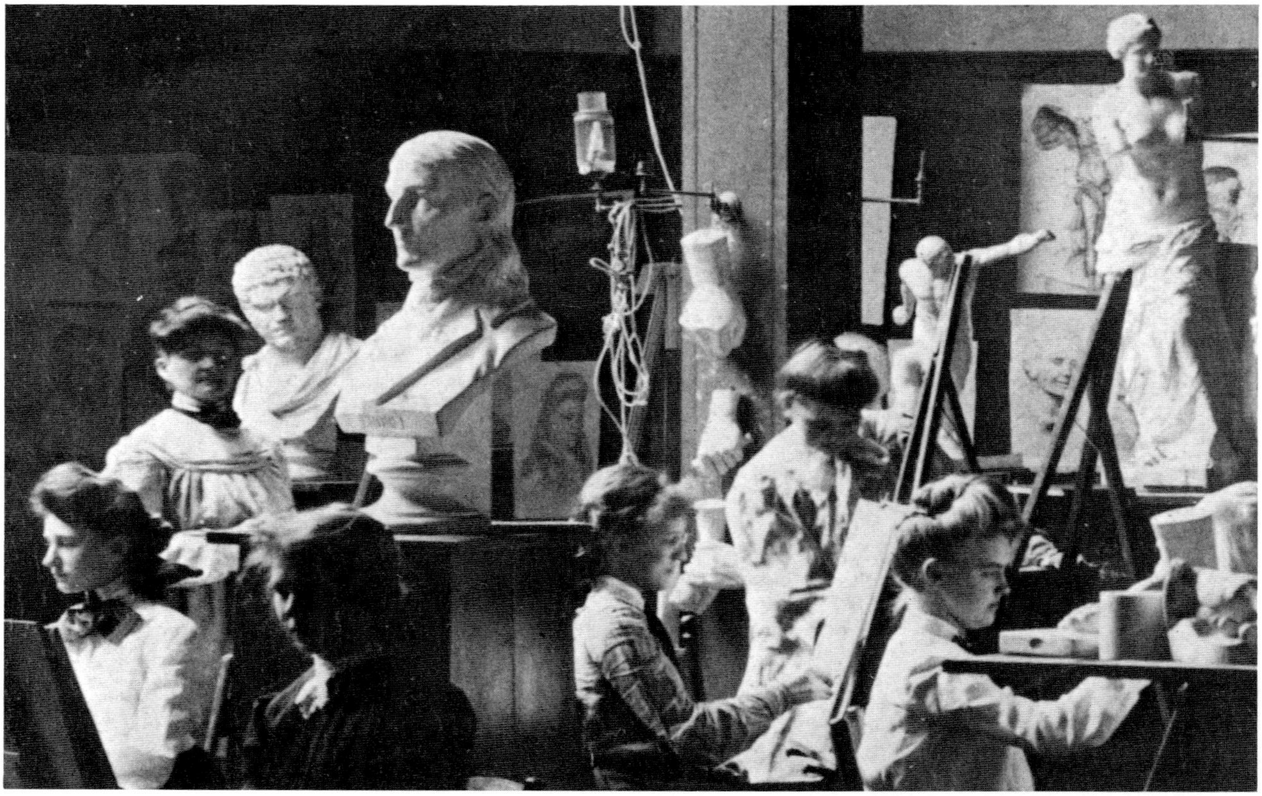

Figure 2. Students in the Tower Studio, about 1906, with plaster casts from Paris. Left side of a photograph given to the art department by Mrs. J. I. Hamaker (M. Ray Parker '12) in 1957. (For the right side, see figure 8).

of presidents have been given only to painters who would create a work of art for the Collection, as well as a likeness.

In the story of Dr. Smith's portrait, we see for the first time how goodwill toward this woman's college in Virginia helped the Collection. On this occasion the sum raised by the Class of 1907 for Dr. Smith's portrait was the artist's fee for head and shoulders only. But William Merritt Chase felt that Dr. Smith's hands ought to be shown, so he simply painted a three-quarter length portrait and included the hands without any additional charge.

*The First Annual Exhibition*

After occasional loan exhibitions in the earlier years, Louise Jordan Smith installed her First Annual Exhibition in 1911. Like most of the Annuals, the first was a loan exhibition from New York. It is unlikely that any other American college or university had committed itself to annual exhibitions as early as 1911. Except for the omission of one Annual during World War I, the Randolph-Macon series has been continuous. The Annual of the Bicentennial year 1976 was the sixty-fifth.

The exhibitions included paintings, sculpture, and graphic arts, both European and American. About 1964 one of Miss Louise's students, Harriet Fitzgerald, herself a painter, wrote: "She understood and was sympathetic to the point of view of Post-Impressionism. She had mingled with its lesser and some of its greater followers in France. Her students were thrilled that she was a personal friend of Henri Rousseau, for instance. But she could see beyond doctrine or idiom or fashion. She saw that there was originality and integrity in American painting."

In 1915 Louise Jordan Smith added a one-semester course in American painting and sculpture to the curriculum in art history. This was five years in advance of any general recognition of the American heritage in art.

### *The Cornerstone of a Collection*

By 1920 the series of annual exhibitions had reached the ninth. Perhaps the presence of George Bellows's "Men of the Docks" (#9; color plate on page 25) in the Ninth Annual Exhibition was what made 1920 a propitious year for starting a collection. Faculty, staff, students, and friends in the community banded together to raise twenty-five hundred dollars to buy "Men of the Docks" from Mr. Bellows as the cornerstone of a permanent collection. The president of the hastily assembled Randolph-Macon Art Association of Lynchburg was T. Moody Campbell, professor of German. The director was Miss Smith.

You may read in the catalogue entry for "Men of the Docks" Dr. Campbell's account of his visit to Mr. Bellows, to whom the painting had been returned after the close of the exhibition. When Dr. Campbell called on the artist and proposed that a permanent collection be started with this painting, Mr. Bellows felt honored and he set a moderate price. He shipped the painting back to Randolph-Macon even before the whole sum had been raised. The campus newspaper, *The Sun Dial*, tells us that the painting stood in its crate, waiting for Miss Smith's last appeal (printed in the issue of May 29, 1920) to bring contributions of exactly one hundred and seventy-six dollars more. Only when this amount had been received was "Men of the Docks" finally uncrated.

Now that it is the custom to think of Bellows's "Men of the Docks" as the cornerstone of the Randolph-Macon Collection, it is interesting to speculate on what the character of the Collection might have become if the choice had fallen on some other work in the Ninth Annual, such as a painting by Childe Hassam, Robert Henri, or William Glackens, or a sculpture by Gutzon Borglum, Malvina Hoffman, or Anna Vaughan Hyatt, all of whom were represented in that Annual. In the account that Dr. Campbell wrote for the first edition of this catalogue he assures us, however, that for him and Miss Smith "Men of the Docks" was clearly the masterpiece of the exhibition. Many think it is still the best painting in the Collection, although at first some viewers grumbled about the "commonplace subject" and the "crude brushwork."

Very important for the future of art at the College is a statement published by the Randolph-Macon Art Association of Lynchburg.[2] It reads: "The Association is proceeding on the assumption that the only way to cultivate good taste in art is to study objects of art frequently, seriously, and at leisure." Randolph-Macon is still proceeding on that assumption.

### *The Fine Arts Fund*

It is easy to imagine why, after five years of continuous fund raising by the Art Association, Miss Smith inspired the students of the 1925–26 session to request the trustees to raise the College fees five dollars per student per year for a Fine Arts Fund, which would finance an exhibition, a play, a concert, and the purchase of works of art. The president of student government that year

2. From a folder in the archives of the College.

was Harriet Fitzgerald, who sponsored the motion and thus performed the first of her many acts in behalf of the Collection.

In 1926 The Randolph-Macon Art Association of Lynchburg was terminated. The Fine Arts Fund has been providing income ever since.

### *The Louise Jordan Smith Fund*

Shortly before her death in December 1928, Louise Jordan Smith made her last will and testament. She left to the College her antiques and paintings, wanting them to be kept together and exhibited as a unit. Her financial assets she left as a trust fund for the purchase of paintings by Randolph-Macon.

Vital for the quality of the Collection is the method she devised for acquiring fewer, but better, pictures. First she limited the frequency of purchases. "The said income shall be used . . . only every second year, this provision being made so as to provide enough money before any expenditure to purchase a real work of art."

In addition, Miss Smith put the selection into the hands of the art department and advisors in museums and universities outside of Lynchburg. Her will says:

> No purchase shall be made except with the written approval of two well recognized experts. My purpose and object in having all contemplated purchases before they are made first approved in writing by well recognized expert judges of pictures and works of art is to keep a high standard of excellence in the things that go into said collection, and to avoid any and all mistakes in the purchase, so far as possible, and I direct the said . . . Bank, to rigidly insist upon this requirement.

Considering these terms, one must conclude that the method of selection by popular vote referred to in the following sentence from *The Sun Dial* of March 20, 1925, had not satisfied Louise Jordan Smith's standards for a collection: "The student body and faculty cooperate with the Board of Trustees in financing the purchase of the pictures selected by vote at each annual exhibit."

Miss Smith left the College at liberty to acquire works of art from any country and in any medium, including sculpture. In 1936, the first year that the Smith Fund could be used, the Annual had not only American paintings, but also works by Beckmann, Degas, Derain, Metzinger, Modigliani, Picasso, and Renoir. One of the four paintings by Renoir was seriously considered for purchase, but a canvas not in the Annual, "Mrs. Scott's House," by Edward Hopper (#102; color plate on page 29), became the first acquisition through the Louise Jordan Smith Fund.

## The Second Period (1928–52)

Beatrice von Keller and Herbert C. Lipscomb, the two persons who built the Randolph-Macon Collection in the second phase of its history—the twenty-four years after Miss Smith's death—followed her new and stricter policy: to purchase a few works of high quality after unhurried searches. Dr. Theodore H. Jack, who was president of the College from 1933 to 1952, heartily concurred. (See #163.)

### *Beatrice von Keller* (1884–1975)

Mrs. von Keller headed the Art Department from 1928 until her retirement in 1952. She had studied at the Royal Academy, Stockholm, and had become familiar with the museums of Paris and Dresden during her married life. As a widow, she had returned to the United States to teach and study. She received her M.A. degree from the University of Chicago before coming to Randolph-Macon. Mrs. von Keller's skill in judging paintings at first sight in dealers' galleries in New York has been described by Agnes Addison Gilchrist: "By some process of unselfconscious and uncerebrated and inarticulate communion, she could divine the true essence of the painting, no matter what idiom it used."[3]

In her trips to the galleries Mrs. von Keller was frequently accompanied by Harriet Fitzgerald, who as painter and trustee of the College still remains in close contact with its activities, particularly in the field of art.

Mrs. von Keller recommended paintings to the trust officers of the Louise Jordan Smith Fund from 1936, the year it was first used, until her retirement in 1952—sixteen years later. During three of these years she was absent to serve as co-director of the Virginia Museum, Richmond, while its director was in the armed services. During this period Dr. Jack called upon Miss Fitzgerald, who, in the matter of purchases, acted as liaison between the College authorities in Lynchburg, Mrs. von Keller in Richmond, and the art market in New York.

Harriet Fitzgerald said this about Beatrice von Keller's judgment of paintings: "She sensed paintings directly and fell in love with them." On the other hand, Mrs. von Keller wrote of Harriet: "She deserves much credit for the Collection's quality."

Mrs. von Keller realized, as Miss Smith had, that a collection that fulfills its educational purpose must include some paintings that are well in advance of popular taste. Some of her acquisitions, such as John Marin's "Taos Mountain" (#130), were made in spite of strong objections from the campus community, and one, Franklin Watkins's "Negro Spiritual" (#179), was kept in the Collection in spite of injured feelings in certain quarters. Mrs. von Keller defended her acquisitions. Eventually even persons who had at first averted their eyes when walking past "that ugly mountain" were able to see its strength.

The Annual Exhibitions during this period continued to include sculpture as well as painting, and French as well as American work, although paintings by Americans predominated. One Annual (1940), however, consisted entirely of twenty-two paintings by eleven French artists, alphabetically from Cézanne to Vlaminck.

3. Agnes Addison Gilchrist, "The Growth of an Art Collection," *Alumnae Bulletin* 50 (November 1956):30–33.

### *Herbert C. Lipscomb* (1882–1973)

Herbert C. Lipscomb, professor and head of the department of Latin, also chairman of the Fine Arts Committee, administered the Fine Arts Fund from its inception in 1926 until his retirement in 1955, a period of twenty-nine years. (See figure 3.) It was Dr. Lipscomb who, in accordance with the wish of the Fine Arts Com-

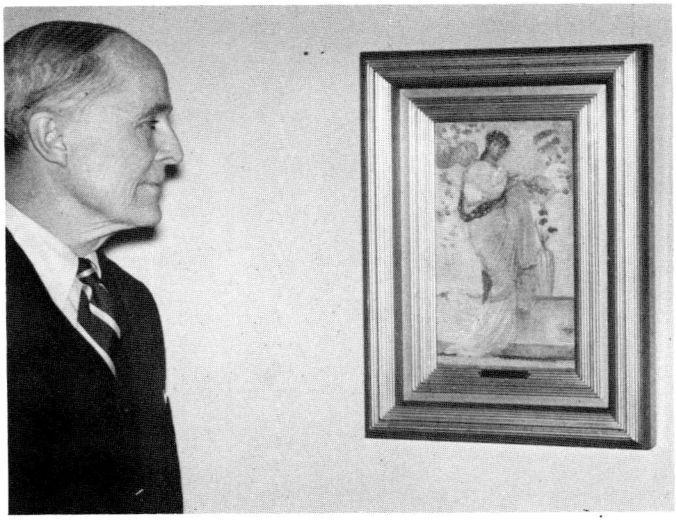

Figure 3. Dr. Herbert C. Lipscomb in 1953, with Whistler's "Tanagra" (#182), his final purchase as chairman of the Fine Arts Committee.

mittee, prevailed on Harry Wehle of the Metropolitan Museum of Art, New York, to prepare a list of American painters who should be represented in the permanent Collection in addition to those, such as Bellows, already included.[4]

For the record, we list below—alphabetically by artist—the sixteen major acquisitions by purchase and commission in this middle period of twenty-four years in the history of the Collection, from 1928 to 1952.

| *Catalogue Number* | *Artist* | *Title* | *Fund* |
|---|---|---|---|
| 18 | John Carroll | "Summer Afternoon" | Smith |
| 19 | John Carroll | "Portrait of Dr. Herbert C. Lipscomb" | Commission |
| 20 | Mary Cassatt | "Sketch of Mother and Daughter Looking at the Baby" | Smith |
| 25 | Thomas Cole | "Corway Peak, New Hampshire" | Fine Arts |
| 66 | Thomas Eakins | "Portrait Sketch of William H. Macdowell" | Fine Arts |
| 95 | Childe Hassam | "Early Evening After Snowfall" | Fine Arts |
| 98 | Robert Henri | "Tom" | Smith |
| 101 | Winslow Homer | "Paris Courtyard" | Fine Arts |
| 102 | Edward Hopper | "Mrs. Scott's House" | Smith |
| 104 | George Inness | "Perugia and the Valley" | Fine Arts |
| 130 | John Marin | "Taos Mountain" | Smith |
| 141 | Georgia O'Keeffe | "Yellow Cactus" | Smith |
| 145 | M. Prendergast | "The Idlers" | Smith |
| 149 | Albert P. Ryder | "A Country Girl" | Fine Arts |
| 157 | John Sloan | "Sun and Wind on the Roof" | Fine Arts |
| 179 | Franklin Watkins | "Negro Spiritual" | Smith |

*Robert G. McIntyre* (1885–1965)

Mrs. von Keller, Dr. Lipscomb, and Dr. Jack in Lynchburg and Miss Fitzgerald in New York evoked the sympathy, the interest, and the aid of some of the most distinguished American dealers of their generation. They included John F. Kraushaar, Albert Milch, Frank K. M. Rehn, and Robert G. McIntyre. These dealers had the want list. They knew not only the names but also the period or style that Randolph-Macon sought and the quality required. The search went on more or less continuously.

The late Mr. McIntyre's friendship and advice when he was president of the Macbeth Gallery, New York (William Macbeth, Inc.), as well as after his retirement, were of greatest assistance. He not only helped to make modest funds buy good paintings, often waiving large portions of his legitimate commission, but also directed numerous gifts to the Collection. For example, Mr. McIntyre's letter of December 11, 1944, to Dr. Jack, offering Theodore Robinson's "Valley of the Seine" (#147), begins: "One of our clients wishes to present a painting to whatever gallery I think would be glad to have it and would appreciate its

4. Dr. Lipscomb described this in his article, "Fiftieth Annual Exhibition: A Significant Anniversary," *Alumnae Bulletin* 54 (June 1961):19–20.

fine quality. . . . I know of no collection more worthy to be the recipient of this fine gift than that of Randolph-Macon."[5]

After Mr. McIntyre and Dr. Jack had met at the presentation of the Bliss gift (described in the next section), their letters showed the development of a warm and humorous relationship. On December 4, 1950, Robert McIntyre wrote: "Through my undying and unflagging interest, my determination to make something worthwhile out of that little school of yours down in the Virginia hinterland, you will soon receive two paintings: . . . You may receive others next year."

An outstanding gift directed to Randolph-Macon by Mr. McIntyre was Rufino Tamayo's "Troubadour" (#166), donated by Stephen C. Clark. This painting is American in the broadest sense of the word.

### *Alfred Stieglitz* (1864–1946)

From Alfred Stieglitz, the photographer at No. 291 Fifth Avenue and later at An American Place, the College purchased John Marin's "Taos Mountain" (#130) and Georgia O'Keeffe's "Yellow Cactus" (#141). The quality of Stieglitz's relationship with Mrs. von Keller is summed up in the dedication that he wrote in her copy of *Letters of John Marin* (privately printed for An American Place, New York, 1931).

> For Beatrice von Keller from Alfred Stieglitz: This book will ever remind her of the wonderful hour—or hours—she and I spent at An American Place looking at Marins and O'Keeffes and Doves and just ever being aware of The Place—M'ch 26/42[6]

### *The Bliss Collection*

The largest and most important group of paintings received by Randolph-Macon as a single gift came from Mrs. Cornelius N. Bliss (later Mrs. A. Conger Goodyear) in 1949 from the estate of her sister-in-law Lizzie P. Bliss, on the advice of Mr. McIntyre, trustee of the estate. (See figure 4.) The forty-one works by Arthur B. Davies in this gift include five oils, six watercolors, twelve drawings, and eighteen prints. Other works by Davies came into the Collection later as gifts from Mrs. Goodyear and from members of the Macbeth family. These gifts have made Randolph-Macon's holding of paintings by Davies one of the four or five largest in the country.

The Bliss collection also contains twelve oils and watercolors by artists other than Davies. Five are by Walt Kuhn.

In 1952 President Jack accepted as an anonymous gift to the College a fireproof, air-conditioned art gallery. It was built that year on a rise at the western end of Quinlan Street, northeast of the main group of College buildings. Constructed only shortly before his retirement and the retirement of Mrs. von Keller as head of the art department, this gallery signaled the end of one era and the start of another.

## The Third Period: 1952–73

A third period in the history of the Collection began in 1952 with Dr. William F. Quillian, Jr., as president of the College and Dr. Mary F. Williams as head of the art department, with a dual appointment as professor of art and curator of the Collection.

### *The Art Gallery*

The Art Gallery (on Quinlan Street) was dedicated in December 1952 with a loan exhibition of American paintings from the National Gallery of Art in Washington. The new building provided security also for several other major exhibitions. At the inauguration of Dr. Quillian in March 1953, sixty-two works from the College Collection were

5. This quotation and the one of December 4, 1950, that follows are from letters in the president's files.

6. Quoted by permission of Georgia O'Keeffe for the Estate of Alfred Stieglitz.

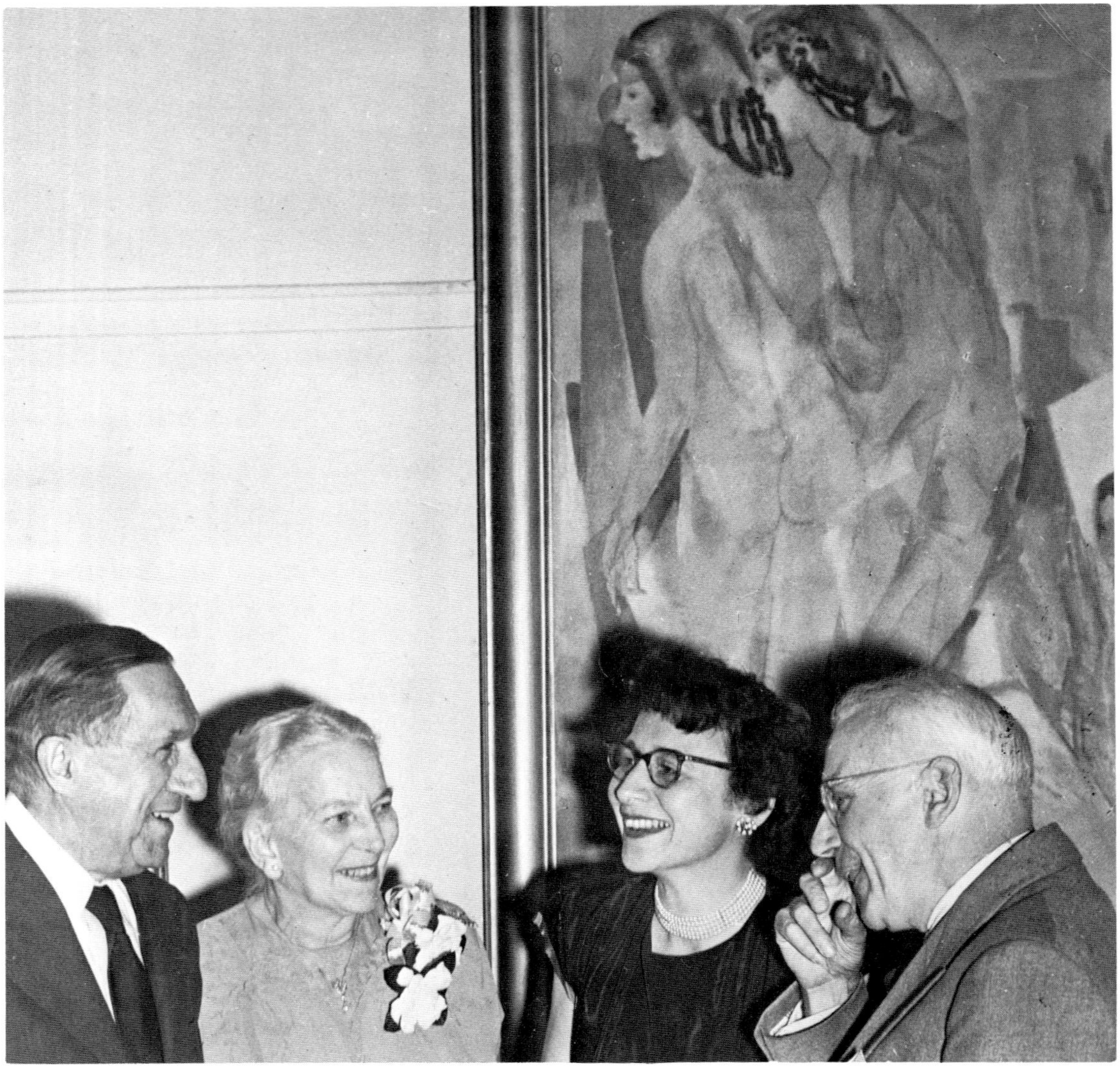

Figure 4. The presentation by Robert G. McIntyre of paintings from the collection of Lizzie P. Bliss, on October 20, 1949, given by Mrs. C. N. Bliss. Left to right: Professor T. Moody Campbell, first president of the Randolph-Macon Art Association of Lynchburg; Mrs. Beatrice von Keller, head of the art department; Harriet Fitzgerald '26, of New York, trustee of the College; and Robert G. McIntyre, president of the Macbeth Gallery (William Macbeth, Inc.). Behind them is "Decoration" (#33), by Arthur B. Davies.

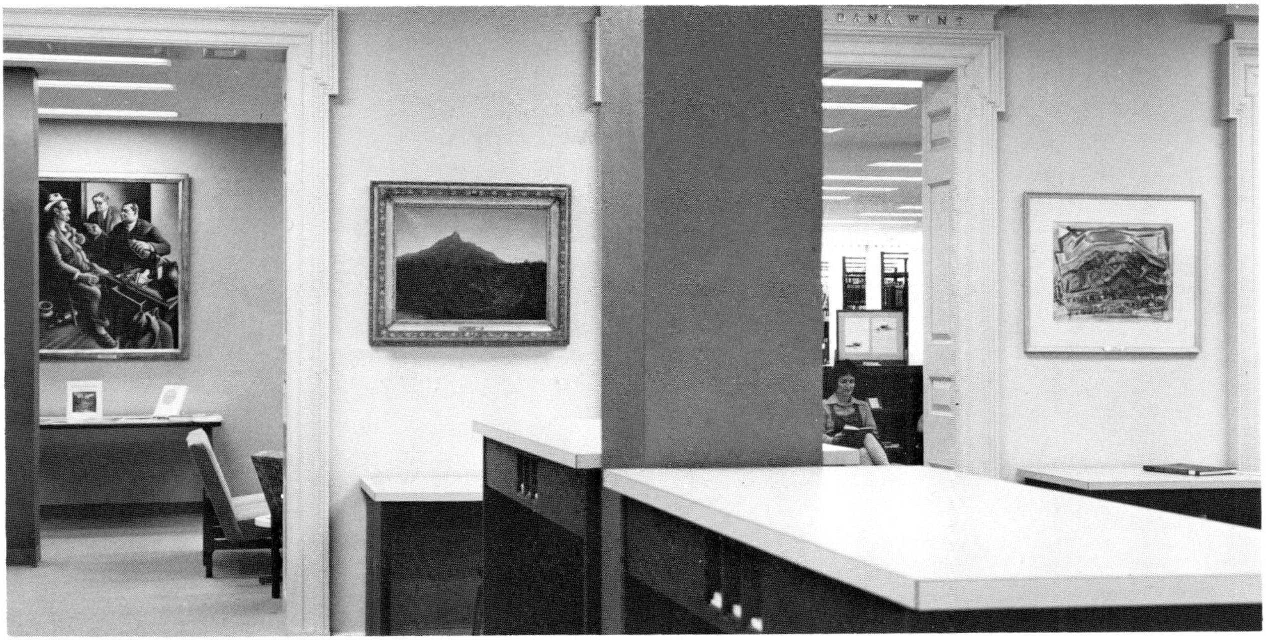

Figure 5. View of the Herbert C. Lipscomb Library, looking into the Charles A. Dana Wing in 1976. Shown from left to right are: "Preparing the Bill" (#10) by Thomas Hart Benton, "Corway Peak, New Hampshire" (#25) by Thomas Cole, a letter written and illustrated with drawings (#209) by Andrew Wyeth, and "Taos Mountain" (#130) by John Marin.

assembled in the gallery. "Eighteenth and Nineteenth Century Paintings from Lynchburg Homes" was shown in 1954, thanks to generous lenders and the assistance of Mrs. E. Alban Watson of Lynchburg. Having the gallery also facilitated a loan of eleven twentieth-century American paintings from the collection of Mr. and Mrs. Roy R. Neuberger of New York in 1956. In 1957, the Phillips Collection in Washington lent eleven paintings by artists represented at Randolph-Macon.

Eventually three special rooms were arranged: the Arthur B. Davies Room, the Louise Jordan Smith Room (see figure 13, below), and the room of the Margaret H. Wright Collection of Graphic Art. For each Annual Exhibition, however, two or more of these rooms had to be dismantled. Except during Annuals, the Art Gallery attracted fewer visitors than the loan exhibitions in the English-Art Building and in Main Hall, where shows changed monthly. Furthermore, the superior lighting and the relative protection of the Charles A. Dana Wing (1967) of the Lipscomb Library made it become virtually an art gallery, one with generous visiting hours. (See figure 5.) In Main Hall, too, some of the best paintings could be seen by visitors and students at all hours. (See figure 6.)

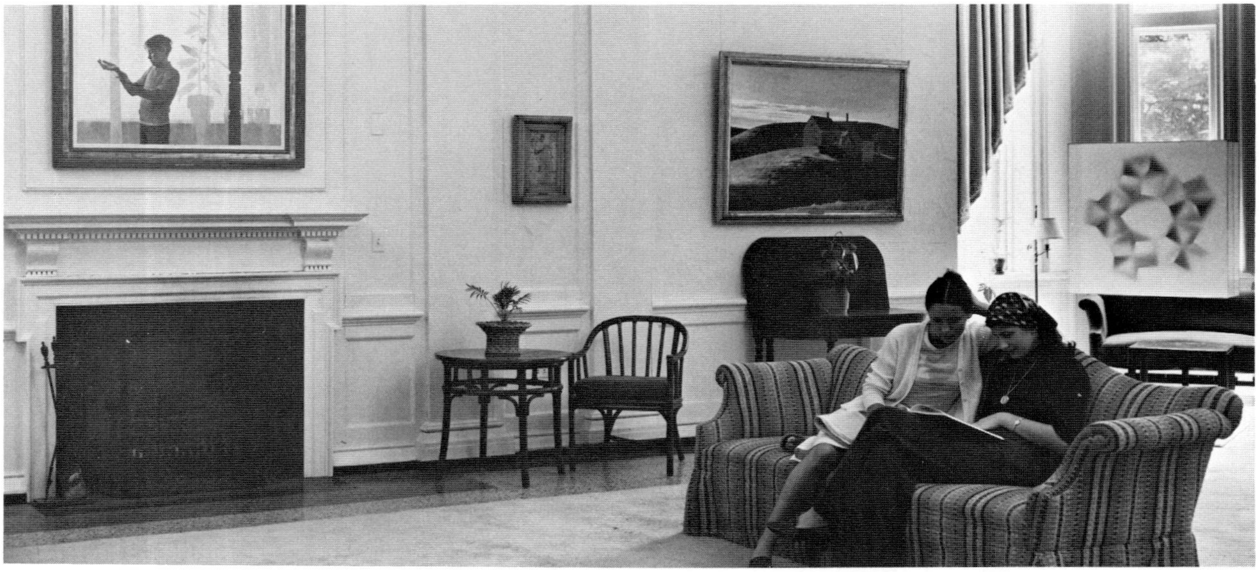

Figure 6. View of Main Hall Lobby (east side) in 1976. Shown from left to right are: "Pulse" (#176) by Robert Vickrey, "Tanagra" (#182) by Whistler, "Mrs. Scott's House" (#102) by Edward Hopper, and the acrylic construction "Shadow Box," made in 1969 by Leo Rabkin (born 1919). "Shadow Box" measures 36¼ × 36¼ × 10½ in. or 92 × 92 × 26.6 cm. and was purchased through the Fine Arts Fund in 1970.

*Some Annuals of 1952–73*

The Annual Exhibition is a testing ground for the selection of paintings for purchase. In January two members of the art department go to New York to borrow paintings from dealers, many of whom already know the College or have been notified in advance. Works that might be purchased are selected, as well as others for comparison of style and quality. During the Annual Exhibition, considerable interest develops as the art department deliberates about a purchase. The choice is announced as the show closes. If the Louise Jordan Smith Fund is to be used, the correspondence to get both the approval of "two well recognized expert judges of pictures" and also the approval of the bank as trustee of the fund may take weeks. This lengthy procedure allows time (to quote the Smith will again) "to avoid any and all mistakes ... so far as possible." The variety and the quality of the Annual Exhibition can be seen in the following descriptions of some of them.

Two were solo exhibitions. The Forty-ninth Annual (1960) was a Jack Levine Retrospective covering 1937–60. It consisted of sixteen works lent by three museums, a corporation, and nine collectors, plus "Café" (#123), which the College was purchasing. A Ben Shahn Retrospective, the Fifty-fifth Annual (1966) celebrated the seventy-fifth anniversary of the College. It was made up of twenty-seven works in all media. Eleven were borrowed from three museums, a college, a university, and four collectors. The rest were available for purchase through Shahn's dealer, Mrs. Edith Gregor Halpert of the Downtown Gallery. The College acquired "It's No Use to Do Any More" (#155) from the "Lucky Dragon" series and the serigraph "Gandhi" (#239).

The Sixtieth Annual (1971) presented portraits by seven available, nationally known painters, one of whom might be chosen to paint the portrait of Dr. Quillian on a commission from the Class of 1954. Philip Pearlstein was selected (#144).

Two Annuals featured American women. The Forty-eighth Annual (1959) included Frankenthaler, Hartigan, MacIver, and O'Keeffe. Painters in the Annual of 1972 (the sixty-first), but not in the earlier one, were Alice Neel, Agnes Martin, Jane Wilson, Marcia Marcus, and Janet Fish. Three sculptresses were also represented by drawings or monotypes: Chryssa, Mary Frank, and Nancy Grossman. Professional painters among the Randolph-Macon alumnae were included in this and other exhibitions.

The Fifty-third Annual in 1964, one of two that featured graphics, included Baskin, Hayter, Lazansky, Munakata, and Peterdi.

Under the frequently used title "Contemporary American Paintings," the twenty-nine works in the Forty-third Annual (1954) included paintings by Hartley, Marin, Marsh, Shahn, Sheeler, Stamos, Tobey, Tomlin, and Weber. Other Annuals had names like "Some New Things"—the title of the Fifty-ninth Annual (1970). It introduced the first loans from the Soho district of New York and from other new galleries. Works by Arakawa, Gene Davis, Donald Lewallen, Robert Mangold, and Robert Ryman appeared in this exhibition.

Had additional funds been available, the Collection might now include works by Kuniyoshi, Tanguy, Motherwell, W. de Kooning, R. Pousette-Dart, or by others whose works have been shown on campus.

*Acquisitions*

By 1958 the financial conditions in America had changed so much that the College took legal steps to obtain more flexible terms for the Louise Jordan Smith Fund. A "real work of art" is still required, but the period for purchase may now be shorter or longer than Miss Smith's original "every second year."

The Fine Arts Fund, like the Smith Fund, is for the purchase of works of art, not paintings exclusively.

The two purchase funds, carefully spent, and one commission by the Class of 1954, for which special contributions were collected, added fifteen major works to the Collection between 1952 and 1973. (See Table on page 14.)

*Gift of the Abingdon Square Portfolio*

In honor of Harriet Fitzgerald '26 the Northern Delaware Chapter of the Alumnae Association purchased and gave to the College in 1968 twelve paintings by members of the Abingdon Square Painters, Inc. This is a cooperative organization for artists in New York. Miss Fitzgerald helped establish it in 1947 and has been its director ever since. The active painters who live in New York, or who still maintain a connection with the group while living elsewhere, are Peggy Anderson, Paul Bond, Mrs. E. Gorham Downing, Harriet Fitzgerald, Eugene Hutner, Donald Louthian, Fred L. Messersmith, Jeanne Morrow, David Sebold, and Sister Theophane. Deceased are Jabez Gray and Nat Koffman.

Miss Fitzgerald carried the Abingdon Square Portfolio, full of matted canvases and watercolors, for exhibition at ten of the eleven institutions to which the American Association of Colleges sent her for a lecture tour in the spring of 1968.

The framing of the twelve paintings before their presentation to the College also honored Miss Fitzgerald. It was the gift of Mrs. Andrew A.

*Major Acquisitions 1952-1973*

| *Catalogue Number* | *Artist* | *Title* | *Fund* |
|---|---|---|---|
| 10 | Thomas Hart Benton | "Preparing the Bill" | Smith |
| 61 | Arthur G. Dove | "Cow # 1" | Fine Arts |
| 87 | Morris Graves | "In the Night" | Smith |
| 91 | Robert Gwathmey | "Front Porch" | Smith and Fine Arts |
| 123 | Jack Levine | "Café" | Smith |
| 128 | Marcia Marcus | "Portrait of Lucas Samaras" | Smith |
| 133 | Henry Lee McFee | "Golden Leaves" | Smith |
| 138 | Carl Morris | "Toward Yesterday" | Smith |
| 144 | Philip Pearlstein | "Portrait of President William F. Quillian, Jr." | Commission |
| — | Leo Rabkin (See figure 6) | "Shadow Box" (construction) | Fine Arts |
| 204 | Dorothy Ruddick | "#9" | Fine Arts |
| 155 | Ben Shahn | "It's No Use To Do Any More" | Smith |
| 165 | Gilbert Stuart | "Portrait of Mrs. Polly Hooper" | Fine Arts |
| 176 | Robert Vickrey | "Pulse" | Smith |
| 182 | James McNeill Whistler | "Tanagra" | Fine Arts |

Smith (Mary Virginia Barnes '35), a member of the Northern Delaware Chapter.

For the exhibition itinerary of the Abingdon Square Portfolio see Appendix C.

### *Gifts and Bequests*

In this period, the largest gifts to the College Collection have been in the graphic arts. These gifts are described in the section on prints.

Gifts of money to be used for framing, permanent labels, and conservation treatment have shown the alumnae's understanding of the maintenance of paintings.

Two alumnae have generously permitted the publication here of the two mid-nineteenth century paintings that they have willed to the College; one is an Edward Hicks (#100), and the other, a family portrait of 1844 (#79).

### *Loan Exhibitions from the Collection*

After examining the table of loan exhibitions from the Collection (Appendix B) one might assume that the College had planned regular circulation of selected paintings during the 1960s. On the contrary, the initiative came either from alumnae or directly from museums. Their requests were complied with because those loan exhibitions created respect for the College and delighted the alumnae. Traveling shows, however, are hard on paintings. Therefore, except for the loan of a single painting now and then, most of the Collection will probably be exhibited hereafter in the Randolph-Macon Art Gallery as an historical survey of American painting.

*Paintings and Special Occasions*

An Arts Symposium on the Creative Process united faculty members and students in year-long preparation for a three-day conference early in March 1960. Jack Levine spoke for art, a retrospective of his work (the Forty-ninth Annual) was on view, and his painting "Café" was purchased.

The Fiftieth Annual Exhibition (1961) titled "Artists on Our Want List" exhibited works by artists not yet represented in the Collection, based on a want list compiled by several knowledgeable advisors. The earliest painting now owned, Gilbert Stuart's portrait of 1811 (#165), was acquired from this exhibition.

In 1966, to celebrate the seventy-fifth anniversary of the founding of the College in 1891, Randolph-Macon offered honorary degrees to a few distinguished women, including Georgia O'Keeffe, (see figure 7), whose "Yellow Cactus" is #141. The first edition of this *Catalogue*, published before the 1965–66 session, was also a seventy-fifth anniversary project.

*Paintings as Teachers*

An article on paintings in the Collection was published in *Arts in Virginia* in the spring issue, 1962. Its title was "Paintings as Teachers." This suggests the role that the Collection plays in the life of the Randolph-Macon community. Living in daily association with such works of art makes an indelible impression upon students. In addition, the Collection serves as a ready laboratory for students who are learning to paint. Other colleges may offer only books about paintings. Here, many a senior paper, written report, or oral presentation started from a Randolph-Macon canvas. From 1952 to 1973 the paintings were often used in courses on art history, both to intensify visual awareness and to help a student develop her personal taste in art. Wherever several paintings were on view, students and visitors found a notebook of information and suggestions for studying each canvas. The statements by artists that are dated between 1958 and 1964 in the present *Catalogue* first appeared in those study sheets.

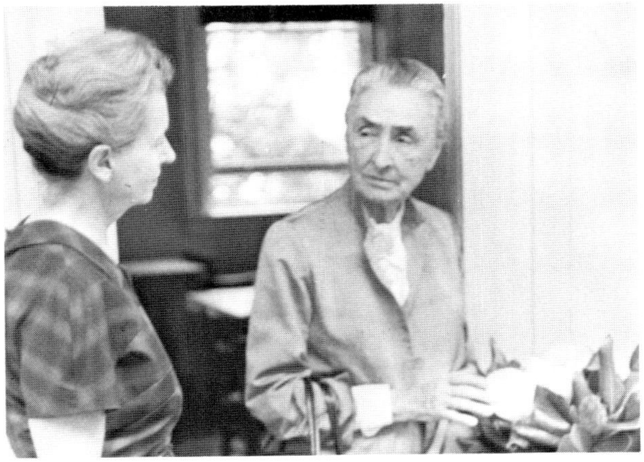

Figure 7. Georgia O'Keeffe (right) with Mary F. Williams, November 1966.

## The Fourth Period: From 1973

Upon the retirement of Mary F. Williams in 1973, the Collection came under the joint care of Elliott R. Twery, chairman of the art department and Robert S. Fuller, acting curator of the Collection.

Safety for the paintings and convenience in viewing them were major reasons for the decision to assemble in chronological order in the Art Gallery on Quinlan Street a number of the most important works. A grant from the National Endowment for the Arts helped make possible certain changes in the interior of the Gallery to improve the exhibition areas. These alterations were initiated by Dr. Kent Ahrens, who taught art history from 1973 to 1976 and was curator from 1975 until his resignation in 1976.

When the paintings were few, a student could study them "frequently, seriously, and at leisure" in Main Hall alone. As more paintings came, they were displayed in fourteen different buildings, making it difficult for them to be seen as a collection.

This catalogue and the installation in the Art Gallery, both prepared during our nation's Bicentennial year, were designed to increase the appreciation of American painting, as exemplified in the Collection of Randolph-Macon Woman's College.

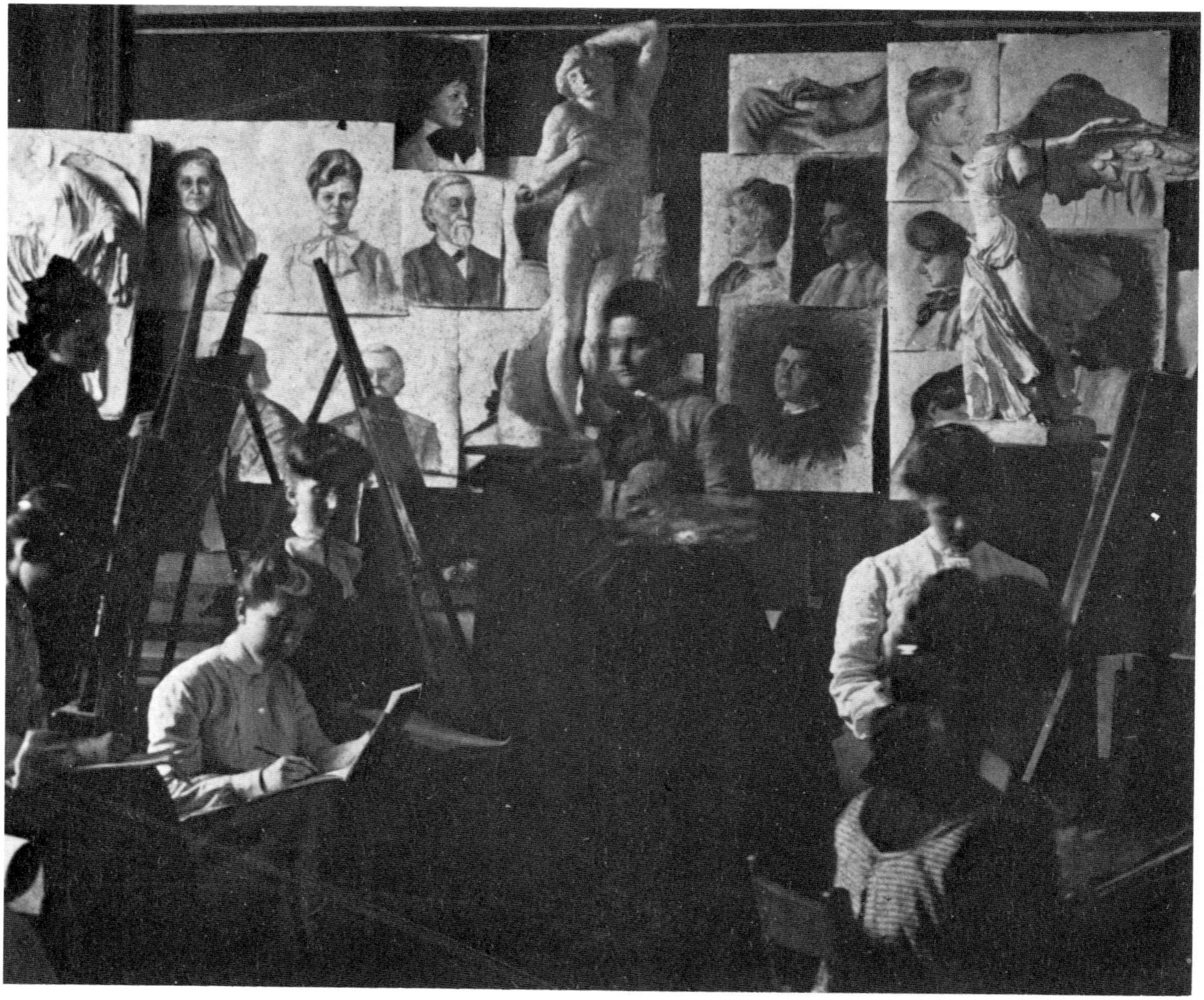

Figure 8. Students in the Tower Studio, about 1906. Right side of a photograph given to the art department by Mrs. J. I. Hamaker (M. Ray Parker '12) in 1957. (For left side, see figure 2).

# Viewed from the Bicentennial Year

## The City of Lynchburg

America's Bicentennial provides an opportunity to celebrate the cooperation in the arts that has always existed between the College and Lynchburg. It is an appropriate time to pay tribute to Lynchburg and to express pleasure that the publication of this *Catalogue of the Collection of American Art* was accepted by the Bicentennial Commission of Lynchburg as one of its projects.

### *In the Tower Studio*

Without realizing that they were initiating adult education in central Virginia in 1893, the wealthy and well-traveled ladies of Lynchburg took the Rivermont Electric Railway and enrolled in Randolph-Macon's art classes. The College was theirs, in a sense, because their families had given an initial endowment of one hundred thousand dollars.

Entering Main Hall, the ladies climbed to the skylighted Tower Studio (see figure 8), where the twenty-five-year-old Miss Louise Jordan Smith (teacher of art and French) handed out paper and charcoal for them to make shaded drawings from the plaster casts she had imported from France. The prestige of this young teacher who had studied at the Académie Julian in Paris led one student to exclaim, "I felt that Paris had been brought to me."[1] Thanks to Miss Louise's competent successors in the studio, special students have continued to come from Lynchburg to this very day.

1. Sallie Lee Mahood, *Autobiography* (Lynchburg, 1965), p. 40.

### *Lynchburg Residents as Teachers*

"Old Man," in figure 9, was etched by Bernard Gutmann, a naturalized American citizen trained in Düsseldorf, who was teaching art privately in Lynchburg when called on to conduct Miss Smith's classes for two years (1895–97) while she returned to Paris on leave for further study.

While "Miss Louise" was abroad, her self-portrait (#158) was shown in the Salon of 1897 in Paris. During the last year of her three years in France, classes in the Tower Studio were taught by Mrs. Sallie L. Mahood, of Lynchburg, represented here by figure 10 (#127). Another native of Lynchburg, Georgia Morgan, whose work appears in figure 11 (#137) and in #136, never completed her Randolph-Macon degree (Class of 1903) but assisted in the College's art classes from 1906–9. Her work, too, was exhibited in the Salon in Paris, as #2789 in the Salon of 1910 (a miniature of a peasant woman).[2] As strong-willed as Miss Smith, Georgia Morgan helped revive the Art Club (1926), helped organize the Civic Art League (1931), was its president the remaining twenty years of her life, and taught art at Lynchburg College for thirty years.[3]

How gratifying that Randolph-Macon could announce, in its catalogue for the 1903–4 sessions, that "Students completing Course 6 are admitted to the life class in the Art Students League in New York and the Académie Julian in Paris,

2. Georgia Morgan's "Scrapbook," in the archives, contains the Salon label for this miniature.

3. For the whole story of these early years, see Ruth Homes Blunt, *The Lynchburg Art Club and Its Affiliates* (Lynchburg, 1962), pp. 6–16.

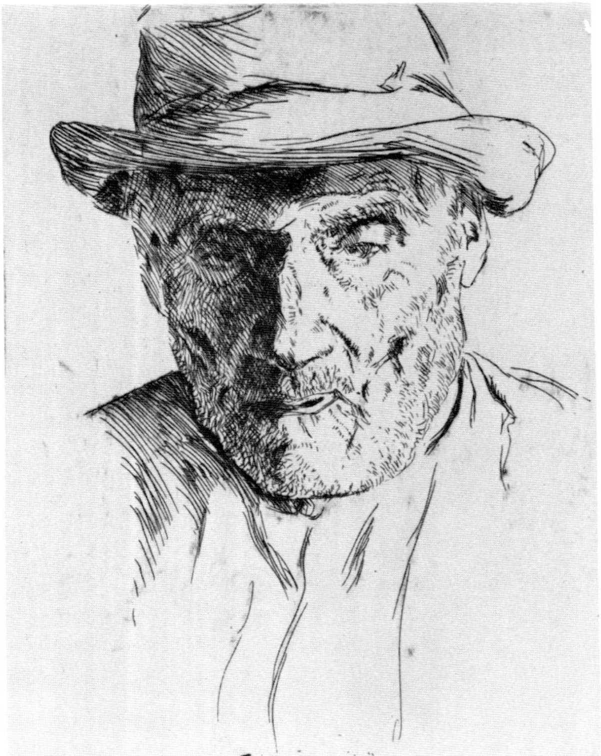

Figure 9. "Old Man," etching by Bernard Gutmann. Gift of Ruth H. Blunt '17, in 1960.

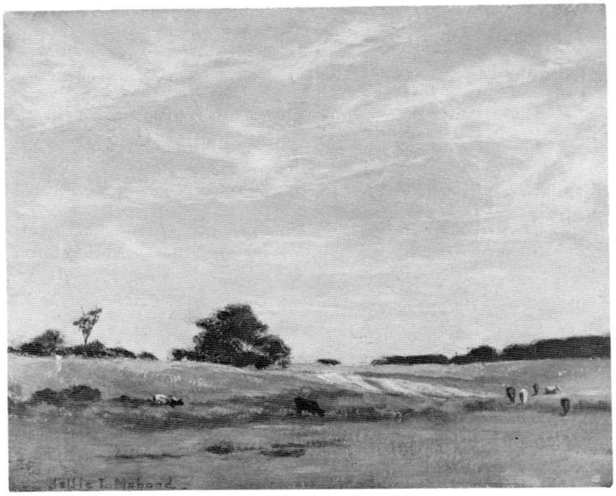

Figure 10. "Sunny Skies" (#127) by Sallie L. Mahood.

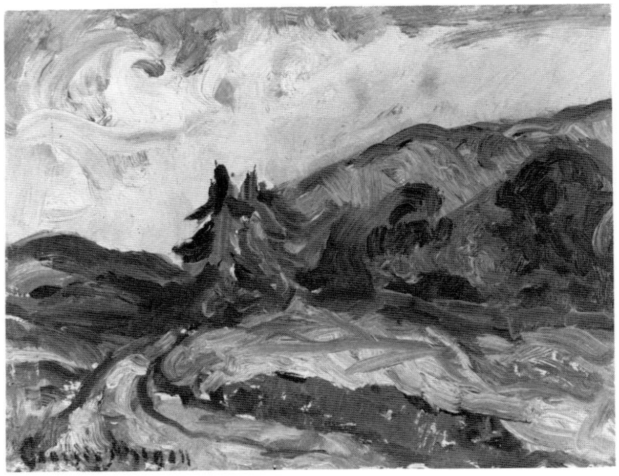

Figure 11. "In Amherst County" (#137) by Georgia Morgan.

France!" Furthermore, for about twenty years, from 1908–29, the students in Randolph-Macon's art department were offered scholarships by the Académie Julian, by the Pennsylvania Academy of the Fine Arts, and, in at least one year, by the Art Students League of New York.

In short, the ladies of Lynchburg gladly climbed to the Tower Studio for the quality of instruction in drawing and painting offered during the thirty-five years of Miss Smith's leadership (1893–1928).

### *In the Art Lecture Room*

With the opening of a new college library in 1929—now the Herbert C. Lipscomb Library—the old library of 1906, erected in memory of Georgie and Lillie Jones, was remodeled and was renamed the English-Art Building.

In the top-floor studio, with its superb view of the Blue Ridge, one of the most colorful personalities to teach painting was the distinguished loyalist refugee from Spain, the painter-sculptor Pierre Daura. He attracted so many adult students to the studio that a morning class with him was scheduled exclusively for them. Mr. Daura taught from 1946 until he resigned in 1953. (See catalogue #26.)

On the second floor, below the studio, a large exhibition hall was created to accommodate loan and Annual Exhibitions and student shows.

To most Lynchburgers "art class" meant learning to draw or to paint, although courses in the history of art had been offered since 1897. Added importance was given to art history by Beatrice von Keller, who headed the art department from 1928 until she retired in 1952. Although she was equipped to teach painting (which she had studied at the Royal Academy, Stockholm), Mrs. von Keller chose to be an art historian and came to Randolph-Macon after receiving an M.A. in art history from the University of Chicago.

The new facilities for art history included a classroom for lectures illustrated by slides and a seminar room with library.

The three courses in art history that attracted the most adult auditors from Lynchburg, starting in the mid-fifties, were the history of ancient, medieval, renaissance, and modern art, taught by Mary F. Williams, Ph.D.; the history of modern painting, taught by Elliott R. Twery, M.F.A.; and the history of American architecture, taught by Robert S. Fuller, M.F.A. Thus, the town and the College became linked through their mutual interest in a second artistic discipline.

### *In Exhibition Rooms*

The regular program of loan exhibitions, the Annual Exhibitions from dealers in New York, and the exhibitions of work by students have also sustained Lynchburg's cooperation with the College that it had helped to found. The exhibition of 1901, described in the press and the *History*,[4] outshines all others in the acclaim it received from the city. Robert C. Ogden, of New York, whose fifteen paintings and two tapestries were on loan, arrived by special train, was welcomed at the railroad station by representatives of the city council and the board of trade, and then was greeted on campus by the mayor of Lynchburg. Before anyone else saw the exhibition, it was viewed at scheduled intervals by "the Lynchburg Orphan Asylum, the teachers of Lynchburg, the pupils of the Lynchburg High School, the pupils of the Lynchburg public schools."[5]

More important in the long run than any single show has been Miss Smith's program of Annual Exhibitions, started in 1911. These Annuals are still as eagerly anticipated in Lynchburg as the Salons are in Paris. Paintings in Annuals were occasionally purchased by residents of Lynchburg (see #15).

4. Roberta D. Cornelius, *The History of Randolph-Macon Woman's College* (Chapel Hill, N.C., 1951), pp. 106-8.
5. *The News* (Lynchburg), April 17, 1901.

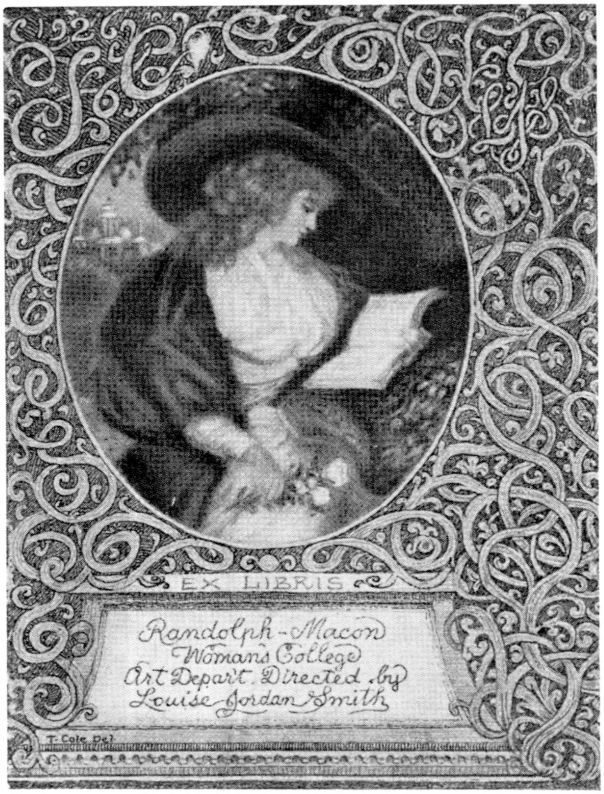


Figure 12. Bookplate of Louise Jordan Smith, a halftone cut (4 × 3 in.; 10.1 × 7.6 cm.) designed by Timothy Cole.

*In the Parlors*

Art lovers of Lynchburg enjoyed meeting the visiting artists whom Miss Louise brought to Virginia. Her program in the early 1920s introduced the etcher Arthur W. Heintzelman (#234) and the etcher-lithographer Joseph Pennell, who spoke on Whistler. A tangible memorial of one such occasion is the bookplate in figure 12, which Timothy Cole, "the last of the wood engravers," designed with "LJS" in the right-hand corner and "1926" in the left. The opportunity to meet the sculptress Anna Vaughan Hyatt in 1922 was another memorable occasion in which visitors from town participated.

*The Lynchburg Randolph-Macon Art Association*

When George Bellows's strong painting "Men of the Docks" came to Lynchburg in the Ninth Annual in 1920, the moment to start a permanent collection had clearly arrived. The citizens participated generously in the Randolph-Macon (or Lynchburg Randolph-Macon) Art Association that was quickly founded to raise money to buy this painting and others over the next six years.

An undated program of the association, now in the archives, states that, "As a joint undertaking it proposes to help foster the lively interest in art noticeable in Town and College. . . . It may appropriate any surplus funds to aid the College in adding to the collection so well begun there on condition that this permanent exhibition will be at all times open to the Lynchburg public."

In her will, Miss Smith expressed the close relationship between the city and the college by stipulating that her antiques and pictures, bequeathed to the College, "be kept together as a unit and held as an art exhibit and to be always open for inspection by the people of Lynchburg." After being placed in the art department, then in the faculty club, many of these objects were reassembled in the Louise Jordan Smith Room in the Art Gallery (shown in figure 13), where they were accessible to the public. As a sentimental gesture on Miss Louise's behalf, her empire sofa (on the right in the photograph) was lent in 1961 to the Lynchburg Art Club, for the opening of its then sparsely furnished new home at 1011 Rivermont Avenue.

*By Public Subscription*

On two occasions the people of Lynchburg have joined with the college community to acquire paintings of primarily historical value—one related to the Civil War and one to the City of Lynchburg. Thanks to the initiative of Mrs. E. Alban Watson, the city's outstanding antiquarian, the College transported to Lynchburg from the mid-

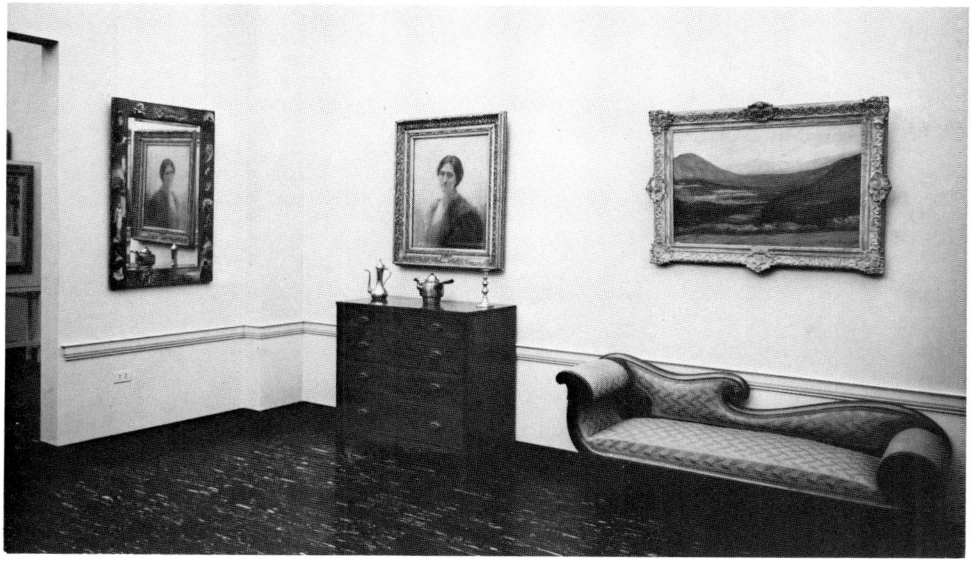

Figure 13. The Louise Jordan Smith Room in the Art Gallery, as it appeared from about 1960 to 1973. Shown from left to right are: "the little mirror in my studio from which my own portrait was painted," the "Self-Portrait" (#158), "Afton Valley" (unnumbered), and some of Miss Smith's furniture, copper, and brass.

west L. M. D. Guillaume's huge canvas depicting "The Surrender of General Robert E. Lee to General Ulysses S. Grant," as it took place in the parlor of the McLean farmhouse at Appomattox, Virginia. This painting, hardly appropriate in Michigan, was available at a reasonable price for suitable public display. The whole sum was collected while the painting was on view in 1954 at Randolph-Macon. Presented to the National Park Service, the painting now dominates the visitors' center at Appomattox.

The other work is August Köllner's wash drawing of Lynchburg in 1845 (#116; see figure 14). In 1953, when no firmly established historical museum existed in Lynchburg, Randolph-Macon decided to become the guardian of this artistic document, on which the painter wrote in pencil, "Lynchburg on the James River, Va. The great staple for Tobacco. . . . June 1845." Keeping Köllner's "Lynchburg" in the city permanently became a project of the community. Fifty-one persons and companies raised the purchase price.[6]

The picture has appeared in several historical exhibitions, including the Bicentennial Exhibition, "Lynchburg, Past and Present: 1786–1976."

### *The Lynchburg Museum System*

The City of Lynchburg's first project for the Bicentennial was repairing the Old Courthouse of 1855, in Greek Revival style, that overlooks from its hill the city and the James River. When the Museum Task Force, as it was called, started plans for the courthouse, several other organizations proposed to restore their particular historic

6. Their names are under glass on the back of the framed picture.

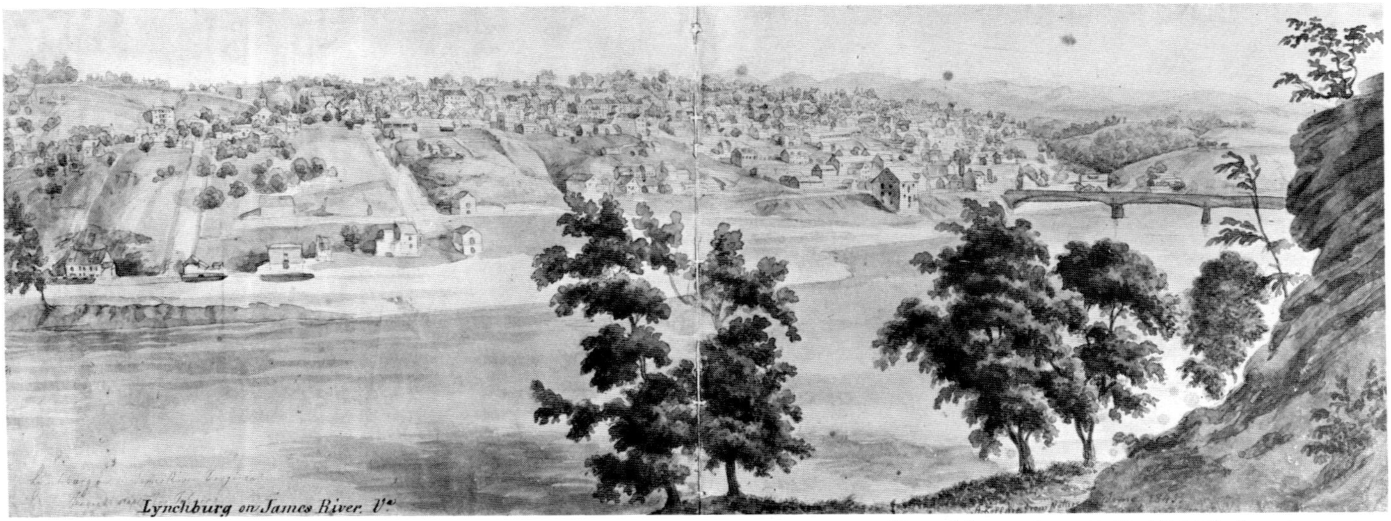


Figure 14. "Lynchburg in 1845" (#116) by August Köllner.

buildings. Fortunately, wise civic leaders devised a municipal museum system based on collaboration rather than competition, and the city council approved. In 1986, when Lynchburg celebrates the Bicentennial anniversary of its founding in 1786, all the projects initiated in 1976 will have been completed.

The Randolph-Macon Art Gallery, although not administered as part of the museum system, nevertheless offers something different and significant. When visitors are touring the historical museum in the Old Courthouse and the other restored buildings, they may also visit a collection of American painting from 1811 to the present.

## The Commonwealth of Virginia

### *The Art Commission*

The Art Commission consists of three architects and two judges of painting and sculpture who meet once a month in Richmond. They are appointed by the governor to review the aesthetic quality of designs for buildings to be paid for by the commonwealth or to be built on state property, as well as of other works of art commissioned or donated, such as memorials and portraits.

Two heads of Randolph-Macon's art department and one alumna have been appointed to serve on the Art Commission: Beatrice von Keller, 1945–50; Elizabeth Nottingham Day '28, 1950–56 (see #53); and Mary F. Williams, 1956–70.

The Art Commission is no rubber stamp. Rejections and constructive criticism are difficult, but the five members meeting in the Capitol have Thomas Jefferson's architecture around them and Antoine Houdon's marble statue of George Washington before them as visible reminders of the high standards of Virginia's art in the past.

### *The Virginia Museum: People*

In 1942 Randolph-Macon lent to the Virginia Museum not a painting but a person—Mrs. Beatrice von Keller. She acted as co-director for fine arts, while Violet M. Pollard (Governor John Garland Pollard's widow) was co-director for

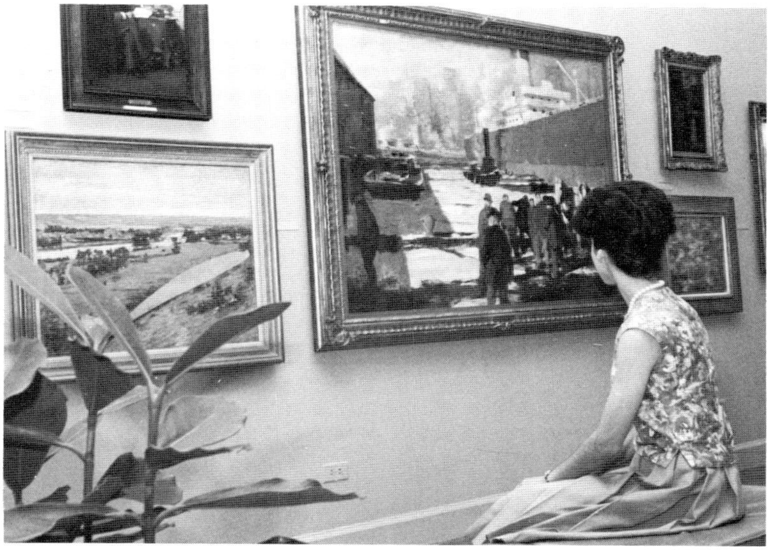

Figure 15. Exhibition in the Virginia Museum of Fine Arts, Richmond, in 1964. Shown from left to right are: part of the "Portrait of Elbert Hubbard" (#22) by W.M. Chase, "Valley of the Seine" (#147) by Theodore Robinson, and "Men of the Docks" (#9) by George Bellows.

business and finance. The two friends served together until 1945, when the director returned from military duties.

In 1968 the Virginia Museum employed Mary F. Williams for one semester as Artmobile advisor. She visited each college on the Artmobile circuit, to review the program with the art departments.

*The Virginia Museum: Paintings*

The Virginia Museum exhibited in 1964 the largest group of paintings ever lent by Randolph-Macon at one time. The *Members' Bulletin* of the museum describes them as "Fifty-four paintings from this remarkable collection, the finest in any Southern college."[7] (See figure 15.)

7. No. 25 (September 1964), p. 1.

In 1969 the Virginia Museum, with its usual expertise, installed in an Artmobile eighteen of Randolph-Macon's paintings and a recorded gallery talk about them. (See figure 16.) The Artmobile visited the museum's chapters and affiliates in twenty-eight communities, as well as sixteen colleges and universities in Virginia. Randolph-Macon alumnae everywhere helped the local institutions welcome school groups and visitors.

## The District of Columbia

*To Washington*

Paintings that have been invited to one-man retrospective exhibitions at the National Gallery of Art in Washington are George Bellows's "Men of the Docks" (#9; color plate on page 25) and Thomas Eakins's "Portrait Sketch of William H. Macdowell" (#66).

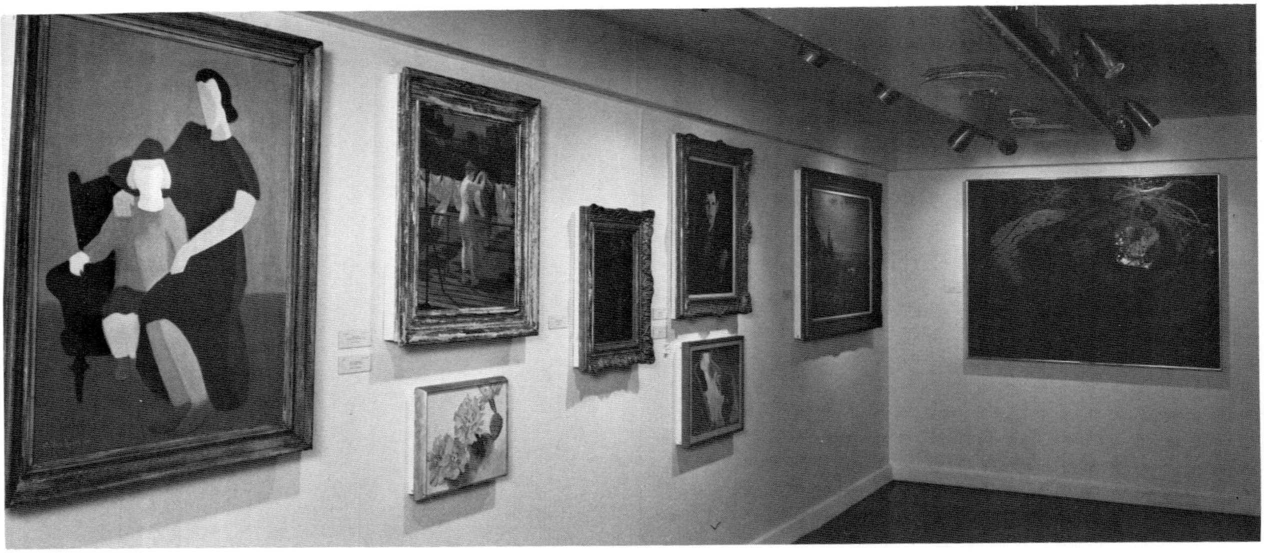

Figure 16. On view in the Virginia Museum Artmobile (left to right): "Child and Mother" (#7) by Milton Avery, "Sun and Wind on the Roof" (#157) by John Sloan, "Yellow Cactus" (#141) by Georgia O'Keeffe, "Paris Courtyard" (#101) by Winslow Homer, "Tom" (#98) by Robert Henri, "Cow #1" (#61) by Arthur G. Dove, "Perugia and the Valley" (#104) by George Inness, and "Toward Yesterday" (#138) by Carl Morris.

*From Washington*

The National Gallery of Art in Washington co-operated with the College by sending a loan exhibition of American portraits and of graphic arts from the Rosenwald Collection for the dedication of the Art Gallery on Quinlan Street in 1952.

The National Endowment for the Arts provided a matching grant for the publication of this revised, enlarged second edition of the *Catalogue*. Simultaneously, the National Endowment for the Arts gave a matching grant to refurbish the interior of the Art Gallery on Quinlan Street.

Visitors from Lynchburg, all of Virginia, and the nation at large, as well as students of all ages are invited to use this *Catalogue* for the greater enjoyment of the Collection of American Painting at Randolph-Macon Woman's College.

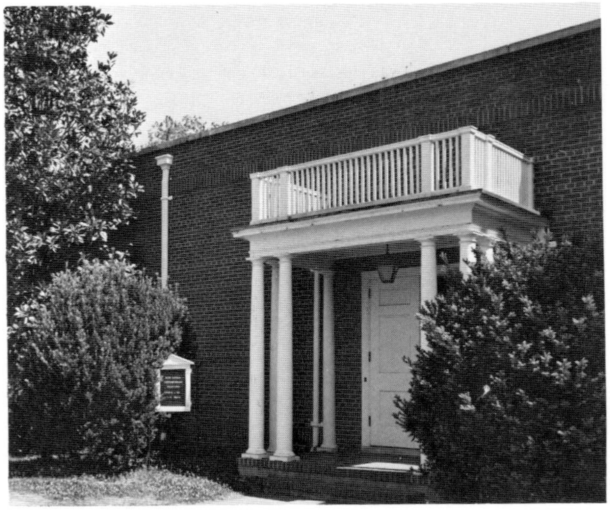

Figure 17. Entrance to the Art Gallery, situated to the north of Main Hall, beyond the playing fields.

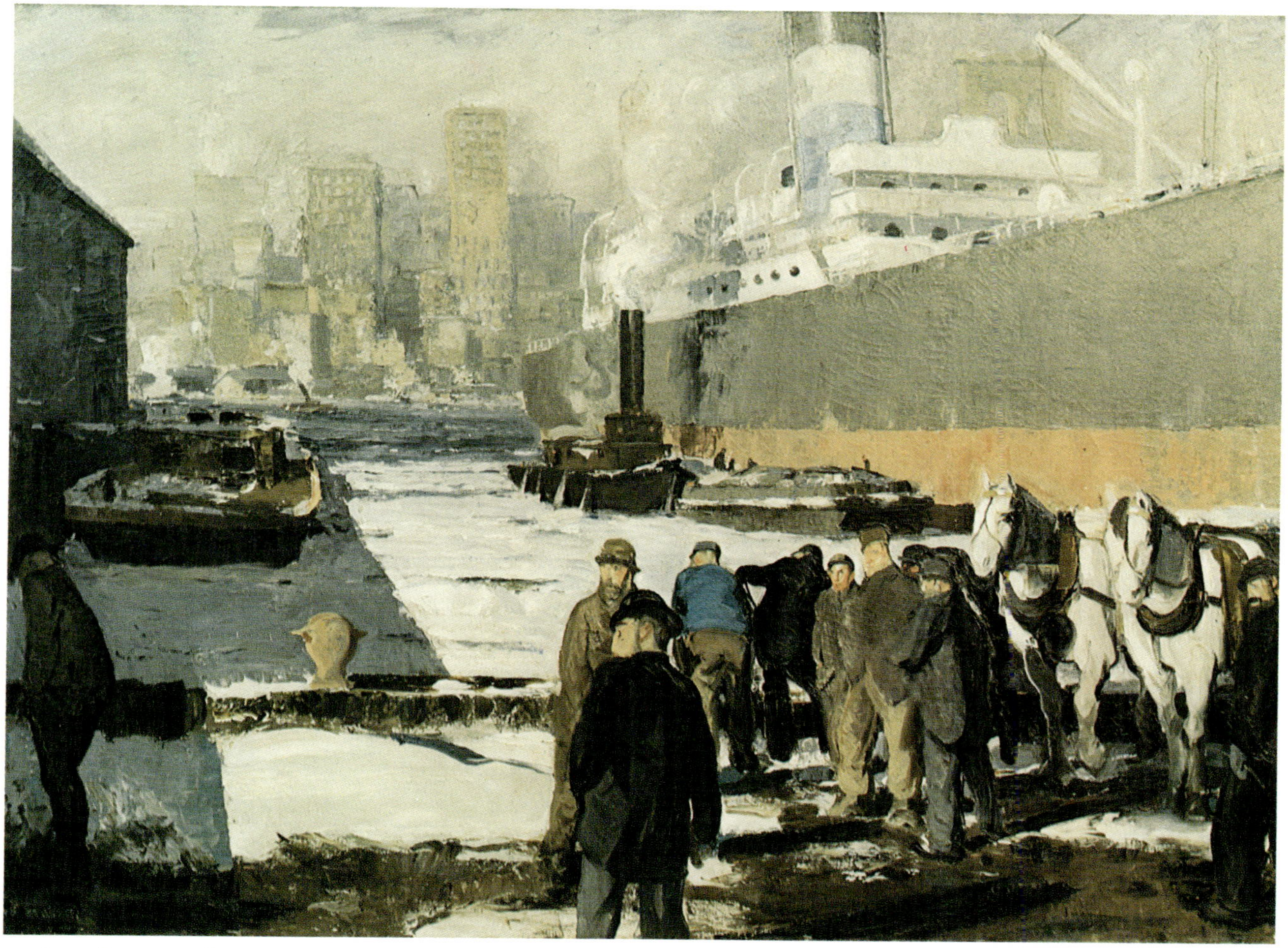

# 9. George Bellows, "Men of the Docks"

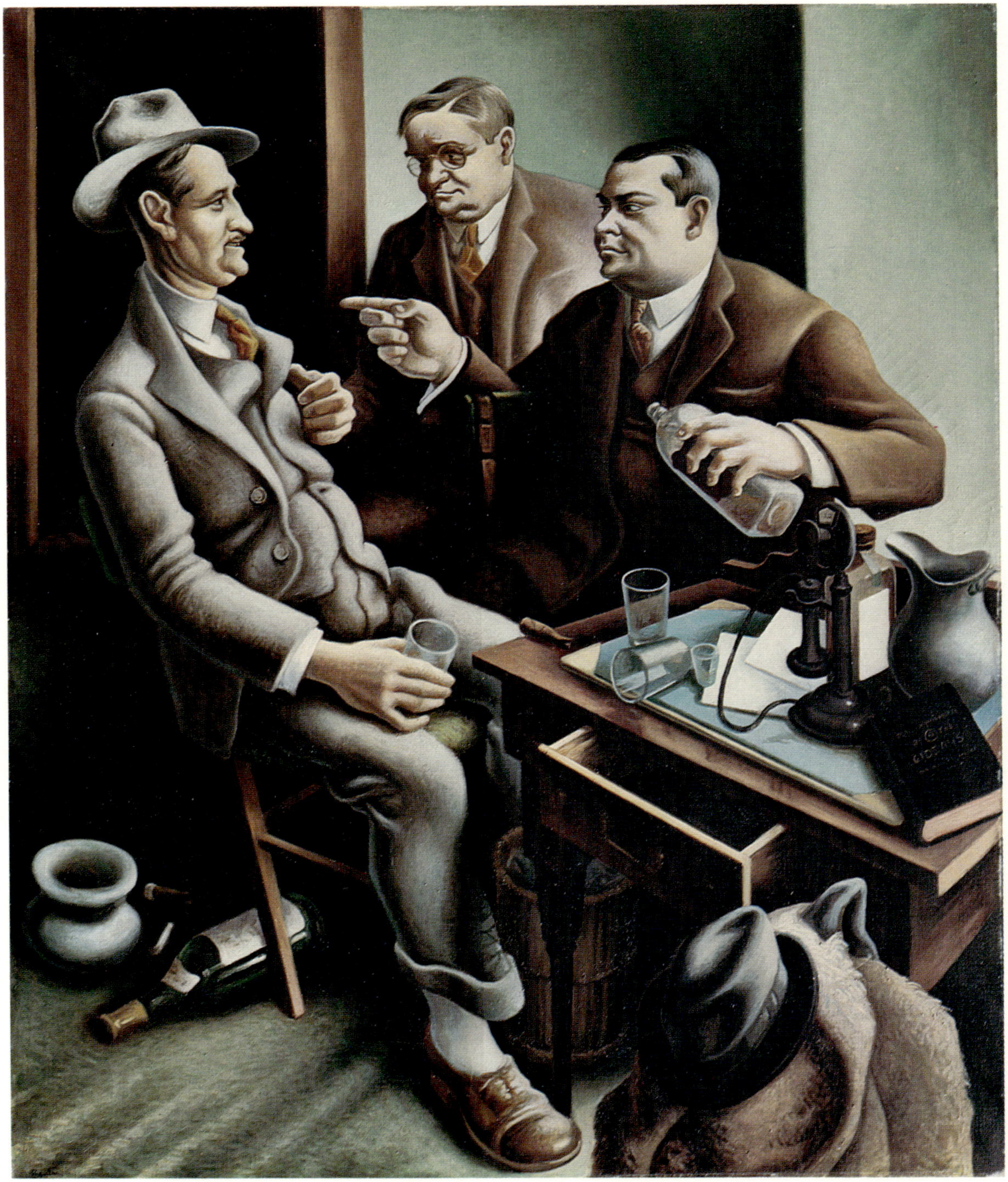

#10. Thomas Hart Benton, "Preparing the Bill"

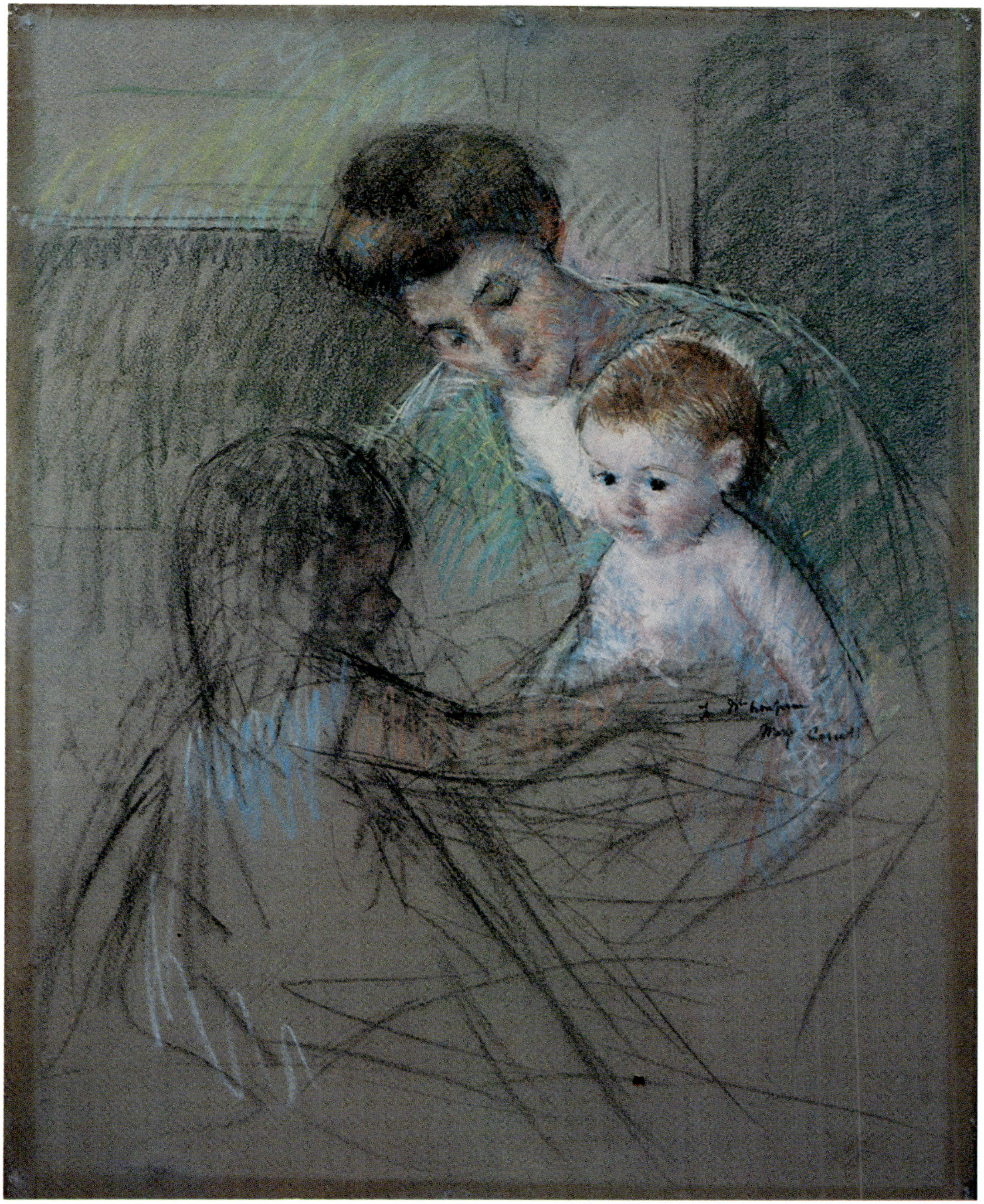

#20. Mary Cassatt, "Sketch of Mother and Daughter Looking at the Baby"

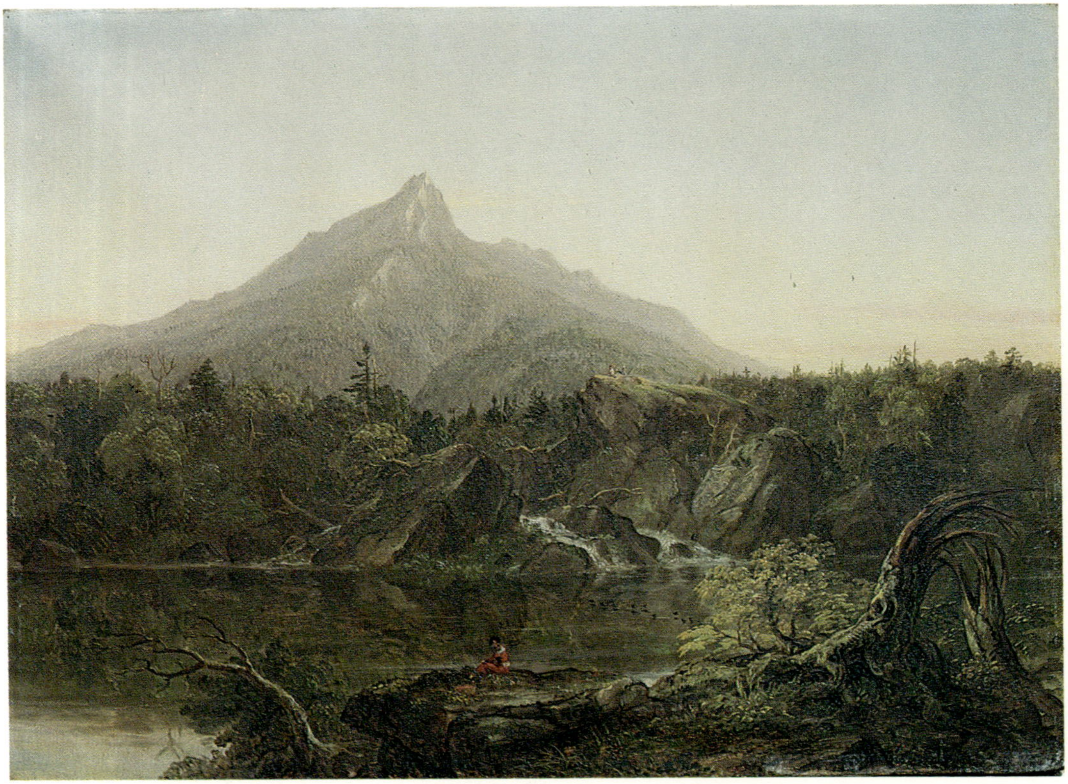

#25. Thomas Cole, "Corway Peak, New Hampshire"

#34. Arthur B. Davies, "Wild He-Goat Dance"

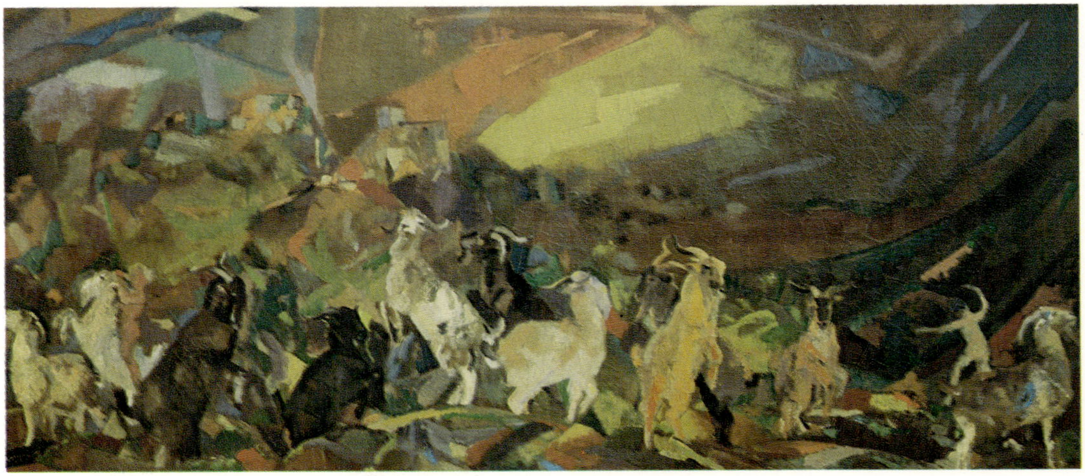

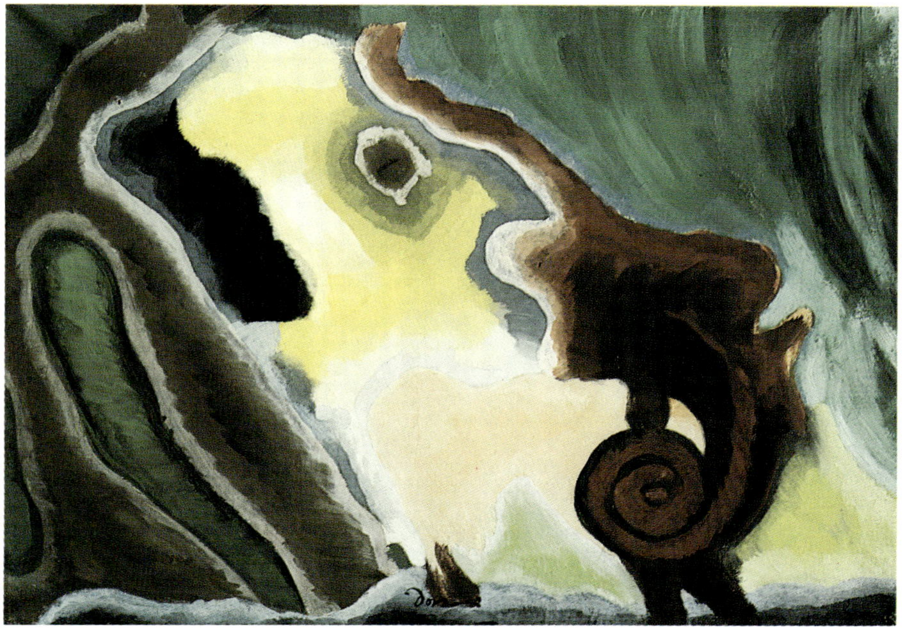

#61. Arthur G. Dove, "Cow #1"

#102. Edward Hopper, "Mrs. Scott's House"

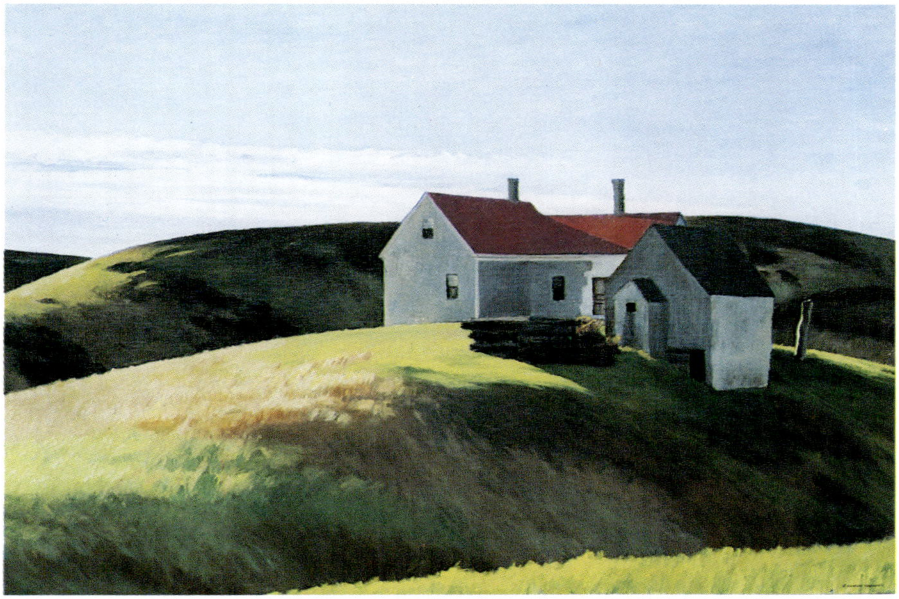

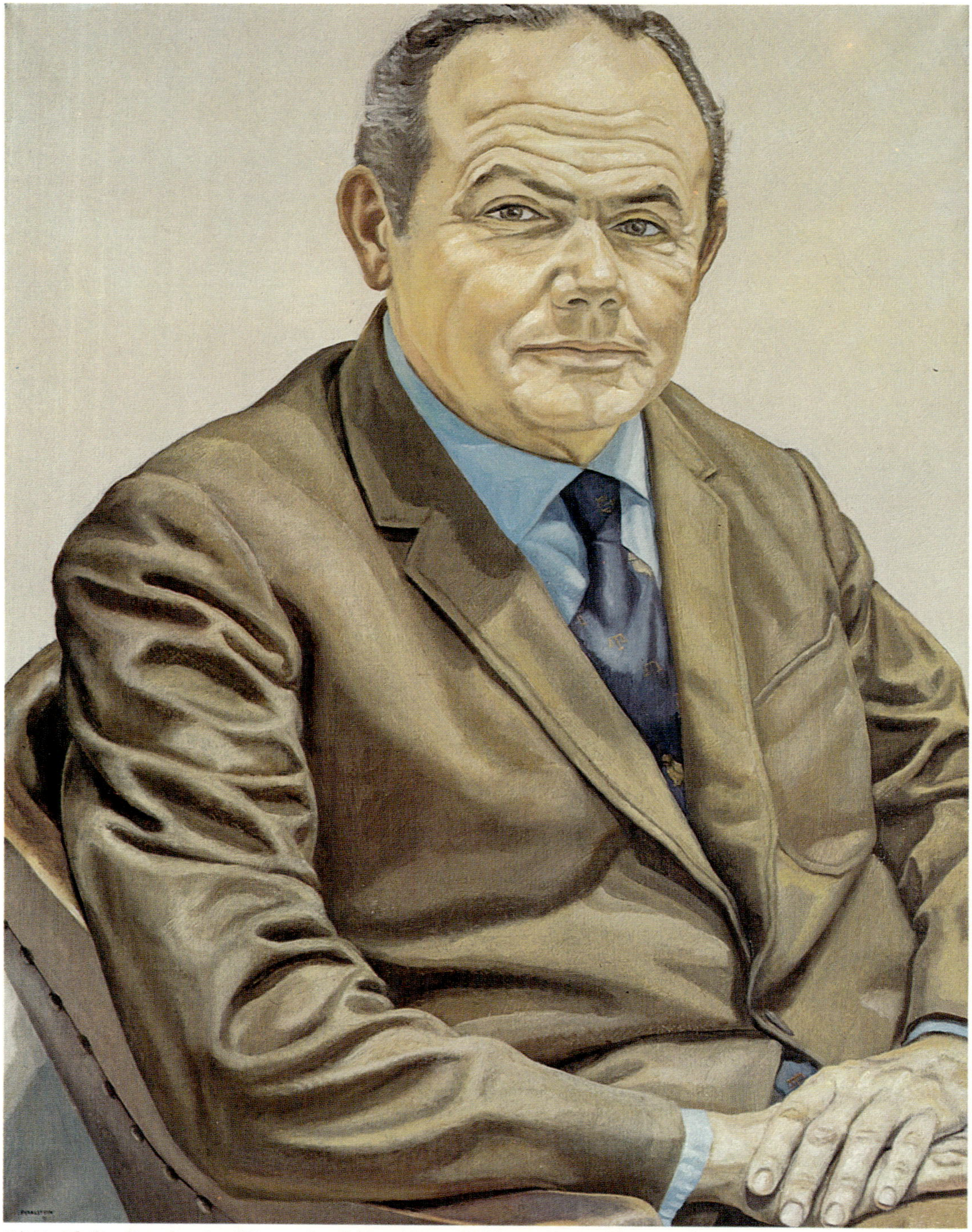

#144. Philip Pearlstein, "Portrait of President William F. Quillian, Jr."

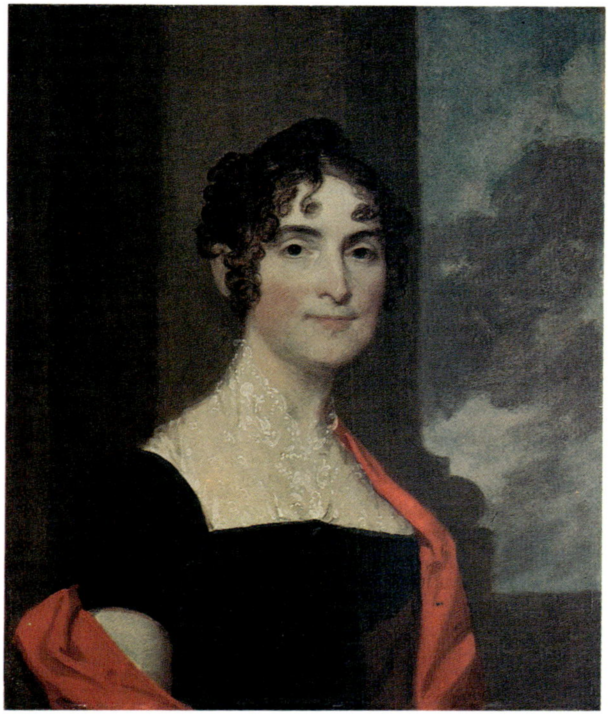

#165. Gilbert Stuart, "Portrait of Mrs. Polly Hooper"

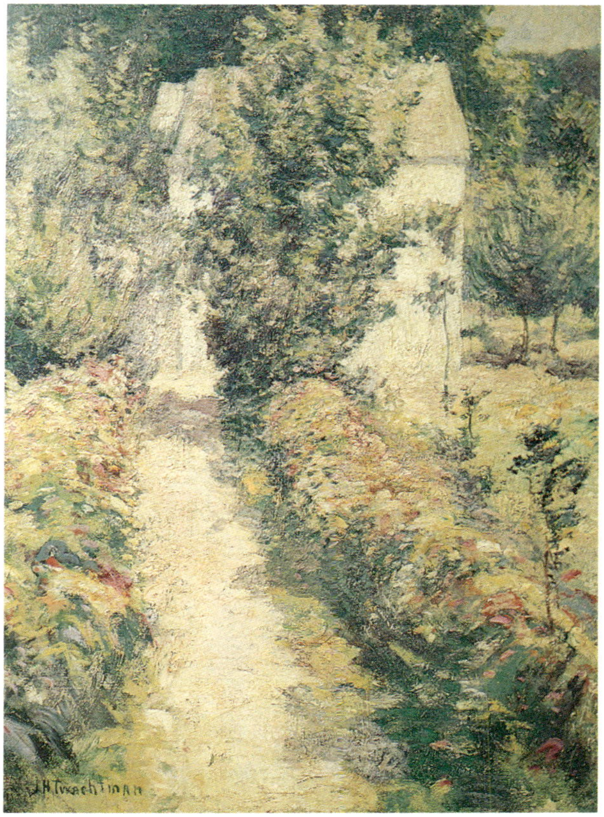

#170. John H. Twachtman, "Azaleas"

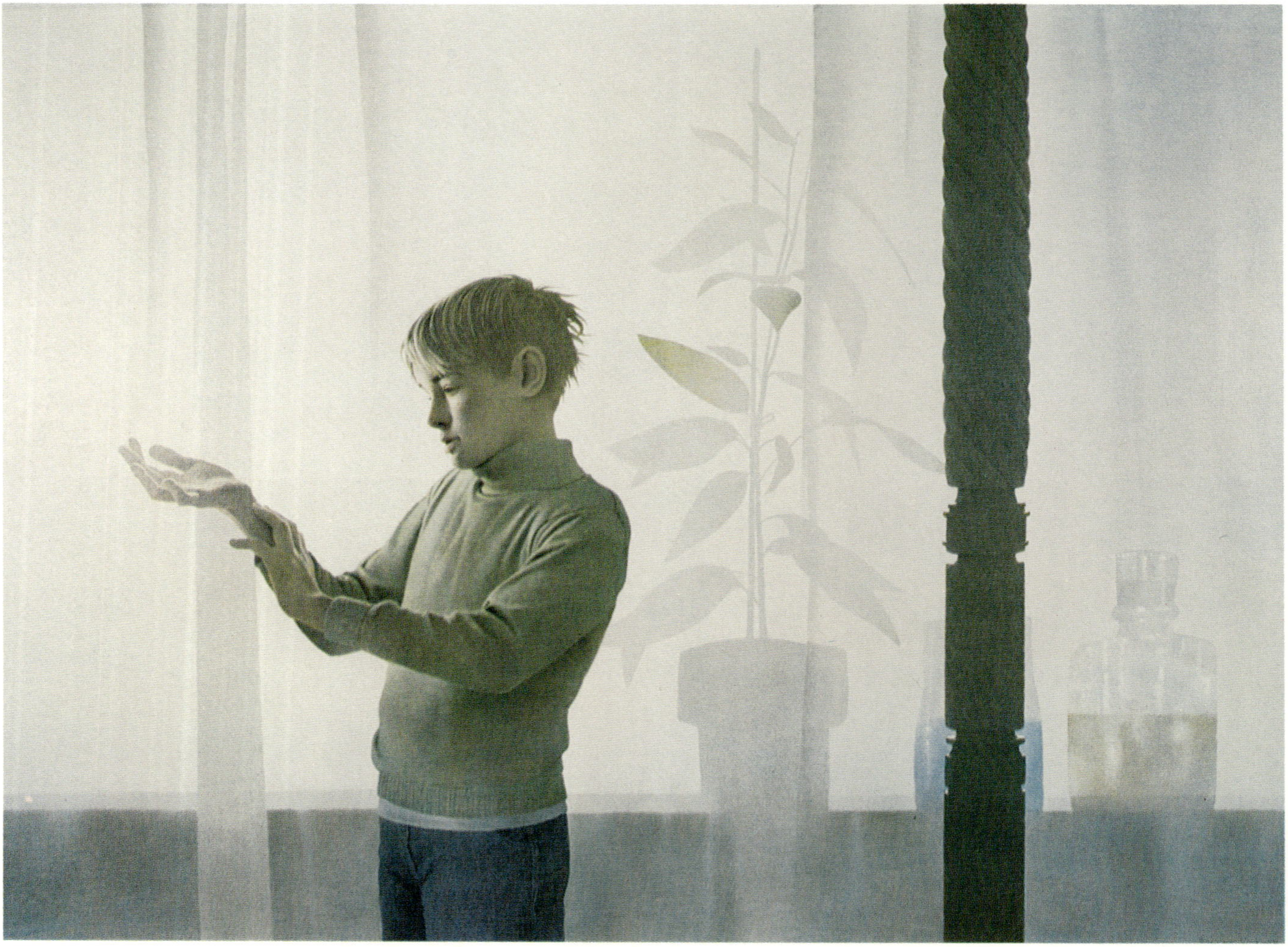

#176. Robert Vickrey, "Pulse"

# Catalogue of the Collection

The year in which a work was created appears directly after the title.

Oil paintings are on canvas, except as noted.

Artists' names appear in capital letters if at least one of their works is reproduced here.

Titles of all entries illustrated in this catalogue are in capital and small capital letters.

Statements by artists were written in 1976, unless another date appears after the artist's name, following the quotation.

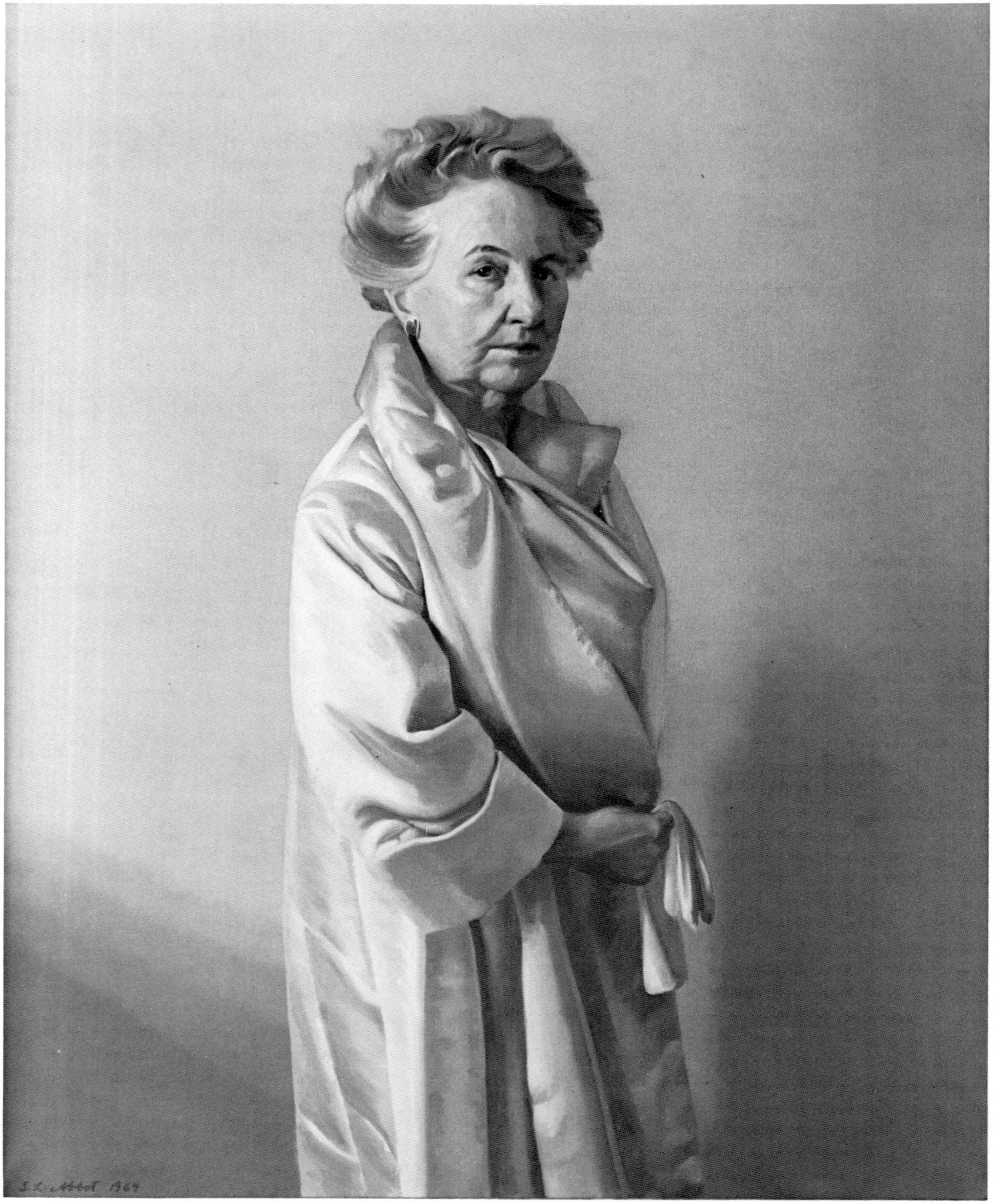

# Paintings

## SCAISBROOKE L. ABBOT

Born 1908

1. PORTRAIT OF CLARA COX BELL (Mrs. W. J. D.) '03
1964

Oil: 44¼ × 36½ in., 112.4 × 92.7 cm.
Signed, lower left: S. L. Abbot 1964
Gift of W. J. Davis Bell, Jr., and Mrs. C. Bell Gurkin, 1964

*When I was asked to do a portrait of Clara Bell, I was delighted. She was my neighbor and old friend, so rather than paint her as a woman of academic accomplishment, I wanted to paint her as I knew her best, a very entertaining companion. She was an indefatigable model and despite her years could stand longer than most people can sit. Her stamina may have come from her pleasure in having a Randolph-Macon Woman's College building named for her.*

Scaisbrooke L. Abbot

Clara Cox Bell Hall, a dormitory opened in the fall of 1964, is named for Mrs. Bell (1881–1975), who served on the board of trustees from 1922 to 1953, its first alumna and first woman member.

Exhibited: "Portraits by Scaisbrooke Abbot," Lynchburg Fine Arts Center, Sept. 28–Oct. 17, 1969, # 9.

Recorded: *The News* (Lynchburg), Oct. 2, 1964, repro.; *Alumnae Bulletin,* 58 (Fall 1964), repro. p. 4.

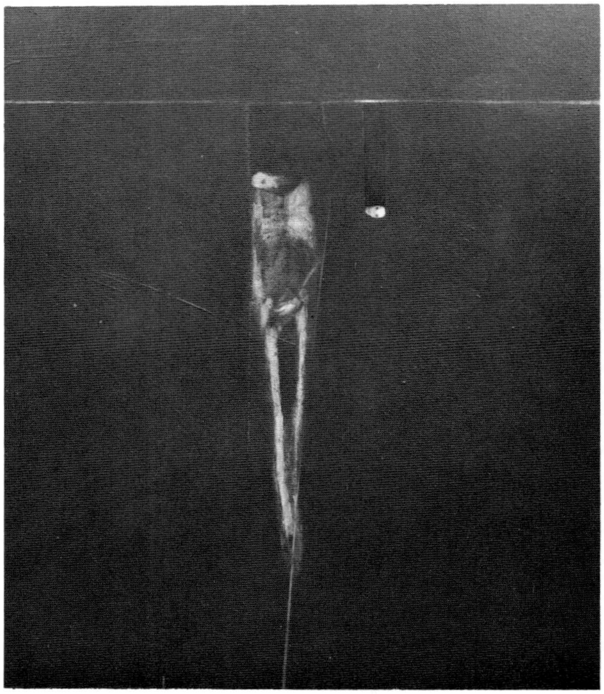

## KEITH ROGERS ALFORD (Mrs. P. K.) '65

Born 1943

2. SAINT CUTHBERT AND KING EDWIN'S HEAD 1974

Acrylic on canvas: 48×40 in.; 101.6×121.9 cm.
Signed and dated, on the back: Keith R. Alford 1974
Fine Arts Fund, 1974

*On one level this painting describes an historical event that came alive to me when I saw Cuthbert's tomb in Durham Cathedral. King Edwin's head was deposited in St. Cuthbert's grave. I imagined the saint, who had lain quietly for a long while, was shocked to be disturbed in the first place and then he was repulsed by the nature of the thing disturbing him.*

*On another level, the painting is about the human spirit. The body of the saint is decaying: it is dead. But his spirit is alive and reacts to the head with revulsion and pity. The saint does not move like a bug which continues to twitch after it has been killed, but moves on impulse rooted in compassion.* Keith Rogers Alford

## MARION BOYD ALLEN
1862–1941

### 3. PORTRAIT OF ANNA VAUGHAN HYATT 1915

Oil: 65×40 in.; 165.1×101.6 cm.
Signed and dated, lower left:
Marian Boyd Allen 1915
Randolph-Macon Art Association, 1922

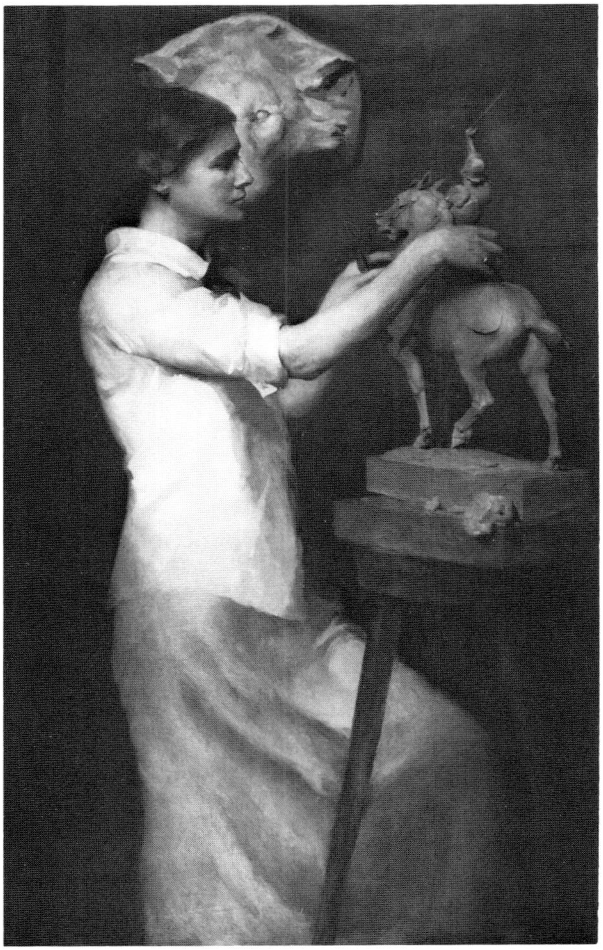

*Mrs. Allen did the portrait in my studio at Annisquam, on Cape Ann, Massachusetts, when I was making an early maquette for my Joan of Arc statue. I think it must have been before I went to Paris to make the first life-sized model of the Joan. . . . Yes, Mr. Huntington did like the painting very much, not only as being good portraiture, but he thought it would in time have some historical value.*

Anna Vaughan Hyatt Huntington (1958)

When Anna Hyatt (1876–1973) came to the College in March 1922 to demonstrate modeling with clay on an armature, this portrait was being shown on campus in the Eleventh Annual Exhibition.

The original bronze equestrian statue developed from the clay sketch shown here was erected on Riverside Drive, New York, in 1915 and a duplicate in Blois, France, in 1921. For other versions see Emile Schaub-Koch, *L'Oeuvre d'Anna Hyatt-Huntington* (Paris, 1949), p. 29.

Mr. Archer M. Huntington, to whom the sculptress was married in 1923, asked to buy this portrait, but the College declined. The original painter, Mrs. William A. Allen of Boston, Mass., was allowed to make a copy in the original dimensions, however. That duplicate (with minor changes in the drapery) is now in the library of the Mariners Museum, Newport News, Va., a museum founded by Mr. Huntington.

Recorded: *International Studio* 57 (Nov. 1915), repro. (before minor alterations in the drapery that were made apparently in 1934) p. 100; *Art and Archaeology* 26 (Sept. 1928), repro. p. 74; *Anna Hyatt Huntington*, American Sculptor Series, No. 3 (New York, 1947), frontispiece; Doris E. Cook, *Woman Sculptor, Anna Hyatt Huntingdon (1876–1973)* (Hartford, Conn., 1976). The cover of the Cook volume reproduces the artist's replica in the Mariners Museum.

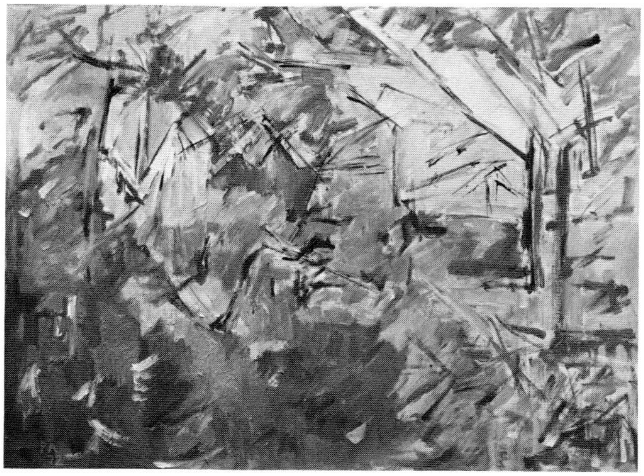

## PEGGY ANDERSON '53

Born 1932

4. Bear Mountain Rocks 1968

Oil on paper: 13 x 16⅜ in.; 33 x 41.5 cm.
Signed, lower left: P. Anderson
Gift of alumnae of the Northern Delaware Chapter, 1968

Exhibited: See Appendix C.

5. View in Woods 1972

Oil: 30 x 40 in.; 76.2 x 101.6 cm.
Signed, lower left: P A 72
Gift of Ida Fitzgerald '28, in 1973

*There is so much patterning in nature that seeing becomes a celebration: the painter's job is to select and create the abstraction that seems true, true to what is there and to her response. There is a cave-like place beside my studio at Meadows of Dan (Virginia) where pine trees grow and light shines through pine needles in the afternoon. The light changes every minute, and the color and the shapes and the planes. I have been trying for years to touch the reality of this place. This canvas represents one of my attempts.*

Peggy Anderson

Exhibited: "Peggy Anderson Exhibition," Pacem in Terris Gallery, New York, Mar. 5–17, 1973, #14; "Twenty-nine Paintings by Peggy Anderson," Randolph-Macon College (Ashland, Va.), Apr. 12–27, 1973, # 13; "Peggy Anderson," Randolph-Macon Woman's College, May 11–13, 1973, #13; Stratford College, Nov. 11–25, 1973, #10; Ferrum Junior College, Sept.-Oct. 1973; Rocky Mount (N.C.) Art Center, Dec. 2–28, 1973, #11.

## RANDOLPH ARNOLD AUFRANC '29

Born 1908

6. PORTRAIT OF DR. BENJAMIN WILLIAM ARNOLD 1950

Oil: 30 x 25 in.; 76.2 x 63.5 cm.

Signed and dated, lower left: Randolph Arnold Aufranc 1950

Gift of alumnae of Massachusetts, 1950

*I used warm colors because my father had a warm personality. The setting was a familiar one, rearranged to make strong design lines. To me the hands are important parts of a portrait, not only from a compositional standpoint, but for character interpretation. My father was always anxious to start posing early, so that he could go out to see the Red Sox play ball. Most of our conversation seemed to be about baseball rather than books.*

Randolph Arnold Aufranc (1959)

Dr. Arnold was Professor of History and Chairman of the Department from 1902 to 1939.

Exhibited: "Loan Exhibition of Paintings by Randolph Arnold Aufranc," at the College, Apr. 25–June 9, 1959, #1.

Recorded: *Alumnae Bulletin* 43 (June 1950), repro. p. 18.

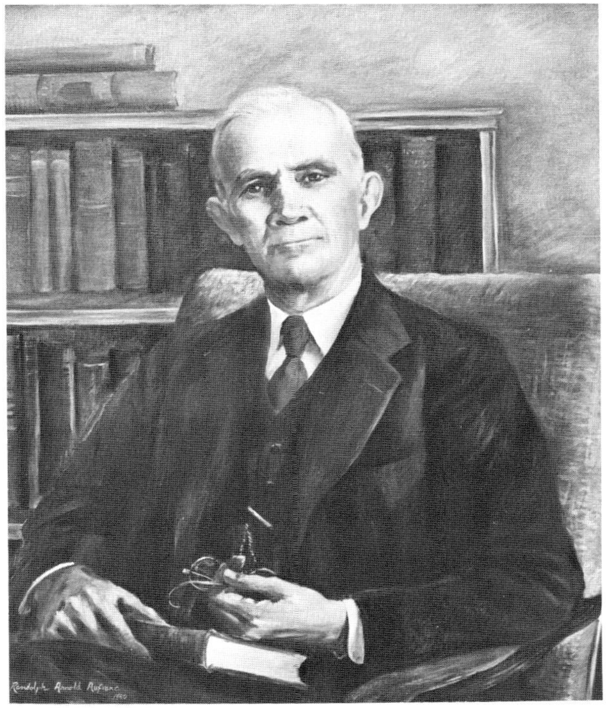

## MILTON AVERY

1893–1965

7. CHILD AND MOTHER 1946

Oil: 36 x 24 in.; 91.4 x 60.9 cm.
Signed and dated, lower left: Milton Avery 1946
Gift of Mr. and Mrs. Roy R. Neuberger, 1956

*Looking over some old gouaches of mine, I was struck by the color scheme of predominant greens of a sketch I had done of my wife and daughter. I decided to see if I could paint an oil with variations of green dominant. "Child and Mother" is the result. The title had no intentional satire—just a relief from the many "Mother and Child" ones.*

Milton Avery (1958)

Exhibited: "Contemporary American Art, the Neuberger Collection," Walker Art Center, Minneapolis, May 24–Aug. 10, 1952, #3; "Milton Avery," Baltimore Museum of Art, Dec. 9, 1952–Jan. 20, 1953, #49; included in all six of the loan and circulating exhibitions of the College Collection during 1964-72, as listed in Appendix B.

Recorded: Virginia Museum, *Members Bulletin* 30 (Sept. 1969), repro. p. 4; *Art Journal* 32 (Winter 72/73), p. 195, repro. p. 194.

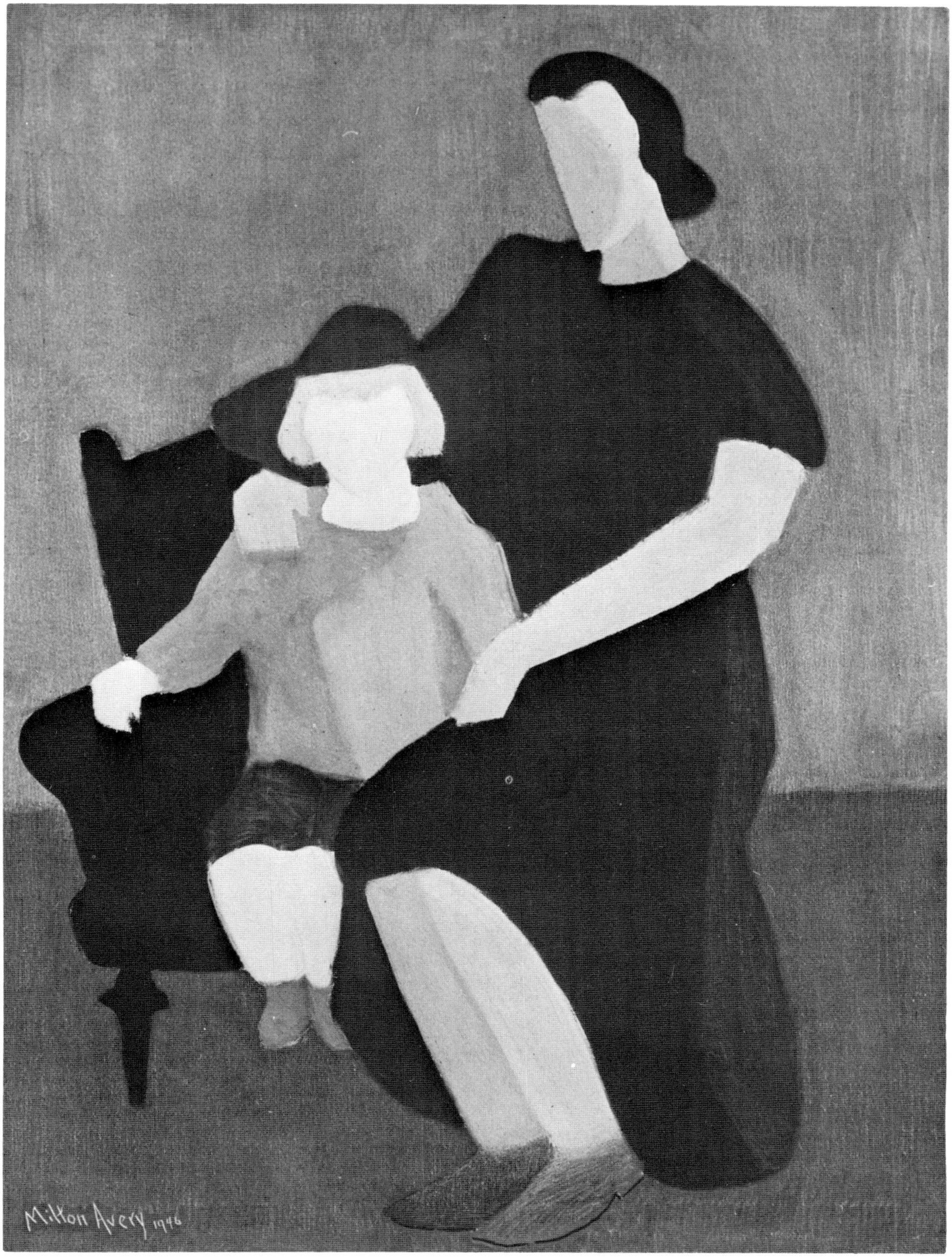
Milton Avery 1946

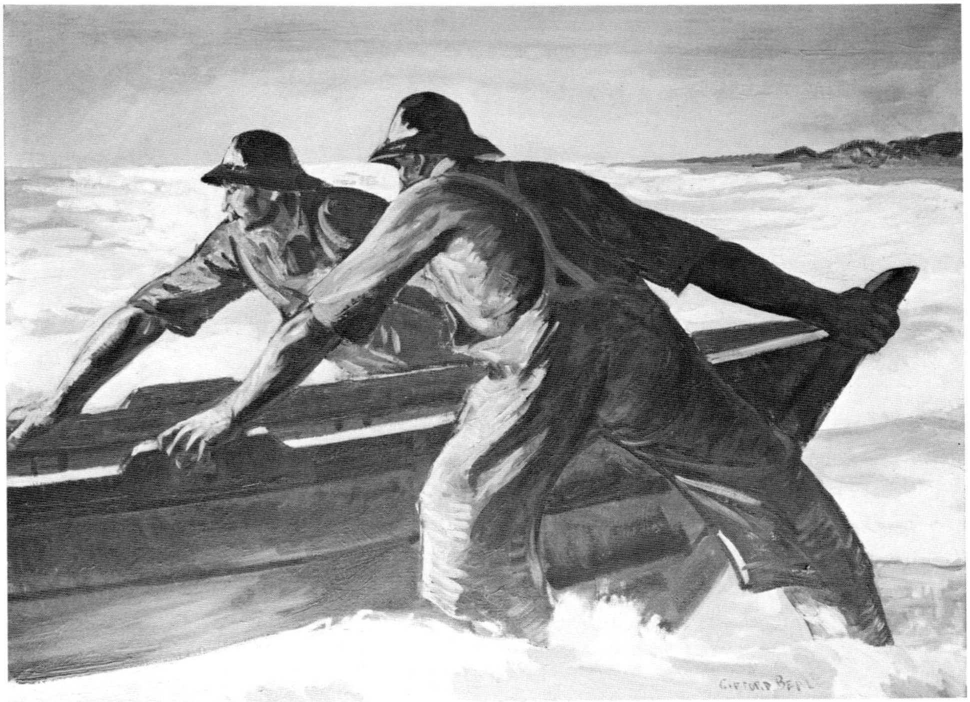

## GIFFORD BEAL

1879–1956

8. Launching the Boat  1930

Oil: 36 × 48 in.; 91.4 × 121.9 cm.
Signed, lower right: Gifford Beal
Fine Arts Fund, 1932

Exhibited: "Twenty-first Annual Exhibition," at the College, Mar. 18–Apr. 16, 1932, #1; "Fifteen Paintings from the Collection of Randolph-Macon Woman's College," circulated by the Alumnae Association between Oct. 1949 and Jan. 1950 to its chapters in Nashville, Birmingham, Atlanta, and Asheville, #1.

Recorded: Homer St. Gaudens, *The American Artist and His Times* (New York, 1941), p. 258.

## GEORGE BELLOWS
1882–1925

9. MEN OF THE DOCKS 1912
(Color plate, page 25)

Oil: 45 × 63½ in.; 114.3 × 161.2 cm.
Painted in New York, February 1912
Signed, lower left: George Bellows
First purchase of the Randolph-Macon Art Association, 1920

*I went to see Mr. Bellows in his studio in New York. He expressed great interest in our plan to start a collection of paintings at Randolph-Macon Woman's College and was pleased that we had selected "Men of the Docks" as the first painting to be purchased by the Art Association. I told him with some hesitation the amount of money we felt we could pay for the picture. His response was immediate and generous. He said that most artists, he being one of them, were less concerned about the price of their pictures than they were about having them in a place where they would be appreciated. He seemed to think the educational aspect of our undertaking was most important. The idea of having his painting where it would be viewed by successive generations of college students certainly appealed to him. Also I had the impression that he considered our idea of purchasing a painting every year, on a shoestring so to speak, was worth encouraging. The fact that the students had entered so enthusiastically into the project evidently impressed him. He said we might have the painting for the sum I had mentioned.*

T. Moody Campbell (1951)

It was as first president of the newly formed Randolph-Macon Art Association that Dr. Campbell (1879–1962) visited Mr. Bellows. This account of the visit was written when Dr. Campbell was professor of German literature at the College.

"Men of the Docks" went to the Panama-California Exposition of 1915 in San Diego instead of "Both Members of the Club"—now at the National Gallery of Art in Washington (Chester Dale Collection)—which Bellows had originally included among his entries. Evidently the exposition committee was alarmed by the postscript that Bellows added to his undated letter accompanying the list of four paintings he had chosen. He wrote:

*P.S. Canvas no. 2 is picture of prize fight and real bloody. So institutions have objected to the subject and refused to hang. . . . I add this note in order that you may object now if you feel that way. G B*[1]

San Diego did object. "Both Members of the Club" is crossed out on Bellows's list and "Men of the Docks" written in above it.

Exhibitions: "Eighty-seventh Annual Exhibition," National Academy of Design, New York, Mar. 9–Apr. 14, 1912, #148, repro.; "One Hundred and Eighth Annual Exhibition," Pennsylvania Academy of the Fine Arts, Philadelphia, Feb. 9–Mar. 30, 1913, #118, repro. (Sesnan Medal); "Twentieth Annual Exhibition of American Art," Cincinnati Museum, May 24–July 26, 1913, #42, repro; "Panama-California Exposition," Fine Arts Gallery, San Diego, Jan. 1915–Dec. 1916, #48; "Ninth Annual Exhibition," at Randolph-Macon Woman's College, Mar. 6-27, 1920, #11; "Memorial Exhibition of the Work of George Bellows," Metropolitan Museum of Art, New York, Oct. 12–Nov. 22, 1925, #15, repro. p. 59; "Main Currents in the Development of American Painting," Inaugural Exhibition, Virginia Museum, Richmond, Jan. 16–Mar. 1, 1936, #108; "New York Realists," Whitney Museum of American Art, New York, Feb. 9–Mar. 5, 1937, #5; "Golden Gate International Exposition," San Francisco, Feb. 18–Oct. 29, 1939, #1223; "George Bellows," Art Institute of Chicago, Jan. 31–Mar. 10, 1946, #14; "Revolution and Tradition," Brooklyn Museum, Nov. 15, 1951–Jan. 6, 1952, #79; "Paintings from College and University Collections," Allen Memorial Art Museum, Oberlin College, Jan. 20–Feb. 15, 1953, #14, repro.; "George Bellows," National Gallery of Art, Washington, Jan. 19–Feb. 24, 1957, #22, repro. p. 60; "George Bellows," Columbus Gallery of Fine Arts, Mar. 21–Apr. 27, 1957, #22; "Modern American Painting: 1915," Fine Arts Gallery of San Diego, Dec. 6, 1962–Jan. 6, 1963, #2, repro. p. 11; "George Bellows," Gallery of Modern Art, New York, Mar. 15–May 1, 1966, #27, repro. p. 22; "In Virginia," Virginia Museum, Richmond, Jan. 18–Feb.

1. Quoted by permission of The Fine Arts Gallery of San Diego.

14, 1971; "Celebrate Ohio," Akron Art Institute, Sept. 25–Nov. 7, 1971; "American Marine Painting," Virginia Museum, Sept. 27–Oct. 31, 1976, and Mariners Museum, Norfolk, Nov. 8–Dec. 12, 1976.

Included in four groups of paintings from Randolph-Macon Woman's College: loan exhibitions to Richmond and to Roanoke, 1964; circulating exhibitions to Florida, 1965, and to Mid-Atlantic states, 1966–67. For galleries and dates see Appendix B.

Recorded: Catalogues of the exhibitions; many reproductions in periodicals (references to these are listed in the material on Bellows in the Frick Art Reference Library, New York); Emma Louise Bellows, comp., *The Paintings of George Bellows* (New York, 1929), repro. p. 34; Peyton Boswell, *George Bellows* (New York, 1942), color repro. p. 58; A. M. Welchons and W. R. Krickenberger, *New Plane Geometry* (Boston, 1952), p. 256, repro. p. 255; Roberta D. Cornelius, *The History of Randolph-Macon Woman's College* (Chapel Hill, 1951), repro. following p. 430; Charles E. Morgan, *George Bellows* (New York, 1965), p. 148, repro. p. 329; Matthew Baigell, *A History of American Painting* (New York, 1971), p. 184, repro. p. 185; *Art Journal* 32 (Winter 72/73), p. 192, repro. p. 193; Mahonri S. Young, *The Paintings of George Bellows,* (New York, 1973), p. 62, color repro. #21; Irwin Unger and H. Mark Johnson, *Land of Progress* (Lexington, Mass., 1975), color repro. p. 543; Jean Stern, "Robert Henri and the 1915 San Diego Exposition," *American Art Review* 2 (Sept.–Oct. 1975), p. 117, color repro. p. 112.

## THOMAS HART BENTON

1889–1975

### 10. Preparing the Bill 1934

(Color plate, page 26)

Oil: 46 × 38 in.; 116.8 × 96.5 cm.
Signed, lower left: Benton
Louise J. Smith Fund, 1958

*Here is the history of the painting. It was executed in the autumn of 1934 with oil paint. It was made from "on the spot" drawings. I was a guest at the party it depicts. During this party the idea that I should make a mural for the Missouri State Capitol was just suggested. A year later, and largely because of the efforts of one of the very gentlemen represented in "Preparing the Bill," I signed a contract for such a mural. After that signing I withdrew the picture from circulation for about fifteen years. The reason should be obvious. I have described the party in "Artist in America."*

Thomas Hart Benton (1958)

This party is described on pages 258–59 of *An Artist in America:*

*In Jefferson City I ran into some old Missouri acquaintances and we had one of those regular hotel room parties where you pour liquids down you and stories out of you until the world begins to spin. When the world was spinning pretty well for me, Ed Barbour, the senatorial incumbent from Greene County and an old friend, said with his good Missouri drawl:*

*"Sa-ay, Tom, you did a picture there for Indiana. Why don't you do one for your home state?"*

*I replied that I was willing and Ed said that he'd get up a bill on the matter for the legislature.*

*Now the world was spinning for me and I took Ed's proposition just to be a part of the spinning and forgot about it. . . . But it seems that Ed and my brother Nat had talked over the business of a Missouri mural before the hotel party, that they had made rather extensive plans which I knew nothing about, and that Ed's question to me was no mere party question but one that had sub-*

*stance to back it up. Anyhow, in a month or so, I got a copy of a bill that was up before the Missouri legislature which recommended that I be hired to do a painting for the state capitol on the history of Missouri.*

Eleven years after the acquisition of "Preparing the Bill" Randolph-Macon's curator wrote in 1969 to congratulate the artist on his eightieth birthday and to ask him "now that the 1930s are so far behind" whether he would identify the three men. She enclosed a halftone reproduction on which he could insert the names. Across the bottom of the sheet he wrote:

*This is a picture of a political meeting in the early 1930's when whiskey could not be consumed without the admixture of ginger ale or other disguising concoctions. What difference does it make who the law makers were? No law makers after Lycurgus are important. These aint.*

Thomas H. Benton

*P.S. These fellows have kids and grand kids—leave 'em alone. Has nothing to do with "Art" anyhow. T.H.B.*

About "Putting the Bill Through," a title used in the *London Studio*, Benton wrote, " 'Preparing the Bill' is correct and original title. Putting a bill 'through' would have to occur on a legislative floor—would it not?"[1]

Exhibited: "Benton Retrospective," Joslyn Art Museum, Omaha, Nov. 14–Dec. 30, 1951, sixth in the unnumbered catalogue; "Thomas Hart Benton," Art Museum of the New Britain Institute, Conn., May 22–Sept. 19, 1954, #24, repro.; "Thomas Hart Benton," University of Kansas Museum of Art, Lawrence, Apr. 12–May 18, 1958, #21; "Randolph-Macon Woman's College Collection," Virginia Museum, Richmond, Sept. 11–Oct. 18, 1964; "Art of the United States 1670–1966," Whitney Museum of American Art, New York, Sept. 28–Nov. 27, 1966, #13, repro. p. 95; "American Prophets," Lowe Art Museum, Coral Gables, Fla., Feb. 22–Mar. 25, 1973; "Thomas Hart Benton," Madison (Wis.) Art Center, Mar. 22–May 3, 1970, p. 12, repro. p. 13.

1. All the above statements by Benton quoted by permission of Jessie Benton.

Recorded: Thomas Hart Benton, *An Artist in America* (New York, 1937), p. 258; *Arts Digest* 9 (Apr. 15, 1935): 12; *London Studio* 15 (June 1938): 326, as "Putting the Bill Through"; John I. H. Baur, *New Art in America: Fifty Painters of the Twentieth Century* (New York, 1957), color repro. p. 131; Mary Frances Williams, "Paintings as Teachers," *Arts in Virginia* 2 (Spring 1962), p. 24, repro. p. 25; *Richmond News Leader*, (Va.), Apr. 27, 1962, repro.; "L'Arte D'Inspirazione Sociale e D'Impegno Civile in America dal 1900 al 1945," *L'Arte Moderna*, VIII / 7 (1969), p. 309, repro. p. 306; Thomas Hart Benton, *An American in Art* (Lawrence, Kans., 1969), repro. p. 105; *Art Journal* 32 (Winter 72/73), p. 195, repro. p. 194; Matthew Baigell, *Thomas Hart Benton* (New York, 1973), repro. 74.

## PETER BLUME

Born 1906

11. CRUCIFIXION 1951

Oil on canvas mounted on masonite: 22 × 25 in.; 55.8 × 63.5 cm.
Signed and dated, upper left: Peter Blume 1951
Gift of Mr. and Mrs. Edward L. Holsten (Nancy Stinnett '24), 1954

*This painting is actually a detail developed from the complete picture called "Shrine," owned by Mr. and Mrs. Edward L. Holsten. There is another detail in the collection of the Whitney Museum called "Man of Sorrows." The motive is Mexican and is a combination of the Mexican Indian and his religious manifestations. This aspect of the "Shrine" represents the robe of Christ, festooned with votive offerings arranged to tell the story of the Crucifixion. Since you have identified the meaning of all "except the little reclining nude woman," I suggest that this figure may be one of the disciples asleep in the garden of Gethsemane.*

Peter Blume (1958)

Exhibited: "Sixtieth Annual American Exhibition," Art Institute of Chicago, Oct. 25–Dec. 16, 1951, #13; "Contemporary American Painting and Sculpture," University of Illinois, Urbana, Mar. 1–Apr. 12, 1953, #14, repro. pl. 107; "Reality and Fantasy, 1900–1954," Walker Art Center, Minneapolis, May 23–July 2, 1954, #13; "Peter Blume in Retrospect," Currier Gallery of Art, Manchester, N.H., Apr. 18–May 31, 1964, and Wadsworth Atheneum, Hartford, July 9–Aug. 16, 1964, #21; "Peter Blume Retrospective," Museum of Contemporary Art, Chicago, Jan. 10–Feb 29, 1976. Included in all six of the loan and circulating exhibitions of the College Collection during 1964–72, as listed in Appendix B.

Recorded: *The News* (Lynchburg), Jan. 9, 1955, repro.; Nathaniel Pousette-Dart, *American Painting Today* (New York, 1956), p. 67; *Arts in Virginia* 2 (Spring 1962), p. 29, with repro.; *Nashville Tennessean*, June 25, 1967, repro.

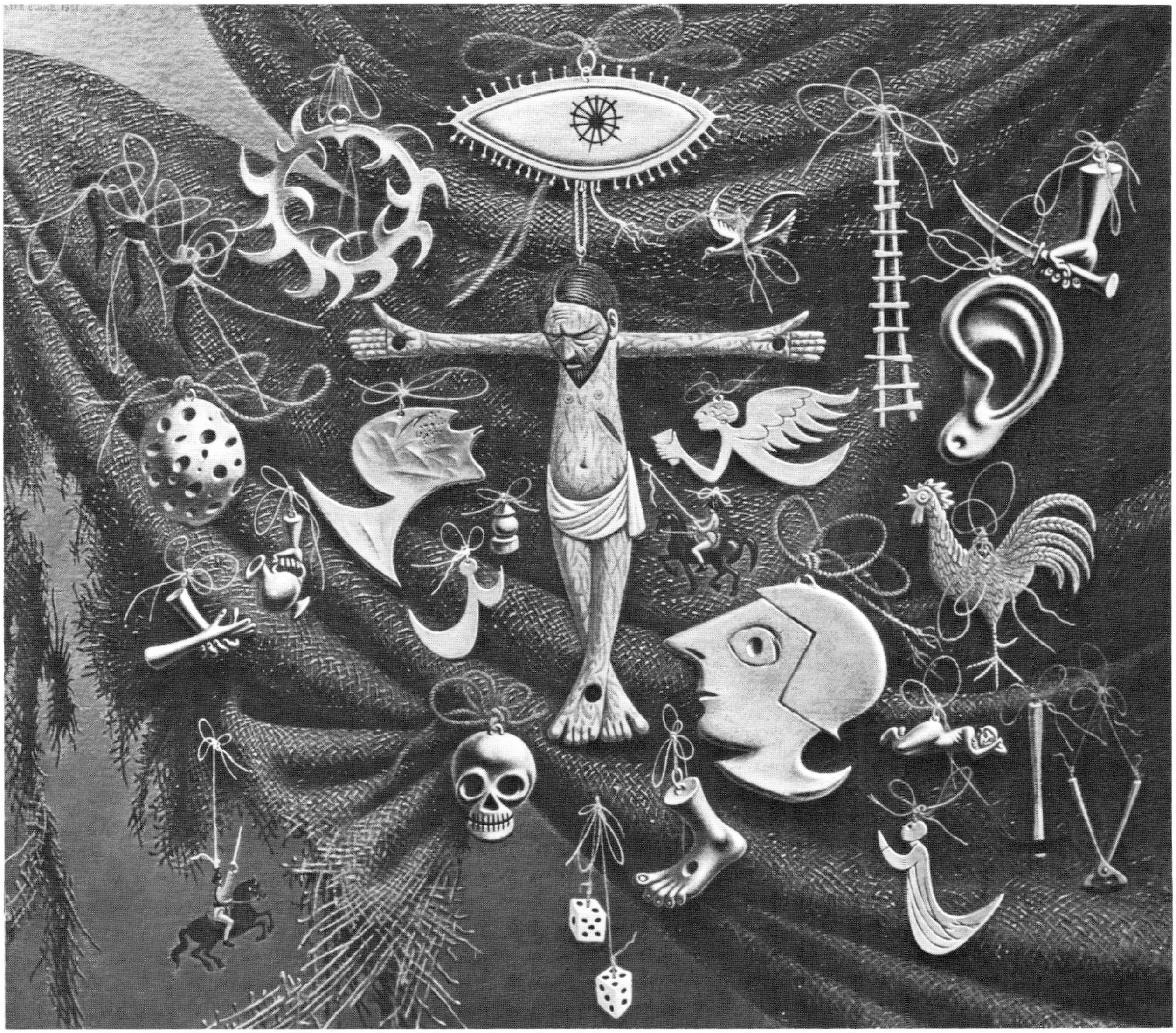

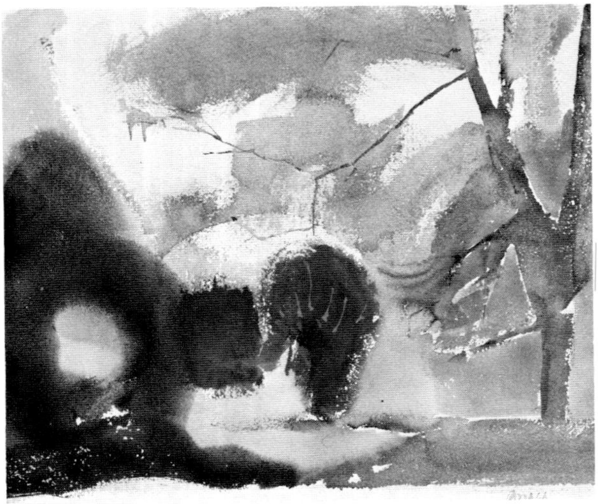

## PAUL BOND

Born 1920

12. River Construction 1952

Casein on paper: 14⅛ × 19⅞ in.; 35.8 × 50.4 cm.
Signed and dated, lower right: May 52 Bond
Gift of alumnae of New York City, 1953

Exhibited: "First Exhibition of Paintings by Paul Bond," Charles Barzansky Galleries, New York, Mar. 8–22, 1954, #7; "Picture of the Week," Sweet Briar College, Nov. 8–14, 1954.

13. CAMPUS 1966
(Reproduced above)

Watercolor: 19 × 22¾ in.; 48.2 × 57.7 cm.
Signed, lower right: Bond 66
Gift of alumnae of the Northern Delaware Chapter, 1968

*Campus is one of a series that evolved out of a commission, 1965–68. It reflects my interest and discovery, rather than the objective purpose of the commission at hand. Watercolor provides me with a medium of chance, involving incongruous relationships, much as casein did during the 1950's. I usually work on four or five at one time: some direct statements; others completed over a period of years.*

Paul Bond

Exhibited: See Appendix C.

## COLLEEN BROWNING

Born 1929

14. RED UMBRELLA 1972

Oil: 25 × 29¼ in.; 63.5 × 74.3 cm.
Signed, upper left: Colleen Browning
Gift of the Cynthia L. Hellman Memorial Fund, 1973

*I've done a whole series of umbrella paintings, as I find that a face enclosed in a sort of protective cage is a very evocative image, with both an inner and an outer meaning. It could be just a woman holding an umbrella; but also someone living in a private world. Perhaps protected or isolated. After all, the circular yoni is the Eastern female sexual symbol and the mandala form would indicate wholeness. The plastic umbrella is like a placenta, so perhaps my women are waiting to be reborn to a clear identity.*

*Finally some personal notes. I used myself as the model, as just about that time I had been knifed in the face. I also bought the red umbrella as a model (it's a tricky thing to paint) and painted with one hand while holding up the open umbrella and peering through it to the mirror—a complicated and somewhat comic operation!*

Colleen Browning

Exhibited: "Colleen Browning—Recent Paintings," Kennedy Galleries, New York, Mar. 18–Apr. 3, 1976, #3, with repro.

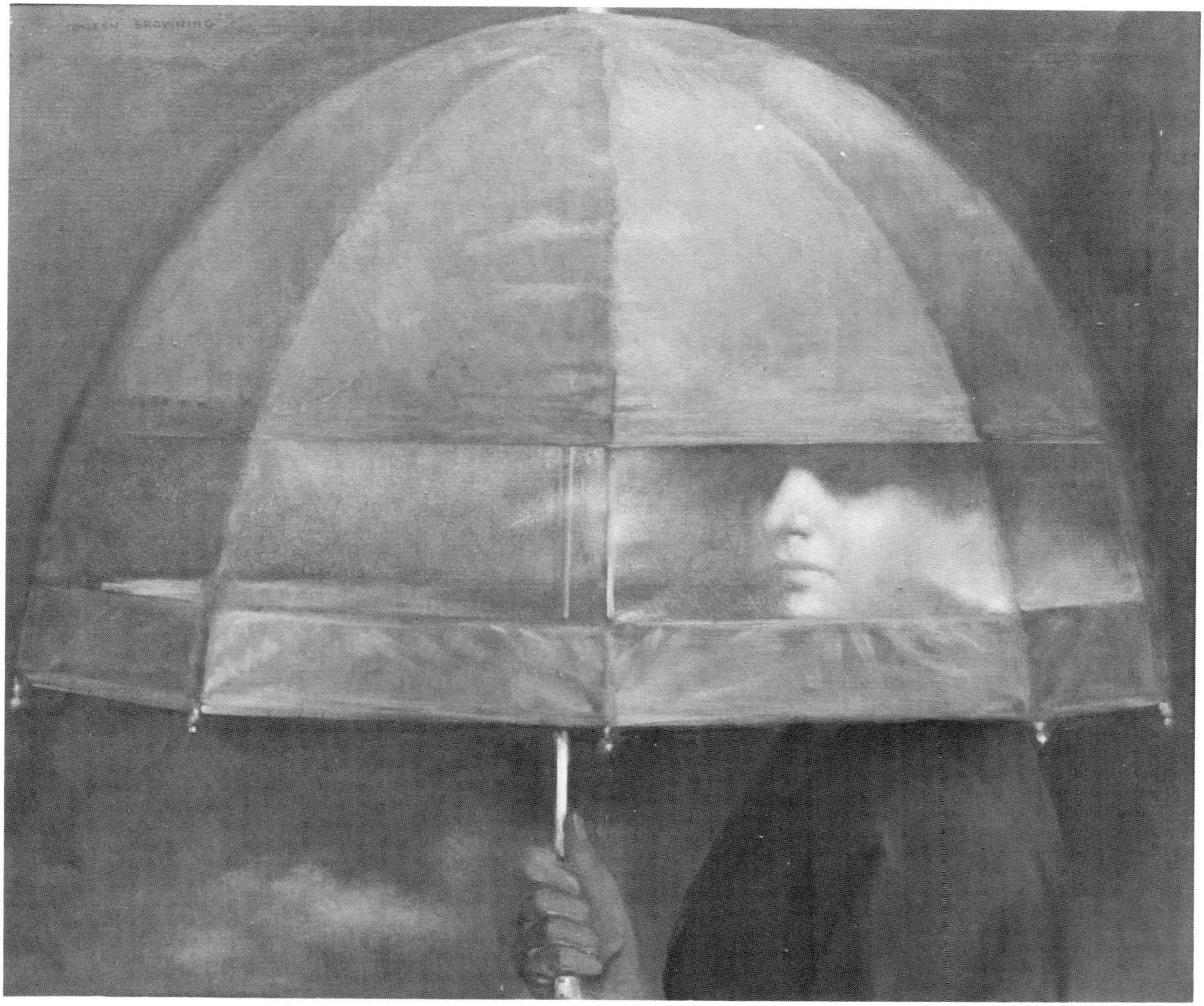

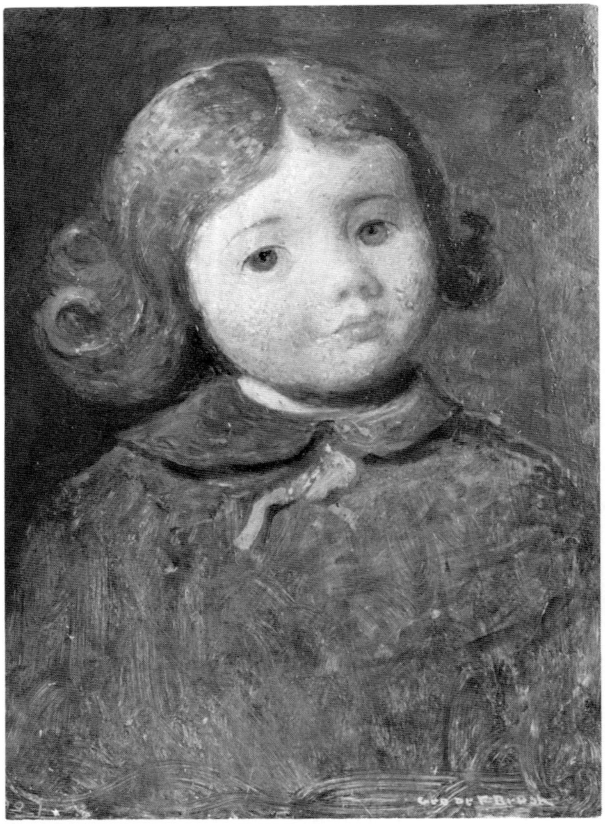

## GEORGE de FOREST BRUSH
1855–1941

15. GEORGIA About 1898

Oil on wood: 12⅞ × 9⅝ in.; 32.7 × 24.4 cm.
Inscribed, lower left: No. 7
lower right; Geo de F Brush
Gift of Gillie A. Larew '03, Annie C. Whiteside '10, and Susan P. Cobbs '27, in 1972

This appears to be a portrait study for the left-hand child in "The Family Group," in which the artist's wife stands holding one child, with four others around her. Sketches for the painting were begun in 1898 in the village of Marlotte, near the Forest of Fontainebleau, where the children posed out-of-doors. Brush finished "The Family Group" in the winter of 1899 in Florence, Italy. The round-faced little Georgia, born on Dec. 2, 1895, must have been three or four years old when this small study was painted. "Georgia," exhibited at the College in the mid-1930s, was purchased by three persons jointly, each of whom kept it in her home either one year or two, according to her share of the cost. Miss Annie C. Whiteside inherited her rights in "Georgia" from her sister Mabel K., one of the three original owners.

Reference: Nancy Douglas Bowditch, *George de Forest Brush, Recollections of a Joyous Painter* (Peterborough, N.H., 1970), p. 105.

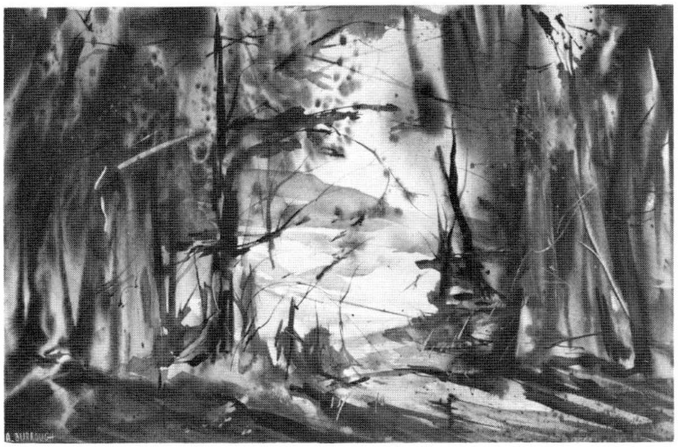

## ANNE K. BURROUGH '41

Born 1919

16. Edge of the Woods 1967

Watercolor: 19¼ × 29 in.; 48.9 × 73.6 cm.
Signed, lower left: A. Burrough
Gift of the artist in memory of Elise Paxton Keebler '14, 1969

*I have worked in many media, with special emphasis on oil and sculpture portraits. However no medium has challenged me as watercolor has. I love its beautiful fluid quality and the lovely accidental effects which can be achieved. A pure virgin wash on sparkling white paper can be a joy forever.*

Anne K. Burrough

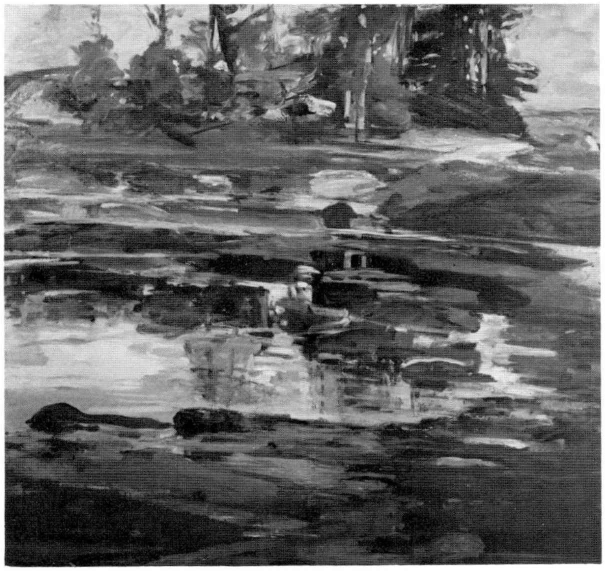

## GRETNA CAMPBELL

Born 1923

17. Landscape, Maine—Reflections, Murray Point 1972

Oil: 50 × 54 in.; 127 × 137.1 cm.
Unsigned
Fine Arts Fund, 1974

*This painting is almost a square of reflections in the shallow water of a Maine cove. The choice of a square canvas is in itself an interpretation. Each kind of rectangle has its own abstract assertion. The canvas is the painter's violin. The force of the diagonals, the pull of the corners of a square is as strong as any horizontal or vertical placed on the square canvas. For some years I have been working with a painting space which recedes in depth along a horizontal from side to side.*

Gretna Campbell

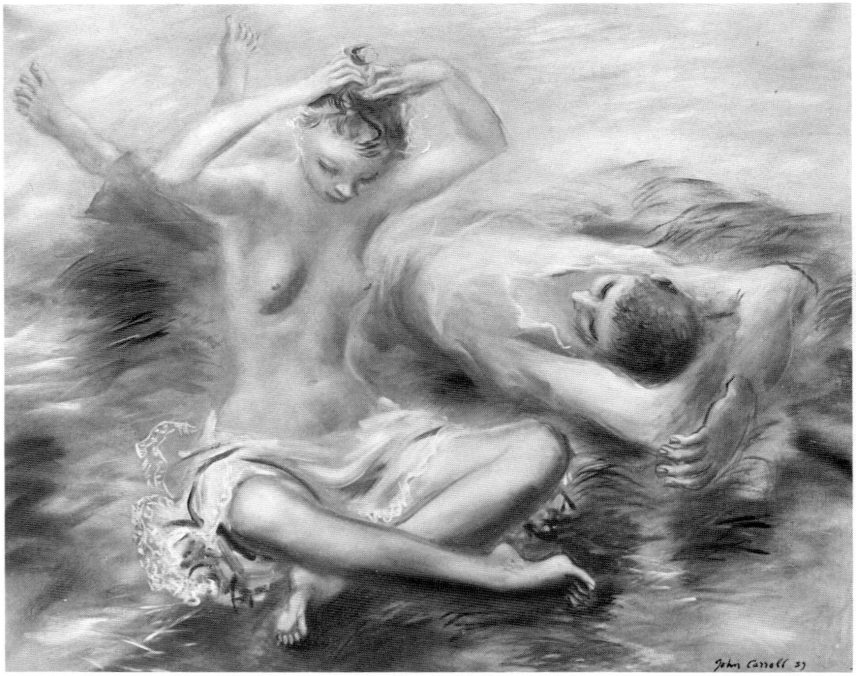


## JOHN CARROLL

1892–1959

18. SUMMER AFTERNOON 1937

Oil: 51 × 63 in.; 129.5 × 160.2 cm.
Signed, lower right: John Carroll 37
Louise J. Smith Fund, 1938

"The girl is Pinky," or Mrs. Carroll, her husband wrote in 1958.

Exhibited: "First Biennial Exhibition of Contemporary American Paintings," Virginia Museum, Richmond, Mar. 12–Apr. 24, 1938, #24, repro.; lent to Sweet Briar College for exhibition, spring 1944; see Appendix B for five exhibitions of the College Collection lent to four southern chapters of the Alumnae Association, 1949–50; to Richmond and to Roanoke, 1964; to four museums in Florida, 1965; and to six Mid-Atlantic states, 1966–67.

Recorded: Sheldon Cheney, *Story of Modern Art* (New York, 1950), repro. p. 592; Margaret Royce, "Art at Randolph-Macon Woman's College," *Commonwealth* 20 (Sept. 1953), repro. p. 25.

# JOHN CARROLL
1892–1959

19. Portrait of Dr. Herbert C. Lipscomb 1949

Oil: 50½ × 40½ in.; 128.7 × 102.8 cm.
Signed, lower right: John Carroll
Gift of Dr. Lipscomb's students through the Alumnae Association, 1949

*Dr. Lipscomb is one of the most interesting people I have painted. It was delightful having him here and since it was one of the hottest seasons ever, we went occasionally to Tanglewood for music in the evening.*

John Carroll (1958)

*John Carroll, on his farm in East Hampton, N.Y., in the foothills of the Catskill Mountains, used as his studio a converted tool shed, simply, but adequately equipped. There he painted with complete absorption in his task. Few were his comments; and when he withdrew at times to view the portrait at a distance, he would hurry back to the easel as if he feared that the impression might fade before it could be transferred to the canvas. Midway in my stay, the artist decided to test the effectiveness of a portrait in profile. This approach he abandoned after the second day of the trial—a decision probably reached after conferring with Mrs. Carroll, for whose judgment he had great respect. In one of the memorable evening discussions, Mr. Carroll declared his allegiance to the Great Tradition in painting and spoke of El Greco and Rembrandt as his "favorites among the old masters."*

Herbert C. Lipscomb (1959)

Regarded for years as the most controversial painting in the collection, this first portrait seemed to many admirers not at all like Dr. Lipscomb (1882–1973), whom they knew as scholar, gentleman, and patron of the arts, the most loved and admired professor on campus. He taught Latin from 1909 until retirement in 1955. The college library, to which he gave his collection of rare books and manuscripts, was named for him in 1959.

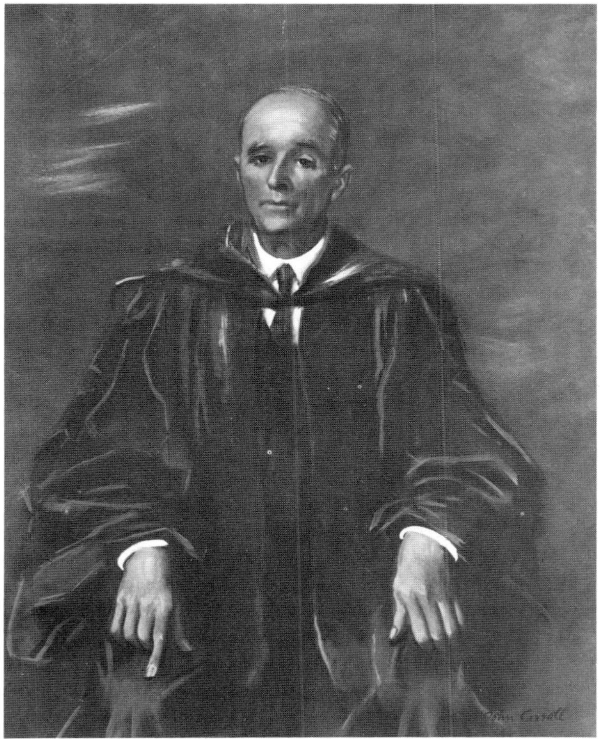

Twelve years of dissatisfaction with the Carroll portrait resulted in a second portrait (see #183, by Winslow Williams).

Exhibited: "Randolph-Macon Woman's College Collection," Virginia Museum, Richmond, Sept. 11–Oct. 18, 1964, #5.

Recorded: Herbert C. Lipscomb, "Reminiscences of the John Carrolls," *Alumnae Bulletin* 52 (June 1959): 2–3; Roberta D. Cornelius, *The History of Randolph-Macon Woman's College,* repro. following p. 430.

## MARY CASSATT
1845–1926

### 20. Sketch of Mother and Daughter Looking at the Baby About 1908
(Color plate, page 27)

Pastel on gray paper: 36½ × 29 in.; 92.7 × 73.6 cm.
Inscribed and signed, center right:
To Mr. Thompson / Mary Cassatt
Louise J. Smith Fund, 1945

This pastel was called "Young Woman with Two Children" until the Smithsonian Institution published Adelyn D. Breeskin's *Catalogue Raisonné* of the works of Mary Cassatt, in which it is #495. To distinguish this group from similar ones showing a woman with a girl and a baby, Mrs. Breeskin gave it the name adopted here. It is a preliminary study related to pastels and to oil sketches for the canvas in the White House, Washington, D.C., now named "Mother Looking Down, Embracing Both Her Children" #501 (1908). The full name of the model, who is identified in several works as "Mother Jeanne," was Jeanne Chauvet. Mrs. Breeskin reminds us that Miss Cassatt preferred using her country neighbors—rather than society matrons—as mothers in her paintings, since she considered the rural models to be more closely concerned with their children.[1]

Provenance: From the artist to Durand-Ruel, Oct. 1908; to Payson Thompson; Thompson Sale, New York, Jan. 29, 1929; acquired from Macbeth Gallery, 1945.

Requested by the Art Institute of Chicago for the Sargent, Whistler, and Cassatt exhibition of 1954. The College declined to lend the work because of the risk in transporting it, and the Art Institute withdrew its request on learning that the medium was pastel.

Recorded: American Art Association, New York, *Thompson Sale,* 1929, #89, repro.; Adelyn D. Breeskin, *Mary Cassatt: A Catalogue Raisonné of the Oils, Pastels, Water Colors, and Drawings,* (Washington, 1970), #495, repro.; *Art Journal* 32 (Winter 72/73), p. 195, repro. p. 194.

1. Adelyn D. Breeskin to Mary F. Williams, May 20, 1976.

## WILLIAM MERRITT CHASE
1849–1916

### 21. Portrait of President William Waugh Smith 1907

Oil: 30 × 25 in.; 76.2 × 63.5 cm.
Signed, lower left: Wm. M. Chase
Gift of the Class of 1907
Conservation treatment: gift of the Class of 1912, in 1962

This was the first painting to belong to the College. The sum collected was Chase's price for the head alone, but he considered Dr. Smith's hands necessary and therefore painted this three-quarter-length portrait for the amount that the Class of 1907 had raised.

Dr. Smith (1845–1912) was president of Randolph-Macon College, Ashland, Va., from 1886 to 1897, and was founder and first president of Randolph-Macon Woman's College from 1893 to 1912, thus serving for four years as president of both colleges.

Exhibited: "Jamestown Exposition," 1907, as part of the display of the Randolph-Macon educational institutions; "Randolph-Macon Woman's College Collection," Virginia Museum, Richmond, Sept. 11–Oct. 18, 1964, #8.

Recorded: *Art Journal* 32 (Winter 72/73), p. 192, with repro.

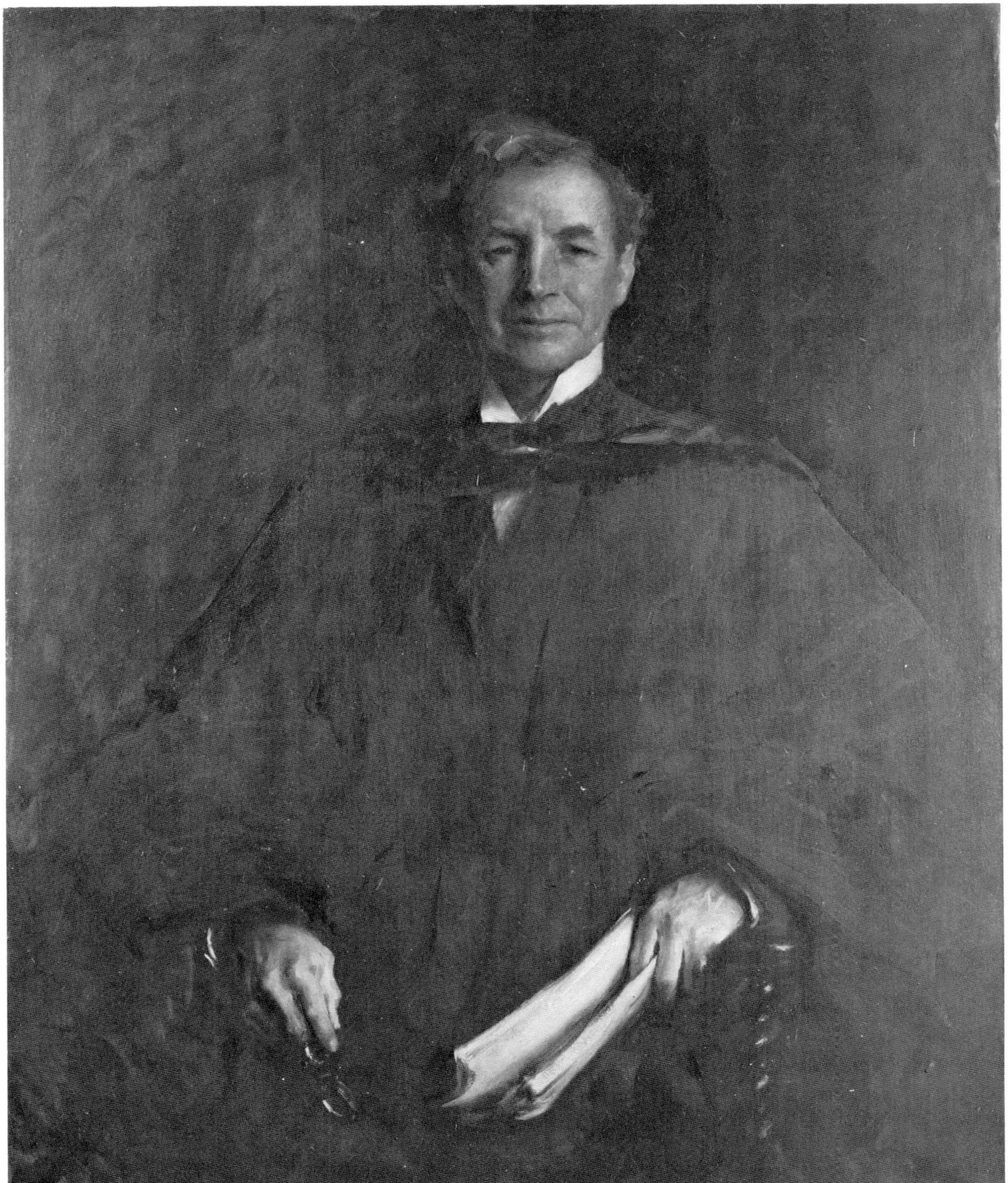

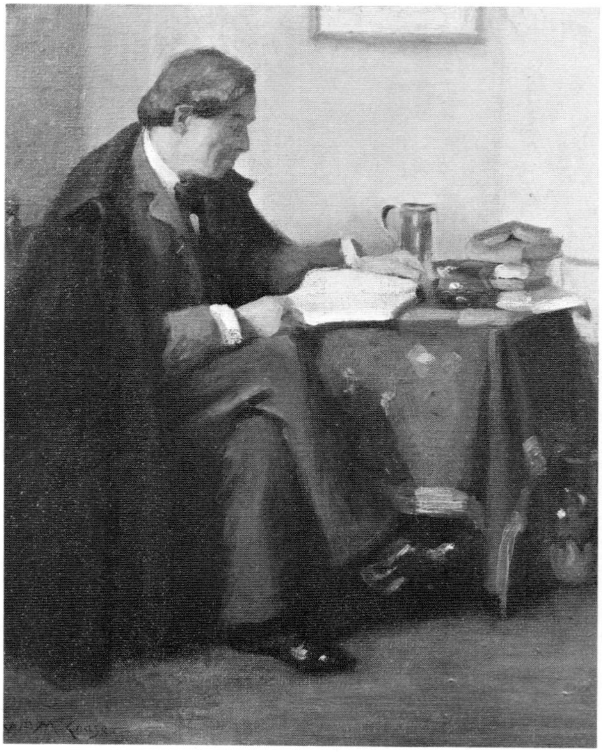

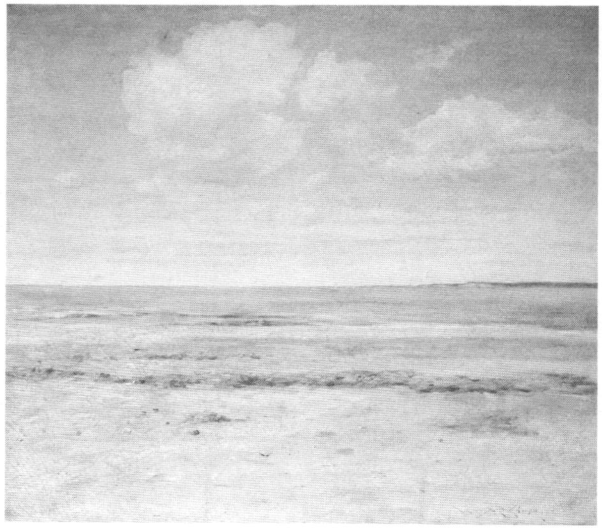

## WILLIAM MERRITT CHASE
1849–1916

22. PORTRAIT OF ELBERT HUBBARD (THE ROYCROFTER) About 1902

Oil: 18 × 15 in.; 45.7 × 38.1 cm.
Signed, lower left: Wm. M. Chase
Gift of Margaret L. Porter '02 in memory of President William Waugh Smith, 1964

Provenance: Collection of John Davis Hatch, Jr.

Exhibited: "Chase Centennial Exhibition," John Heron Art Institute, Indianapolis, Nov. 1–Dec. 11, 1949, #49, repro.; "William Merritt Chase," Parrish Art Museum, Southampton, Long Island, N.Y., June 30–July 27, 1957, #62, repro.; see Appendix B for exhibitions of the College Collection at Richmond, 1964, and in six Mid-Atlantic states, 1966–67.

Recorded: Catalogues of the exhibitions; *Alumnae Bulletin* 57 (Spring 1964), p. 23, with repro.

23. THE DESERTED BEACH About 1907

Oil: 35 × 40 in.; 88.9 × 101.6 cm.
Signed, lower right: Wm. M. Chase
Gift of the artist, 1907

Probably Shinnecock, near Southampton, Long Island, N.Y., where Chase had a summer home.

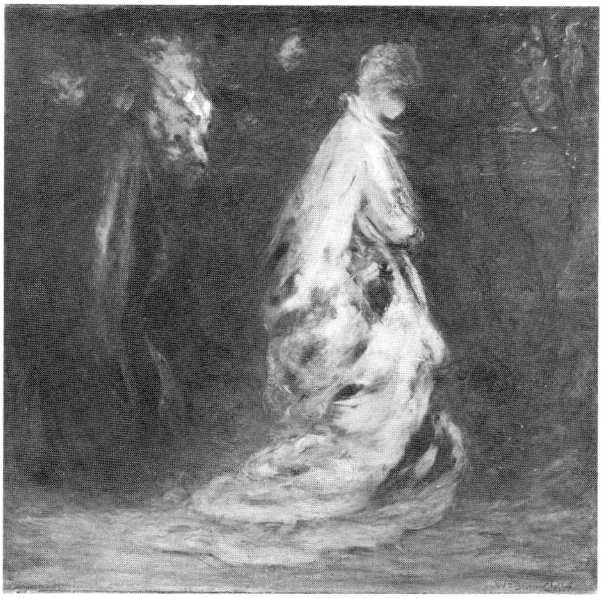

## WILLIAM BAXTER CLOSSON

1848–1926

24. The Parting

Oil: 30 × 30 in.; 76.2 × 76.2 cm.
Signed, lower right: Wm. Baxter Closson
Gift of Mr. and Mrs. Chauncey J. Blair, 1976

## THOMAS COLE

1801–48

25. Corway Peak, New Hampshire 1844
(Color plate, page 28)

Oil: 18 × 24 in.; 45.7 × 60.9 cm.
Signed and dated, lower center: T. Cole 1844
Cut into lower stretcher bar: T. Cole
Painted across center back: Corway Peak, New Hampshire
Fine Arts Fund, 1948

Today this peak in the White Mountains is known by its Indian name, Chocorua. The following quotation explains why the painting is called "Corway Peak, New Hampshire."

*How rich and sonorous that word Chocorua is! Do not, O reader, commit the sin of which the Yankee inhabitants are guilty, and into which stage-drivers will tempt you, of flattening the majestic roll and melancholy cadence of the word into "Corway." Does not its rhythm suggest the wildness and loneliness of the great hills?*[1]

Exhibited: It is not known whether in the following sentence Louis L. Noble was referring to this "Corway Peak" of 1844 or to Cole's earlier one, exhibited at the National Academy of Design in 1835: "When his American autumnal and forest views, 'Corway Peak' and 'The Tornado in the Forest,' for instance, were first seen in London, they were condemned as false to nature, particularly in color."[2] Shown in five exhibitions of the College Collection listed in Appendix B: at Richmond and at Roanoke, 1964; at Tampa, Orlando, Gainesville, and Jacksonville, 1965; in six Mid-Atlantic states, 1966–67; and in the Virginia Museum's Artmobile, 1969–70.

1. Thomas Starr King, *The White Hills: Their Legends, Landscape, and Poetry* (Boston, 1859), p. 141.

2. Louis L. Noble, *The Course of Empire, Voyage of Life and Other Pictures of Thomas Cole, N. A.* (New York, 1853), p. 173.

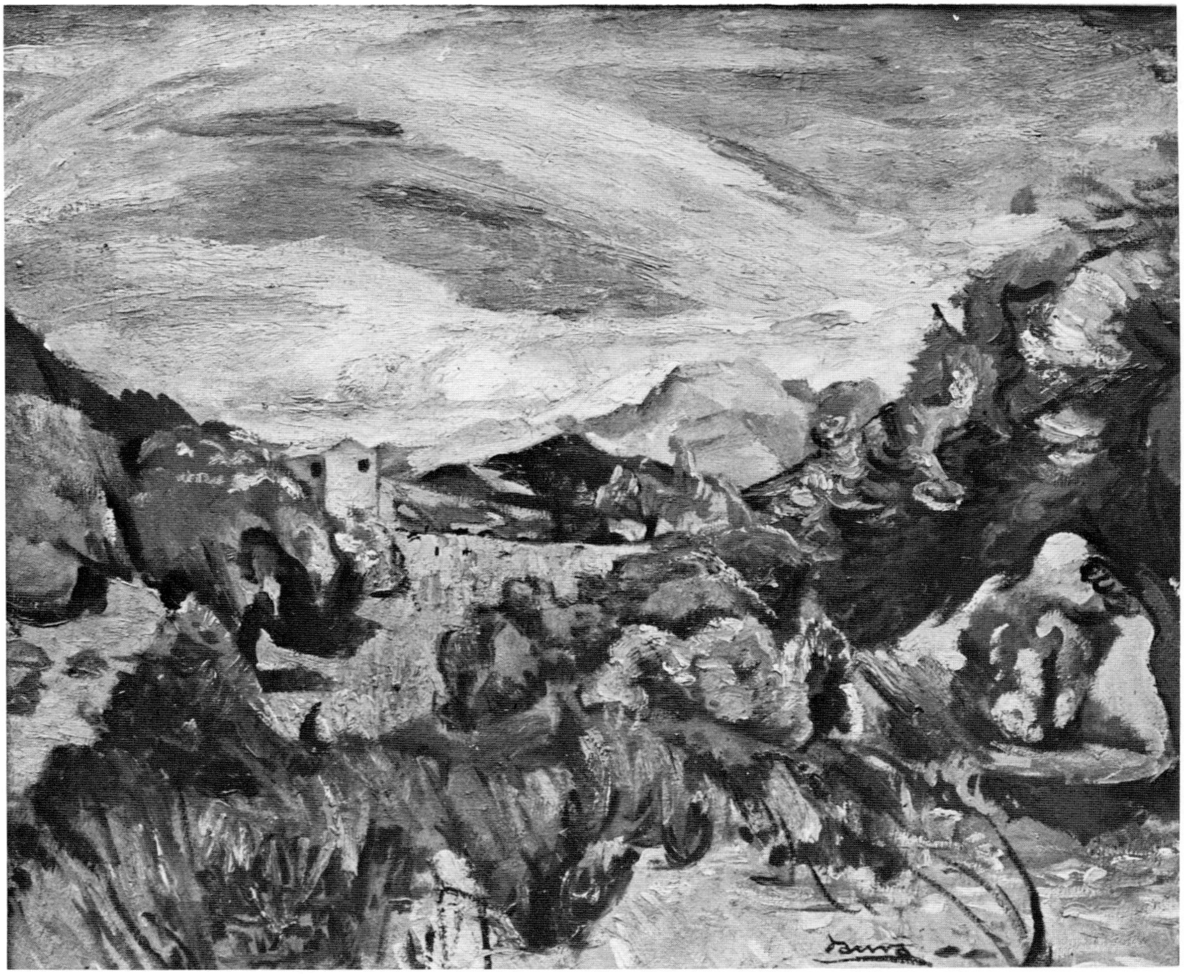

PIERRE DAURA
1896–1976

26. LOZZI, ISLAND OF CORSICA 1928

Oil: 23 × 28 in.; 58.4 × 71.1 cm.
Signed, right of center: Daura
Given in 1950 "In Appreciation of Mr. Daura's Work by Members of the Classes of 1947, '48, '49 and '50."

*This painting done in 1928 would indicate a transition from the two-dimensional static character of my preceding work to a more dynamic lyricism, a more tormented exalted vision which presided over my work before receding back to pure abstraction.*

Pierre Daura (1959)

Exhibited: "The Lynchburg Art Center Begins Its Series of One Man Shows Presenting the Works of Pierre Daura," Nov. 1–15, 1953, #15; "Randolph-Macon Woman's College Collection," Virginia Museum, Richmond, Sept. 11–Oct. 18, 1964, #10.

# ARTHUR B. DAVIES

1862–1928

Forty-one works by Arthur B. Davies from the collection of Lizzie P. Bliss were given to the College in 1949 by Miss Bliss's sister-in-law, Mrs. Cornelius N. Bliss, after consultation with Robert G. McIntyre, president of the Macbeth Gallery (William Macbeth, Inc.) and trustee of the estate of Miss Bliss. That gift consisted of five oils and several watercolors, drawings, and prints. Other works by Davies, also from the Lizzie P. Bliss collection, were given in 1952 by the same donor, then Mrs. A. Conger Goodyear. Paintings by Davies have been given also by members of the Macbeth family at various times.

References to major exhibitions

1918 Macbeth: "Loan Exhibition of Paintings, Watercolors, Drawings, Etchings, and Sculpture by Arthur B. Davies," Macbeth Galleries, (*sic*), New York, 1918.
1930 Memorial: "Memorial Exhibition of the Works of Arthur B. Davies," Metropolitan Museum of Art, New York, 1930.
1962 Centennial: "Arthur B. Davies, a Centennial Exhibition," Munson-Williams-Proctor Institute, Utica, N.Y., and circulated to six other museums, 1962-63.

Bibliography

Catalogues of the exhibitions of 1918, 1930, and 1962.
Royal Cortissoz, *Arthur B. Davies,* American Artists Series, Whitney Museum (New York, 1931) (contains a list prepared by the artist's widow, Dr. Virginia M. Davies, of the artist's known works).
Duncan Phillips and others, *Arthur B. Davies: Essays on the Man and His Art,* The Phillips Publications, no. 3, (Washington, 1924).

The nine oils that have been dated (#27–35), are catalogued chronologically; the eight other oils (#36–43) are then catalogued alphabetically by title, followed by the seven watercolors. For drawings by Davies see #185–201; for prints, see # 211–29.

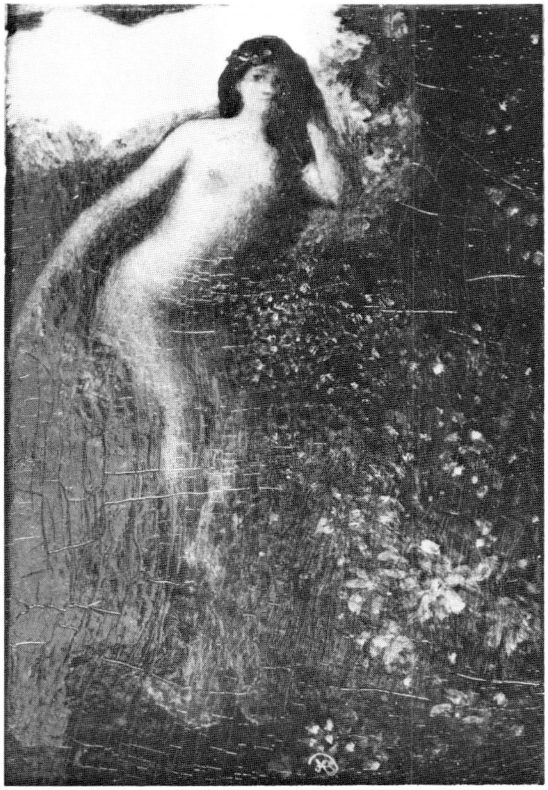

27. NIXIE About 1893
Oil on wood: 6 × 4 in.; 15.2 × 10.1 cm.
Signed, bottom center, with a monogram: AB enclosed in a D
Gift of Mrs. Robert W. Macbeth, 1950

The dimensions given here differ from those in the catalogue of the Centennial Exhibition, but are correct.

Exhibited: 1962 Centennial, #4. The date given above was determined by Harris Prior, who prepared the 1962 Centennial exhibition.

Recorded: Cortissoz, p. 30 as in the collection of Mrs. William Macbeth.

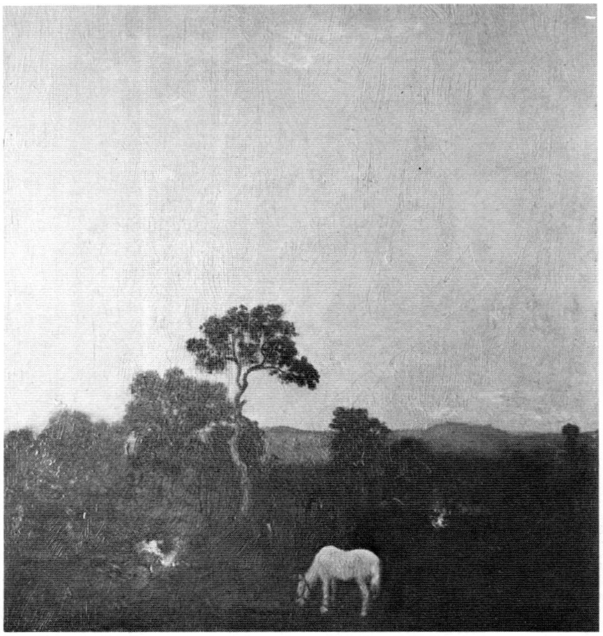

## ARTHUR B. DAVIES (cont.)

28. Music in the Fields 1895

Oil: 20 × 8¼ in.; 50.8 × 20.9 cm.
Signed, bottom center: A. B. Davies
Gift of Mrs. Robert W. Macbeth, 1950

Recorded: Cortissoz, p. 29, with height and width reversed; the date as above.

29. Gypsy Encampment in the Ramapo Hills 1896

Oil on wood: 14 × 11¾ in.; 35.5 × 29.8 cm.
Signed, bottom center: A. B. Davies
Signed and dated on the back in chalk:
A. B. Davies 1896
Gift of Mrs. Robert W. Macbeth, 1950

Exhibited: 1962 Centennial, #8; "Randolph-Macon Woman's College Collection," Virginia Museum, Richmond, Sept. 11–Oct. 19, 1964, #11.

Recorded: Cortissoz, p. 26, as "Gypsy Camp."

30. Flora 1900

Oil: 16 × 13¼ in.; 40.6 × 34.2 cm.
Signed, bottom center: A. B. Davies
Gift of Mrs. William Macbeth, 1950

Recorded: Cortissoz, p. 25, dated as above.

31. Primitive Man 1903

Oil: 28¼ × 23 in.; 71.4 × 58.4 cm.
Signed, bottom, left of center: A. B. Davies
Gift of Mrs. A. Conger Goodyear, 1952

Exhibited: 1930 Memorial, #36.

Recorded: Cortissoz, p. 31, dated as above; Catalogue of the 1930 Memorial Exhibition, repro.

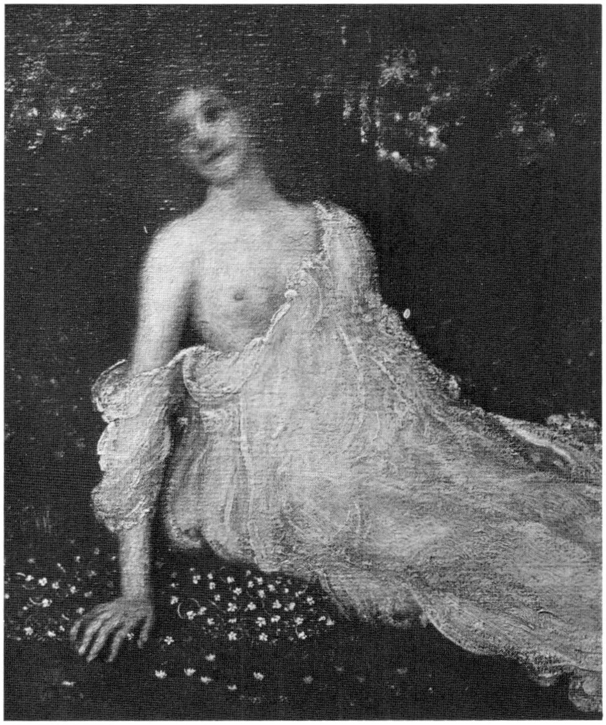

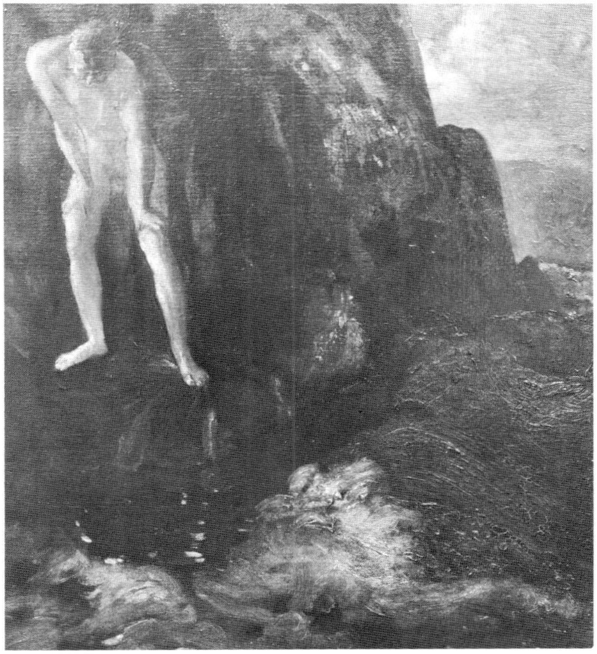

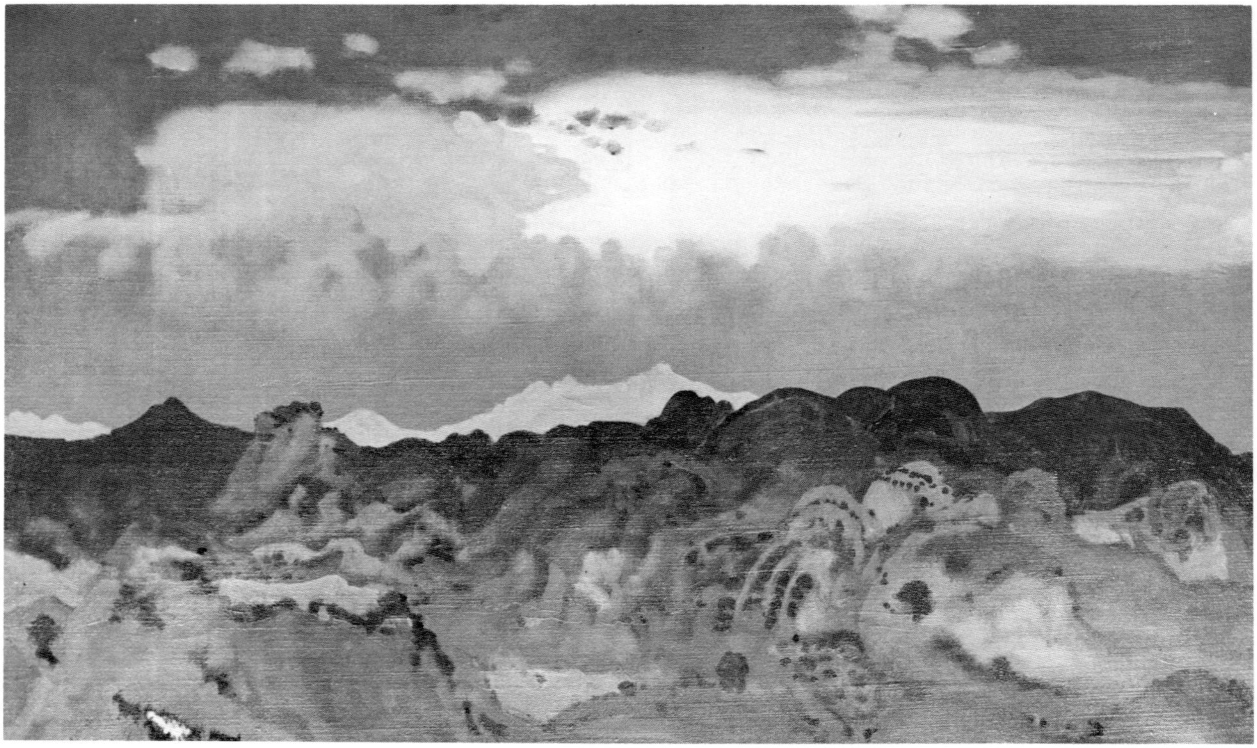

## ARTHUR B. DAVIES (cont.)

32. ACHAEA, GREECE Exhibited 1918

Oil: 18 × 30 in.; 45.7 × 76.2 cm.
Signed, lower left: A. B. Davies
Gift of Mrs. C. N. Bliss, 1949

Exhibited: 1918 Macbeth, #38; Brooklyn Museum, N.Y., June 5, 1926, as "Achara"; 1930 Memorial, #60.

Recorded: catalogues of the exhibitions of 1918 and 1930. *Arts and Decoration* 8 (Jan. 1918), repro. p. 112; reproduced, catalogues of the 1918 Macbeth and 1930 Memorial exhibitions; Cortissoz, p. 20, as "Achaia," with 1920 given as the date.

33. DECORATION Exhibited 1918

Oil sketch on canvas: 58½ × 38 in.; 148.5 × 96.5 cm.
Unsigned
Gift of Mrs. C. N. Bliss, 1949

Exhibited: 1918 Macbeth, #41.

Recorded: Catalogue of the 1918 Macbeth Exhibition.

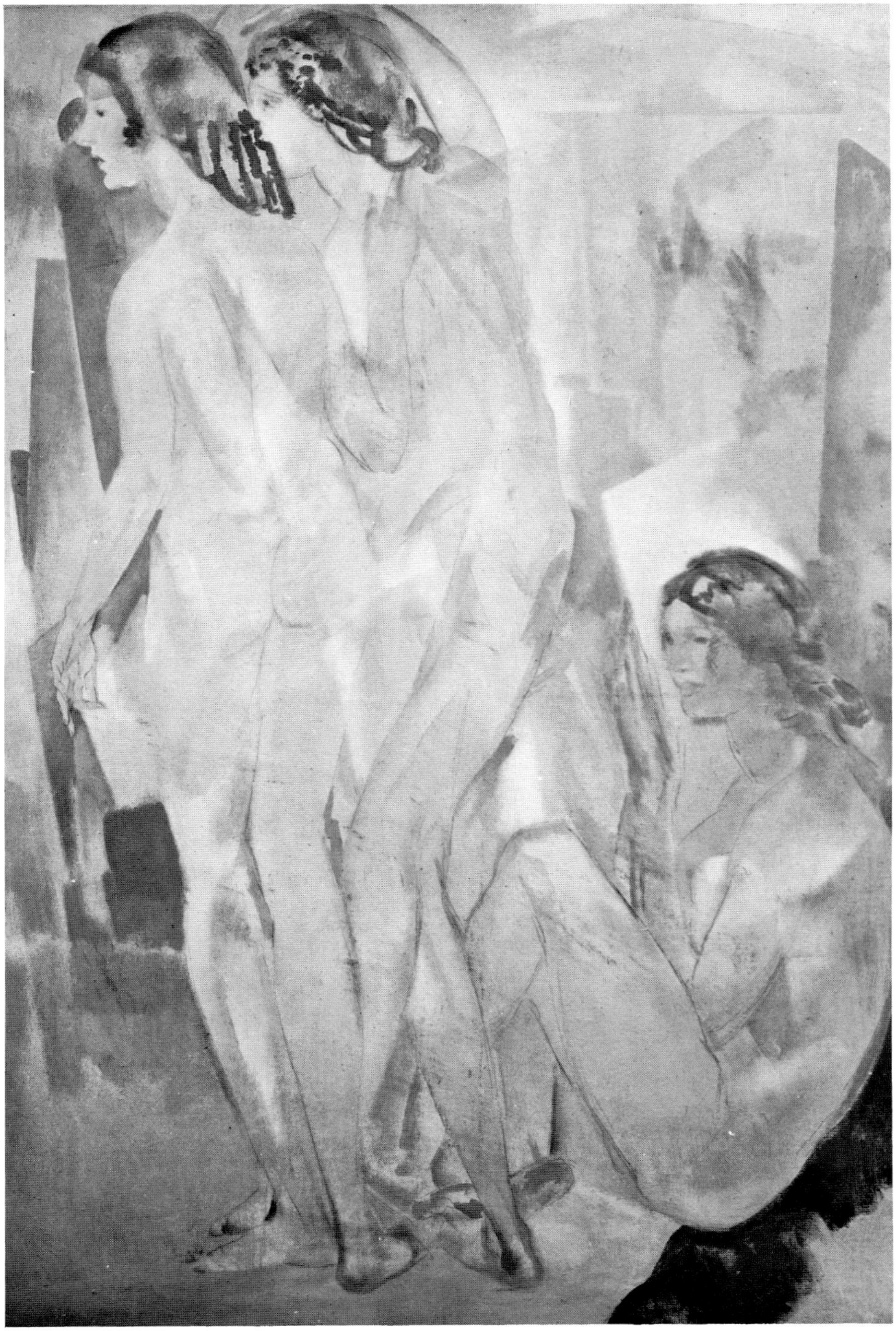

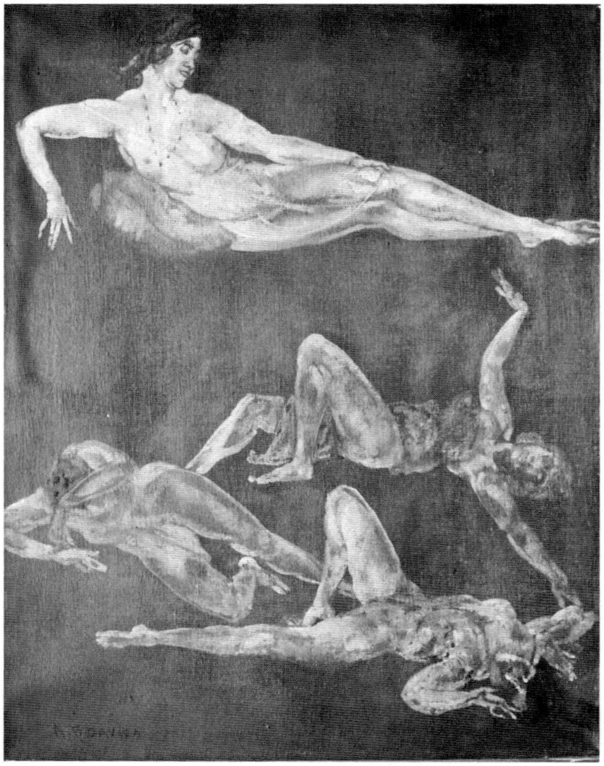

## ARTHUR B. DAVIES (cont.)

34. WILD HE-GOAT DANCE 1920
(Color plate, page 28)

Oil: 18 × 40 in.; 45.7 × 101.6 cm.
Signed lower left: A. B. Davies
Gift of Mrs. A. Conger Goodyear, 1952

Exhibited: 1930 Memorial, #119; 1962 Centennial, #52; shown in five exhibitions of the College Collection listed in Appendix B: at Richmond and at Roanoke, 1964; at Tampa, Orlando, Gainesville, and Jacksonville, 1965; in six Mid-Atlantic states, 1966–67; and in the Virginia Museum's Artmobile, 1969–70.

Recorded: Reproduced in catalogues of the 1930 and 1962 exhibitions; F. Newlin Price, "Davies the Absolute," *International Studio* 75 (June 1922), repro. p. 215; Cortissoz, p. 35.

35. FOUR DANCING FIGURES 1924

Oil: 22 × 17 in.; 55.8 × 43.1 cm.
Signed, lower left: A. B. Davies
Gift of Mrs. C. N. Bliss, 1949

Recorded: Cortissoz, p. 25, dated as above.

36. An Olympiad

Oil: 10½ × 13⅜ in.; 26.6 × 33.9 cm.
Signed, bottom center: A. B. Davies
Gift of Mrs. William Macbeth, 1950

37. Connecticut River Valley

Oil on wood: 5⅜ × 9⅜ in.; 13.6 × 23.8 cm.
Signed, lower left: ABD
Gift of Mrs. Robert W. Macbeth, 1950

38. Half Faded Blossom

Oil: 7 × 15¾ in.; 17.7 × 40 cm.
Unsigned
Gift of Mrs. C. N. Bliss, 1949

39. Long Island Shore

Oil on wood: 6⅛ × 10⅛ in.; 15.5 × 25.7 cm.
Signed, lower left: ABD
Gift of Mrs. William Macbeth, 1950

Recorded: Cortissoz, p. 28, with slightly smaller dimensions.

40. On Hampstead Heath

Oil: 7½ × 12⅝ in.; 19 × 32 cm.
Signed, bottom, left of center: A. B. Davies
Gift of Mrs. William Macbeth, 1950

41. Pastoral

Oil: 8¼ × 12¾ in.; 20.9 × 32.3 cm.
Signed, lower right: A. B. Davies
Gift of Mrs. William Macbeth, 1950

Recorded: Cortissoz, p. 30.

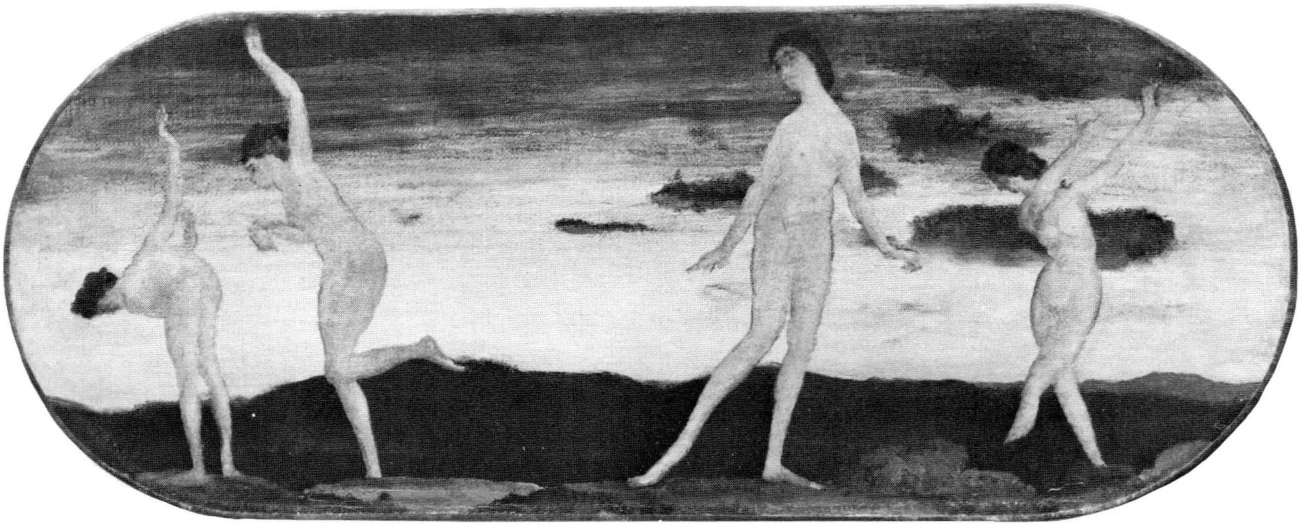

42. Star in the North

Oil on oval canvas: 9 × 19 in.; 22.8 × 48.2 cm.
Unsigned
Gift of Mrs. C. N. Bliss, 1949

Exhibited: Randolph-Macon Woman's College Collection," Virginia Museum, Richmond, Sept. 11–Oct. 18, 1964, #13.

Recorded: Cortissoz, p. 33; *The News* (Lynchburg), Oct. 16, 1949, repro.; *Arts in Virginia* 2 (Spring 1962), p. 28, repro. p. 27.

43. Sweet Ariel Clouds

Oil on wood: 6¼ × 10⅛ in.; 15.8 × 25.7 cm.
Signed, lower right: ABD
Gift of Mrs. William Macbeth, 1950

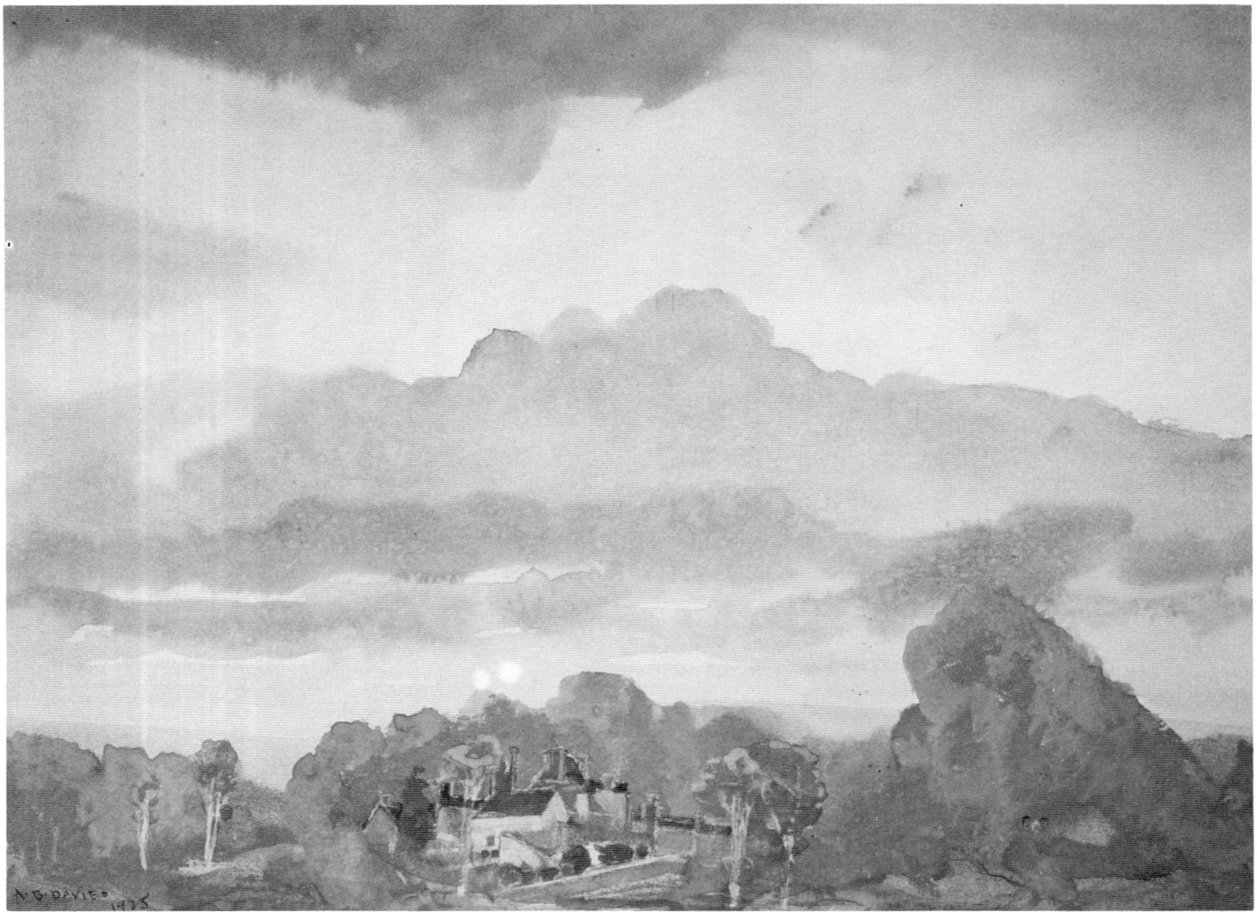

## ARTHUR B. DAVIES (cont.)

44. OUTSKIRTS OF PARIS 1925

Watercolor: 10½ × 14½ in.; 26.6 × 36.8 cm.
Signed and dated, lower left: A.B. Davies 1925
Gift of Mrs. Robert W. Macbeth, in memory of her husband, 1945

Exhibited: "Twenty-fourth Annual Philadelphia Water Color Exhibit," Pennsylvania Academy of the Fine Arts and Philadelphia Water Color Club, 1926; "Seventh International Exhibition of Watercolor Paintings," Art Institute of Chicago, 1927; "Annual Fine Arts Exhibition of the Minnesota State Fair," 1927; the College Collection, Virginia Museum, Richmond, Sept. 11–Oct. 18, 1964, #12.

Six watercolors given by Mrs. C. N. Bliss, 1949

45. By the River

12 × 7 in.; 30.4 × 17.7 cm.
Signed, lower left: ABD

46. Three Nudes in Landscape

9 × 6⅞ in.; 22.8 × 17.4 cm.
Signed, lower left: A. B. Davies

47. Nudes in Landscape (three)

On tan paper: 11¾ × 6¾ in.; 29.8 × 17.1 cm.
Signed, lower left: A. B. Davies

48. AMBER GARDEN

12¾ × 9½ in.; 32.3 × 24.1 cm.
Signed, lower left: ABD

Formerly known as "Two Nudes with Tree." The present title comes from Davies's aquatint "Amber Garden," which is a mirror image of this watercolor. Compare with #212, reproduced on page 185.

49. Kneeling and Seated Nudes (two)

9⅛ × 6⅞ in.; 23.1 × 17.4 cm.
Unsigned

50. Three Nudes

11¾ × 6⅞ in.; 29.8 × 17.4 cm.
Signed, lower left: ABD

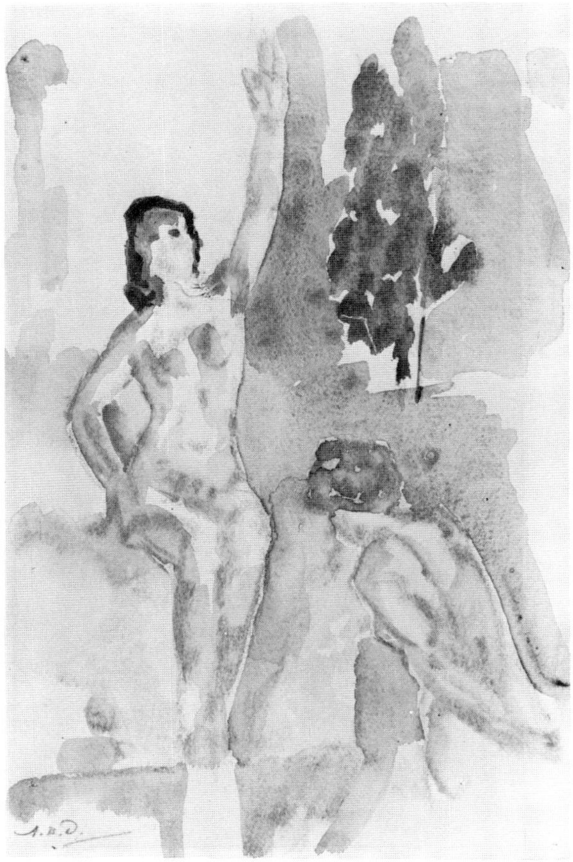

Drawings by Davies begin with #185.

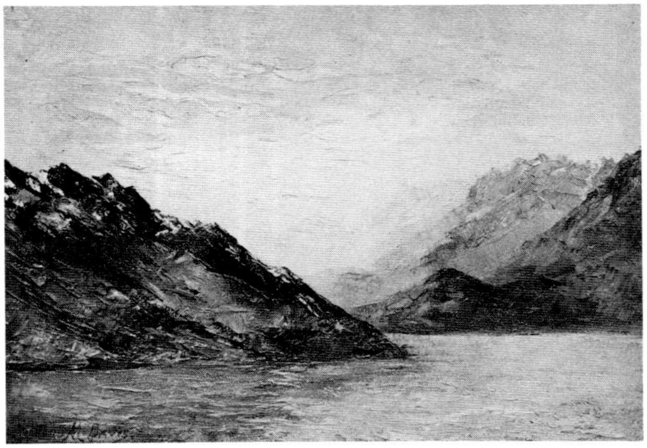

## LEONARD M. DAVIS
1864–1938

51. LAKE BENNETT, ALASKA

Oil on cardboard: 7 × 10 in.; 17.7 × 25.4 cm.
Signed, lower left: Leonard M. Davis
Purchased with admission fees to the Fourth Annual Exhibition, 1914

## STUART DAVIS
1894–1964

52. THE FOUNTAIN 1941

Gouache: 11½ × 15½ in.; 29.2 × 39.3 cm.
Signed, lower right: Stuart Davis
Gift of the American Academy of Arts and Letters (Childe Hassam Fund), 1946

*I do not recall my specific interest in the various items of subject matter in my gouache "The Fountain." Let us say it is a still life and that the elements involved were picked at random as a challenge in composition.*

Stuart Davis (1963)

Exhibited: "Randolph-Macon Woman's College Collection," Virginia Museum, Richmond, Sept. 11–Oct. 18, 1964, #15; "Stuart Davis Memorial Exhibition," organized by and exhibited at the National Collection of Fine Arts, Washington, and circulated to the Art Institute of Chicago, to Whitney Museum of American Art, New York, and to Art Galleries, University of California at Los Angeles, May 25–Dec. 5, 1965, #76; "Stuart Davis," circulated by the United States Information Agency and the Smithsonian Institution, National Collection of Fine Arts, to the Museum of Modern Art, Paris, Feb. 15–Mar. 15, to Amerika Haus, Berlin, Apr. 22–May 21, and to the American Embassy Gallery, London, June 7–24, 1966, #27; "Art on Paper," Weatherspoon Art Gallery, University of N.C. at Greensboro, Nov. 14–Dec. 17, 1971, #4. See Appendix B for exhibitions of the College Collection in six Mid-Atlantic states, 1966–67.

Recorded: In catalogues of the Memorial Exhibition and exhibitions in Paris, Berlin, London, and Greensboro; *Art Journal* 32 (Winter 72/73), p. 195, repro. p. 194.

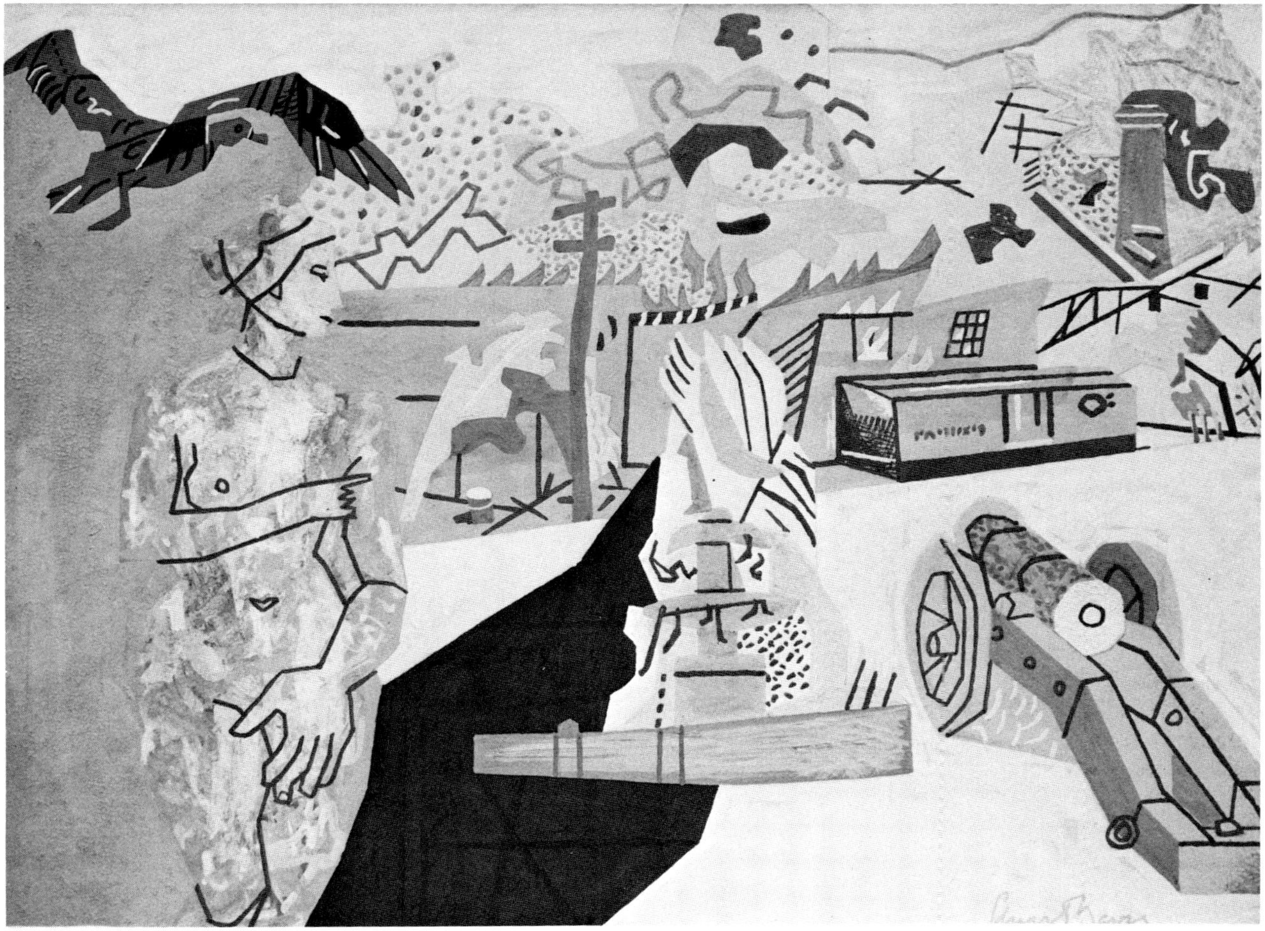

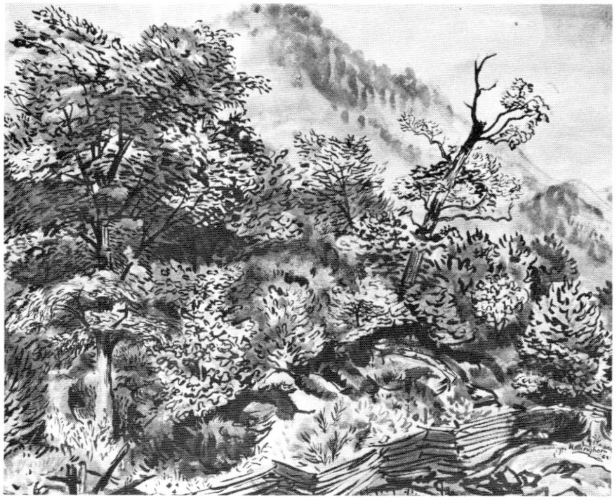

## ELIZABETH NOTTINGHAM DAY '28

1907–56

53. Edge of the Wood 1952

Watercolor: 19½ × 23½ in.; 49.5 × 59.6 cm.
Signed and dated, lower right: Nottingham '52
Memorial Gift of the Class of 1928, in 1958

Exhibited: "Water Colors by Elizabeth Nottingham Day," Traveling Exhibition #69, circulated in Virginia by the Virginia Museum, Richmond, in 1957–58; "Elizabeth Nottingham Day Memorial Exhibition," at the College, Apr. 25–June 3, 1958, #15; "Randolph-Macon Woman's College Collection," Virginia Museum, Sept. 11–Oct. 18, 1964, #16.

Recorded: *An Artist Abroad: Letters by Elizabeth Nottingham Day. . .* , (privately printed, Orange, Va., 1959), repro. p. 125.

## WÖRDEN DAY '34

54. By the River 1941

Oil: 25 × 30 in.; 63.5 × 76.2 cm.
Signed and dated, lower right:
E. Wörden Day 24/2/41
Fine Arts Fund, 1941

Exhibited: "Esther Wörden Day," Virginia Museum, Richmond, Oct. 25–Nov. 13, 1941, #10.

55. View at Kingston, New York 1941

Oil: 25 × 30 in.; 63.5 × 76.2 cm.
Signed and dated, lower right:
E Wörden Day 8/19/41
Gift of Beatrice von Keller, 1953

56. Industrial City 1942

Watercolor: 14½ × 21¾ in.; 36.8 × 55.2 cm.
Signed and dated, lower left:
E. Wörden Day 10/10/42
Gift of Mrs. J. Garland Pollard, Jr., 1969

57. Wilderness III 1960

Oil on masonite: 49½ × 58¾ in.; 125.7 × 149.2 cm.
Signed, lower right: Wörden Day (followed by a monogram)
Gift of Julie Marshall, 1963

*I seek in my own work to touch the Reality behind forms, whether visible or invisible. This Reality goes beyond the three-dimensional world of effect, to the forces which create the effect. Still further inner journeys carry me to the constant behind the forces. The only constant behind the irreversible flux, evolution of the cosmos, is Light. There is no ultimate, absolute form, space, or time. Color-Light alone is the only constant. It is the Reality that is not out there, but here. And here is Now. And Now is the only constant that always has been, is now, and will always be.*

*Indeed the best of abstract art is truly out of this world into the fourth (and beyond) dimension of*

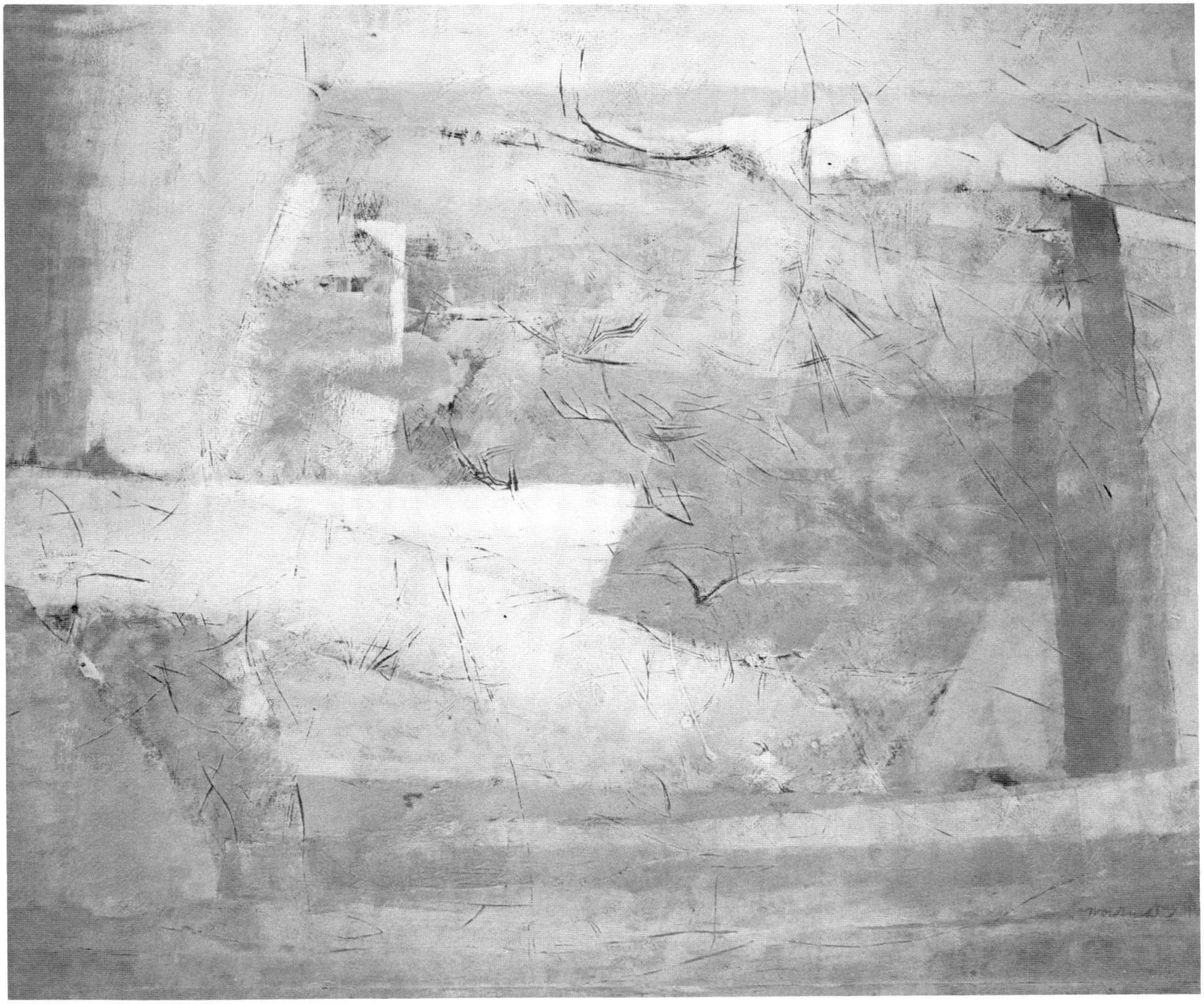

*Color-Light. Ours is an age of the grey dawning of a new consciousness, requiring a new mental species, a spiritual evolution.*

Wörden Day[1]

1. Quoted by permission of Wörden Day, who wrote it in 1957 to Mrs. Robert B. Scott (Harriet Wyche '57).

Exhibited: "Randolph-Macon Woman's College Collection," Virginia Museum Richmond, Sept. 11–Oct. 18, 1964, #17.

Recorded: *Wörden Day* (Montclair [N.J.] Art Museum, 1959), pp. 2–7; Andrew C. Ritchie, *Abstract Painting and Sculpture in America* (New York, 1951), p.150.

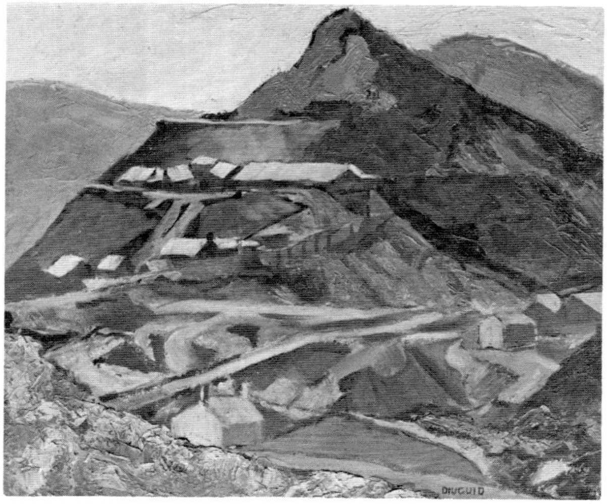

## MARY SAMPSON DIUGUID ex-'05
1883–1968

58. Slate Mines in Wales

Oil: 20 × 24 in.; 50.8 × 60.9 cm.
Signed, lower right: Diuguid
Gift of Mrs. Kirk Perrow, Jr., in honor of the artist, 1968

59. South Carolina

Watercolor: 19¼ × 22¾ in.; 48.9 × 57.7 cm.
Signed, lower right: Diuguid
Gift of Mrs. Kirk Perrow, Jr., in honor of the artist, 1968

## BURHAN DOGANCAY
Born 1925

60. Big E (Walls 70 Series) 1970

Acrylic on canvas: 60 × 60 in.; 152.4 × 152.4 cm.
Signed and dated on the back, top right: B Dogancay 1970 N.Y.C.
Gift of Mrs. Erik T. Kjellstrom, in honor of Louise B. Schutz '71, 1971

*The "Walls 70" series focuses on twentieth century billboard culture—torn posters, words, and images on urban walls. These elements give a mixture of* trompe l'oeil *and colorful design.*

*In "Big E" fragments from today's commercial world survive in a single large block letter E. The curling edges of torn posters reveal other layers beneath. You may say, "Uninteresting. Those posters have been defaced, the slogans are crude, the words are disorderly." But look further. I am sure you'll find beauty and honest expressions.*

Burhan Dogancay

Literature on the series: "Back to the Walls," *Art Gallery* 14 (Oct. 1970):17, 74–75.

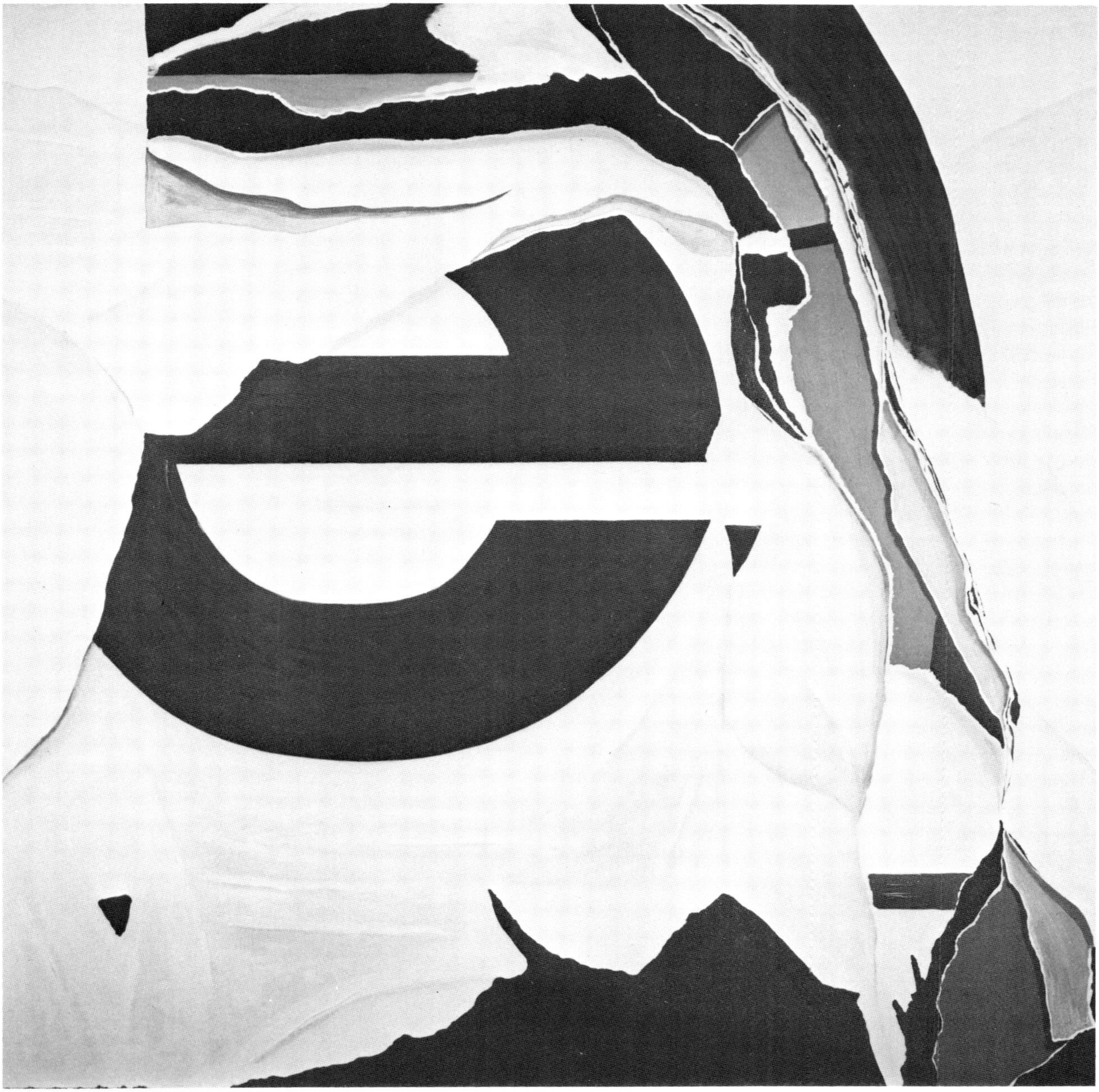

## ARTHUR G. DOVE

1880–1946

### 61. Cow #1 1935
(Color plate, page 29)

Tempera and wax emulsion on canvas: 15 × 21 in.; 38.1 × 53.3 cm.
Signed, center bottom: Dove
Fine Arts Fund, 1957

Acquired from Mrs. Edith Gregor Halpert, owner and director of the Downtown Gallery, New York, as one of the twenty paintings and two pastels that came to light ten years after Arthur G. Dove's death, when household effects belonging to his estate were being moved because the storage warehouse was to be torn down. As a group, they were exhibited at the Downtown Gallery in 1956, but the little catalogue of that "Special Exhibition / Feb. 28–Mar. 24, 1956" does not include "COW #1." This title does, however, appear in the folder of a Dove exhibition shown in 1939 at Alfred Stieglitz's gallery in New York, An American Place, as: "19. Cow #1 . . . 1935."

Exhibited: "Arthur G. Dove," An American Place, 509 Madison Avenue, New York, Apr. 10–May 17, 1939, #19; "Forty-sixth Annual Exhibition," at the College, Apr. 28–June 4, 1957, #5; "Dove Retrospective Exhibition," organized by and exhibited at the University of California, Los Angeles, and circulated to six other museums, 1958–59, #48; "Art Between the Two World Wars," Randolph-Macon College (Ashland, Va.), Apr. 10–12, 1964; "Arthur Dove," organized by the Museum of Modern Art, New York (private showing Dec. 2–6, 1968), and circulated to seven other museums, 1968–69, #16; "Arthur Dove," organized by and exhibited at the San Francisco Museum of Art and circulated to four other museums, 1974–76, #87. Shown in five exhibitions of the College Collection listed in Appendix B: at Richmond and at Roanoke, 1964; at Tampa, Orlando, Gainesville, and Jacksonville, 1965; in six Mid-Atlantic states, 1966–67; and in the Virginia Museum's Artmobile 1969–70.

Recorded: Frederick S. Wight, *Arthur G. Dove* (Berkeley and Los Angeles, 1968), #48; *Arts in Virginia* 2 (Spring 1962), p. 27, repro. p. 26; *Artform* 1 (June 1963), repro. p. 25; *Art Journal* 32 (Winter 72/73), repro. p. 193; Barbara Haskell, *Arthur Dove* (San Francisco, 1974), color repro. p. 87.

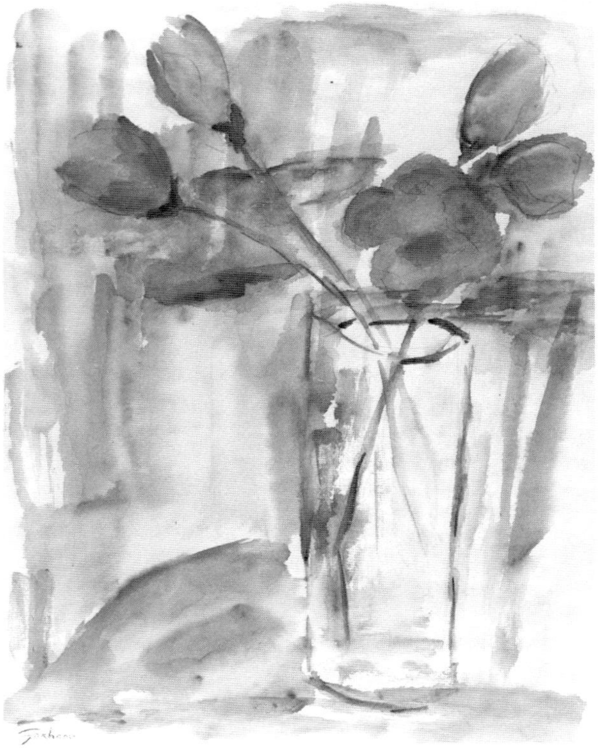

## E. GORHAM DOWNING (MRS.)

### 62. The Red Roses 1965

Watercolor: 15½ × 11¾ in.; 39.3 × 29.8 cm.
Signed, lower left: Gorham
Gift of the artist, 1976

*Painted in the studio of the Abingdon Square Painters in New York. It was exciting because of the freshness of the flowers and a challenge by virtue of the medium, watercolor on rice paper.*

E. Gorham Downing

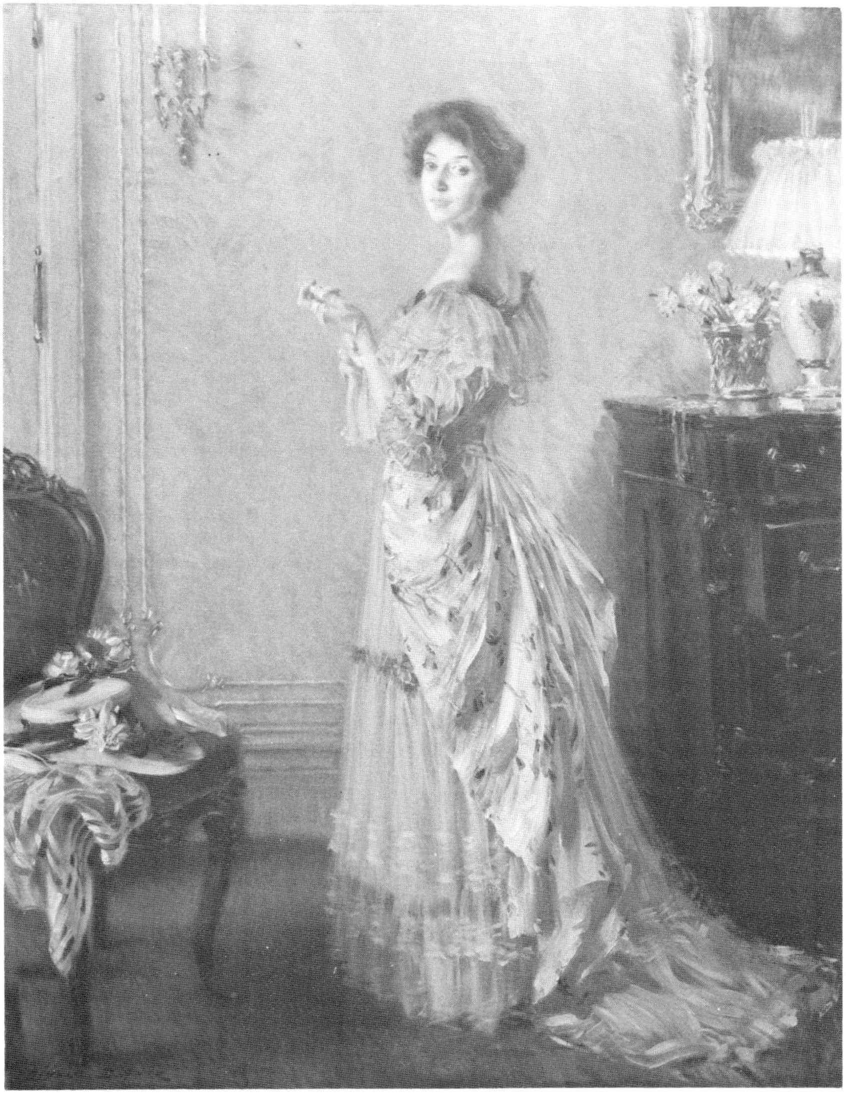

## EDWARD DUFNER

1871–1956

63. Grandmother's Gown

Oil: 39½ × 30½ in.; 100.3 × 77.4 cm.
Signed, lower left: Edward Dufner
Gift of the artist, 1926

Exhibited: "Fifteenth Annual" at the College, 1926.

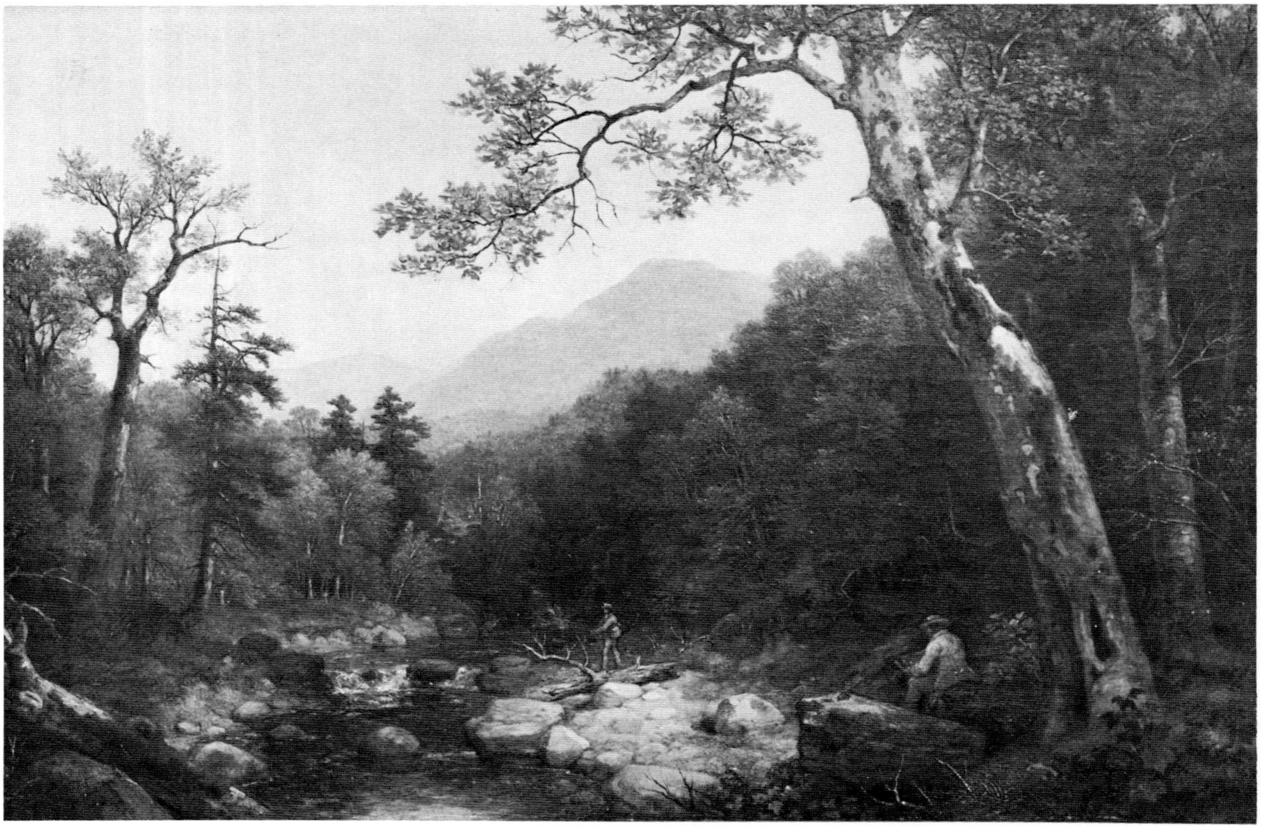

## ASHER BROWN DURAND

1796–1886

64. THE SKETCHER 1870

Oil: 21 × 32 in.; 53.3 × 81.2 cm.
Signed and dated, lower left: A. B. Durand 1870
Gift of Mr. Thomas F. Torrey II, 1954

The art historian David B. Lawall found the right title for this painting when he discovered that Durand exhibited only one painting in 1870, namely, "The Sketcher." For the first edition of this catalogue, the words "with Fisherman and Artist" were added to "Landscape" simply for identification.

About these two men Lawall says:

*The artist in the painting, it seems to me, illustrates the idea of the imitation of nature, while the fisherman stands for the idea of life in harmony with nature. Both are Stoic ideas. The painting would then be an exposition of Durand's Stoicism, of his aesthetic, and of his morality; therefore, a most interesting painting.*[1]

Provenance: Originally acquired by Thomas F. Torrey of New York (1844–1905), grandfather of the donor.

Exhibited: "Forty-fifth Annual Exhibition," National Academy of Design, 1870, #403; "Randolph-Macon Woman's College Collection," Virginia Museum, Richmond, Sept. 11–Oct. 18, 1964, #19; "A. B. Durand," Montclair (N.J.) Art Museum, Oct. 24–Nov. 28, 1971, #83.

Recorded: David B. Lawall, *A. B. Durand 1796–1886* (Montclair, 1971), p. 67, repro. p. 107.

1. D. B. Lawall to M. F. Williams, April 16, 1969; quoted by permission.

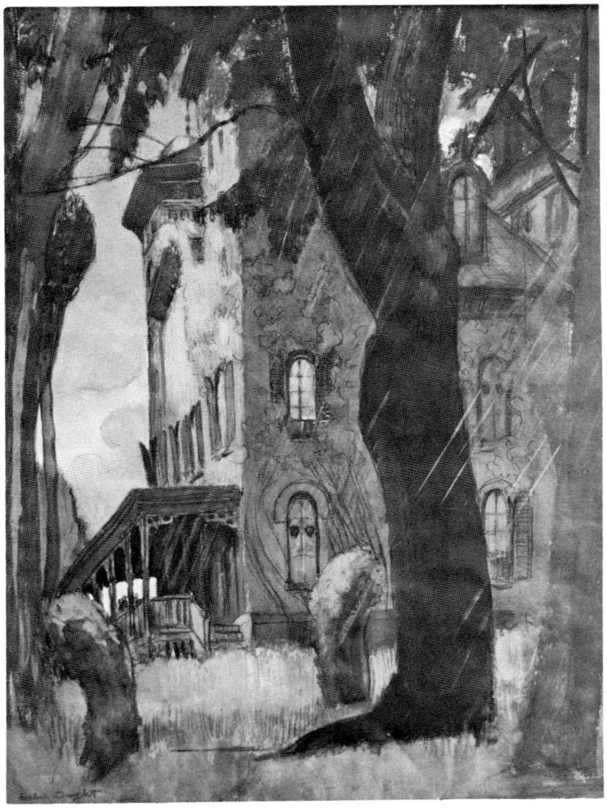

## MABEL DWIGHT
1876–1955

65. The Haunted House

Watercolor: 17½ × 13 in.; 44.4 × 33 cm.
Signed, lower left: Mabel Dwight
Acquired about 1933

## THOMAS EAKINS
1844–1916

66. Portrait Sketch of William H. Macdowell
About 1891

(Reproduced on page 78)

Oil: 28 × 22 in.; 71.1 × 55.8 cm.
Unsigned
Fine Arts Fund, 1941

William H. Macdowell, an engraver, was the father-in-law of the artist, who painted him at least six times. This oil study has lines ruled across it, through the pigment, as if for transfer. The vertical line can be seen in the hair over the high point of the forehead. The two horizontal lines intersect that line under the brighter eye and on the back of the hand.

Hoopes believes that this oil sketch was painted before the almost identical but unfinished watercolor, nearly the same size, owned by the Baltimore Museum of Art. The two may be compared on page 84 of his book.

During conservation treatment the signature recorded by Goodrich (#261) was found to be on a linen liner, not on the pigment-supporting canvas.

Provenance: Mrs. Thomas Eakins, Estate of Mrs. Thomas Eakins (in which this painting was listed as No. 26).

Exhibited: "Thomas Eakins Memorial Exhibition," Metropolitan Museum of Art, New York, Nov. 5–Dec. 3, 1917, #36; "Memorial Exhibition of Thomas Eakins," Pennsylvania Academy of the Fine Arts, Philadelphia, Dec. 23, 1917–Jan. 13, 1918, #52, repro. p. 87; "Eakins Exhibition," Baltimore Museum of Art, Dec. 1, 1936–Jan. 1, 1937, #21; "Thomas Eakins Centennial Exhibition," Carnegie Institute of Technology, Pittsburgh, Apr. 1–June 1, 1954, #92; "Fifteen Paintings from the Collection of Randolph-Macon Woman's College," circulated by the Alumnae Association between Oct. 1949 and Jan. 1950 to its chapters in Nashville, Birmingham, Atlanta, and Asheville; "Picture of the Week," Sweet Briar College, Oct. 26–Nov. 13, 1955; "Thomas Eakins, A Retrospective Exhibition," National Gallery of Art, Washington, Oct. 8–Nov. 12, 1961; Art Institute of Chicago, Dec. 1–Jan. 7, 1962; Philadelphia Museum of Art, Feb. 1–Mar. 18, 1962, #59; "Thomas Eakins Retrospective Exhibition," Whitney Museum of American Art, New York, Sept. 22–Nov. 21, 1970, #55, repro. p. 54. See Appendix B for exhibitions at Richmond and at Roanoke, 1964; at Tampa, Orlando, Gainesville, and

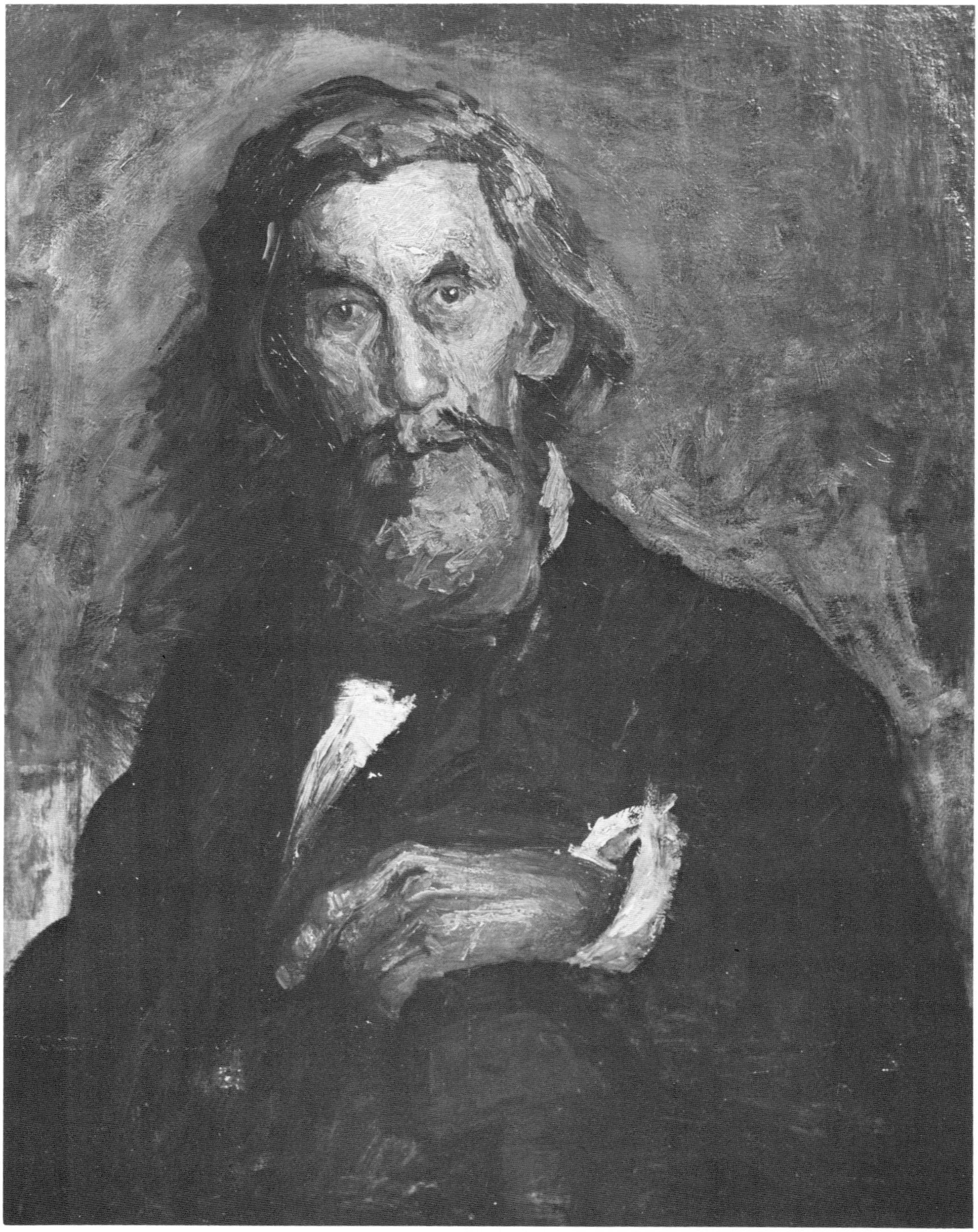

## THOMAS EAKINS (cont.)

Jacksonville, 1965; and in six Mid-Atlantic states, 1966-67.

Recorded: Catalogues of the exhibitions; Lloyd Goodrich, *Thomas Eakins, His Life and Work* (New York, 1933), #261, p. 183; Roland McKinney, *Thomas Eakins* (New York, 1942), repro. p. 102; *Thomas Eakins, a Retrospective Exhibition* (Washington, 1961), #59, repro. p. 92; *Arts Magazine* 36 (Jan. 1962), repro. p. 22; *Life*, July 23, 1971, color repro. p. 55; Donelson F. Hoopes, *Eakins Watercolors* (New York, 1971), p. 84, repro. #14; *Art Journal*, 32 (Winter 72/73), p. 195, repro. p. 193.

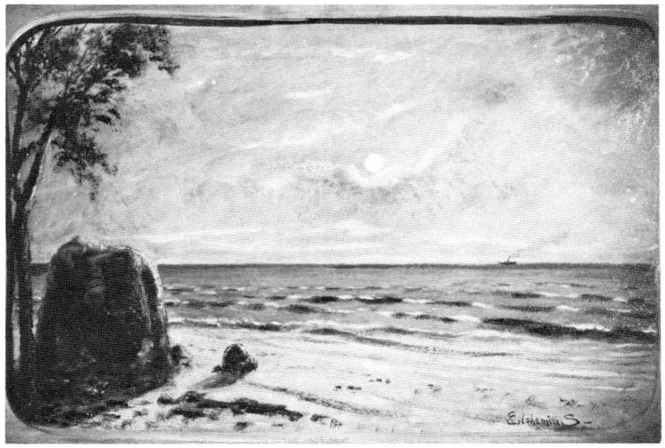

## LOUIS M. EILSHEMIUS
1864–1941

67. MOONLIT SEA About 1916

Oil on cardboard: 20½ × 30⅜ in.; 52 × 77.1 cm.
Signed, lower right: Eilshemius
Gift of Mr. and Mrs. Alan H. Temple, 1949

The approximate date has been established through comparison with two other paintings in which the large rock at the left also appears. They are "Bather on the Rocks" and "Tragedy," both of 1916 and both reproduced in *Masterpieces of Eilshemius* with introduction by Hugh Stix (New York, 1959).

What appears to be a frame deep enough to cast a shadow on the left and across the top is really part of the painting.

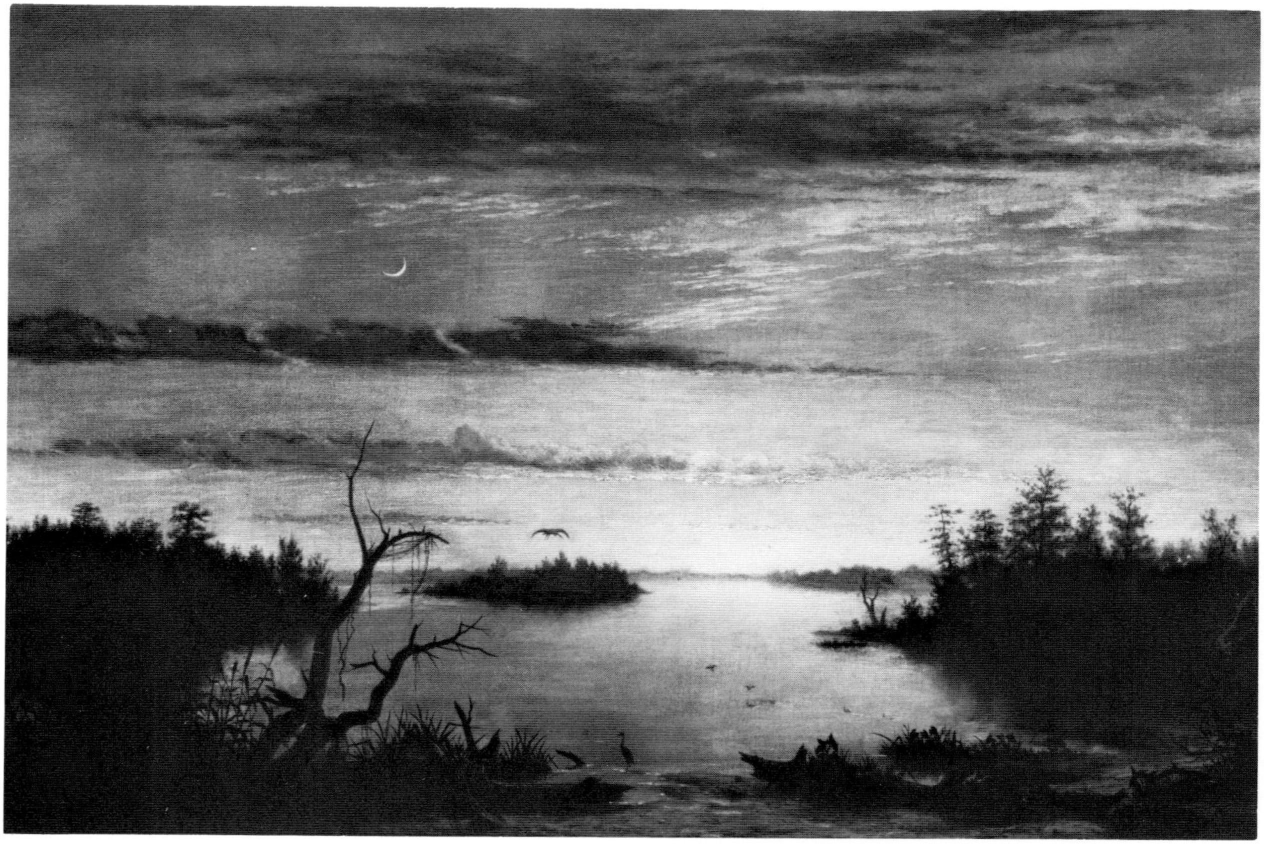

FLAVIUS J. FISHER
1832–1905

68. Dismal Swamp

Oil: 30 × 50 in.; 76.2 × 127 cm.
Unsigned
Gift of Mrs. Robert N. Winfree, 1976

## HARRIET FITZGERALD '26

Born 1904

69. Negro Children with Landscape 1936

Oil: 30 × 24 in.; 76.2 × 60.9 cm.
Unsigned
Fine Arts Fund, 1936

70. Aunt Maria 1937

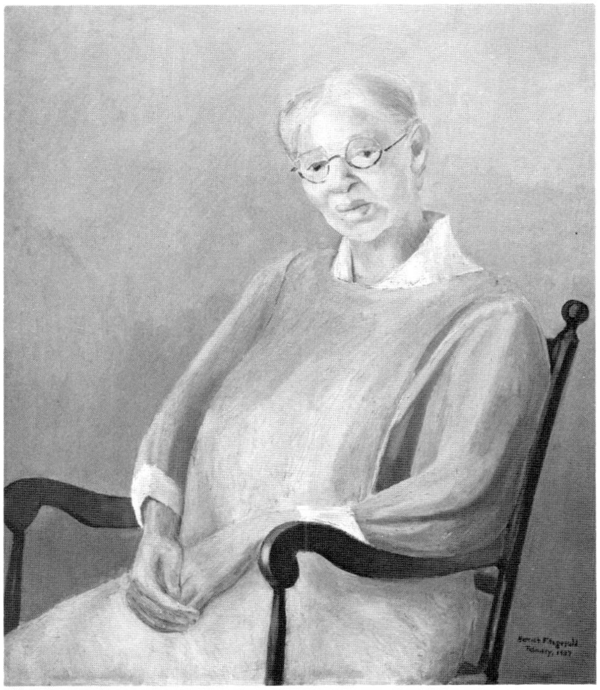

Oil: 40 × 30 in.; 101.6 × 86.3 cm.

Signed and dated, lower right:
Harriet Fitzgerald / February 1937
Commissioned by students and alumnae, 1938

Alumnae will remember Mrs. Maria Graves, faithful servant of Randolph-Macon from its opening in 1893 until she gradually retired during the 1940s to the apartment maintained for her on campus, where she died in 1952 in her eighties or nineties. The *History*[1] records her impression of the raw new college and her gift of money for a science building.

Recorded: *The News* (Lynchburg), Jan. 31, 1937, and Apr. 19, 1952; *Richmond Times-Dispatch,* Nov. 3, 1950; *Alumnae Bulletin* 45 (June 1952): 43.

71. North Danville 1938

Oil: 30 × 26 in.; 76.2 × 66 cm.
Signed and dated, lower right: H. Fitzgerald 1938
Fine Arts Fund, 1938

1. Roberta D. Cornelius, *The History of Randolph-Macon Woman's College* (Chapel Hill, N.C., 1951), pp. 32, 274.

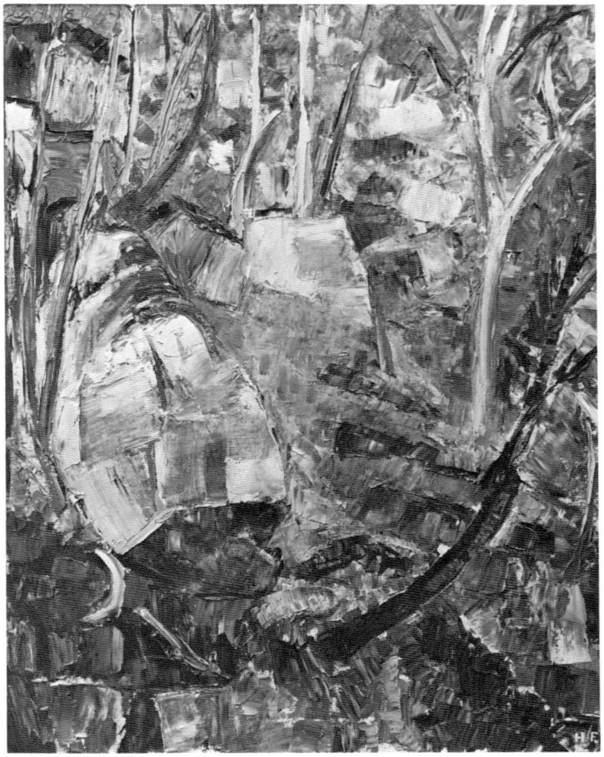

## HARRIET FITZGERALD '26

72. 1957 FOREST SERIES #4 1957

Oil: 28 × 22 in.; 71.1 × 55.8 cm.
Signed, lower right: H.F.
Gift of Ethel Watson, 1958

*I'm in a state of transition and I want to say what I have to say in paint, not words. I can talk about other people's paintings, but I've never been able to talk about my own. I can say that this painting is one of a series which I have been adding to since 1948, all painted either in Bear Mountain Park or Haines Falls, N.Y. This was painted at the latter place.*

Harriet Fitzgerald (1959)

Exhibited: "Harriet Fitzgerald Exhibition," Charles Barzansky Galleries, New York, Feb. 3–15, 1958, #17; "Randolph-Macon Woman's College Collection," Virginia Museum, Richmond, Sept. 11–Oct. 18, 1964, #21.

73. Blowing in the Wind 1967

Oil: 36 × 30 in.; 91.4 × 76.2 cm.
Signed and dated, lower right: H F 67
Gift of the artist, 1968

74. March Mountain 1967

Oil: 36 × 30 in.; 91.4 × 76.2 cm.
Signed and dated, lower left: H F 67
Gift of Mrs. Andrew A. Smith (Mary Virginia Barnes '35), 1968

75. Night Landing About 1967

Oil on paper: 18 × 22¾ in.; 45.7 × 57.7 cm.
Unsigned
Gift of the artist through alumnae of the Northern Delaware Chapter, 1968

Exhibited: See Appendix C.

76. PORTRAIT OF PRESIDENT WILLIAM A. WEBB 1968

Oil: 30 × 24 in.; 76.2 × 60.9 cm.
Signed and dated, lower right: H F 68
Gift of Mrs. Addison White (Carolyn C. Webb '25), 1968

*To paint a portrait from a photograph is a dubious procedure, and more so when one has not known the subject in life. I undertook the commission from Dr. Webb's daughter because the abstract excellence of the photograph (with which I had long been familiar) seemed to offer a very strong structural theme. His son, Dr. Stanford Webb, agreed to sit for me in order to suggest the actuality of colors and textures. I kept the statement as simple as possible and focused on the painting as an abstraction, which is the way I approach any portrait.*

Harriet Fitzgerald

Dr. Webb was president of the College from 1913–19.

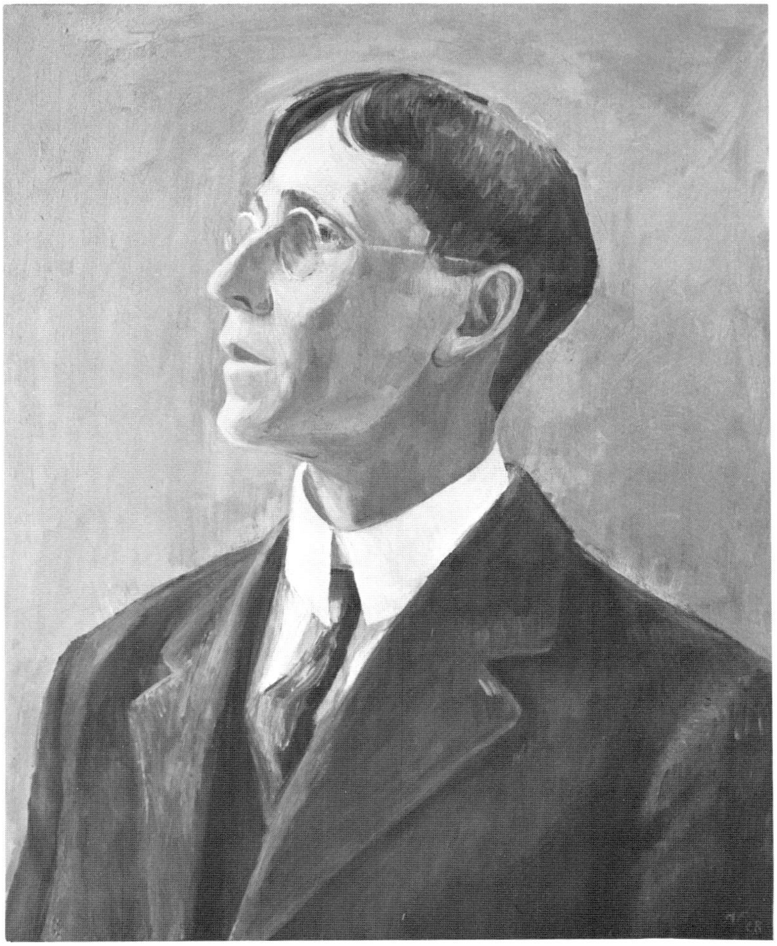

77. Tuscan Landscape 1969
(Reproduced on page 84)

Oil: 36 × 30 in.; 91.4 × 76.2 cm.
Signed and dated, lower left: H F 69
Gift of the artist, 1971

*I have painted in the area of this Italian landscape many times for more than ten years. My positions, looking across a wide valley to mountains beyond, have been in the vicinity of the little 16th century church of San Clemente on the mountain above Fiesole. Small settlements in a broad expanse of space, patterns of cultivated land punctuated by cypress trees and wooded*

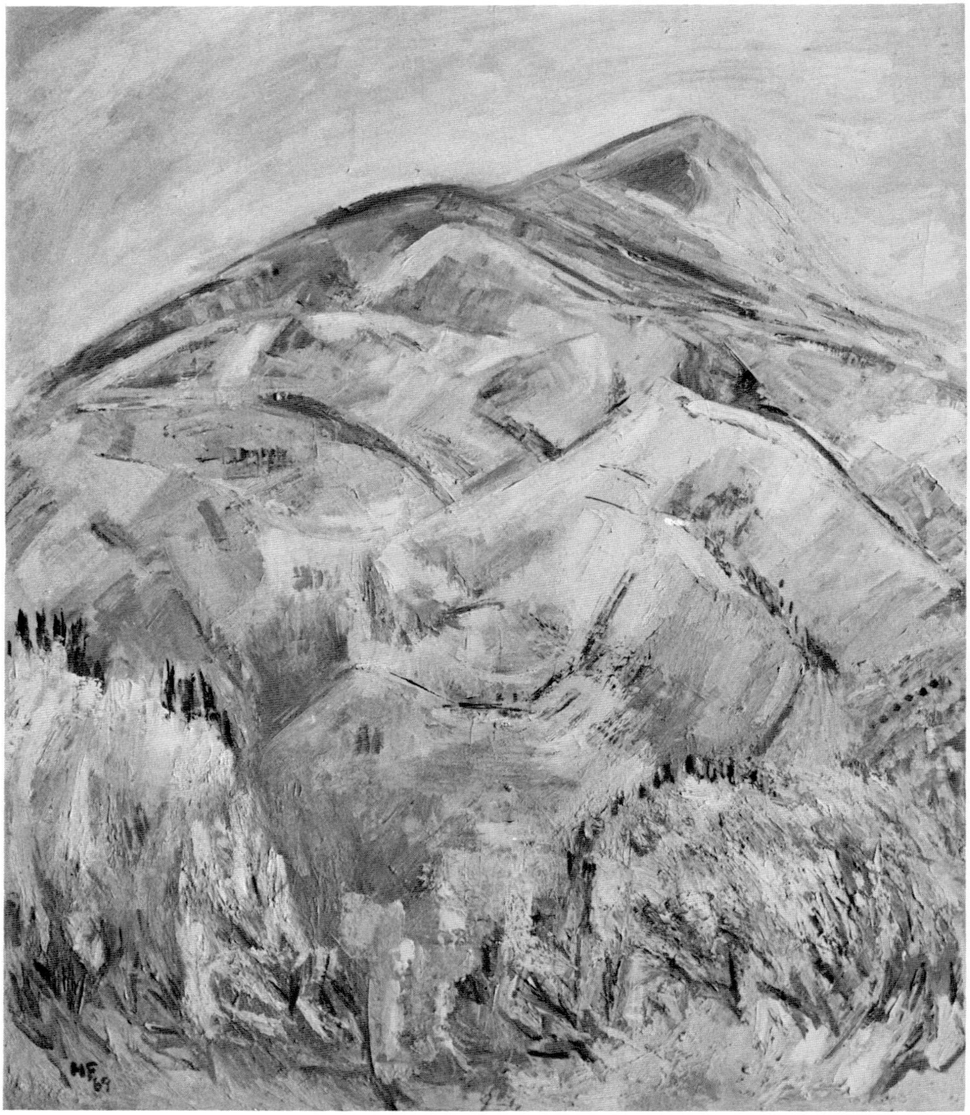

*areas, all these offer focal points in a rich variety of shape and texture. Painted in my studio at Meadows of Dan, Virginia, after a return from Italy. I wanted to simplify and intensify the abstract pattern away from the constant flow of new suggestions.*

Harriet Fitzgerald

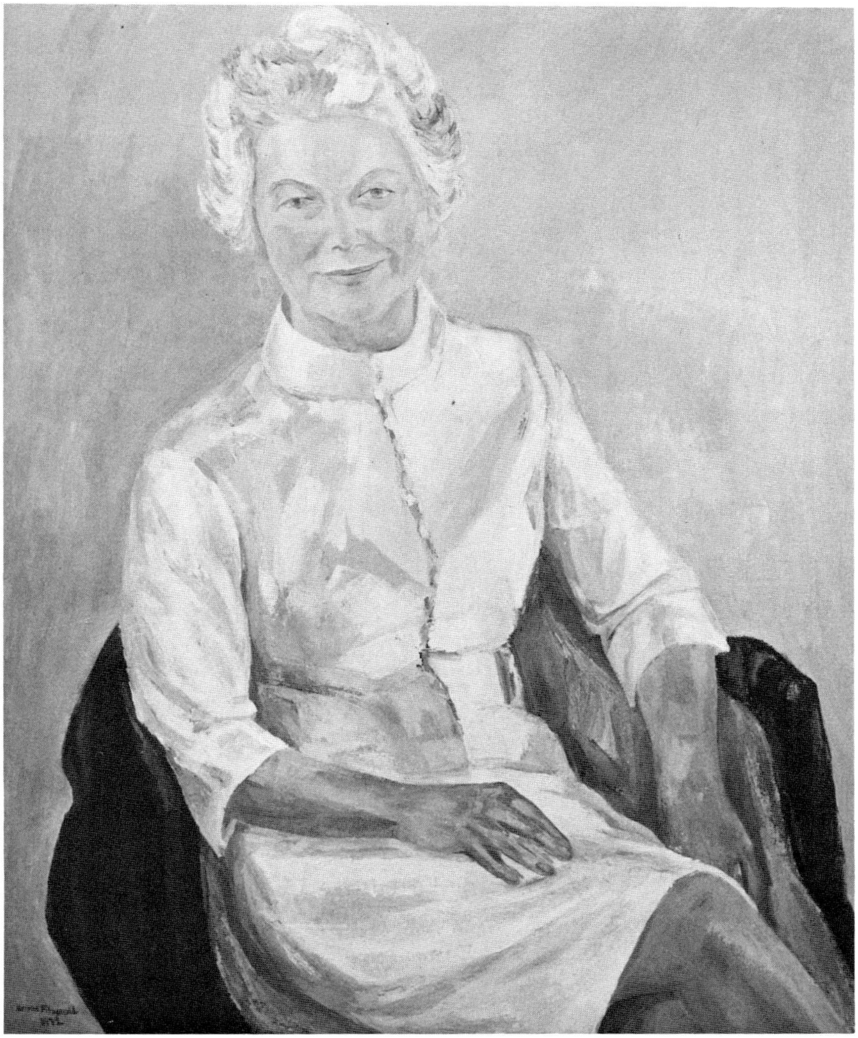

78. PORTRAIT OF ANNE JETER RIBBLE (MRS. J. M.) '26 1972

Oil: 46 × 36 in.; 116.8 × 91.4 cm.
Signed, lower left: H. Fitzgerald
Commissioned and owned by the Alumnae Association, 1972

*It is sometimes difficult to undertake portraits of one's closest friends and relatives, because emotional involvement can get in the way. On the other hand, the relationship sets up a constant monitor toward the interpretation that is emerging. I wanted to paint this portrait and I found the undertaking a great challenge. The sitter gave me patient and intelligent help. Some portraits catch the impression of a moment in the life of the subject. In contrast, however, it was my intention to suggest the presence of a personality over a more lasting period of time.*

Harriet Fitzgerald

*Sitting for a portrait by Harriet Fitzgerald is a delightful, enriching experience, because her conversation, as she paints, is filled with discussions of philosophy, politics, and people. The studio called "The Pot of Gold" looks out in the rear to woods green with trees, in the front to a field calm with grazing cattle and baby calves. While posing I often thought of one of Harriet's Negro friends who said, "I'd ruther just sit for Miss Harriet than clean and wash clothes for someone else." That month at the Meadows of Dan in Virginia was an experience I shall always cherish.*

Anne Jeter Ribble

Recorded: *Alumnae Bulletin* 41 (Winter 1973), repro. p. 16.

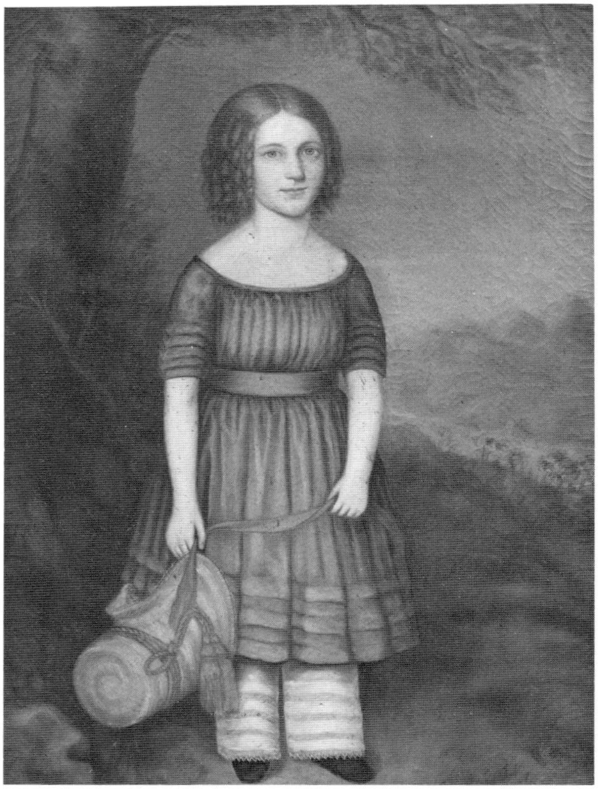

## GEORGE W. FITZWILSON

Active in the 1840s

79. PORTRAIT OF MARY ELIZABETH MORGAN 1844
(Mrs. August Forsberg, 1839–1918)

Oil: 46 × 34¼ in.; 116.8 × 87 cm.
Unsigned

This painting is not in the Collection, but has been included in the catalogue through the courtesy of the subject's daughter, Mrs. John H. Davis (Hilda Forsberg '01), who has included it in her will as a bequest to the College.

## KARL FORTESS

Born 1907

80. LOVE IS REAL 1964

Oil: 40 × 24 in.; 101.6 × 60.9 cm.
Signed, lower left: K. Fortess
Gift of Mr. and Mrs. Sam Golden, 1968

*This painting is the third version of a painting called "Portrait." The 1st painting had an entire tree painted on a piece of paper that was nailed to the stump. The 2nd had a self-portrait in place of the tree. The 3rd version has the slogan "Love is Real." All three paintings were a continued exploration of man's effect on the landscape, in all cases man's contrivance with the real elements that exist in the landscape around us. This also involves the mood I impose on nature.*

Karl Fortess

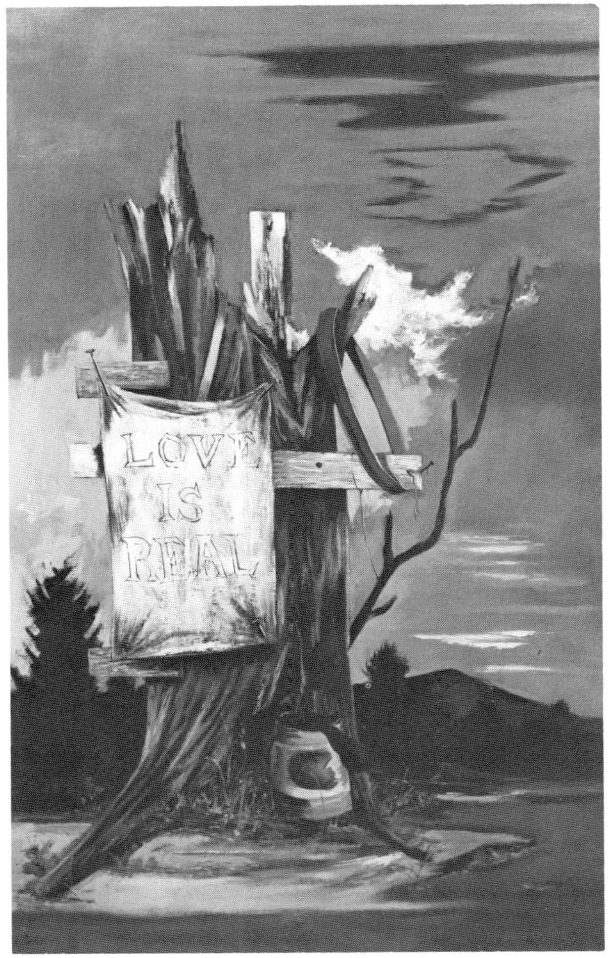

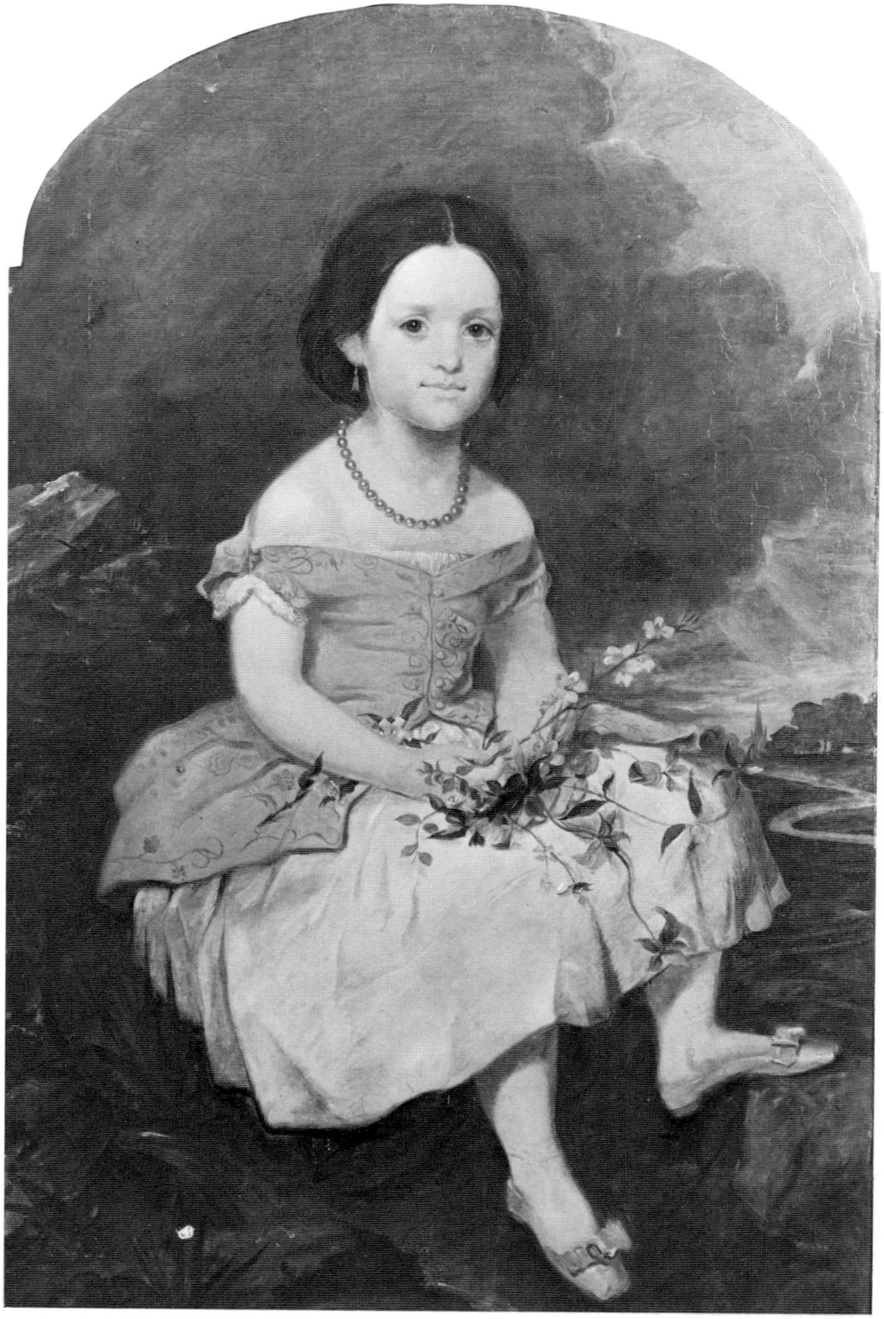

## TREVOR T. FOWLER

Active 1829–69

81. PORTRAIT OF LENA ELIZABETH BONDURANT, AGE SIX 1859

Oil: 48 × 30 in.; 121.9 × 76.2 cm.
Signed and dated, center back: Trevor T. Fowler 1859
Gift of Lena Bondurant Henderson and Mrs. Annie Henderson Young (daughters of the subject), 1950

*Trevor T. (or Thomas Trevor) Fowler, a portrait painter of Louisville, was invited to come to our mother's plantation home Waveland, in Louisiana on the Mississippi River, to paint the family portraits, that is, her father and mother and herself. He spent six months on the plantation as their guest. That was in 1859.*

Lena Bondurant Henderson (1951)

This portrait was treated in 1953 to conceal bullet holes and cuts inflicted during the Civil War, when troops occupied Waveland.

Exhibited: See Appendix B for exhibitions of the College Collection at Richmond, 1964, and in six Mid-Atlantic states, 1966–67.

Recorded: *Nashville Tennessean*, July 16, 1967, repro.

## FREDERICK CARL FRIESEKE

1874–1939

82. REST

Oil: 26 × 32 in.; 66 × 81.8 cm.
Signed, lower right: F. C. Frieseke
Fine Arts Fund, 1930

Exhibited: "Paintings by C. F. Frieseke, Gardner Symons, and James R. Hopkins," Minneapolis Institute of Arts, January 1917.

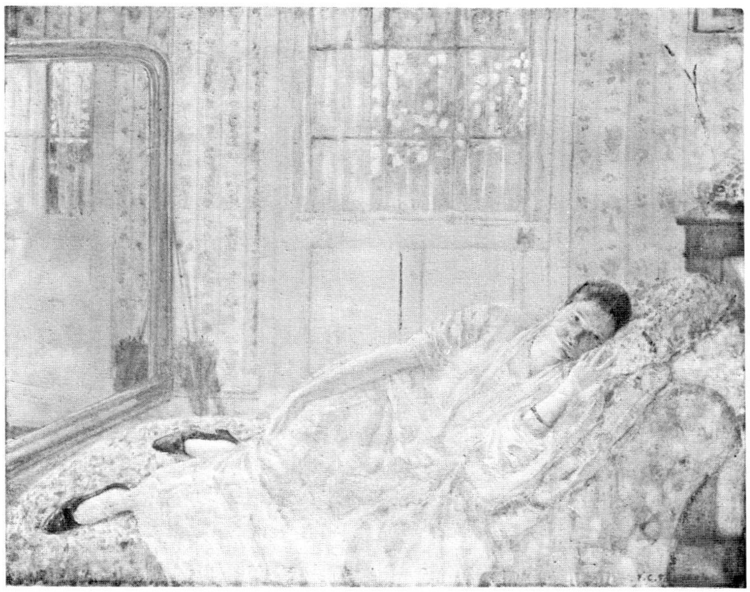

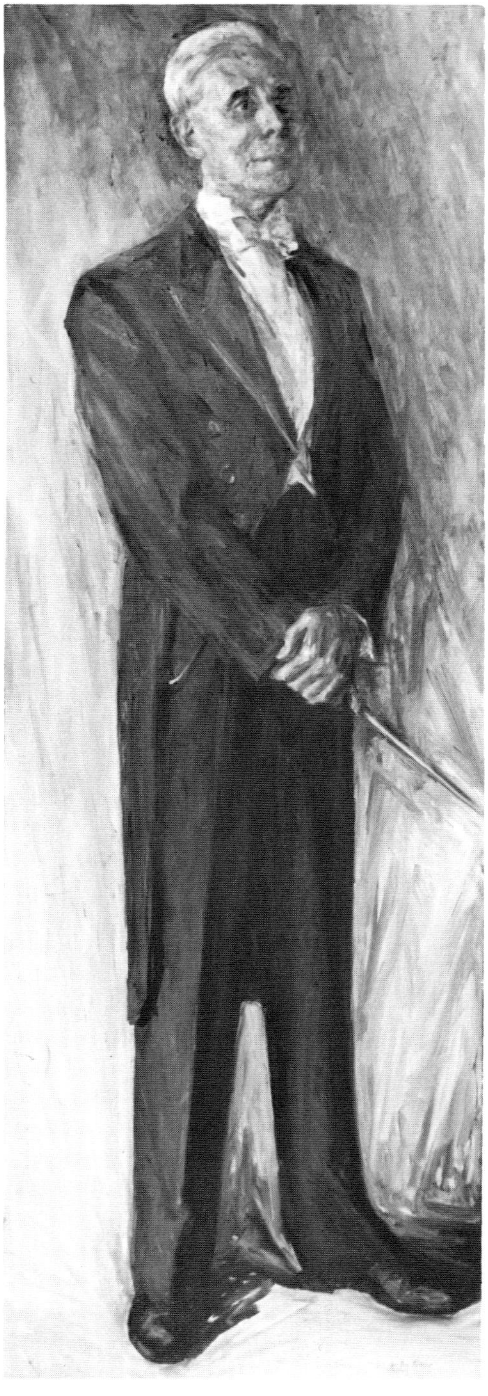

## CAROLYN GORTON FULLER

Born 1921

83. The Conductor
(Portrait of Pedro Sanjuan, 1886–1976)
1961

Oil: 72½ × 24½ in.; 184.1 × 62.2 cm.
Signed and dated, lower right:
Carolyn Gorton Fuller 10/25/61
Gift of Mr. and Mrs. C. Wesley Goyer, Jr., 1964

*I am interested in the painter's visual relationship to the sitter, often representing children from above, as adults usually see them. Because Pedro had been conductor of the Madrid Philharmonic for many years, I chose to paint him as players in the first row of the orchestra would have seen him. He stood posing on the top of a desk. I stood at my easel on the floor below him. I was more interested in the angularity of his almost El Grecoesque figure and in value than in color or photographic representation.*

Carolyn Gorton Fuller

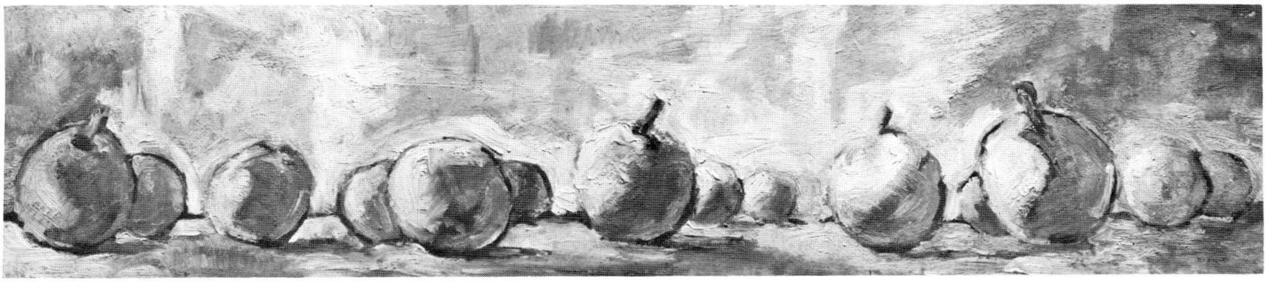

## ROBERT S. FULLER

Born 1923

84. YELLOW APPLES 1959

Oil on masonite: 7 × 30¾ in.; 17.7 × 78.1 cm.
Unsigned
Gift of fifteen families of the College faculty, 1961

Exhibited: "Robert Simmons Fuller," Charles Barzansky Galleries, New York, Dec. 4–16, 1961, #13; "Randolph-Macon Woman's College Collection," Virginia Museum, Richmond, Sept. 11–Oct. 18, 1964, #24.

Recorded: *The News* (Lynchburg), Dec. 12, 1961; *The Sun Dial* (Lynchburg), Dec. 14, 1961.

85. ROUND TABLE NO. 1 1961

Oil: 35 × 24 in.; 88.9 × 60 cm.
Signed, lower right: R. S. Fuller 61
Acquired in 1961 in place of an earlier painting bought through the Fine Arts Fund, 1955

*In still life I find ample material for exploration and experimentation in color, value, form, and space. If this result of that seeking gives you pleasure, I have been doubly rewarded, because the picture has been, in addition to an exciting painting experience for me, a link between you, the viewer, and me, the artist.*

Robert S. Fuller (1963)

Exhibited: "Robert Simmons Fuller," Charles Barzansky Galleries, New York, Dec. 4–16, 1961, #21; "Randolph-Macon Woman's College Collection," Virginia Museum, Richmond, Sept. 11–Oct. 18, 1964, #23.

Recorded: *The News* (Lynchburg), Dec. 3, 1961, with repro.

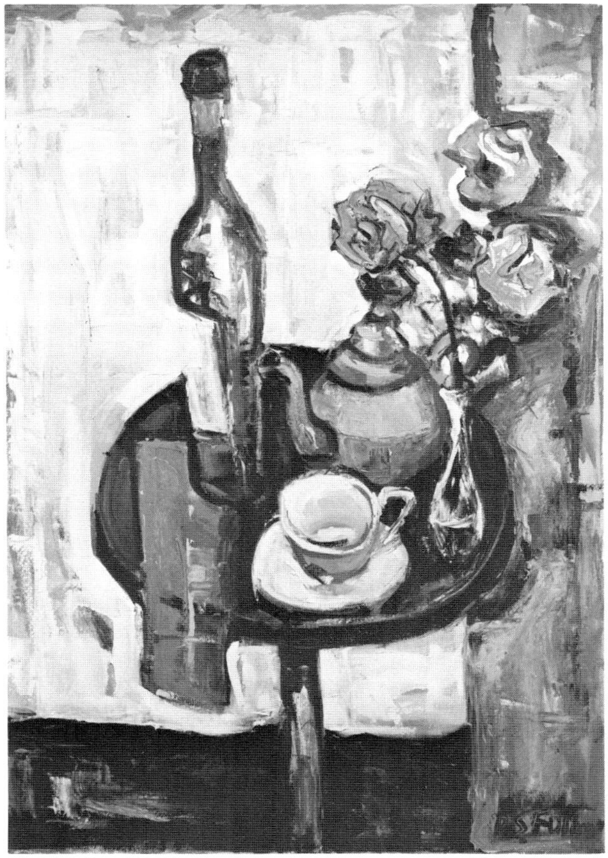

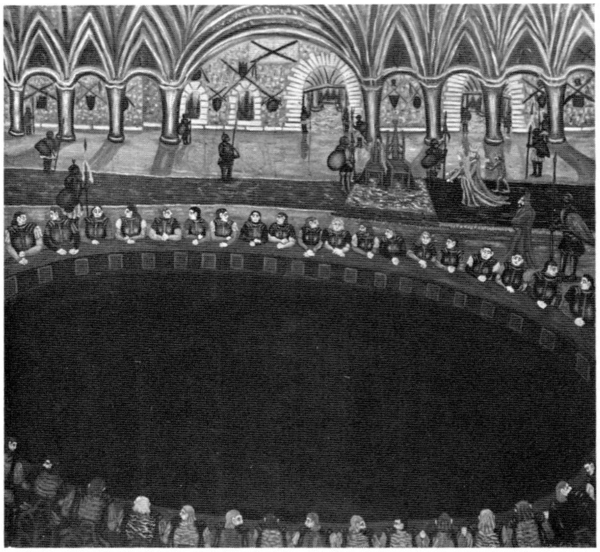

## VICTOR JOSEPH GATTO

1893–1965

86. Knights of the Round Table 1944

Oil: 52 × 52 in.; 132 × 132 cm.
Signed, lower right: Victor Joseph Gatto
Gift of Bess Barzansky (Mrs. Charles), in honor of her daughter Barbara Barzansky '67, in 1968

Exhibited: "Exhibition of Paintings by Victor Joseph Gatto," Charles Barzansky Galleries, New York, Oct. 19–Nov. 4, 1944, #5.

Recorded: "Gatto, a Barnstorming Primitive" (signed M. R.), *Art Digest* 19 (Nov. 8, 1944): 9.

## MORRIS GRAVES

Born 1910

87. In The Night 1943

Sumi ink on rice paper: 28½ × 26 in.; 72.4 × 66 cm.
Unsigned
Louise J. Smith Fund, 1962

This is one of a series of paintings of birds at night. The "Eagle" in the Phillips Gallery, Washington, D.C., is very similar, but horizontal in shape. The title also belongs to at least five other works by Graves.

When in 1963 a study sheet prepared for students was submitted to Morris Graves for approval (he was then living in Ireland), he crossed out two adjectives that described him and also one that referred to his bird paintings in a flattering way. He did leave unaltered, however, the following excerpts from the recommendations written by two experts, as required for acquisitions through the Smith Fund. Both are from museum directors, both dated 1962.

*Although it does not bear his signature I would consider it unquestionably one of his fine ink paintings of about 1943. The crumpled paper which is difficult to mount is also characteristic of that period. The brushwork is extraordinarily strong and typical of his best work. In spite of the bubble in the mounting I think it would be an excellent addition to the collection.*

*From the photograph it looks like an excellent Graves to me. . . . This is good Graves at a good time. . . . I would not concern myself about the bubble. It is at least certain that Graves likes a crinkled effect which presupposes that the paper does not lie flat.*

Exhibited: "Fifty-first Annual," at the College, Mar. 6–21, 1962, #10; see Appendix B for exhibitions of the College Collection at Richmond, 1964, in six Mid-Atlantic states, 1966–67, and in the Artmobile, 1969–70; "Art on Paper," Weatherspoon Art Gallery, University of N.C. at Greensboro, Nov. 14–Dec. 17, 1971, #8; "The Drawings of Morris Graves," an exhibition organized by the American Federation of Arts and circulated to six museums, Sept. 1975–Sept. 1976, #14.

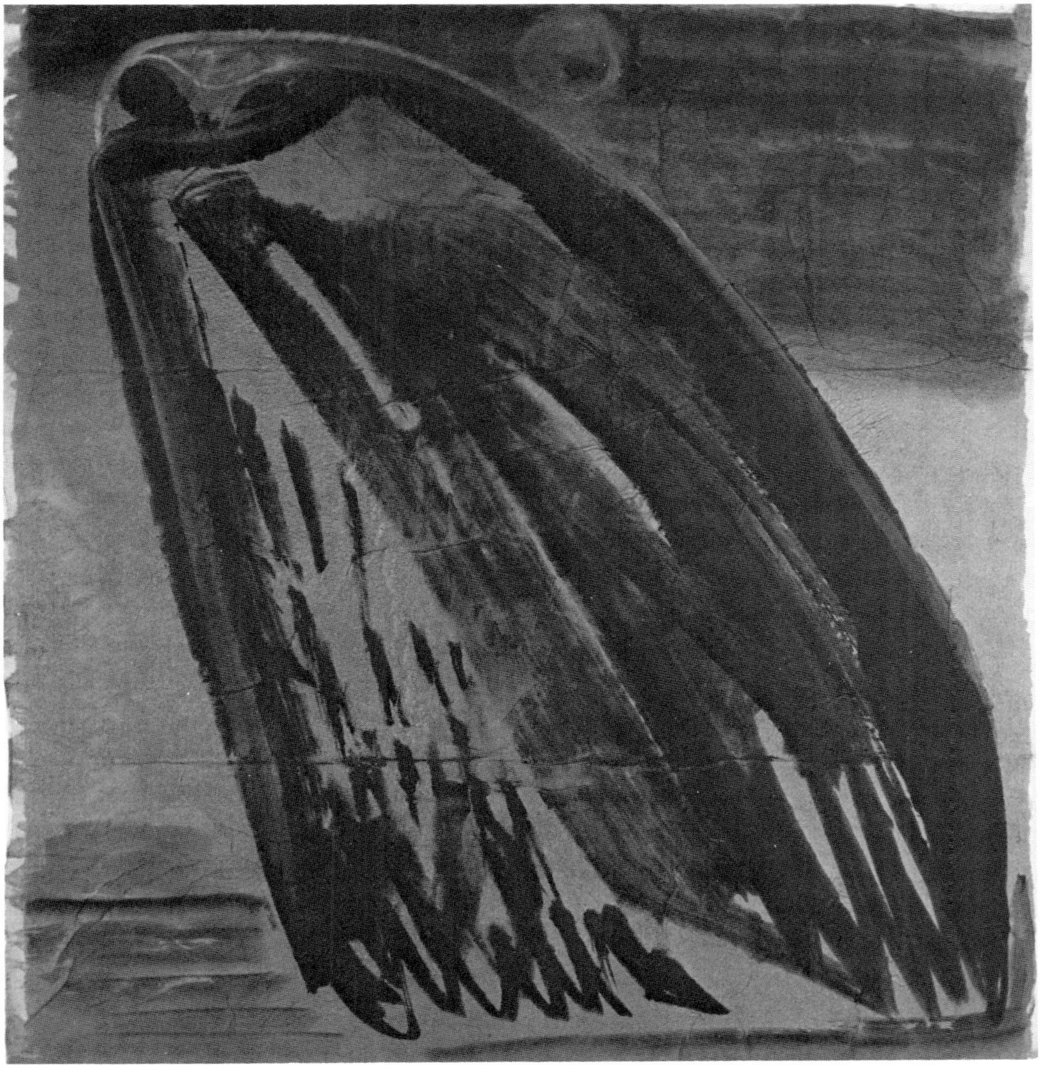

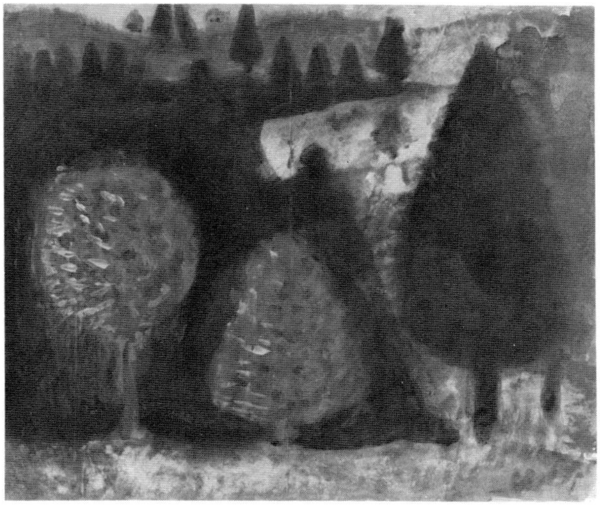

## JABEZ GRAY

1908–50

88. LANDSCAPE About 1949

Oil on paper: 20 × 24 in.; 50.8 × 60.9 cm.
Unsigned
Gift of The Abingdon Square Painters, Inc., 1968

The artist was a member of the Abingdon Square Painters.

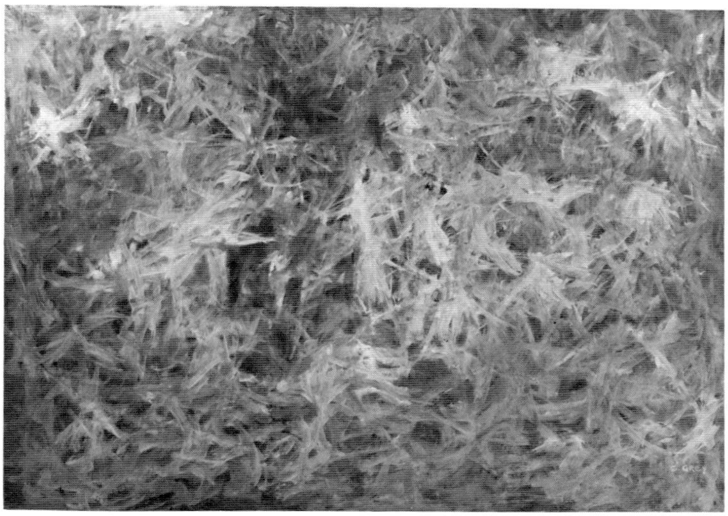

## ESTELLE GREY (MRS. CARL ASHBY)

89. SEA GULLS AND WAVES 1964

Oil: 53½ × 76 in.; 135.8 × 193 cm.
Signed, lower right: E. Grey
Gift of Dr. and Mrs. David H. Dawson, 1968

*This is a personal reaction to the environs of Cape Cod. From 1944 to the present my husband and I have spent many summers there at Wellfleet, North Truro, and Provincetown. The different moods of weather and the variety of topography have been especially fascinating. I have tried to catch the spirit of continually moving waves, the freedom of the gulls in flight, and the motion of the atmosphere along the Cape.*

Estelle Grey

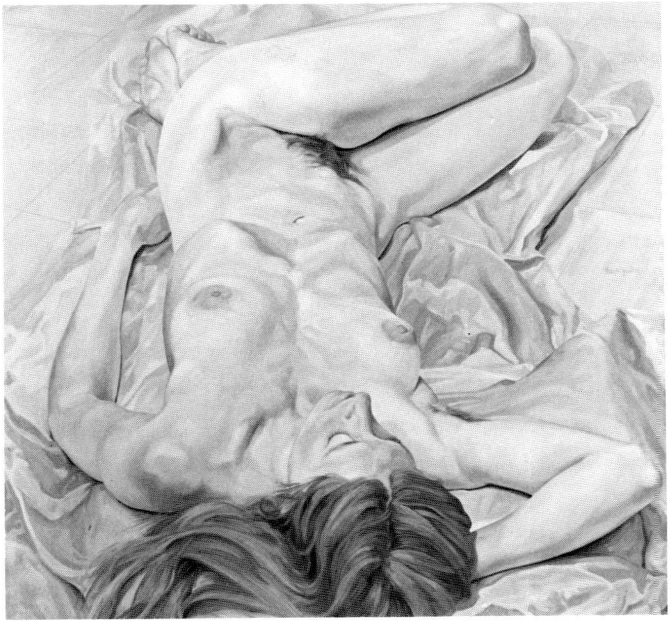

## THEOPHIL GROELL

Born 1932

90. Rose Chapeau 1974

Oil: 36 × 38 in.; 91.4 × 96.5 cm.
Signed and dated, center right:
theophil groell 74
Louise J. Smith Fund and Fine Arts Fund, 1976

*The title "Rose Chapeau" best explains my thoughts about painting the nude, for it is derived from the name of the particular model, Rosaire. "Chapeau" refers to the importance in the composition of her head and hair. The model is not simply an object or form used to carry on a tradition. She is a real person, a friend, and not "Nude on Orange Satin." All my paintings grow from the particular model and her whole nature. I do not try to force an attitude upon her that she cannot assume.*

*While painting, I work exceedingly close to the model in a small, confined studio with the windows covered to prevent the daylight from entering. This assures me a continuity of light source as I work on the painting both day and night. Everything in the work is fully developed and explicitly described. I am very conscious and deliberate about planning the folds in the surrounding cloths and draperies. I do this in order that their linear movements "echo" the movements found in the gesture of the figure.*

*My strongest influences have come from the fresco paintings of the Italian Renaissance (Giotto, Masaccio, and Piero della Francesca in particular), for in these paintings are found the subtle fusion, in line and color, of the figure and its environs.*

Theophil Groell

Exhibited: "Dodd-Groell-Gelber," Sewell Art Gallery, Rice University, Houston, Feb. 4-Mar. 21, 1975, and Summit (N.J.) Art Center, Apr. 6-26, 1975.

Recorded: *An Exhibition of Paintings by Dodd-Groell-Gelber*, with notes by Lawrence Campbell (New York, Green Mountain Gallery, 1975), #11, repro. p. 14.

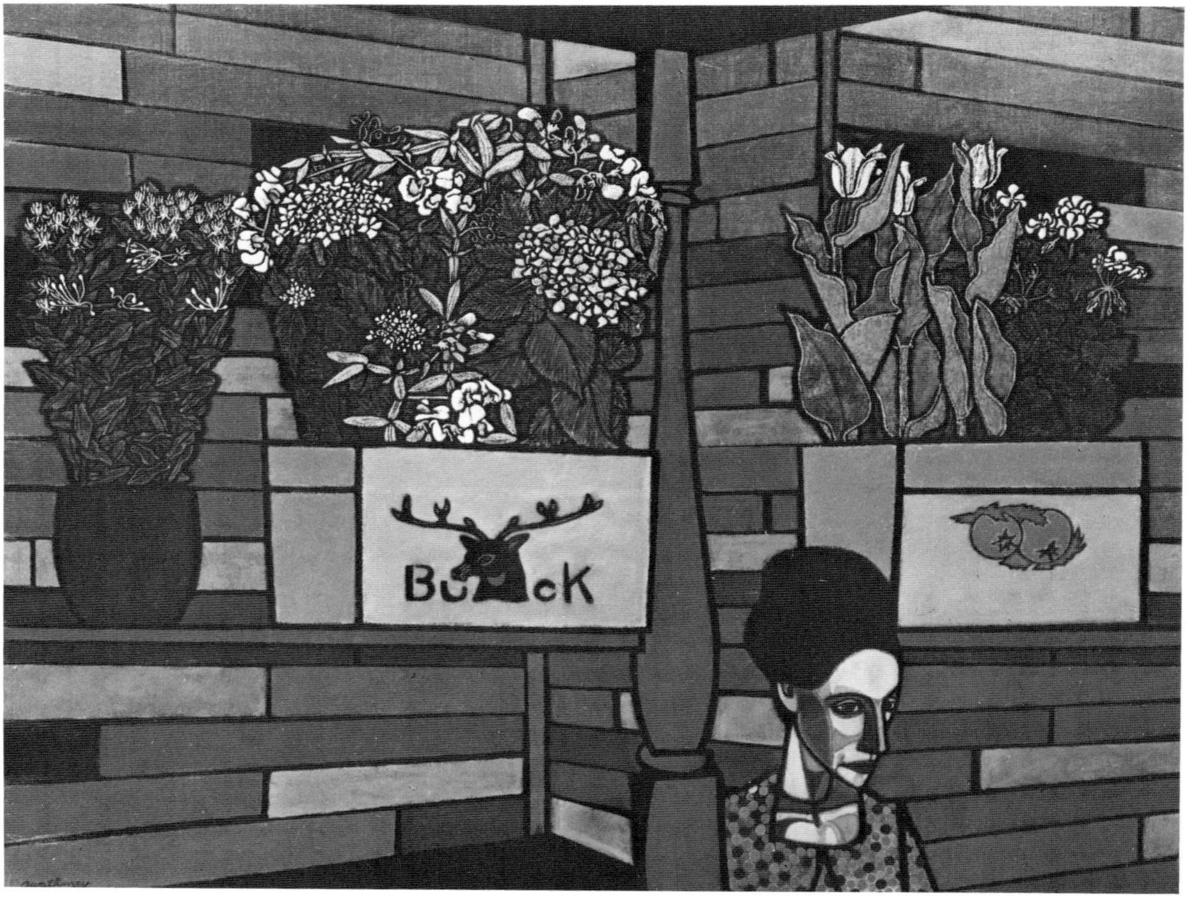


ROBERT GWATHMEY
Born 1903

91. FRONT PORCH 1966

Oil: 32 × 41 in.; 81.2 × 104.1 cm.
Signed, lower left: Gwathmey
Smith Fund and Fine Arts Fund, 1967

*On the other side of the tracks so much of the activity takes place outside the poor abode, the front porch, the street. The search for beauty is suggested by the flowers and the utilization of the emptied grocery boxes with their stenciled images. A woman sits awaiting a neighbor's company.*

*Art is the conceptual solution of complicated forms, the perceptual fusion of personality and experience, not humble ornamentation of surface pyrotechnics. Beauty never comes from decorative effects but from structural coherence. Art never grows out of the persuasion of polished eclecticism or the inviting momentum of the bandwagon.*

Robert Gwathmey

Exhibited: "Fifty-sixth Annual Exhibition," at the College, Mar 5–21, 1967, #12; "Encounters," Johnson C. Smith University, Charlotte, N.C., Oct. 26–Dec., 1968, #27; "Referendum 70," Terry Dintenfass, Inc., New York, Sept. 15–Oct. 3, 1970; "Randolph-Macon at Reynolda House," Winston-Salem, N.C., Mar. 17–26, 1972, #3.

## ELIZABETH VAUGHAN HALL ex-'21

Born 1897

92. CHESTNUT WOODS IN FALL 1962 or early 1963

Oil: 16 × 20 in.; 40.6 × 50.8 cm.
Signed, lower right: Elizabeth Hall
Gift of alumnae of Atlanta, 1964

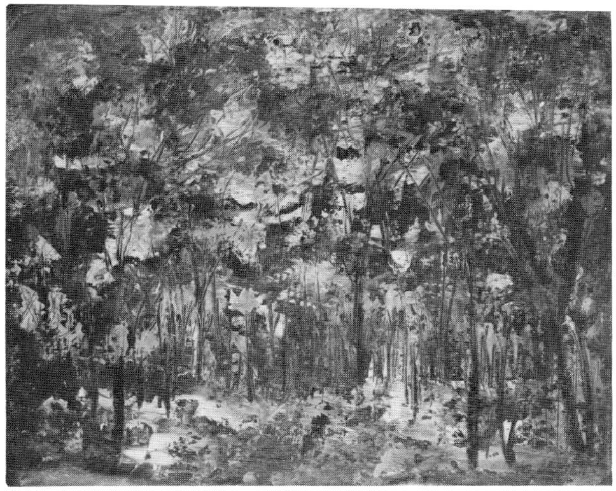

*This painting which has been exhibited under three titles, none of which seems just right ("Fall in the Bois de Vincennes," "In a Yellow Wood," "Chestnut Trees in Fall"), was done here in my studio in Atlanta from a small watercolor sketch made as I sat in my car one damp Sunday afternoon in the Bois de Vincennes. The chestnut leaves were so yellow, on the ground and on the trees, that there was a yellow glow on everything. That brilliant yellow determined the color, texture, and feeling.*

*What is now the finished painting was done as underpainting originally, but nothing I tried to do to it seemed as good as what was already on the canvas, so, with a few strokes here and there, I left it as it was. If my painting takes you along the path through this yellow wood, then my problem has been solved.*

Elizabeth Vaughan Hall (1964)

Exhibited: Atlanta Art Association, spring 1963, as "In a Yellow Wood"; "Elizabeth Hall Exhibition," Fred Reed Gallery, Atlanta, May 1963; "Paintings by Elizabeth Vaughan Hall," at the College, Oct. 19–Nov. 17, 1963, #21; "Elizabeth Hall," Dzirkalis Galleries, Atlanta, Dec. 1–15, 1963; "Randolph-Macon Woman's College Collection," Virginia Museum, Richmond, Sept. 11–Oct. 18, 1964, #26.

93. Hilltop Village in Spain 1964

Oil on cardboard: 16 × 20 in.; 40.6 × 50 cm.
Signed and dated, lower right: Elizabeth Hall 64
Gift of Susan Dabney '15, in 1969

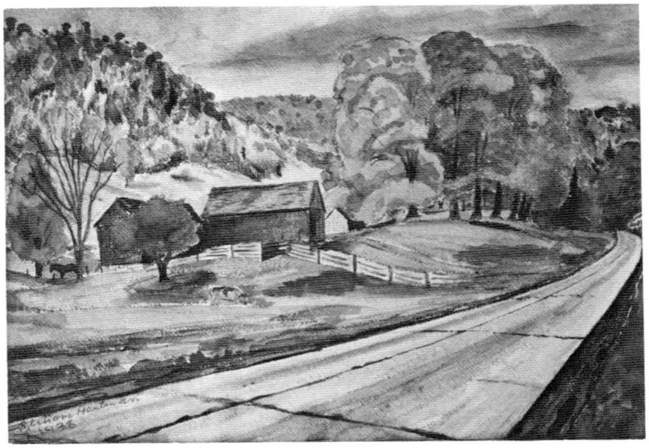

## BERTRAM HARTMAN
1882–1960

94. Connecticut Highway to Waramug 1938

Watercolor: 15 × 22¼ in.; 38.1 × 56.5 cm.
Signed and dated, lower left: Bertram Hartman 1938
Gift of six alumnae living in New York City, honoring the fiftieth anniversary of the College, 1943

*Being very proud of our Alma Mater on her fiftieth anniversary, we felt that giving a painting was one way we could express our love and congratulations. We chose this particular picture because, though it was done in Connecticut, it reminds us of Virginia, and also because there is something about the open road, universal and timeless, that appealed to all six of us.*

Norma Chambers '27 (1943)

Exhibited: "Fifteen Paintings from the College Collection" circulated by the Alumnae Association to its chapters in Nashville, Birmingham, Atlanta, and Asheville, Oct. 1949–Jan. 1950, #6.

## CHILDE HASSAM
1859–1935

95. Early Evening After Snowfall 1906

Oil: 30 × 25 in.; 76.2 × 63.5 cm.
Signed and dated, lower left: Childe Hassam 1906
Fine Arts Fund, 1936

Provenance: Ellsworth H. Augustus, Cleveland; Estate of Ellsworth H. Augustus.

Exhibited: "Fifteen Paintings from the Collection of Randolph-Macon Woman's College," circulated by the Alumnae Association between Oct. 1949 and Jan. 1950 to its chapters in Nashville, Birmingham, Atlanta, and Asheville; "American Impressionism," Stratford College, Danville, Va., Apr. 8–15, 1962. See Appendix B for exhibitions of the College Collection at Richmond and at Roanoke, 1964, and in six Mid-Atlantic states, 1966–67.

Recorded: *Art News* 35 (Nov. 7, 1936) reproduces the painting and identifies the city as New York; *Art Journal* 32 (Winter 72/73): 195, with repro. on cover.

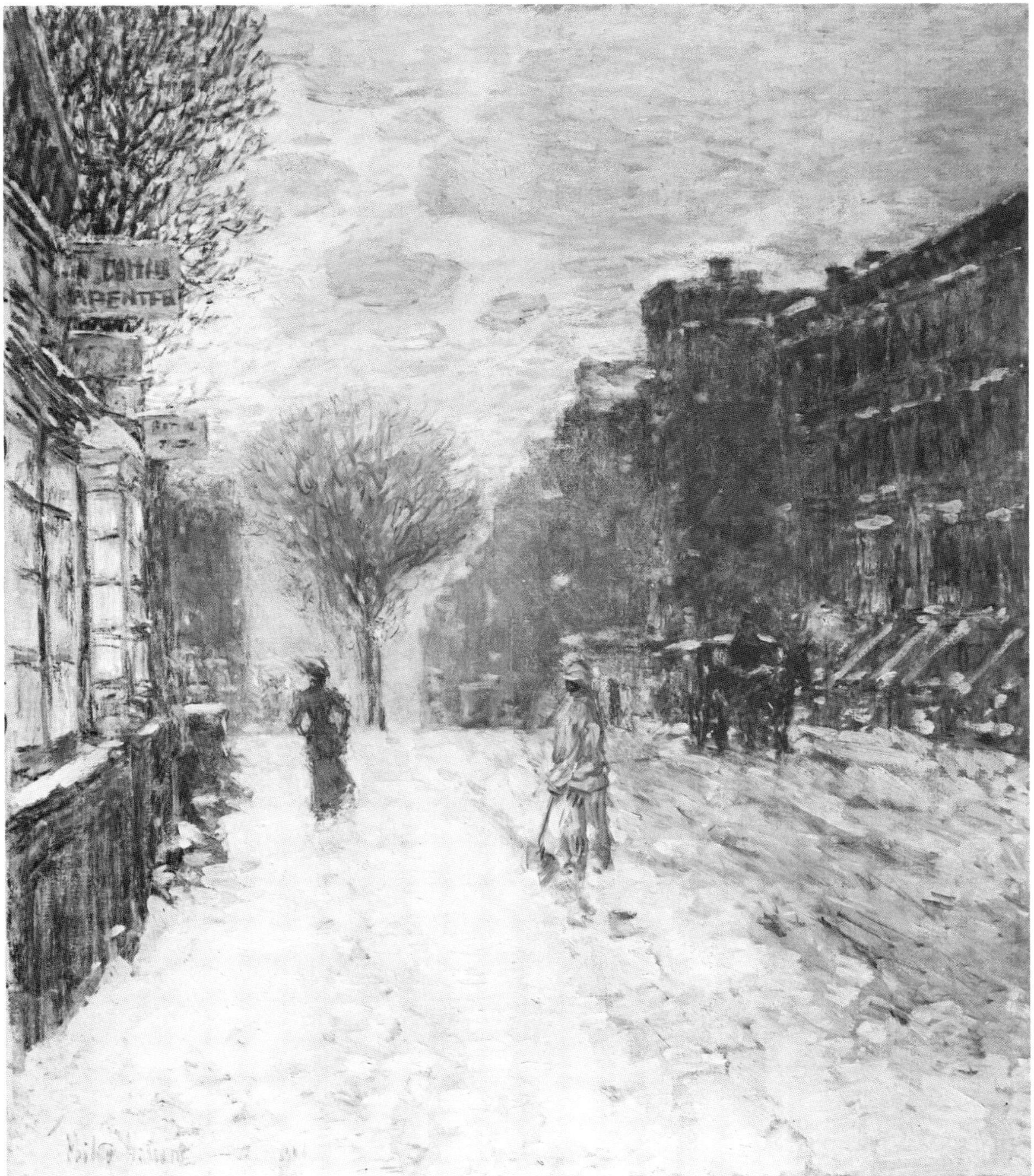

## Erik Haupt

Born 1891

96. Portrait of Charles A. Dana, A.B., M.A., LL.D. 1957

Oil: 44 × 36 in.; 111.7 × 91.4 cm.
Signed, lower right: Erik Haupt
Gift of Charles A. Dana, 1967

The eastern extension (1967) of the Lipscomb Library (1929) is named the Charles A. Dana Wing "in honor of a generous and outstanding philanthropist" who gave a matching grant toward its construction.

## Mildred Hayward

1889-1967

97. Mexican Lotus Leaves with Red Flowers

Oil: 40 × 30 in.; 101.6 × 76.2 cm.
Signed, lower left: Mildred Hayward
Gift of Mr. and Mrs. Chauncey J. Blair, 1976

Exhibited: "Art in Embassies Program" of the Department of State, American Embassy in Tokyo, Japan, Dec. 1966–Feb. 1969; American Embassy in Reykjavik, Iceland, Jan. 1970–Nov. 1972.

## ROBERT HENRI

1865–1929

98. TOM 1926

Oil: 24 × 20 in.; 60.9 × 50.8 cm.
Signed, lower right: Robert Henri
On the back: N 36 Robert Henri "Tom"
Louise J. Smith Fund, 1950

*"Tom" was painted by Robert Henri in the summer of 1926 in his home "Corrymore" on Achill Island, Ireland. Corrymore was previously the home of Charles Cunningham Boycott whose harsh oppressive treatment of the peasantry caused his retreat to England, because they would neither serve nor sell to him, thus giving the word "boycott" to the English language.*

Violet Organ (1958)

Henri's carefully kept records were in the possession of his sister-in-law, Miss Violet Organ of New York, until her death in 1959.

Only a short time before painting "Tom," Robert Henri had occupied the Tower Studio at Randolph-Macon Woman's College, where he painted the portrait of Mrs. Robert C. Watts, April 9–16, 1926.

Provenance: Collection of Carl Tucker, New York.

Exhibited: "Survey of American Paintings," Sweet Briar College, Oct. 24–Nov. 5, 1938; J. L. Hudson Company, Detroit, Jan. 1942; Syracuse Museum of Fine Arts, Jan. 1947; Mattituck Historical Society (Conn.), May 1947; Des Moines Art Center, Sept. 1949; "Celebrate Ohio," Akron Art Institute, Sept. 25–Nov. 7, 1971. Shown in five exhibitions of the College Collection listed in Appendix B: at Richmond and at Roanoke, 1964; at Tampa, Orlando, Gainesville, and Jacksonville, 1965; in six Mid-Atlantic states, 1966–67; and in the Virginia Museum's Artmobile, 1969–70.

Recorded: *Arts in Virginia* 2 (Spring 1962), p. 24, repro. p. 25; *The News* (Lynchburg), Nov. 12, 1950, with repro.; *Nashville Banner*, July 14, 1967, repro.

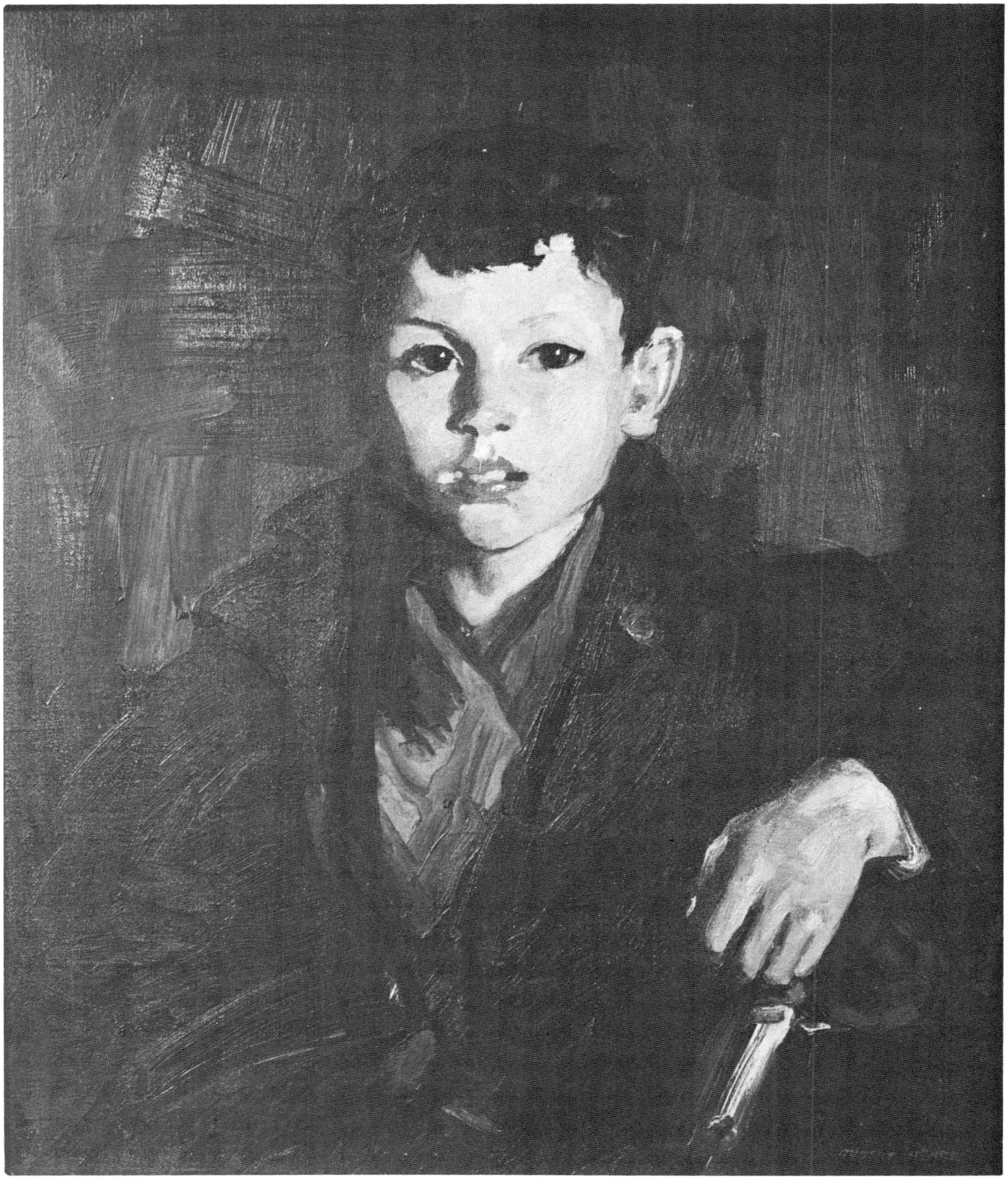

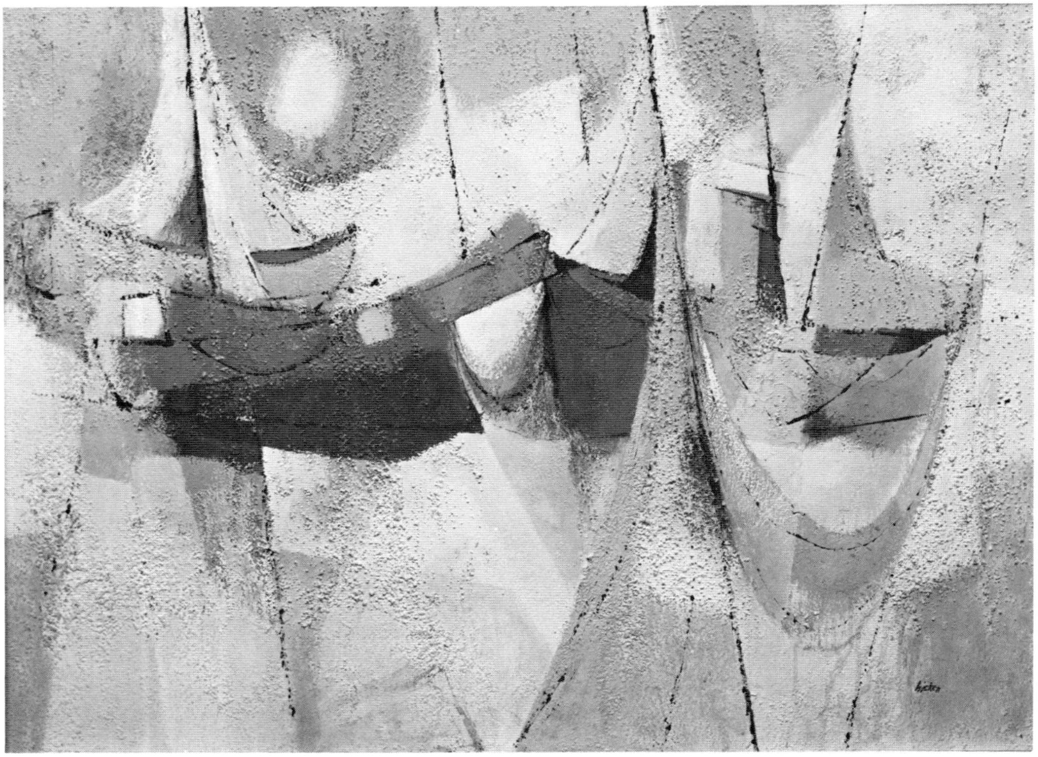

## PHILIP HICKEN

Born 1910

99. Marine Forms In the 1960s

Oil: 36 × 48 in.; 91.4 × 121.9 cm.
Signed, lower right: hicken
Gift of Mr. and Mrs. Clifford B. Moller (Polly Elkins '45), 1968

*One of a series executed in the 1960's from preliminary sketches made on the Island of Nantucket, Mass. The intent was to employ the design elements of form, line and color, without completely divorcing the source of the original inspiration—canvas sails and sturdy wooden hulls—dominant elements in their own right in the Island way of life.*

Philip Hicken

## EDWARD HICKS

1780–1849

100. A Peaceable Kingdom About 1840–45

Oil: 17½ × 23½ in.; 44.5 × 59.6 cm.
Unsigned

This painting is not in the Collection, but is in the catalogue through the courtesy of Phyllis Crawford '20, who has included it in her will as a bequest to the College.

Exhibited: "Edward Hicks, A Gentle Spirit," Andrew Crispo Gallery, New York, May 16-June 28, 1975, #13, with color repro. in the catalogue.

Recorded: Eleanore Price Mather, in her introduction to the catalogue of the exhibition mentioned above, places this work in Hick's middle period, for two reasons. The lion is seated instead of standing and William Penn appears with Indians, instead of with Quakers as in his earlier paintings. This work, she says, is very similar to the one in the Brooklyn Museum.

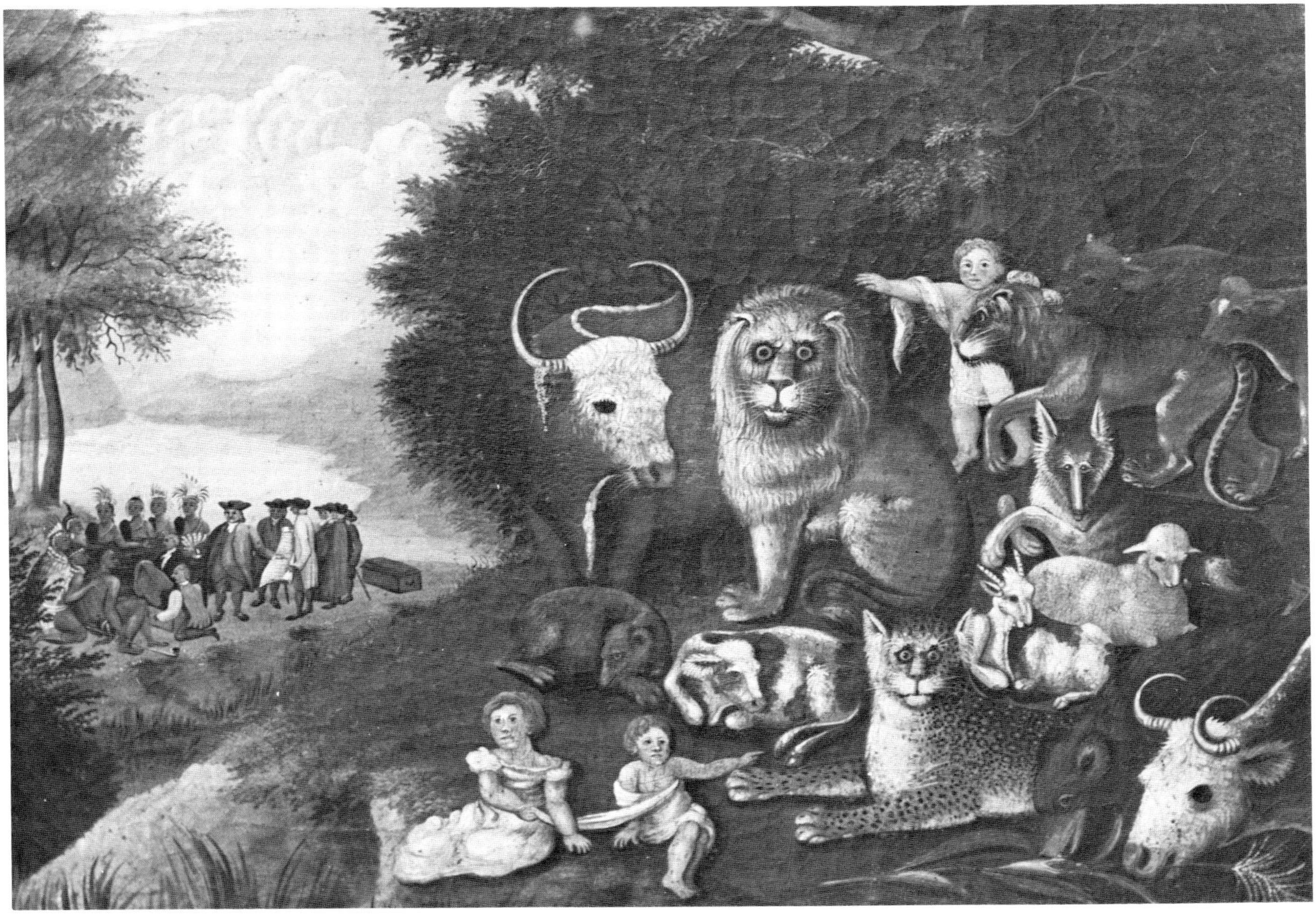

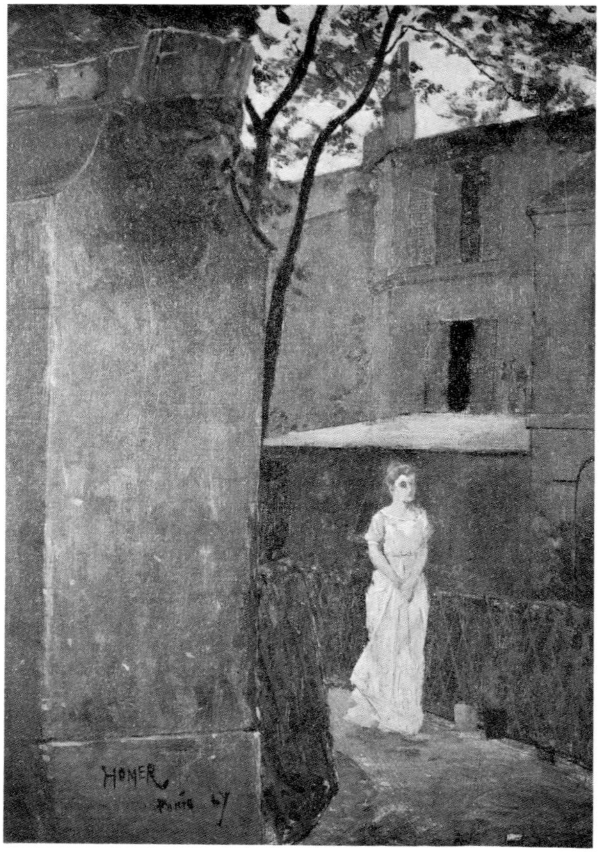


## WINSLOW HOMER
1836–1910

101. PARIS COURTYARD 1867

Oil: 16¾ × 12 in.; 42.5 × 30.4 cm.
Signed and dated, lower left: Homer Paris 67
Fine Arts Fund, 1945

*It is one of the six Paris paintings mentioned by me in my book on Homer, page 39.*

Lloyd Goodrich (1958)

Provenance:

*Homer's "Paris Courtyard" was one of a large number of his early works given to the Carnegie Institute, Pittsburgh, in the twenties by Homer's sister-in-law, Mrs. Charles S. Homer. At that time Homer's early work was not appreciated, and in 1941 the Institute sold them (crazy people!). They were purchased by the Milch and Babcock Galleries on joint account.*[1]

Robert G. McIntyre (1953)

Mrs. Jacob H. Rand of Brooklyn and New York bought "Paris Courtyard" in 1942 and later sold it to the Macbeth Gallery, from which the College acquired it.

Exhibited: "Winslow Homer," Babcock Galleries, New York, Dec. 8–31, 1941, #6; "Yankee Painter, Winslow Homer," University of Arizona Art Gallery (Tucson), Oct. 11–Dec. 1, 1963, #119; shown in five exhibitions of the College Collection listed in Appendix B: at Richmond and at Roanoke, 1964; at Tampa, Orlando, Gainesville, and Jacksonville, 1965; in six Mid-Atlantic states, 1966–67; and in the Virginia Museum's Artmobile, 1969–70.

Recorded: Lloyd Goodrich, *Winslow Homer* (New York, 1944), p. 39; Catalogue of the Arizona exhibition, p. 88.

1. Robert G. McIntyre to Herbert C. Lipscomb, March 14, 1953.

## EDWARD HOPPER
1882–1967

102. Mrs. Scott's House 1932
(Color plate, page 29)

Oil: 26 × 50½ in.; 66 × 128.2 cm.
Signed, lower right: Edward Hopper
Louise J. Smith Fund, 1936

*Regarding your picture, "Mrs. Scott's House" by Edward Hopper, in getting ourselves off to Cape Cod, your first letter was mislaid. I'm glad to have your second copy. Mr. Hopper asks me to look after this matter. I'm far the more garrulous and this picture is one of my favorites. That foreground of tall grass would wring the heart of anyone who feels strongly about this unique part of the Cape.*

*All Cape Cod grass is special. No weeds grow on Cape Cod, everything that comes out of the ground is beautiful. In "Mrs. Scott's House" that hill is grass en masse, glorified by "a sun descending."*

*Mrs. Scott died more or less recently. She was a prim, kind New England lady whose house (surprisingly, containing [of late years] all the modern conveniences) was spotless. Her heirs have shown no disposition to sell the house or do any damage to that hill.*

*Railroad tracks run across the little valley that lies beneath it. As E. Hopper worked there late afternoons, the man in the caboose at the end of the late N.Y., N.H. & H. train always waved in most friendly fashion.*

*We neglected saying "Mrs. Scott's House" is situated at South Truro, down near the end of Cape Cod, Mass. That hill obscures the view of the sea, a partly surrounded arm of the Atlantic. The house, kept in good repair, is old, it is quite humble, as is the best of this Cape (to our point of view) and doubtlessly built by the people who fished or sailed on its seas, but is no proud Captain's House.*

*Take whatever you see fit of the foregoing (E. Hopper has already edited a lot of what he feels irrelevant). We love having one of the specially prized Hopper creations snug and serene among you. Yes, that picture certainly has serenity.*

*[Added in pencil:] Quite on my own, I add—That picture surely is destined to outlive much of the dense fog of ignorance & arrogance that has come to gain ground in our day. You will do well to guard a relic of the spiritual, yet unobtrusive whose value belongs to time and history.*

*Milton says something inimitable about books, why not applicable to pictures—in the "Areopagitica." You are nearer to it than I—if Milton still prevails in women's colleges. This shamefully garbled—what sticks in my memory—"Books—not absolutely dead things. Nay, they do contain, as in a vial, the purest efficacy & extraction of the living intellect that bred them, embalmed & treasured up, on purpose to a life beyond life."*

*You have a responsibility, and do not change its frame!*

Jo N. Hopper (1958)

The foregoing letter written at South Truro, Mass., dated September 5, 1958, was followed by one of April 9, 1965, in which Mrs. Hopper referred again to "Mrs. Scott's House."

*By those who know this picture, her [presence] was missed at the big Whitney Retrospective [of 1964]. . . . I'm sure "she" was invited but you had other engagements for her this time. . . . We feel Mrs. Scott's House is among the 15 or so finest canvases of E.H.*

When informed that this painting had not been invited to the big show that went from New York to Chicago, Detroit, and St. Louis, she wrote from Truro on October 21, 1965:

*It was sadly missed by those who know. But you must be told neither E. Hopper nor I had any say in this matter. We weren't even there before the show went on. . . . I'd love for E.H. to have a show where we were consulted. E. H. so mild & meek. Not really, but silent.*

Jo N. Hopper (1965)

Exhibited: "International Exhibition," Rockefeller Center, New York, 1933, #22, repro. p. 10; "One Hundred and Thirtieth Annual Exhibition," Pennsylvania Academy of the Fine Arts, Philadelphia, Jan. 27–Mar. 3, 1935, #79 (Temple Gold Medal); "The 1936 International Exhibition of Paintings," Carnegie Institute of Technology, Pittsburgh, Oct. 25–Dec. 6, 1939, #53, repro, p. 29; "An American Show," Cincinnati Art Museum, Oct. 1–Nov. 5, 1948, #28; "Fifteen Paintings from the Collection of Randolph-Macon Woman's College," circulated by the Alumnae Association between Oct. 1949 and Jan. 1950 to its chapters in Nashville, Birmingham, Atlanta, and Asheville, #8; "Edward Hopper Retrospective Exhibition": Whitney Museum of American Art, New York, Feb. 11–Mar. 26, 1950, Museum of Fine Arts, Boston, Apr. 13–May 14, 1950, Detroit Institute of Fine Arts, June 4–July 2, 1950, #40; "Edward Hopper," University of Arizona Art Gallery (Tucson) Apr. 20–May 19, 1963, #22; included in four groups of paintings from Randolph-Macon Woman's College: a loan exhibition to Richmond, 1964; circulating exhibitions to Florida, 1965, and to six Mid-Atlantic states, 1966–67; and the Artmobile of the Virginia Museum, 1969–70. For dates and galleries see Appendix B.

Recorded: Catalogues of the exhibitions; *Art News* 35 (Nov. 7, 1936), repro. p. 18; *Alumnae Bulletin* 19 (June 1936), repro. p. 2; American Artists Group, *Edward Hopper* (New York, 1945), repro.; *Arts in Virginia* 2 (Spring 1962), p. 28 with repro.; *Art Journal* 32 (Winter 72/73), p. 195, repro. p. 194.

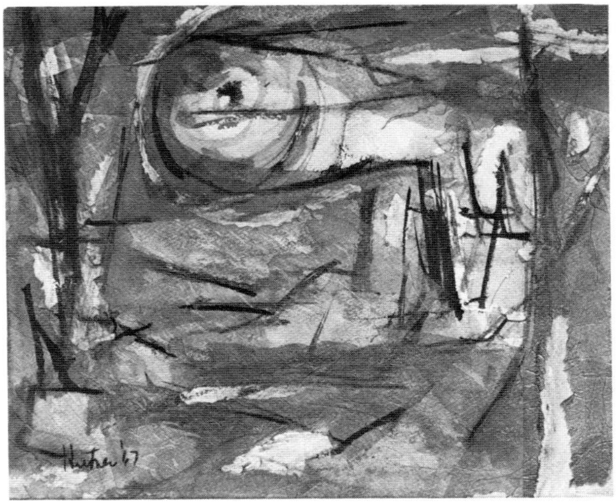

## EUGENE HUTNER

Born 1921

103. SUNSET 1967

Collage: 12¼ × 15⅜ in.; 31.7 × 39 cm.
Signed, lower left: Hutner '67
Gift of alumnae of the Northern Delaware Chapter, 1968

*This collage is based on a visual experience which excited me. Stimulated by what I had seen in the world around me, I reorganized this experience into a totally new form. Through the use of shapes, textures, color, and line, I changed reality into a series of completely different visual effects. I intensified the original spatial and color relationships to create for myself and the onlooker a new emotional experience. I believe art has to have a personal and individual communication, even though it is bound to be affected by twentieth century concepts of color and spatial tensions.*

Eugene Hutner

Exhibited: See Appendix C.

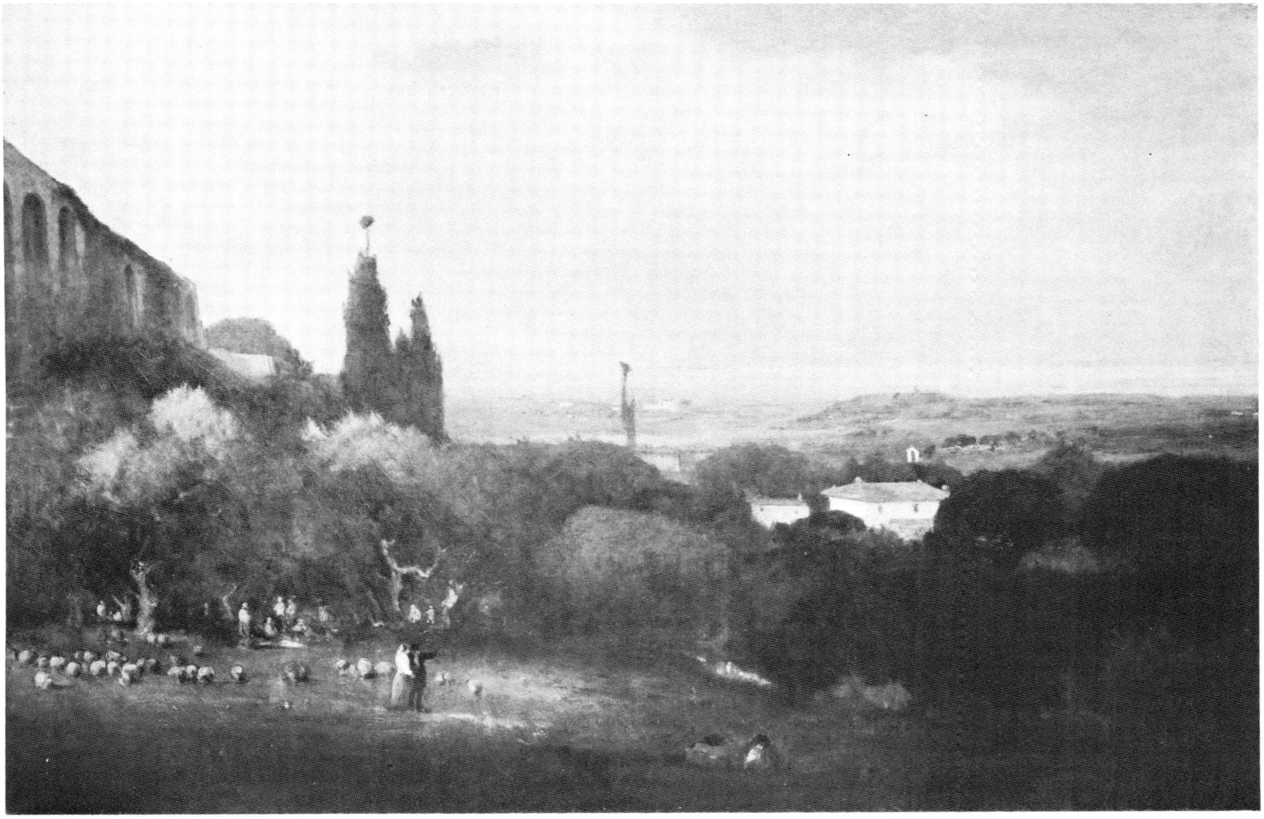

## GEORGE INNESS

1825–94

104. PERUGIA AND THE VALLEY
(Scene Near Perugia) 1874

Oil: 30 × 45 in.; 76.2 × 114.3 cm.
Signed and dated, lower left: G. Inness 1874
Fine Arts Fund, 1942

Although LeRoy Ireland's description of this painting in his book on Inness concludes, "The town of Perugia in the distance," it is possible that the white hill-town far across the valley in the center of the painting is actually Assisi, while the walls of Perugia rise on the immediate left.

Provenance: Mrs. Oliver Peabody, Boston, catalogue No. 6; George H. Ainslie, New York, 1912; to John F.

Braun, Philadelphia, on July 16, 1918; from Ferargil Gallery, New York.

Exhibited: National Academy of Design, New York, 1874 or more probably 1875, as "Scene Near Perugia," #358; "Exhibition of Thirty-Eight Paintings by the late George Inness, N.A., from the Ainslie Collection and Others," New York School of Applied Design for Women, Apr. 6–May 6, 1912, #6; Inness and Wyant Exhibition, New York School of Applied Design for Women, June–Sept. 1912, #6; American Art Association, Jan. 20, 1913, #109, repro.; "George Inness and A. H. Wyant," City Art Museum, St. Louis, Feb. 1914, #11; "Paintings by George Inness," University (of Texas) Art Museum, Austin, Dec. 12, 1965–Jan. 30, 1966, #53. See Appendix B for exhibitions in Richmond, 1964; in six Mid-Atlantic states, 1966–67; and in the Virginia Museum Artmobile, 1969–70.

Recorded: *Catalogue: Sale of Emerson McMillin Collection* (American Art Association, New York, Jan. 1913), #109, repro.; *The Art World and Arts and Decoration* 10 (Jan. 1919), repro. p. 118 as "Perugia of the Valley"; *Art News* 24 (Feb. 27, 1926), repro. p. 9; LeRoy Ireland, *The Works of George Inness* (Austin, Texas, 1965), #677, with repro. p. 166.

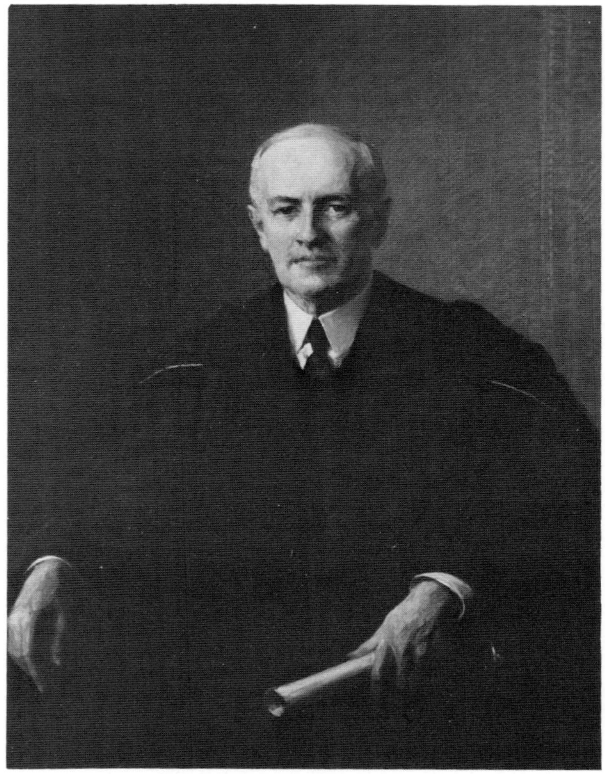

## ERNEST LUDVIC IPSEN
1869–1951

105. PORTRAIT OF DEAN NATHAN A. PATTILLO
1931

Oil: 48 × 36½ in.; 121.9 × 92.7 cm.
Signed and dated, upper left: E. L. Ipsen 1931
Gift of the Classes of 1930 and 1931 through the Alumnae Association, 1931

Dr. Pattillo was acting president of the College three times and was dean from 1907–36.

Recorded: Roberta D. Cornelius, *The History of Randolph-Macon Woman's College*, repro. following p. 430; *Alumnae Bulletin* 25 (Nov. 1931), repro. on cover.

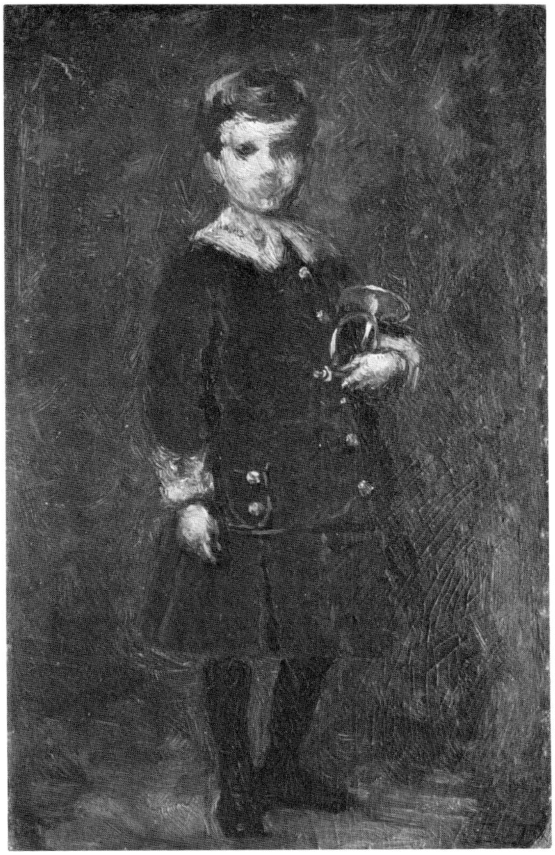

# EASTMAN JOHNSON

1824–1906

106. THE LITTLE PRINCE

Oil on cardboard: 13 × 8¼ in.; 33 × 20.9 cm.
Signed, lower right: E. J.
Gift of Mr. Robert G. McIntyre to Harriet Fitzgerald '26 and her gift to the College in 1948

Recorded: *The News* (Lynchburg), Aug. 1, 1948, with repro.

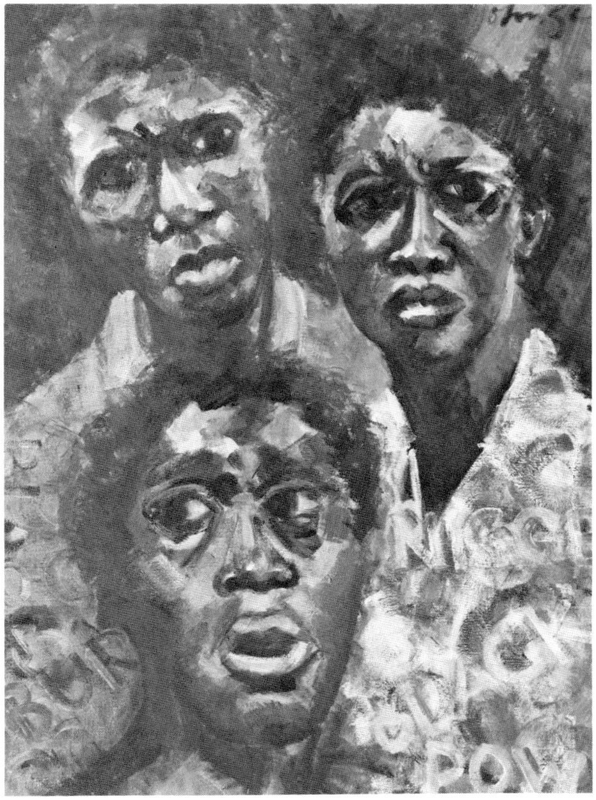

# JOHN EDWARD JOHNSON

Born 1938

107. NIAGARA

Oil: 40 × 30 in.; 101 6 × 76.2 cm.
Signed, top right: Johnson
Gift of Dr. and Mrs. David H. Dawson, 1968

If the artist could be located, he would be asked whether the title of this canvas refers to the meeting of black reformers who gathered at Niagara Falls, Canada, in 1905 to plan a more militant attack on discrimination.

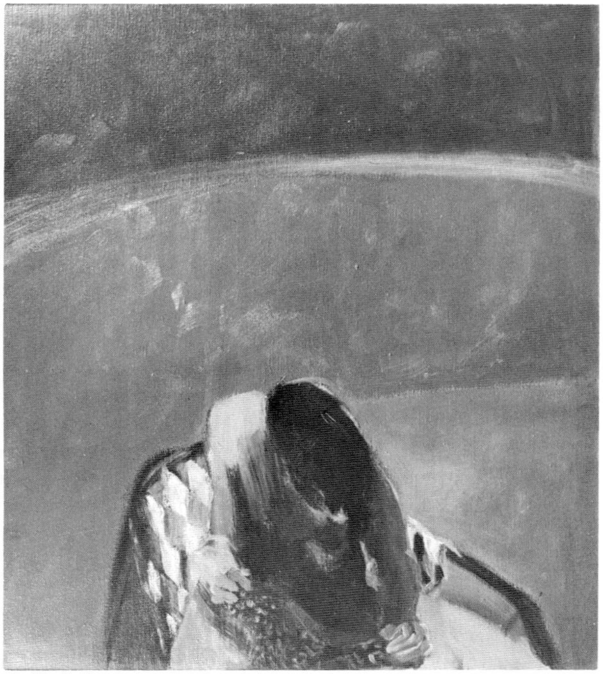

## PATRICIA KEARNEY

Born 1925

108. FIGURE IN A ROOM #1 1966

Acrylic on canvas: 46 × 40 in.; 116.8 × 101.6 cm.
Unsigned
Accepted from the artist in 1967, at her request, in exchange for an earlier work given anonymously in 1965.

*My concern is in working out certain formal problems within a rather narrow, self-imposed limitation. Several overlapping and adjacent shapes happen to develop into a figure, because I seem to be object-oriented. The remainder of the canvas is articulated with one or two colors in wide expanses. Their contrast with the "busy" color of the "figure" intrigues me. Rich color kept within a closely confined value range offers a fascinating formal challenge.*

*This painting is frankly "contentless" in that I had no notion of commenting on or telling a story about the image. The "story" is about color, shape, and value relations.*

Patricia Kearney (1967)

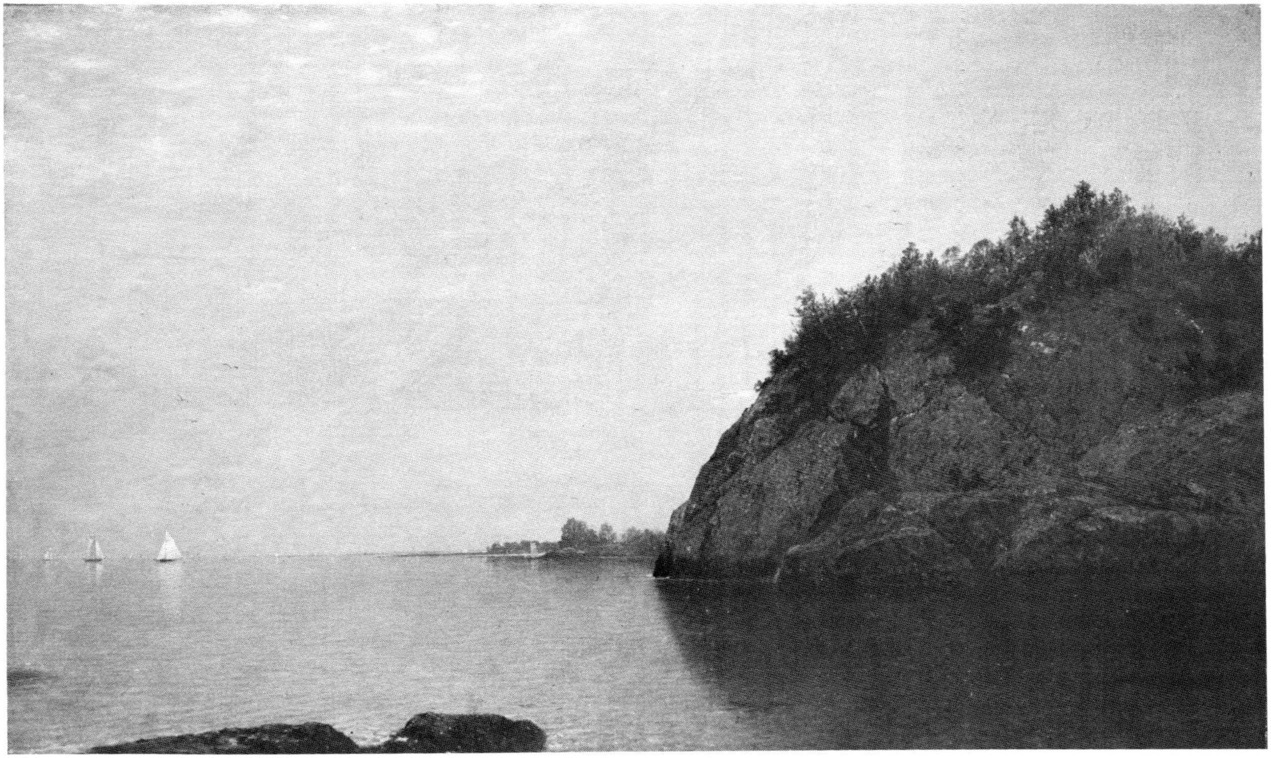

## JOHN FREDERICK KENSETT

1818–72

109. ON THE CONNECTICUT SHORE 187[?]

Oil: 28 × 45¾ in.; 71.1 × 116.2 cm.
Signed and dated, lower right: F.K. '7[?]
Gift of Mr. Thomas F. Torrey II, 1955

Provenance: From the collection of Thomas F. Torrey (1844–1905) of New York, grandfather of the donor.

Recorded: *The Advance* (Lynchburg), Mar. 16, 1956, with repro.

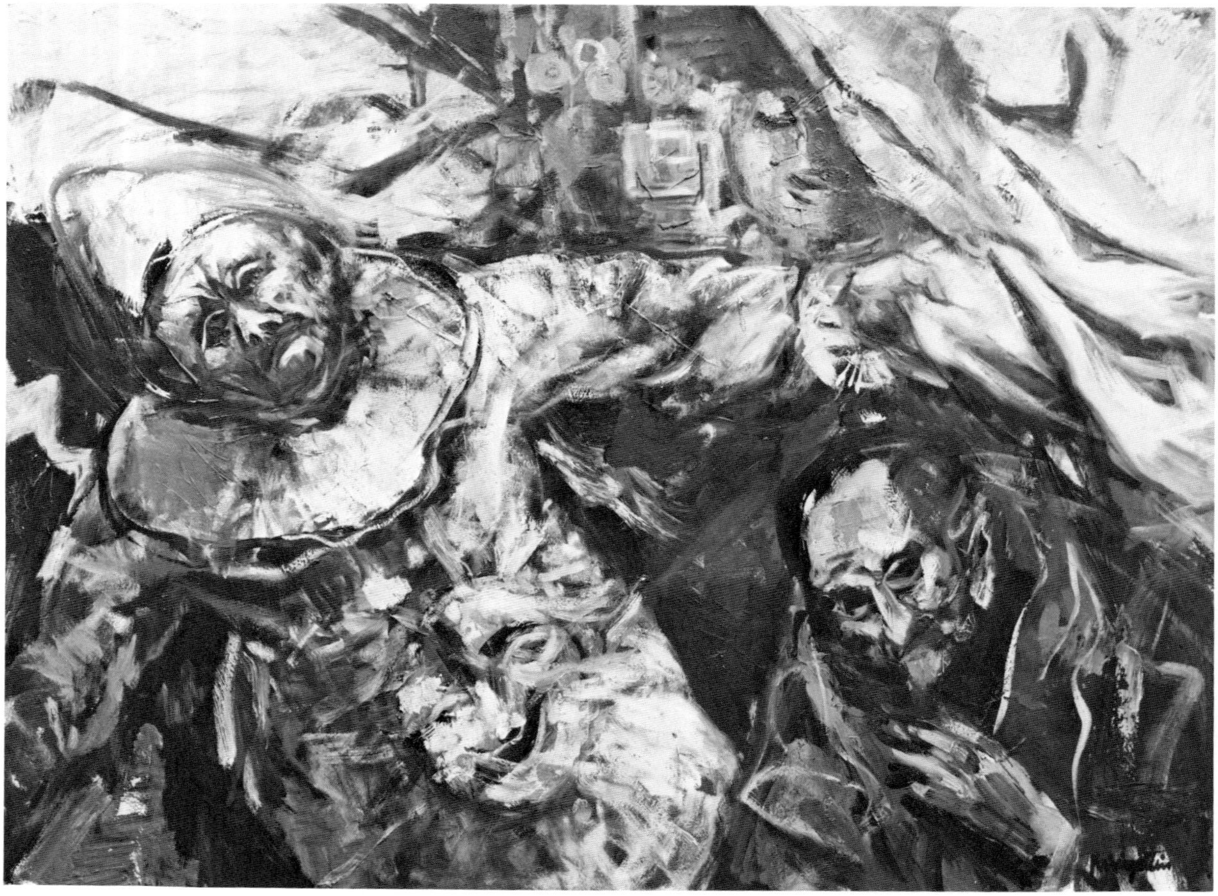

## JONAH KINIGSTEIN

Born 1923

110. CLOWNS UNVEILING 1966

Oil on masonite: 36 × 48 in.; 91.4 × 121.9 cm.
Signed, lower right: Kinigstein
Gift of Mr. and Mrs. Leonard Bocour, 1968

*One of a series of anti-clerical paintings depicting Christ as a clown and being revealed as such in many grotesque circumstances. At other times it is the pope turned into a clown in a circus-like masquerade dream sequence. Religion in general is taken to task and dramatized as society in love with carnival costumes and pranks.*

Jonah Kinigstein

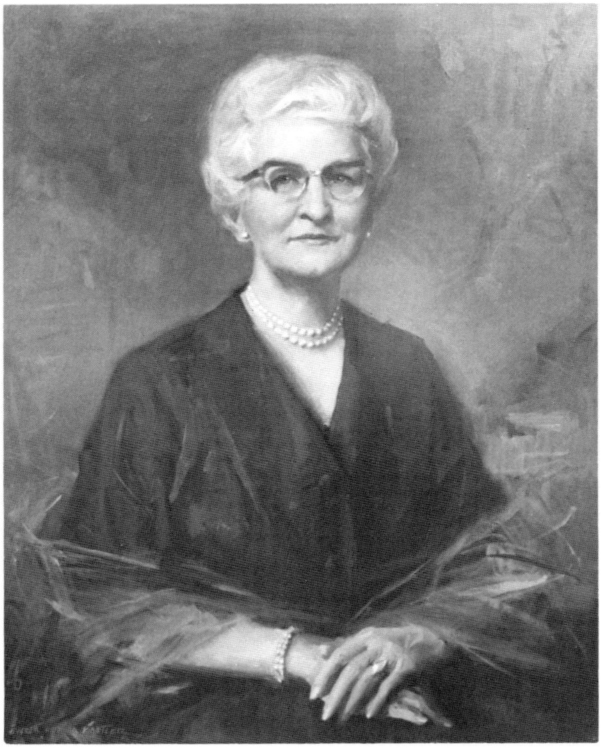

## EVERETT RAYMOND KINSTLER

Born 1926

111. PORTRAIT OF SALLIE FRANKLIN CHEATHAM (Mrs. W. B.) 1966

Oil: 36 × 28 in.; 91.4 × 71.1 cm.
Signed, lower right: Everett Raymond Kinstler
Inscribed on the back: posthumous portrait
Gift of Owen R. Cheatham, 1966

Cheatham Dining Room, which connects Bell Hall with Wright Hall, was donated by Mr. Cheatham in 1964 and named in honor of his mother (1876–1962).

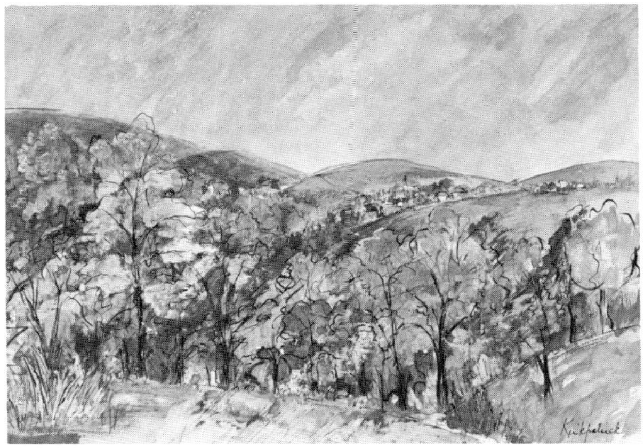

## MARGARET M. KIRKPATRICK

1898–1967

112. APPROACH TO LYNCHBURG 1960

Ink and gouache: 13½ × 19¼ in.; 34.2 × 48.9 cm.
Signed, lower right: Kirkpatrick
Gift of friends of the artist, 1960

*When taking the train at Norfolk to return to Lynchburg, I usually choose a seat on the left-hand side of the coach to be assured of the first possible view of the mountains. On one occasion the foothills came into view when it was late in the day. It was late in the season too. All colors were present, but muted. The pattern of trees, mountains, sky, and a tiny pocket of habitation gave a feeling of welcoming serenity. All of this I went home and attempted to note.*

Margaret M. Kirkpatrick (1962)

Exhibited: "Margaret Kirkpatrick Exhibition," Lynchburg Art Center, Oct. 2–16, 1960; "Paintings by Margaret Kirkpatrick," Hollins College, Feb. 9–23, 1964.

Recorded: *The News* (Lynchburg), Jan. 10, 1961.

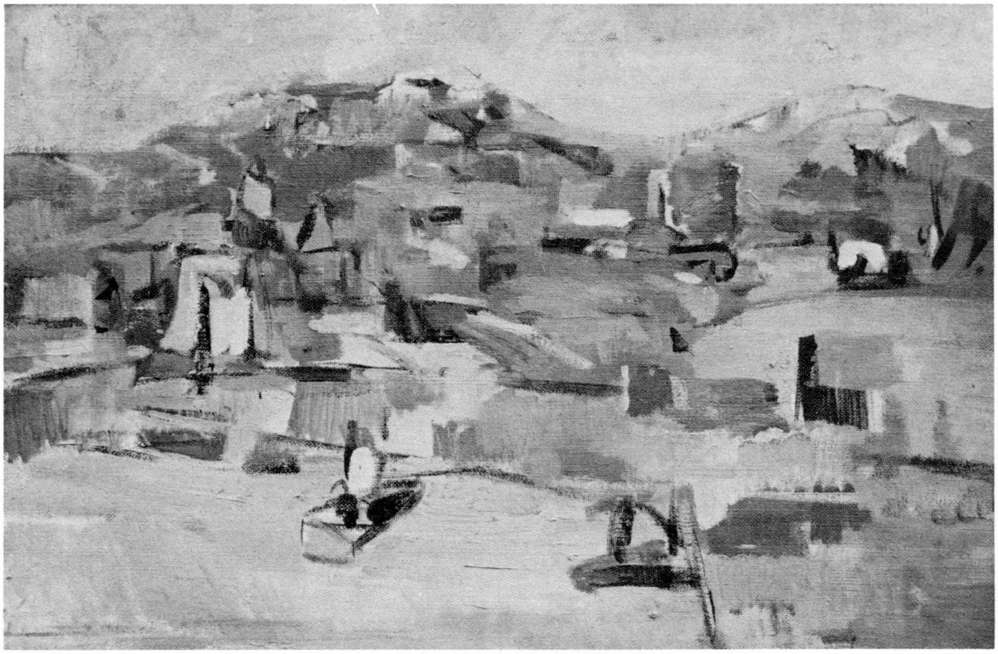

## NAT KOFFMAN

1910–50

113. LANDSCAPE ABSTRACTION

Oil: 22 × 33 in.; 58.8 × 83.8 cm.
Unsigned
Gift of Harriet Fitzgerald '26, in 1952

*Selectivity and a new and heightened order are necessary to make the material supplied us by nature of value in interpreting life. Since our scope is limited and a definite viewpoint is necessary, we find ourselves constantly rejecting the overabundant riches of nature and taking just those things that point up the unified expression. Not only that, we find ourselves most naturally rearranging and distorting forms as though we had been responsible for their growth.*

Nat Koffman[1]

1. Quoted from *The Notebook of Nat Koffman* (Abingdon Square Publication, New York, 1951), p. 34, by permission of Harriet Fitzgerald, Executrix of the Estate of Nat Koffman.

114. Landscape

Watercolor: 19½ × 25½ in.; 49.5 × 64.7 cm.
Signed, lower right: N. Koffman
Gift of Norma Chambers '27, in 1952

115. Landscape

Watercolor: 12⅞ × 16 in.; 32.7 × 40.6 cm.
Unsigned
Gift of alumnae of Northern Delaware Chapter, 1968

Exhibited: See Appendix C.

## AUGUST KÖLLNER
1813–83

116. LYNCHBURG IN 1845
(Reproduced on page 22)

Wash drawing: 7 × 18½ in.; 17.7 × 46.9 cm.
Signed and dated, lower right:
A. Köllner from Nature June 1845
Gift of members of the faculty and staff, alumnae, members of the Lynchburg Historical Society, and friends, 1953

In pencil in the lower left corner: "Lynchburg on the James River, Virginia. The great staple for Tobacco." When readying his topographical drawings and watercolors for exhibition, Köllner used to add large, clear identifications in ink near his original (penciled) notations. This new label in ink reads: "Lynchburg on James River, Va." The double page seems to have been the center of his sketchbook.

Exhibited: "Lynchburg Historical Society Exhibition," Lynchburg Art Center, Mar. 14–21, 1954; "Image of an Age," Lynchburg Fine Arts Center, Apr. 7–May 3, 1963, #43, repro. on wraparound cover; "Randolph-Macon Woman's College Collection," Virginia Museum, Richmond, Sept. 11–Oct. 18, 1964, #32; "Bicentennial Exhibition, Lynchburg Past and Present, 1786–1976," June 20–July 30, 1976.

Recorded: *The News* (Lynchburg), May 28, 1953, with repro., June 7, 1953, June 19, 1953, with repro.; *The Daily Advance* (Lynchburg), June 20, 1953, editorial; *Richmond Times Dispatch*, June 26, 1953; *Iron Worker* 20 (Winter 1955–56), repro. p. 2; "Lynchburg in Virginia, Nineteen Hundred and Seventy Six, Lynchburg Bicentennial Commission," a community calendar with the painting reproduced on the cover.

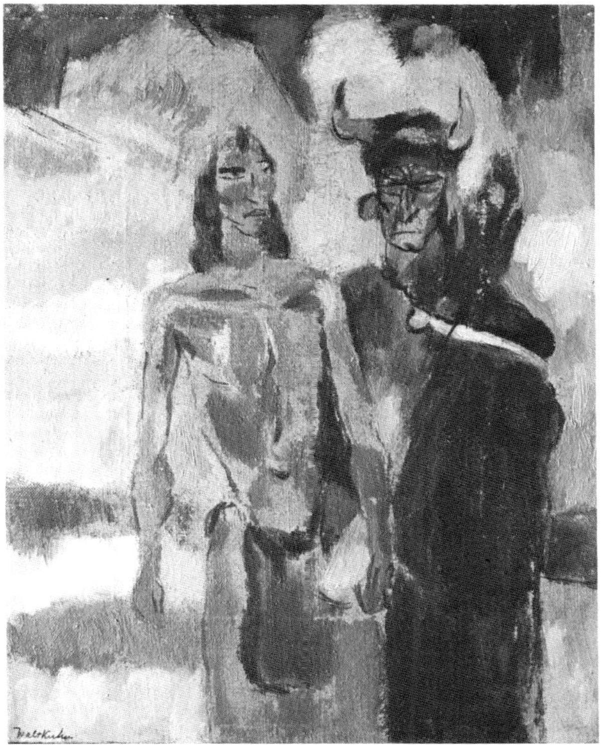

## WALT KUHN
1880–1949

117. MEDICINE About 1918–20

Oil: 10½ × 8 in.; 26.5 × 20.3 cm.
Signed, lower left: Walt Kuhn
Gift of Mrs. C. N. Bliss, 1949

From Kuhn's series "An Imaginary History of the West," painted between 1918 and 1920. Most of the paintings (twenty-nine) are in the Colorado Springs Fine Arts Center. Its nearly identical "Medicine" is signed, dated, and titled by Kuhn.

Exhibited: with others of the series, Montross Gallery, New York, January 1922; "Randolph-Macon Woman's College Collection," Virginia Museum, Richmond, Sept. 11–Oct. 18, 1964, #33.

Recorded: Colorado Springs Fine Arts Center, *Walt Kuhn: An Imaginary History of the West* (Colorado Springs, 1964), p. 4.

## WALT KUHN (cont.)

118. The Song

Gouache: 17¾ × 13¾ in.; 45 × 34.9 cm.
Signed, lower right: Walt Kuhn
Gift of Mrs. C. N. Bliss, 1949

Exhibited: "Art on Paper," Weatherspoon Art Gallery, University of North Carolina, Greensboro, Nov. 14–Dec. 17, 1971, #11.

119. Near Portsmouth

Oil: 13 × 18½ in.; 33 × 46.9 cm.
Unsigned
Gift of Mrs. C. N. Bliss, 1949

120. Vase of Flowers 1924

Oil on wood: 13 × 12 in.; 33 × 30.4 cm.
Unsigned
Gift of Mrs. C. N. Bliss, 1949

121. Indian Warriors 1918–20

Watercolor: 7½ × 11½ in.; 19 × 29.2 cm.
Signed, lower right: Walt Kuhn
Gift of Mrs. C. N. Bliss, 1949

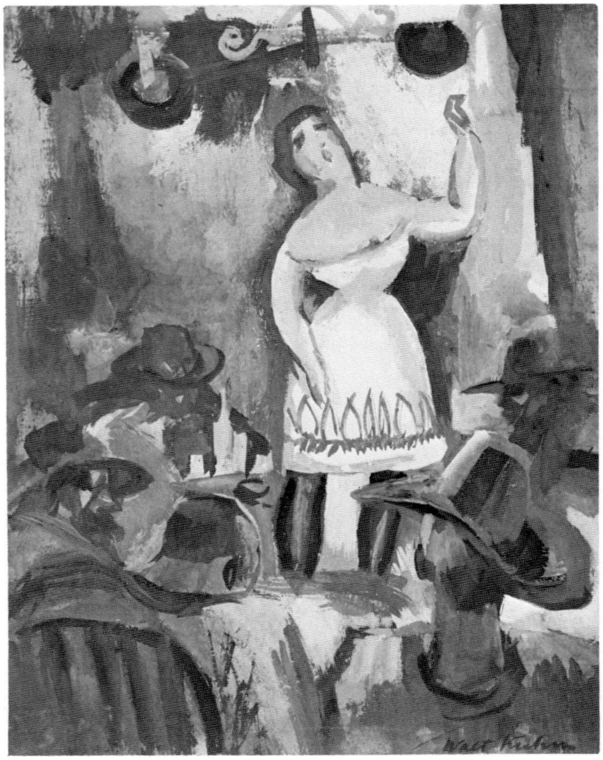

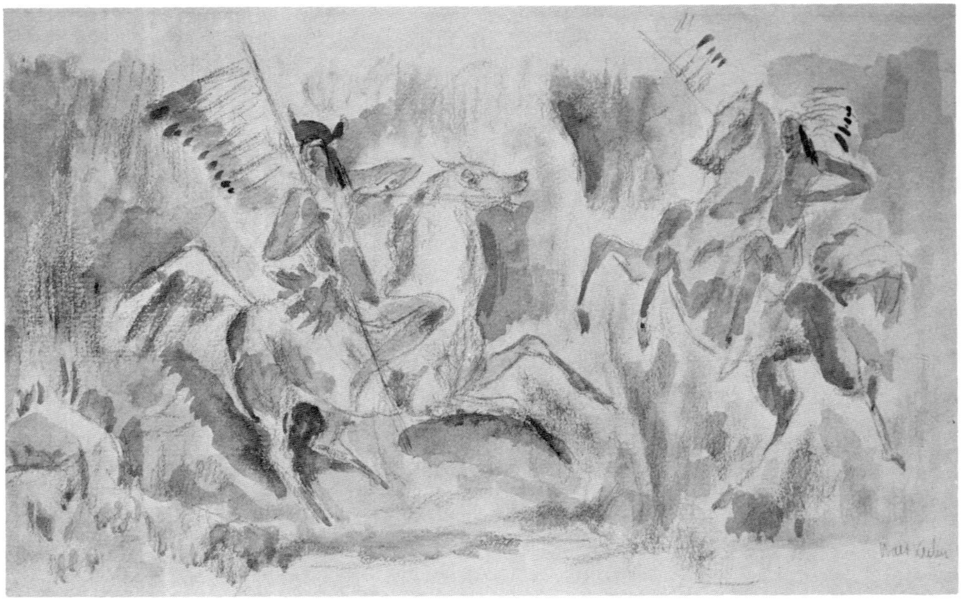

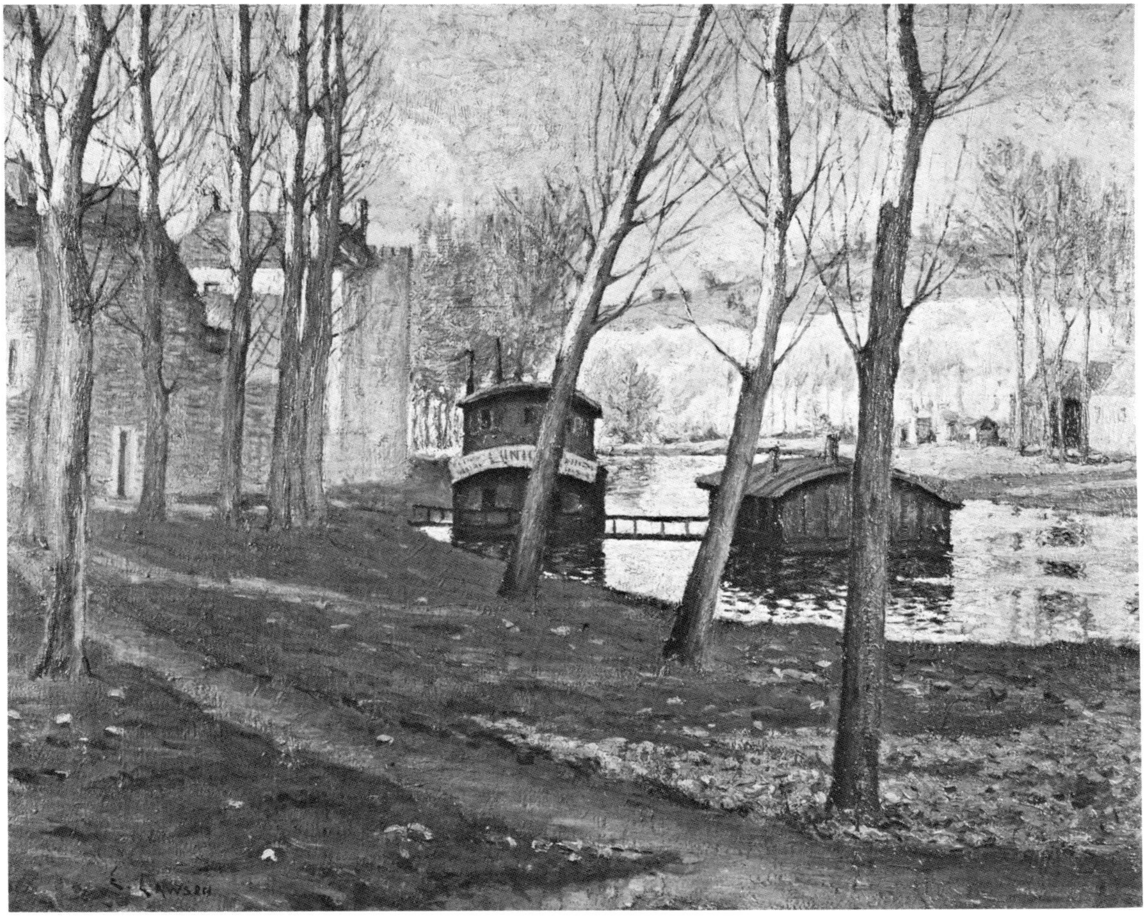

## ERNEST LAWSON

1873–1939

122. MORET-SUR-LOING About 1893

Oil: 26 × 32 in.; 66 × 81.2 cm.
Signed, lower left: E. Lawson
Purchased about 1927

Before the publication of Henry and Sidney Berry-Hill's book on Lawson in 1967, this painting was called merely "River Scene." They have identified the location as Moret, near the Forest of Fontainebleau, where Lawson met the French Impressionist, Alfred Sisley. Lawson also set up his easel across the Loing River at a point shown in the very center of this canvas. There he produced "Church at Moret-sur-Loing," a slightly smaller painting (20 × 24¼ in.; 50.8 × 62.2 cm.), now privately owned.

Exhibited: "Randolph-Macon Woman's College Collection," Virginia Museum, Richmond, Sept. 11–Oct. 18, 1964, #34; the College Collection in the Artmobile circulated by the Virginia Museum, 1969–70, #11; "Ernest Lawson Retrospective," ACA Galleries, New York, Nov. 27- Dec. 24, 1976, #48 with repro.

Recorded: Henry and Sidney Berry-Hill, *Ernest Lawson, American Impressionist* (Leigh-on-Sea, England, 1967), p. 25, repro. #13; Virginia Museum, *Members Bulletin* 30 (Oct. 1969), repro. p. 6; *The News* (Lynchburg), Mar. 9, 1970, repro.; Mahonri Young, *The Eight* (New York, 1973), color repro. p. 84.

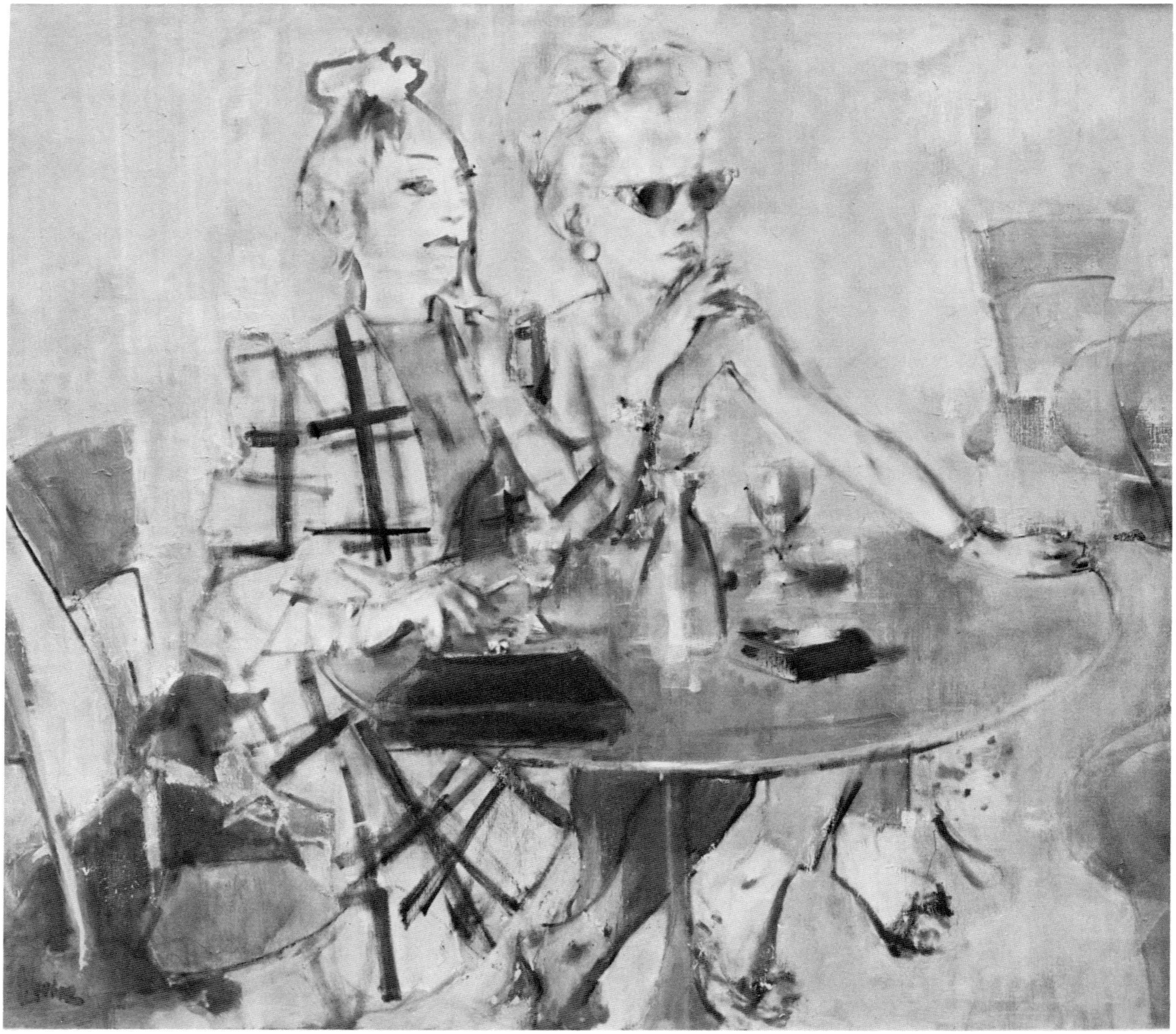

## JACK LEVINE

Born 1915

123. CAFÉ 1960

Oil: 42 × 48 in.; 106.6 × 121.9 cm.
Signed, lower left: J. Levine
Louise J. Smith Fund, 1960

"Yes, I finished it. I said what I wanted to say," Mr. Levine answered when asked whether the girl at the left was still only sketched. He added, "If a thing is drawn right, what else needs to be done to it?" In fact, the chair at the left and the purse on the table were painted, he said, to go with the linear style of the left-hand figure. "The color scheme is orange and oyster white. . . . When we were abroad we used to see these divorced girls sitting in cafés looking the world over. As a man, I couldn't help being interested in them."

The College took an option on this painting before it was finished. At that stage the girls were sitting in a circular booth, not on separate chairs. The poodle was more conspicuous, and the front edge of the table was considerably lower.

Mr. Levine came to the College to speak at the "Arts Symposium on the Creative Process," March 3–5, 1960, at which time seventeen of his paintings were exhibited.

Exhibited: "Paintings by Jack Levine," Forty-ninth Annual Exhibition," at the College, Mar. 4–23, 1960, #17; included in all six of the loan and circulating exhibitions of the College Collection, 1964–1972, as listed in Appendix B.

Recorded: "Our Symposium Painter, Jack Levine," *Alumnae Bulletin* 53 (Apr. 1960), p. 9, repro.; *The News* (Lynchburg), Mar. 3, 1960; *Creativity in Art and Education,* a booklet on the Arts Symposium (Lynchburg, 1961), repro. p. 12; *New York Times Book Review,* Mar. 18, 1962, repro. p. 5; Frank Getlein, *Jack Levine* (New York, 1966), repro. p. 129; *Art Journal* 32 (Winter 72/73), repro. p. 193.

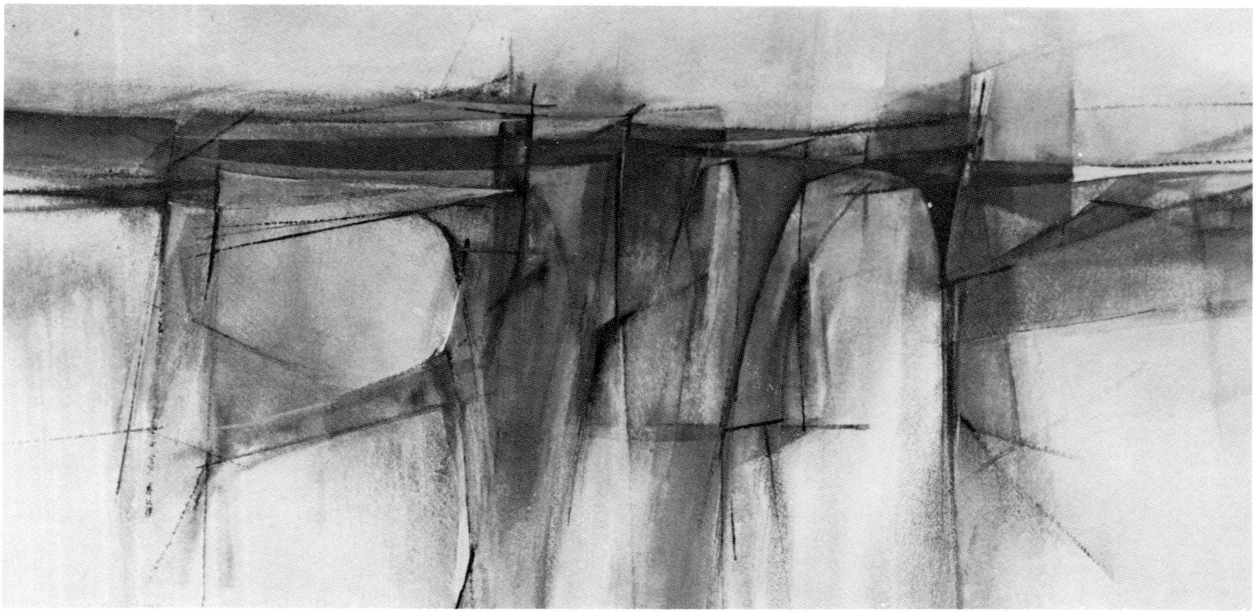

## DONALD LOUTHIAN

Born 1929

124. The Bridge 1963

Casein: 11½ × 24 in.; 29.2 × 60.9 cm.
Signed, lower left: Louthian 1963
Gift of the alumnae of the Northern Delaware Chapter, 1968

*I try to invent appropriate vivid symbols of the environment rather than involve myself in a naturalistic rendering of it. It is hoped that the viewer's own experience and memory will combine with my symbols, giving each person an individual participation in the painting.*

Donald Louthian

Exhibited: See Appendix C.

## LUIGI LUCIONI

Born 1900

125. Red Barn in the Hills 1933

Oil on masonite: 9 × 15 in.; 22.8 × 38.1 cm.
Signed and dated, lower left: L. Lucioni 1933
Gift of Robert G. McIntyre, 1949

*It is hard now, so many years later, to recall how I felt about my little painting, "Red Barn in the Hills." And yet, strangely enough, I remember it very vividly.*

*It was during early September when I had finished my larger canvases and I used to take trips north of my home in Manchester (Vermont) to get away from the over-civilized atmosphere of Manchester itself. I parked my car on a little dirt road away from the main highway and climbed a little knoll. I was surprised to find what seemed like an abandoned red barn and a pasture with hills rising rather sharply beyond them. The clear September sun lighted up this cluster of buildings and it seemed to me to stand there as a symbol of endurance against the rather rugged hills, holding its own in a very severe climate. Actually, it turned out that it was not abandoned; a farmer and a herd of cows appeared later, in time for the milking.*

*I painted very fast and furiously that day and tried to capture the impression that the scene had made on me. Several years later I passed by that spot again, and sure enough the barn was still there and my first impression of rugged endurance seemed justified to me.*

Luigi Lucioni (1959)

126. Road to Stowe 1931

Oil: 14 × 17 in.; 35.5 × 43.1 cm.
Signed, lower right: Lucioni 31
Gift of Annie Kate Gilbert '13 and Mary Sims, 1973

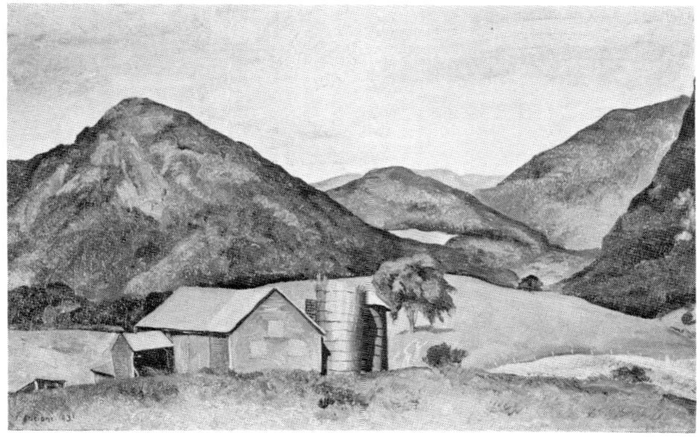

## SALLIE L. MAHOOD (Mrs. John A.)

1864–1953

127. Summer Skies
(Reproduced on page 18)

Oil on cardboard: 8 × 10 in.; 20.3 × 25.4 cm.
Signed, lower left: Sallie L. Mahood
Gift of Julia Mahood, 1965

Painted at Martha's Vineyard, Mass. This gift answered Randolph-Macon's request for a painting for its group of works by teachers of painting at the College. Mrs. Mahood instructed in art during the 1897–98 session. Her son Alex Blount Mahood gave, also in 1965, a copy of *Sallie Lee Mahood, 1864–1953: Autobiography,* edited by him and by Mrs. Alfonso Umana (Helen McGehee '42) and privately published in Lynchburg in 1965.

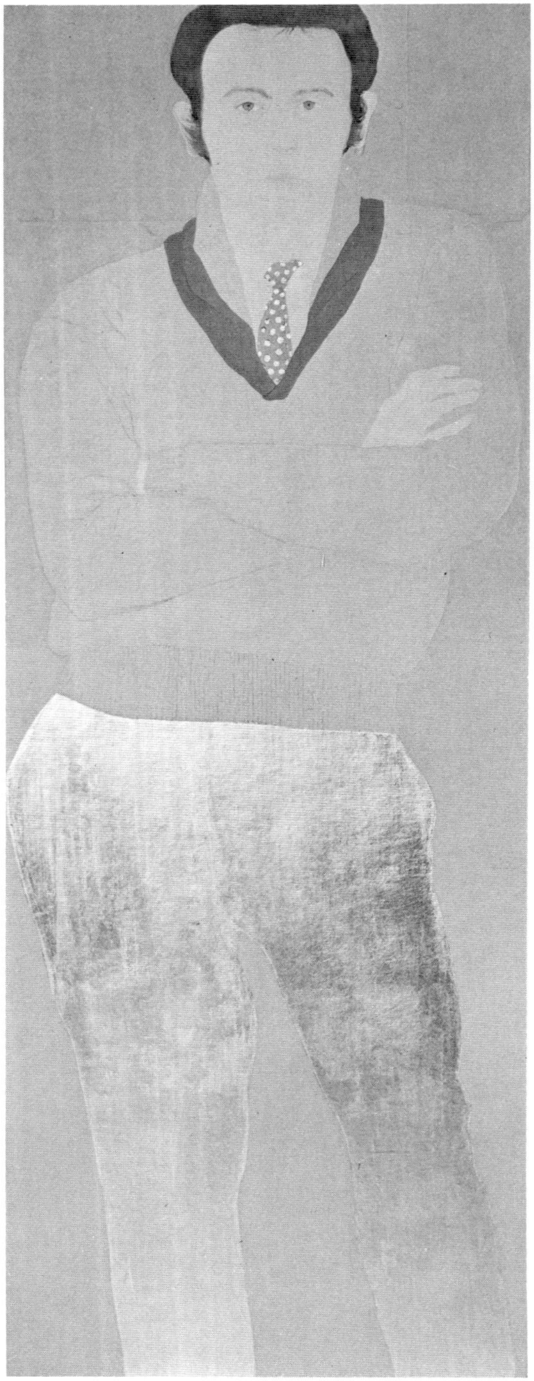

## MARCIA MARCUS

Born 1928

128. Portrait of Lucas Samaras 1965

Oil and aluminum leaf on canvas: 67½ × 24⅝ in.; 171.4 × 62.5 cm.
Unsigned
Louise J. Smith Fund, 1972

*I prefer paintings to be seen rather than talked about, so shall only mention the facts of the portrait. Lucas posed over a period of five months, probably on the average of two or three times a week. This gave me the leisure to carry the painting as far as I could without the pressure that can take place when the sitter is obviously bored, restless or reluctant to continue. At the end he pointed out the amusing fact that the closer I came to completing the painting, the more brushes I dropped. Over the years his observation has proved to be true, especially when the work has been very concentrated.*

Marcia Marcus

Exhibited: "1965 Mid-Year Show," Butler Institute of American Art, Youngstown, Ohio, June 27–Sept. 6, #120; "1965 Annual Exhibition of Contemporary Painting," Whitney Museum of American Art, New York, Dec. 8, 1965–Jan. 30, 1966; "American Painting 1966," Virginia Museum, Richmond, May 16–June 12, 1966; "Contemporary Portraits," circulating exhibition of the Museum of Modern Art, New York, exhibited in seven institutions, Feb. 2, 1969–Feb. 22, 1970.

Recorded: Cecil Vincent Donovan, "American Painting 1966," *Arts in Virginia* 6 (Spring 1966), p. 8, with repro.

## HERMAN MARIL

Born 1908

129. Approaching Storm 1962

Oil: 48 × 36 in.; 121.9 × 91.4 cm.
Signed, lower left: Herman Maril 1962
Gift of Mr. and Mrs. Jules Horelick, 1968

*The ideas in my paintings most always have as their source some visual experience. I enjoy reacting to my environment. This was painted on Cape Cod. But the true strength of a work, I believe, lies in its abstract painting structure. Everything should be expressed in the language of paint on the two-dimensional surface.*

Herman Maril

Exhibited: "Faculty Exhibition," University of Maryland, Baltimore, Oct. 1967.

Recorded: Emery Grossman, *Art and Tradition* (New York, 1968), repro., with artist standing in front of the painting, p. 103.

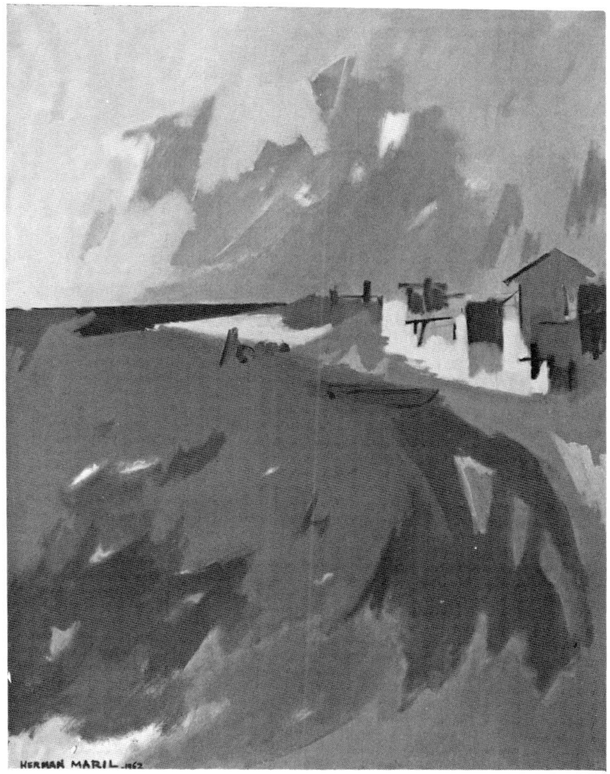

## JOHN MARIN
1870–1953

130. TAOS MOUNTAIN 1929

Watercolor: 17 × 22 in.; 43.1 × 55.8 cm.
Signed and dated, lower right: Marin '29
Louise J. Smith Fund, 1942

John Marin's impressions of the mountains of New Mexico are revealed in the following two letters, both of 1929. Strand is Paul Strand, the photographer. Alfred Stieglitz, also a photographer, was Marin's champion in New York.

*Taos, New Mexico, June 22, 23, 25*
*One of these, I don't know which*

*My dear Strand,*

*Yep, here I am. . . . All my pictures this year will have labels tagged to them, as this is so and so mountain, I'd have you understand. . . . I am sort of laying out spots, places, points of observations, staking claims for future use.*[1]

*Taos, New Mexico, July 21, 1929*
*My dear Stieglitz,*

*The batch is growing, quite a batch in quantity. . . . The One who made this country, this big level seeming desert table land cut out slices. They are the canyons. Then here and there he put mountains atop. Astanding here you can see six or seven thunderstorms going on at the same time.*[2]

The concern that Stieglitz expresses in the following letter was due to the fact that in June 1942 Mrs. von Keller, head of the art department, was about to take an extended leave of absence from the College.

1. *Selected Writings of John Marin*, ed. Dorothy Norman (New York, 1949), pp. 127–28. Quoted by permission of Dorothy Norman and John Marin, Jr.

2. Ibid., pp. 129–30.

*An American Place*
*509 Madison Ave.*
*New York City [undated]*

*Dear Miss (sic) von Keller,*

*Yes, I had worried about the Marin. You see, I am a man with heart trouble and much too conscientious for a time like this. I like all edges and workmanship kept clean.*

*I'm afraid you're in for a difficult time if the public is supposed to make up its mind about a painting. And to have the committee reach any decision—that's like expecting the state of the world suddenly to become peaceful overnight! I'm afraid we would all drop dead on the spot, and the world would be unpeopled. That might be a real beginning. What a grin real art would have on its countenance! But real art, I have a notion, will ever survive.*

*Joking aside, I see, in rereading your letter, that it is not the committee alone which must come to a decision, but there are several "authorities" on art to decide whether it is a good choice. And that, you see, will take more time. Well, take it from me, the Marin that was sent to you is an A-plus example of this.*

*I have a weak spot for Virginia. There is no Marin in Virginia to my knowledge. Your school is a center of enlightenment for young women, so I am particularly eager that they should live with one of Marin's finest pictures. For such, I repeat, is this particular Marin which you are privileged to live with for the time being.*

*Sincerely yours,*
*Alfred Stieglitz*[3]

*June 16, 1942*

*My dear Miss (sic) von Keller:*

*A few days ago Mr. [Sheldon] Cheney appeared to look at the Marin you selected. And yesterday, Mr. [Frank K. M.] Rehn. Both said they would write to you, confirming your selection. As the picture*

3. This letter and the one that follows are quoted by permission of Georgia O'Keeffe, for the Estate of Alfred Stieglitz.

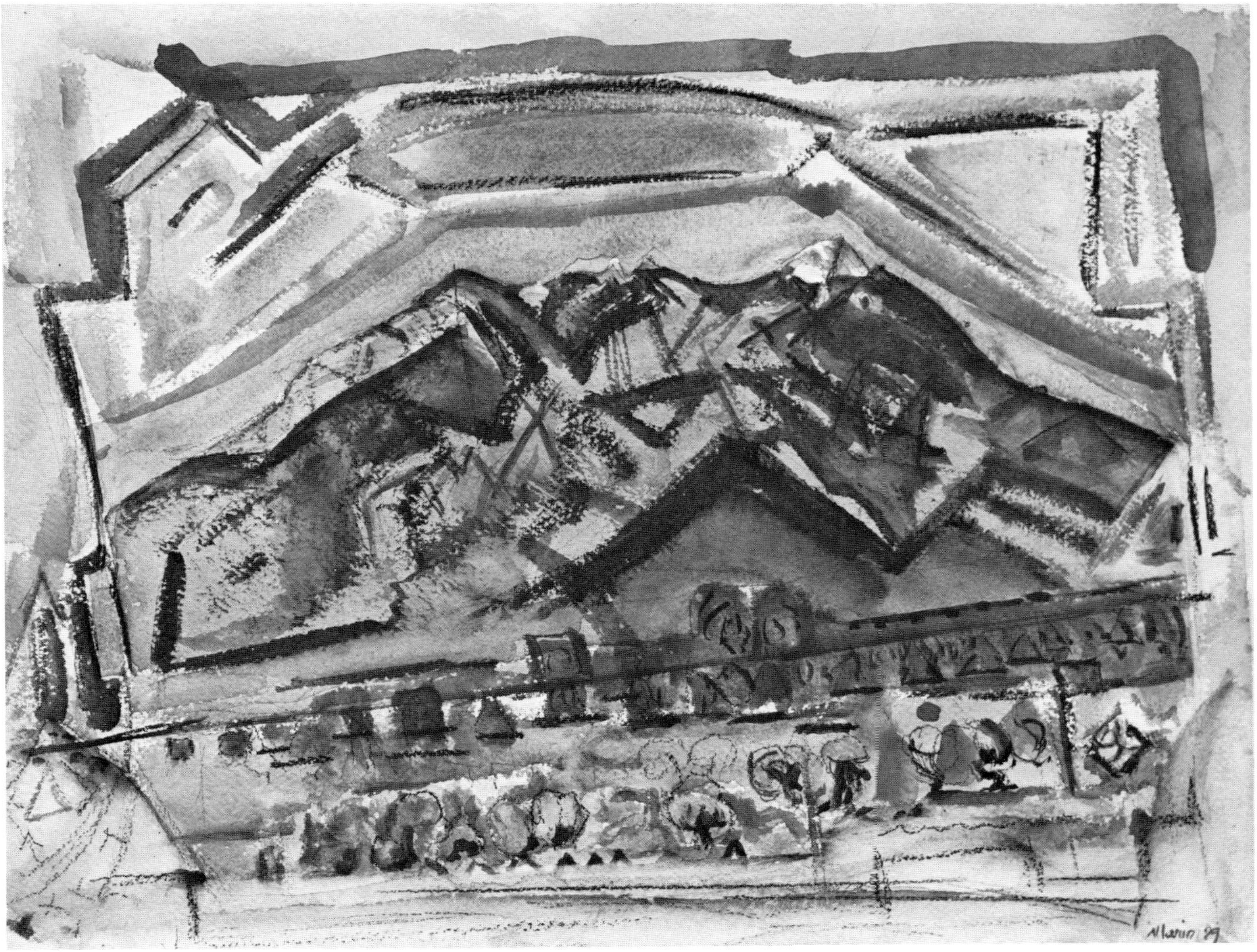

*stands here it looks more and more beautiful. I am glad you chose it. It will undoubtedly lead to much healthy controversy because it exudes health, ruggedness, and is a masterpiece of painting.*

*With cordial greetings and thanks,*

*Alfred Stieglitz*

Van Deren Coke (*Marin in New Mexico*, p. 30) says that Marin painted "Taos Mountain" from a site near Arroyo Seco looking southeast toward Pueblo Peak.

Exhibited: In all seven exhibitions of the College Collection, 1949–72, see Appendix B; "University Collections," a traveling exhibition (which included also Randolph-Macon's painting "The Idlers," by

Maurice Prendergast) organized by the American Federation of Arts under the sponsorship of the College Art Association, circulated in Europe by the United States Information Agency between June 30, 1956, and Aug. 1, 1957, to Malmö, Sweden; to Utrecht, Holland; to three places in England: Birmingham, London, and Newcastle-upon-Tyne; to two places in Belgium: Brussels and Liège; to two places in France: Lyons and Besançon; and to two German cities: Marburg and Tübingen; "Art between the Two World Wars," Randolph-Macon College (Ashland, Va.), Apr. 10–12, 1964; "Marin in New Mexico, 1929 & 1930," an exhibition organized by the University Art Museum, University of New Mexico at Albuquerque, exhibited there and in Texas at San Antonio and Fort Worth between Nov. 18, 1968, and May 12, 1969, #27.

Recorded: College Art Association of America, *University Collections* (about 1956), #31, repro. pl. 20 on p. 17; #31 in the catalogues published in Malmö, Utrecht, and Brussels; #23 in the catalogue for Lyons; Agnes Addison Gilchrist, "The Growth of an Art Collection," *Alumnae Bulletin* 50 (Nov. 1956), pp. 30-34, repro. p. 30; Mary Frances Williams, "Paintings as Teachers," *Arts in Virginia* 2 (Spring 1962), p. 24, repro.; Van Deren Coke, *Marin in New Mexico, 1929 & 1930* (Albuquerque, 1968), #27, repro. p. 25; Sheldon Reich, *John Marin* (University of Arizona, Tucson, 1970), vol. 2, # 29.57; *Art Journal* 32 (Winter 72/73), p. 195, repro. p. 193.

## ANTONIO P. MARTINO

Born 1902

131. FOUR HOUSES 1951

Oil: 26¼ × 40¼ in.; 66.6 × 102.2 cm.
Signed, lower right: Antonio P. Martino
Gift of the National Academy of Design (Henry Ward Ranger Fund), 1951

*My painting "Four Houses" was painted from a small study which I made in Manayunk, January, 1951. Manayunk is a suburb which lies just Northeast of Philadelphia. The houses first attracted my attention because of the unusual color relationships. This resolved itself into a felt massiveness of the patterns of houses, sky and snow and ground shapes. I tried to develop this weight with the power of the colors—the warmth of the houses, yellow, warm blues, warm grays played against the cool blues of the snow and the heavy sky. The slight roll of the foreground seemed to accent this overall weightiness by contrast with the horizontal and vertical forms of the buildings.*

Antonio P. Martino, N.A. (1958)

Exhibited: "One Hundred and Twenty-sixth Annual," National Academy of Design, New York, 1951, #57, repro.; "Henry Ward Ranger Centennial Exhibition," National Academy of Design, New York, Sept. 24–Oct. 12, 1958.

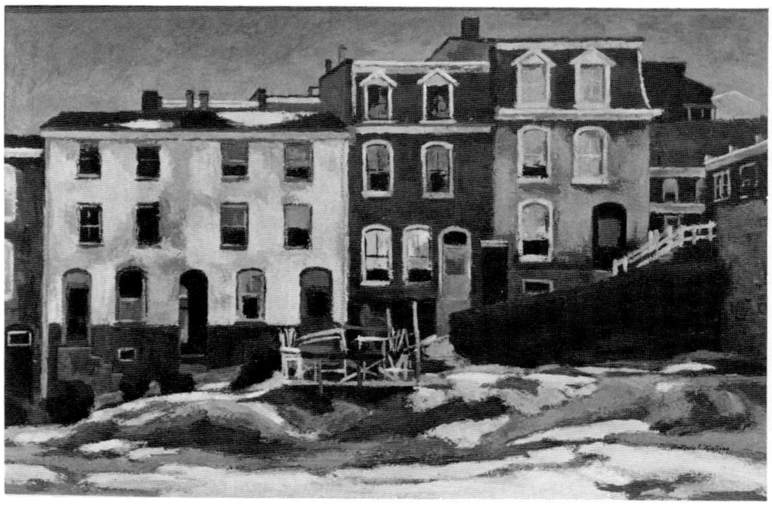

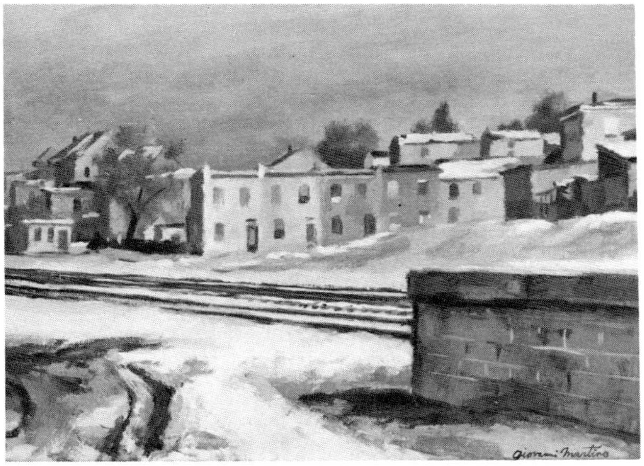

## GIOVANNI MARTINO

Born 1908

132. WINTER DAY 1954

Oil: 12 × 16 in.; 30.4 × 40.6 cm.
Signed, lower right: Giovanni Martino
Gift of the Salmagundi Club, 1955

*"Winter Day" was painted in 1954 on the scene in Manayunk, Pennsylvania. It was early in the morning. In this particular scene I was interested in the patterned stucco walls of homes in the middle distance which, when bathed in sunlight, contrasted nicely with the serenity of the sky and snow-covered foreground. The old stone wall to the right intensifies spatial relations and adds to the integration of the scene. I am not externally conscious of these things while painting.*

Giovanni Martino (1963)

Exhibited: Salmagundi Club Auction Exhibition, 1955.

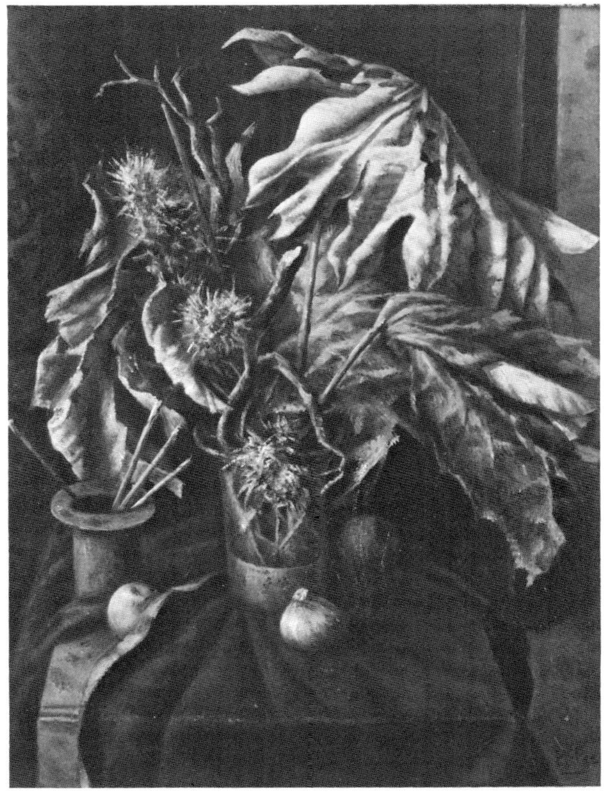

## HENRY LEE McFEE

1886–1953

133. GOLDEN LEAVES 1940

Oil: 40 × 30 in.; 101.6 × 76.2 cm.
Signed, lower right: McFee
Louise J. Smith Fund, 1953

Exhibited: See Appendix B for exhibitions of the College Collection at Richmond, 1964, and in six Mid-Atlantic states, 1966–67.

Recorded: Fine Arts Foundation of Scripps College, *Henry Lee McFee* (Claremont, Cal., 1950), repro.

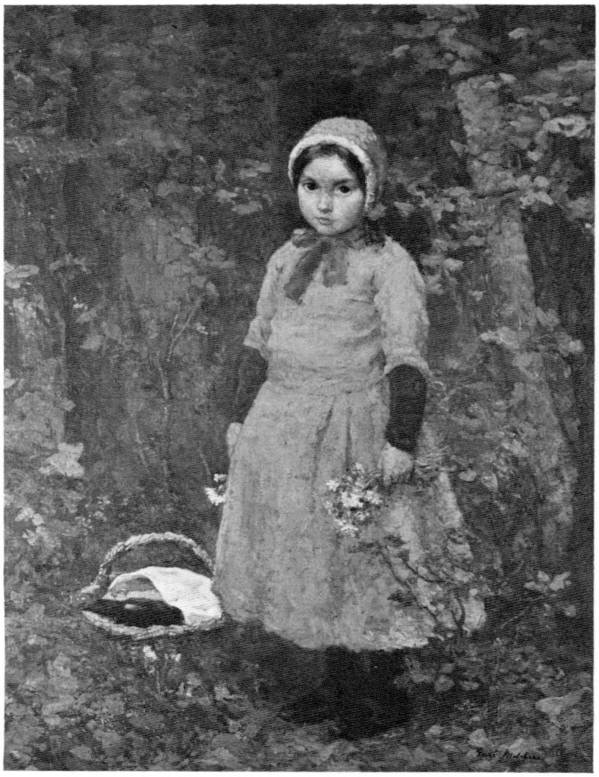

## GARI MELCHERS

1860–1932

134. LITTLE RED RIDING HOOD 1897

Oil: 52 × 39 in.; 132 × 99 cm.
Signed, lower right: Gari Melchers
Fine Arts Fund, 1938

Painted in Egmond-am-See, the Netherlands.

Provenance: Estate of Gari Melchers; Mrs. Gari Melchers.

Exhibited: "Gari Melchers Memorial Exhibition," Virginia Museum, Richmond, Jan. 17–Feb. 28, 1938, #86, repro.; "French Impressionists Influence American Artists," Lowe Art Museum, Coral Gables, Fla., Mar. 19–Apr. 25, 1971, #101.

Recorded: *The News* (Lynchburg), May 4, 1938, and Mar. 16, 1943; *Alumnae Bulletin* 31 (June 1938): 40.

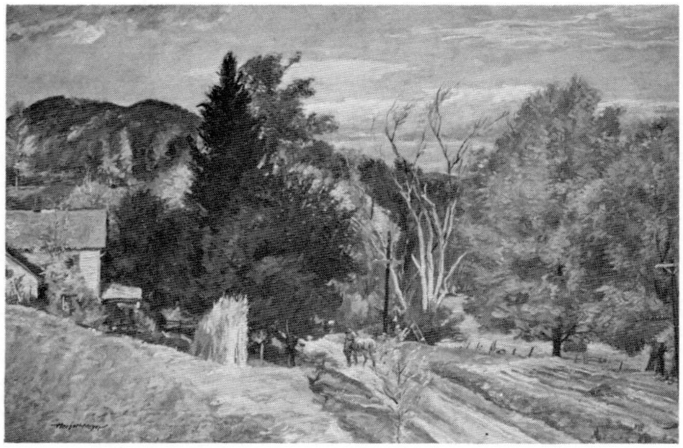

## HERBERT MEYER

1882–1961

135. END OF HARVEST, DORSET [Vt.] 1943

Oil: 21 × 32 in.; 53.3 × 81.2 cm.
Signed, lower left: Herbert Meyer
Dated on top stretcher bar: 11/13/43
Gift of Mrs. Reginald Marsh, 1962

Exhibited: "Thirty-fourth Annual Exhibition," Art Association of Newport, R.I., 1945, #36.

# GEORGIA MORGAN ex-'03

1869–1951

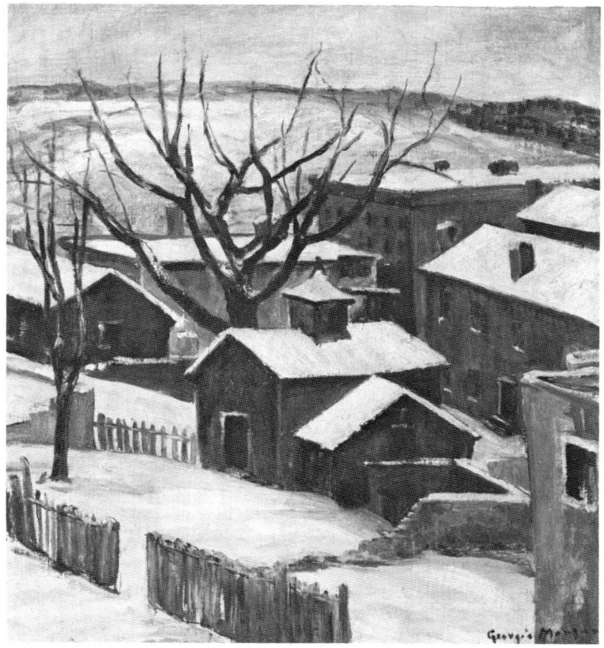

136. Abandoned Stable in Snow
(Deserted Stables) 1938

Oil: 24 × 22 in.; 60.9 × 55.8 cm.
Signed, lower right: Georgia Morgan
Fine Arts Fund, 1938

The stable formerly stood back of 814 Court Street, Lynchburg. The artist was instrumental in having it converted during the 1930s into a clubhouse for the Lynchburg Antiquarian Club, of which she was a member.[1] For other activities of this painter refer to the chapter called "Viewed from the Bicentennial Year."

Exhibited: "Forty-fifth Annual Exhibition," National Association of Women Painters and Sculptors, Feb. 1936; "Exhibition of Paintings: Georgia Morgan," Lynchburg College, May 31–June 8, 1938, #41 (as "Snowy House Tops"); "Georgia Morgan Exhibition," at the College, Apr. 1939, #19 (as "Deserted Stables"); Richmond Academy of Science and Fine Arts, Apr. 7–22, 1940, #24 (as "Old Abandoned Stable in Snow"); an exhibition of the Salons of America, Inc. (Forum Galleries, New York), at an unknown date (as "Abandoned Stable"); "Georgia Morgan Retrospective Exhibition," at the College, Nov. 1950, #17; "Lynchburg Civic Art League Exhibition (Georgia Morgan Memorial)," Nov. 1–15, 1952, and Oct. 23–Nov. 17, 1957. (A painting named "Deserted," mentioned in notices of exhibitions as early as 1935, is apparently a different work.)

Recorded: Ruth H. Blunt and Eva Moore, "Portrait of an Artist," *Alumnae Bulletin*, 46 (Apr. 1953): 26; Ruth H. Blunt, *The Lynchburg Art Club and Its Affiliates* (Lynchburg, 1962), p. 44.

137. In Amherst County

(Reproduced on page 18)

Oil on masonite: 7½ × 10¼ in.; 19 × 26 cm.
Signed, lower right: Georgia Morgan
Gift of Robert S. Fuller, 1968

1. See Blunt and Moore, "Portrait of an Artist," p. 26.

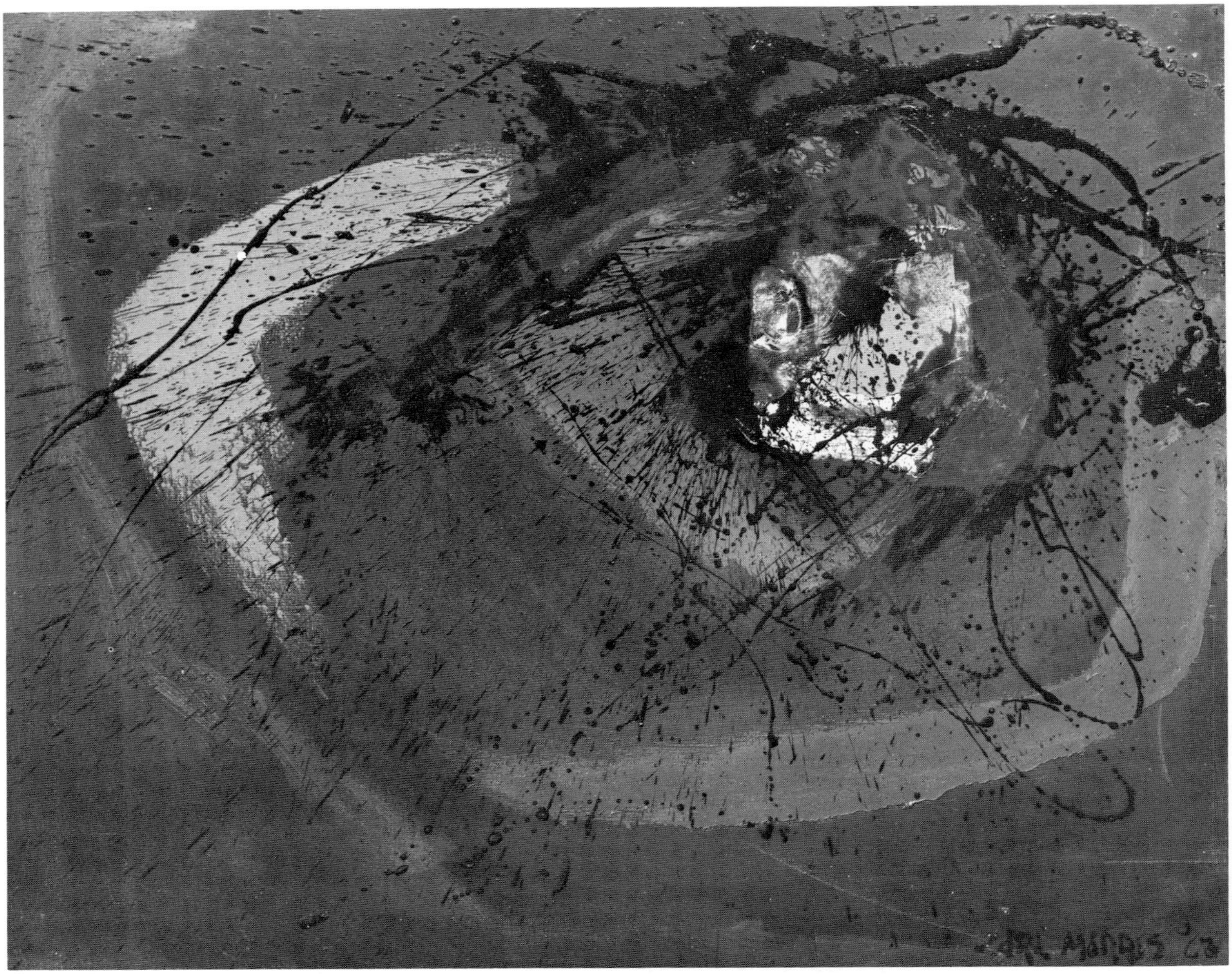

## CARL MORRIS

Born 1911

138. Toward Yesterday 1963

Oil: 46 × 58 in.; 116.8 × 147.3 cm.
Signed and dated, lower left: Carl Morris '63
Louise J. Smith Fund, 1965

*From a group of paintings around 1963, centering principally on the germinal force, the beginning or becoming that marks the metamorphosis of energy into form. "Toward Yesterday" defines the genesis of this energy.*

Carl Morris

Exhibited: See Appendix B for the exhibition of the College Collection circulated to six Mid-Atlantic states, 1966–67, #21, and the exhibition in the Virginia Museum's Artmobile, 1969–70, #14.

## GEORGE MORRISON

Born 1919

139. Parlor 1959

Oil: 36 × 42 in.; 91.4 × 106.6 cm.
Signed, lower left: G. Morrison 1959
Gift of Mr. and Mrs. Sam Golden, 1968

*This is one of many abstract paintings done in the 1950's, based on structural elements, with a concern for texture and colored surfaces.*

George Morrison

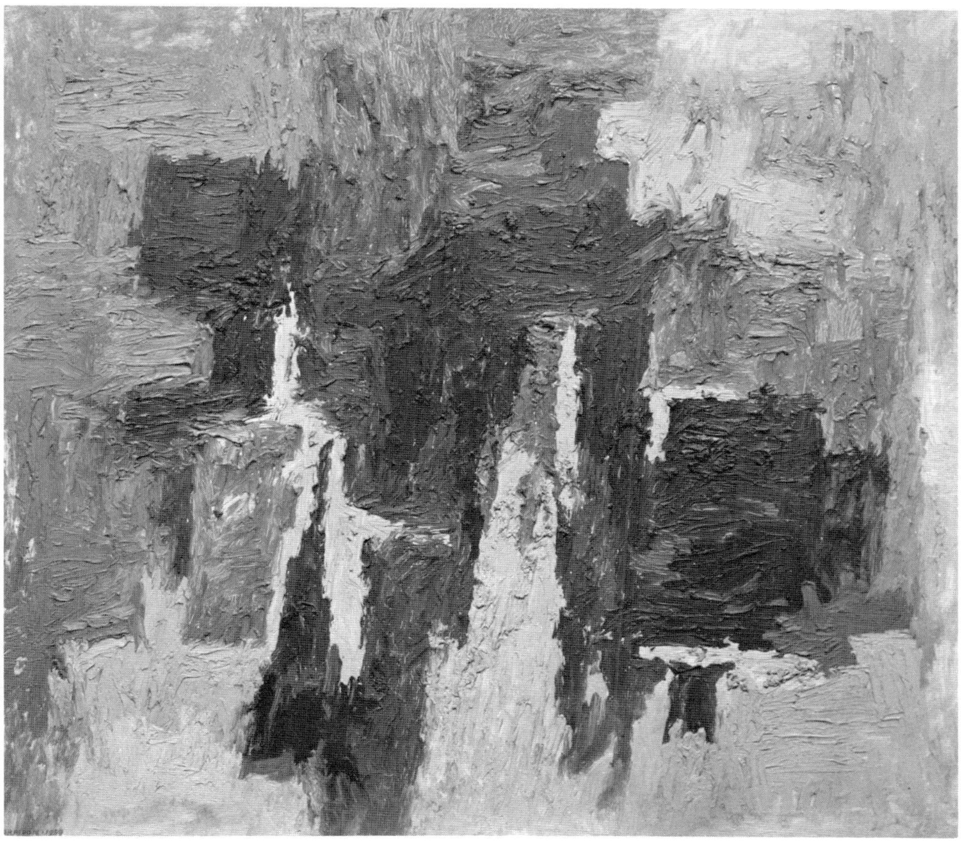

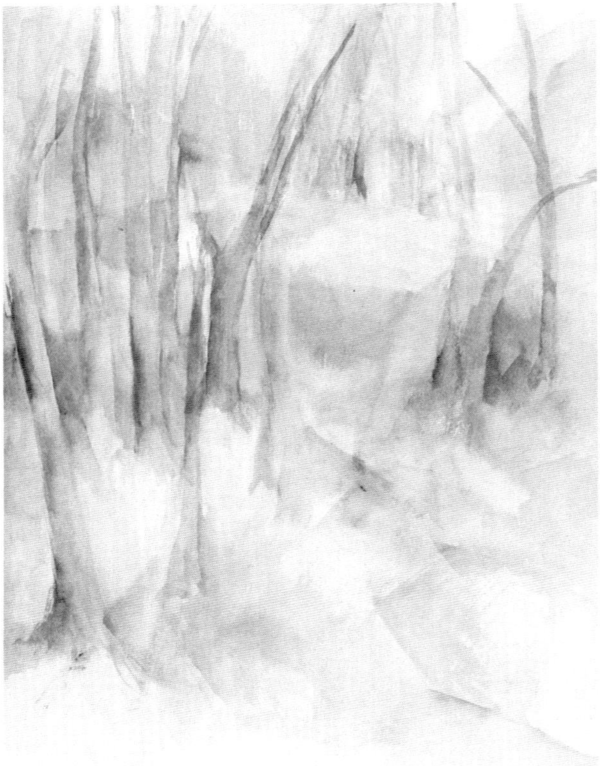

## JEANNE MORROW

140. Wood in April 1968

Watercolor: 23¼ × 17½ in.; 59.6 × 44.4 cm.
Unsigned
Gift of alumnae of the Northern Delaware Chapter, 1968

*For me painting is a response, an adventure, a thanksgiving. I try to express feeling with the force that draws it; thus, the wonder stirred by the spring light in the woods. This was painted at Meadows of Dan, in the mountains near Danville, Virginia.*

Jeanne Morrow

Exhibited: See Appendix C.

## GEORGIA O'KEEFFE

Born 1887

141. Yellow Cactus 1940

Oil: 12 × 16 in.; 30.4 × 40.6 cm.
Unsigned
Louise J. Smith Fund, 1944

*The yellow cactus blooms in the spring and to me this seems a very good portrait of it.*

Georgia O'Keeffe

It took more than a year to bring "The O'Keeffe" to Randolph-Macon. The work of recommending paintings for purchase by the College fell on Harriet Fitzgerald '26 from 1942 to 1945 while Mrs. von Keller, head of the art department, was in Richmond as co-director of the Virginia Museum. On May 19, 1943, Miss Fitzgerald wrote to President Jack:

*I have a report to make.*

*I have seen Mr. Stieglitz twice and found him unwilling to come below [his price] on the O'Keeffe. . . . He says that he wants us to have the O'Keeffe and that he will hold it for us for a year, during which time he is certain we can get [the money]. He says that he will turn down any other offer on the picture, no matter who makes it or how much they offer to pay. . . . He believes in institutions like ours. . . . He feels that, while all of her paintings are beautiful, this is "a gem, one of the perfect paintings."*

*I had two long talks with him. He really is a wonderful old man with a truly rare quality. Talking with him you feel that, through his creative, philosophical discourses—for that is what his conversations are—through the humor, the ruthless realism of his opinions, there radiates a terrific sense of goodness.*

*But he is very old and not to be disagreed with. He is not only unwilling to budge from his price . . . but he is also unwilling to send [the painting] to Lynchburg for inspection.*

*After he let the Marin go down on approval last spring I thought that he would do the same with the O'Keeffe this time. But even Marin is not*

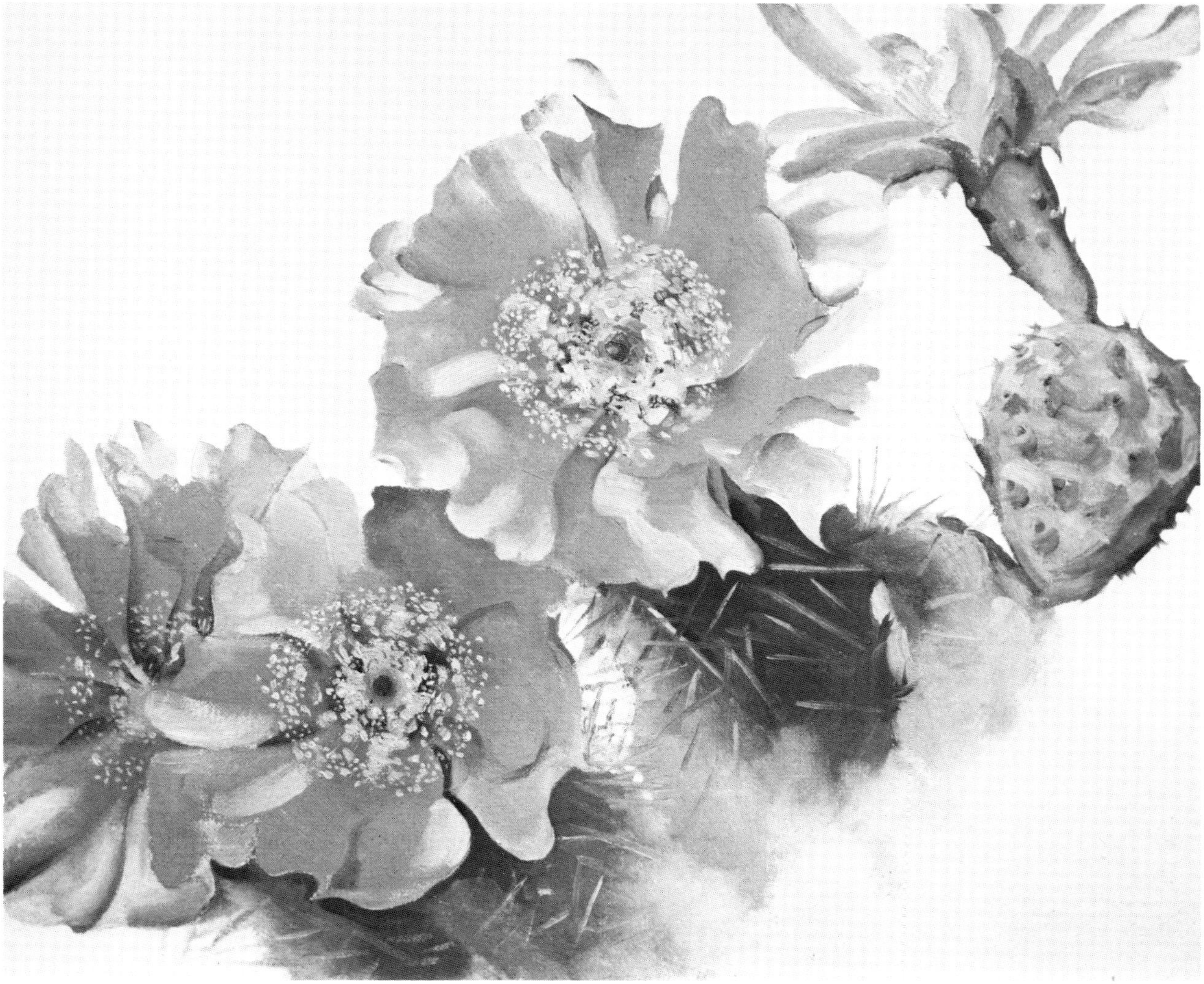

*O'Keeffe. She is God on earth to him and there is just no arguing about holy things.*[1]

On May 19, 1944, exactly one year after Miss Fitzgerald's "report," quoted above, Mr. Stieglitz wrote formally to Dr. Jack, acknowledging the purchase. Then in an undated longhand letter he notified him of the shipment and added:

*It's a rare O'Keeffe. Rare of the rare ones. . . . Thanks for your kind invitation to visit your College. And participate in a little celebration. I can't travel. Am old & have a bad heart—I'll send your letter to Miss O'Keeffe who is in New Mexico. She needs the altitude & the life in her secluded home far away from all "art" centers.*
*My thanks for your active interest and kindness,*
*Alfred Stieglitz*[2]

Exhibited: "Exhibition of Georgia O'Keeffe," An American Place, New York, Jan. 27–Mar. 11, 1941, #1; "Art Between the Two World Wars," Randolph-Macon College (Ashland, Va.), Apr. 10–12, 1964; included in all seven exhibitions of the College Collection, see Appendix B.

Recorded: Harriet Fitzgerald, "Georgia O'Keeffe," *Alumnae Bulletin* 38 (Nov. 1944), pp. 1–4, repro. p. 1; Mary Frances Williams, "Paintings as Teachers," *Arts in Virginia* 2 (Spring 1962), p. 27, repro. p. 24; Mary Frances Williams, "The Randolph-Macon Woman's College Collection," *Art Journal* 32 (Winter 72/73), p. 195, repro. p. 194.

Accounts of the conferring of an honorary doctorate on Georgia O'Keeffe on September 26, 1966, are in: *Randolph-Macon Today* (October 1966), p. 1; *The News* (Lynchburg), Sept. 18 and 27, 1966; *Alumnae Bulletin* 60 (Fall 1966): 22; *The Daily Advance* (Lynchburg), Sept. 27, 1966. See figure 7.

1. Quoted by permission of Harriet Fitzgerald.

2. Quoted by permission of Georgia O'Keeffe, for the Estate of Alfred Stieglitz.

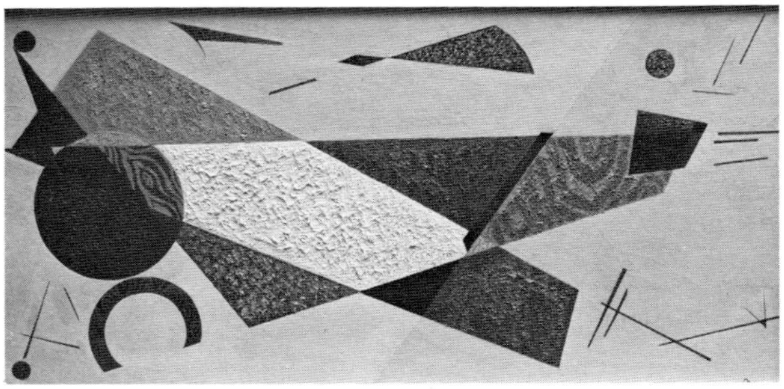

## WILLIAM BISHOP OWEN
1895–1963

142. ABSTRACTION 1954

Oil on masonite: 11½ × 24½ in.; 29.2 × 62.2 cm.
Signed, lower right: Owen
Fine Arts Fund, 1955

*This represents my attempt to escape from the conventional traditions of naturalism with its emphasis on three-dimensional form and space portrayal. For me it was an affirmation that "decoration" in the elevated sense had again come into its own. I am pleased to consider this painting of mine a piece of decoration.*

William B. Owen (1958)

Professor Owen taught drawing and painting at the College from 1953 until he resigned in 1956.

Exhibited: "Forty-fourth Annual Exhibition," at the College, Apr. 23–June 5, 1955, #36.

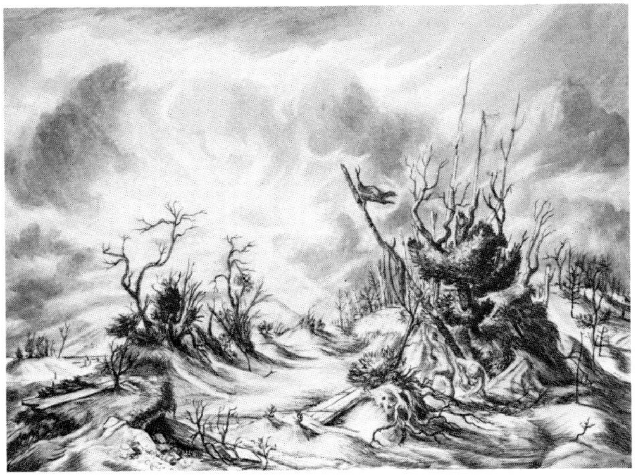

## WILLIAM C. PALMER

Born 1906

143. END OF A HOLIDAY 1937

Ink and watercolor: 23¾ × 28½ in.; 60.3 × 72.3 cm.
Signed and dated, lower center: William C. Palmer 1937
Gift of Robert G. McIntyre, 1948

*Air, light, and water have always stimulated my imagination and been the basic content of my work. Nature in its uncontrolled growth or in its peaceful aspects has been the background of my paintings. Man's effort to control or enjoy his environment has been secondary. These, plus the mystery of the unknown, have produced paintings in the same spirit as this painting. It records an outing on an untamed beach on the Canadian shore of Lake Ontario, where for many years my summers were spent in our camp on the Bay of Quinte. In this natural and unspoiled setting I was able to live in close communion with nature.*

William C. Palmer (1959)

Exhibited: "Fifteen Paintings from the Collection of Randolph-Macon Woman's College," circulated by the Alumnae Association between October 1949 and January 1950 to its chapters in Nashville, Birmingham, Atlanta, and Asheville, #11.

## PHILIP PEARLSTEIN

Born 1924

144. PORTRAIT OF PRESIDENT WILLIAM F. QUILLIAN, JR. 1971
(Color plate, page 30)

Oil: 42 × 32 in.; 106.6 × 81.2 cm.
Signed, lower left: Pearlstein 71
Gift of the Class of 1954, other alumnae, and friends, 1972

*Dr. Quillian's portrait was one of a long-continuing series of more than seventeen portraits, commissioned and otherwise, done in the past couple of years. So that is really what my life is all about. On this occasion I do not want to launch into what should become a major article on my view on art. Neither do I want to come up with a folksy / chummy recollection, because it would be false to the aesthetic position—an embattled one, I might add—that my paintings represent for me.*

Philip Pearlstein

*In my five days of sitting for Philip Pearlstein in his top floor studio in New York City, I found him to be an intelligent, warm, humane person. He is a family man, obviously proud of his son and his two daughters, all of whom have been subjects for his paintings.*

*At the first sitting he sketched the entire figure with considerable detail. After he had been at work about an hour, I asked if my portrait would run off the canvas (a characteristic of his portraits). He replied with a kind of impish smile, "It has just run off." In the afternoon of the second day he said he felt the body was too short and so in about thirty minutes he repainted the bottom fifth of the canvas, lowering the arms and the overlapped hands. As he painted, we either conversed or listened to music ranging from an Indian Raga to a César Franck symphony.*

*This portrait is unmistakably "a Pearlstein," and I like it for that reason. Others can debate whether or not it is a good likeness—while I listen from the sidelines in amused satisfaction.*

William F. Quillian, Jr.

Recorded: *Alumnae Bulletin* 65 (Summer 1972), p. 44, with repro.; *The News* (Lynchburg), May 14, 1972, with repro.; *Art Journal* 32 (Winter 72/73), p. 192, with repro.

## MAURICE PRENDERGAST

1859–1924

### 145. The Idlers About 1916–18

Oil: 21 × 32 in.; 53.4 × 81.2 cm.
Unsigned
Louise J. Smith Fund, 1949

Provenance: Charles Prendergast (1924); Thomas Cochran; given by Mr. Cochran in 1928 to the Addison Gallery, Andover, Mass.; released by the Addison Gallery about 1946 to William Macbeth, Inc., with other paintings by artists overrepresented in its collection.

Exhibited: "The Prendergasts, Retrospective Exhibition of the Work of Maurice and Charles Prendergast," Addison Gallery of American Art, Andover, Mass., 1938, #82; "University Collections," a traveling exhibition (which included also Randolph-Macon's watercolor by John Marin, "Taos Mountain") organized by the American Federation of Arts under the sponsorship of the College Art Association, circulated in Europe by the United States Information Agency between June 30, 1956, and Aug. 1, 1957, to Malmö, Sweden; to Utrecht, Holland; to three places in England: Birmingham, London, and Newcastle-upon-Tyne; to two places in Belgium: Brussels and Liège; two places in France: Lyons and Besançon; and to two German cities: Marburg and Tübingen; "From the Archives of American Art, The Role of the Macbeth Gallery," a traveling exhibition of the American Federation of Arts, shown first in the AFA Gallery, New York, Oct. 10–29, 1962, and circulated from Nov. 12, 1962, to July 21, 1963, to museums in Tampa (Fla.), Oklahoma City, Flint (Mich.), Columbia (S.C.), and Albany, #26; "The Eight," Southern Vermont Art Center, June 22—July 21, 1963, #52; shown in five exhibitions of the College Collection listed in Appendix B: at Richmond and at Roanoke, 1964; in Tampa, Orlando, Gainesville, and Jacksonville, 1965; in six Mid-Atlantic states, 1966–67; and in the Virginia Museum's Artmobile, 1969–70; "Maurice Prendergast," University of Maryland Art Gallery, Sept. 1–Oct. 6, 1976.

Recorded: Addison Gallery, *Handbook of Paintings* (Andover, Mass., 1939), repro. p. 68; *University Collections* (about 1956), #39, repro. p. 13; #39 in the catalogues published in Malmö, Utrecht, and Brussels; #31 in the catalogue for Lyons; Agnes Addison Gilchrist, "The Growth of an Art Collection," *Alumnae Bulletin* 50 (Nov. 1956), pp. 30–34, repro. p. 30; *Art Journal* 32 (Winter 72/73), p. 195, with repro.

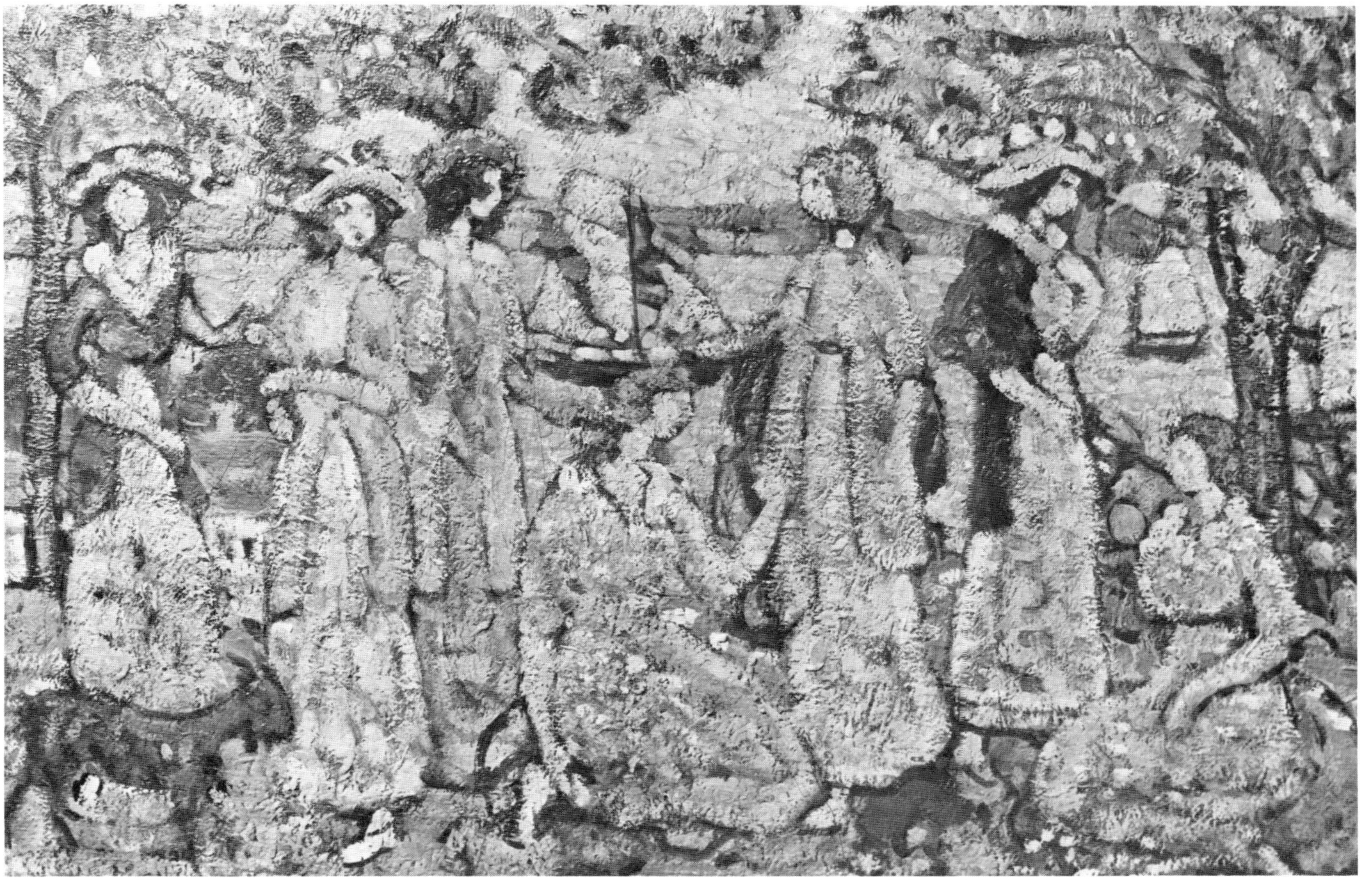

## Alfredo Ramón
Born 1922

146. Nuestra Andalucia 1968

Oil: 27½ × 40 in.; 69.8 × 101.6 cm.
Signed and dated, lower left:
Alfredo Ramón 1968
Gift of the artist and his wife
(Betty Uelsmann '45), 1969

## THEODORE ROBINSON
1852–96

147. VALLEY OF THE SEINE 1892

Oil: 26 × 32 in.; 66 × 81.2 cm.
Signed, lower right: Th. Robinson
Gift of Francis M. Weld, 1945

Painted in Giverny, looking down on the hamlet of Vernon, on the Seine River near Paris, during Theodore Robinson's last visit to France. In his diary, preserved at the Frick Art Reference Library, New York, Robinson wrote in June 1892:

*4 Commenced a "Vue de Vernon" most charming in the morning sunlight. I will try two canvases, one, the later, will try by cloud shadows, to have the river light against its banks—foreground and parts of meadow beyond in shadow. Cathedral and parts of bridge, etc., in bright sunlight.*
*5 Worked on my "Vue de Vernon No. 2" was sadly bothered by wind—and one smart shower.*
*6 Worked at my "Vue de Vernon"—It is begun with too modified color—I must try for more purity. And not to work beyond the hour chosen for the effect—tis most important.*
*9 Commenced a "Vue de Vernon" grey day for 2½ or 3 hours. Charming—but the sunlight, with floating shadows I find more so.*
*14 Yesterday and today—windy and too cold for comfort—worked on the grey "Vernon."*[1]

For perhaps the first time since the canvases left Robinson's own hands, three views of this scene were reunited at the Theodore Robinson exhibition organized by and exhibited at the Baltimore Museum of Art in 1973 before being circulated to four more museums. In contrast with the two other paintings, the one belonging to the Corcoran Gallery of Art, Washington (Baur #242), is clearly sunny. The version at the Addison Gallery, Andover, Mass. (Baur #240), is partly sunny, partly cloudy. Randolph-Macon's (Baur #241) shows a gray day, warmed by patches of rose in the clouds. The river is "light against its banks." Because Monet lived at Giverny and the two men were friends, we can imagine them as they compared these three canvases that Robinson switched on and off his easel as sun and rain altered light and color.

1. Quoted by permission of the Frick Art Reference Library.

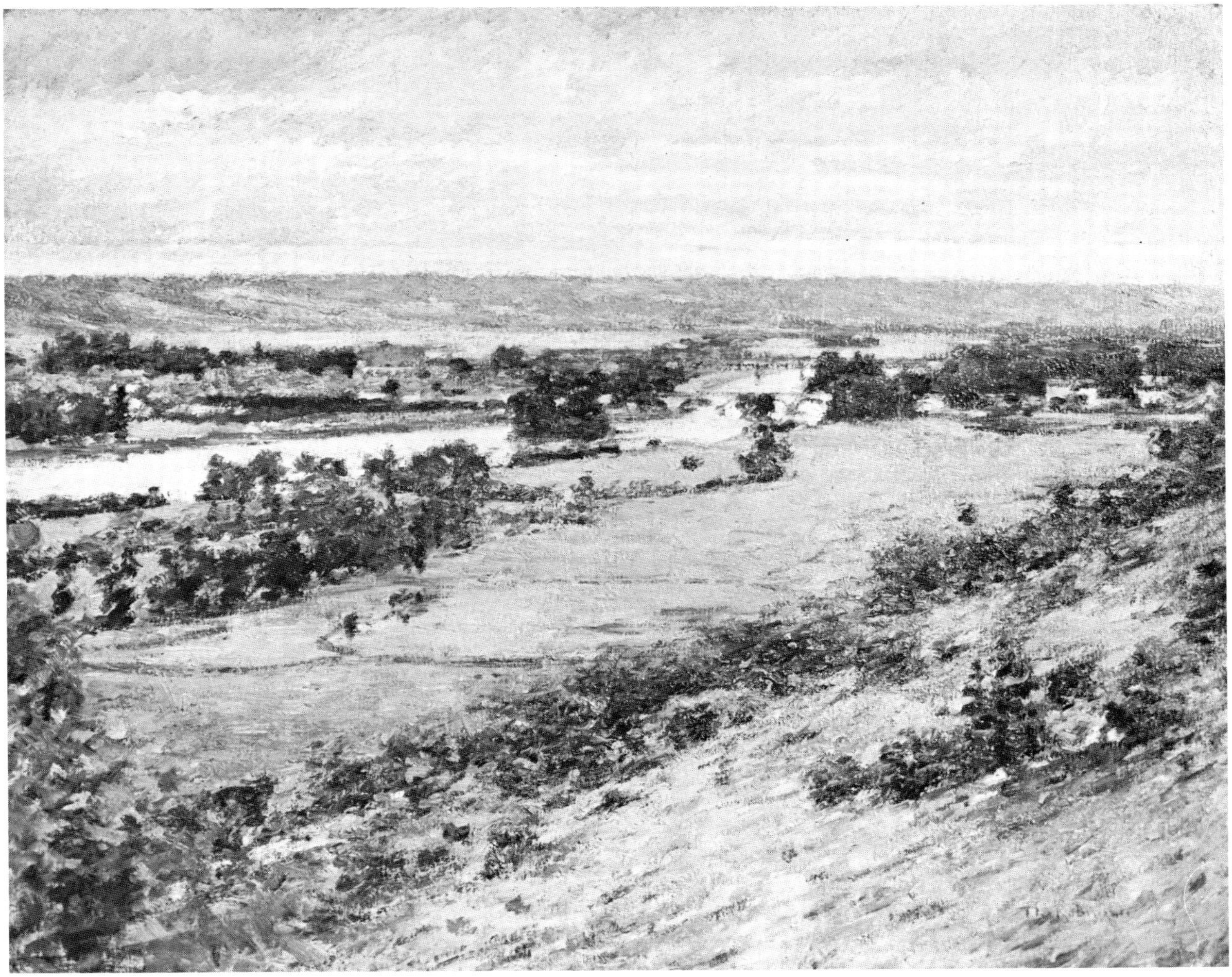

Provenance: Collection of Duncan Phillips, Washington, from whom it passed in 1926 to William Macbeth, Inc.; sold to Francis M. Weld in 1927.

Exhibited: "Theodore Robinson, First Exhibition since 1895," Macbeth Gallery, New York, Apr. 9–May 8, 1943, #9; see Appendix B for four exhibitions of the College Collection: to four southern chapters of the Alumnae Association, 1949–50; to the Virginia Museum, Richmond, 1964; to six Mid-Atlantic states, 1966–67; and to the Artmobile of the Virginia Museum, 1969–70; "French Impressionists Influence American Artists," Lowe Art Museum, Coral Gables, Fla., Mar. 19–Apr. 25, 1971, #154, repro. p. 84; "Theodore Robinson," organized by the Baltimore Museum of Art and circulated May 1, 1973–Feb. 24, 1974, #44, repro. p. 45.

Recorded: J. I. H. Baur, *Theodore Robinson* (New York, 1946), #241, p. 34; Catalogue of the Baltimore exhibition of 1973; Kennedy Galleries, *Theodore Robinson, American Impressionist* (New York, 1966), p. 14; *Art Journal* 32 (Winter 72/73), p. 195 with repro.

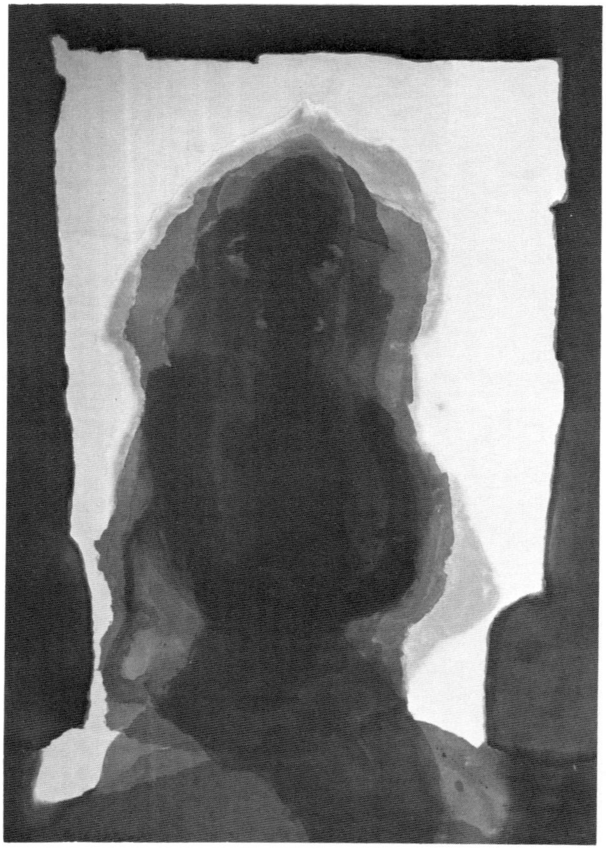

## RUTH BLACKWELL ROGERS '67

Born 1945

148. YELLOW WINDOW 1972

Acrylic on canvas: 66 × 45½ in.; 167.6 × 115.5 cm.
Signed, lower left: Blackwell Rogers
Fine Arts Fund, 1973

*In this painting I was trying to make visible the aura of the figure. The feelings given off by that person, even the surrounding air. The person is directly in front of a window; light from the window accentuates the aura effect and darkens the face. I tried to make the figure, the aura, and the light co-equal in creating the experience. From what experience did the painting grow? Talking intently with someone.*

*People often ask about the medium. I stained raw canvas (flat on the floor) with thin acrylic paint.*

Ruth Blackwell Rogers

Exhibited: Graduate Show, Ackland Museum, University of North Carolina at Chapel Hill, June 1972.

Recorded: Reviewed in *North Carolina Anvil*, June 10, 1972.

# ALBERT PINKHAM RYDER
1847–1917

## 149. A Country Girl About 1903

Oil: 9½ × 5¾ in.; 24.1 × 14.6 cm.
Signed, lower right: Ryder
Fine Arts Fund, 1947

Provenance: "A Country Girl," according to the late Robert G. McIntyre, president of William Macbeth, Inc., went to his firm directly from the artist and is mentioned in the company's stock book Number 2 for 1903. It was sold in 1905 to William S. Hurley of Brooklyn, N.Y.

Because forgeries exist, the following statements by Mr. McIntyre are important for authentication of "A Country Girl" as an original by Ryder.

*Twenty or more years ago I was driving with some friends to a house party at Valhalla, N.Y., and about six o'clock we stopped at a road house for dinner. I noticed pictures on the walls in several of the rooms, and of course being curious I looked them over. In one room I was quite startled to see this Ryder and asked the proprietor how she came by it. Then she told me how Mr. Hurley helped her start the restaurant and gave, or lent, her pictures to decorate the rooms.*[1]

*Later she consigned the Ryder to a New York dealer who sold it to Dr. L. Pierce Clark of New York whose widow and daughters, Mrs. T. D. Cairns of Chicago and Mrs. Frederick L. Strong of New York, inherited it. They owned it at the time you purchased it for the gallery.*[2]

Robert G. McIntyre (1947)

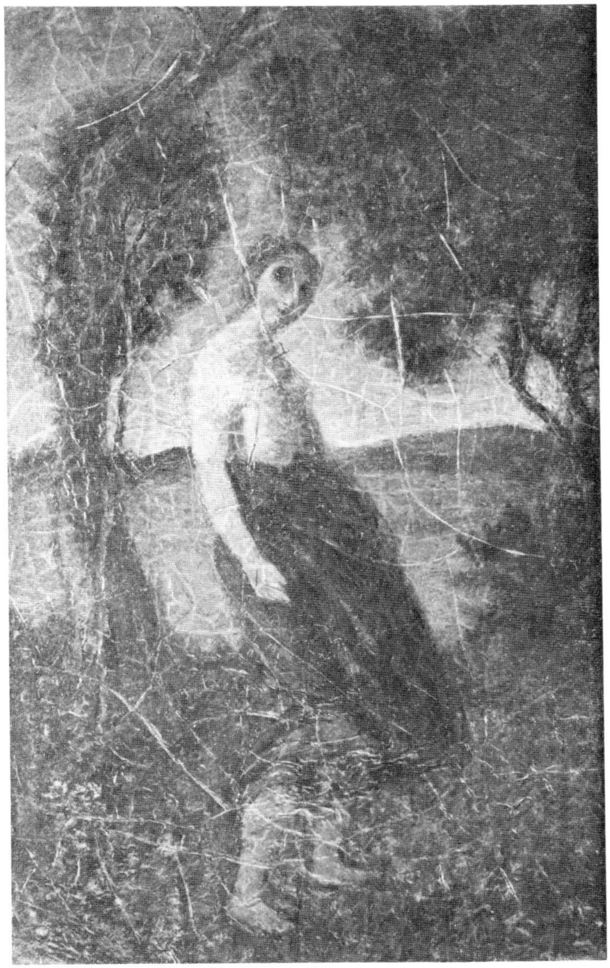

Exhibited: Shown twice under the name "An Idyll": "American Forerunners," San Francisco Museum of Art, Oct. 20–Dec. 3, 1936, and "American Artists of the Nineteenth and Twentieth Centuries," Babcock Galleries, New York, May 1944, #3. Shown twice as "A Country Girl": "Albert Pinkham Ryder Centenary Exhibition," Whitney Museum of American Art, New York, Oct. 18–Nov. 30, 1947, #4, and "Albert Pinkham Ryder Retrospective Exhibition," Corcoran Gallery of Art, Washington, Apr. 7–May 21, 1961, #34; included in four groups of paintings from the College: loan exhibitions to Richmond and to Roanoke, 1964; circulating exhibitions to Florida, 1965, and to six Mid-Atlantic states, 1966–67. For galleries and dates see Appendix B.

Recorded: Catalogues of exhibitions and *Art in America* 25 (Oct. 1937), repro. p. 171; Lloyd Goodrich, *Albert Pinkham Ryder* (New York, 1959), repro. pl. 24.

1. Robert G. McIntyre to Herbert C. Lipscomb, March 10, 1947.

2. McIntyre to Lipscomb, March 27, 1947.

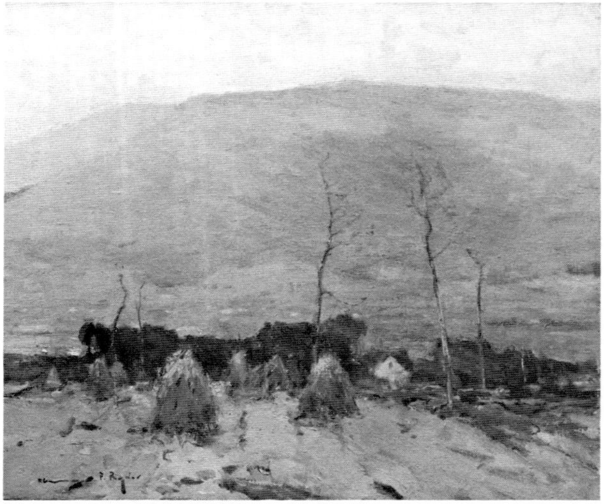

## CHAUNCY FOSTER RYDER
1868–1949

150. Vermont Hills

Oil: 30½ × 25 in.; 77.4 × 63.5 cm.
Signed, lower left: Chauncy F. Ryder
Purchased 1922

Exhibited: "One Hundred and Fifteenth Annual Exhibition," Pennsylvania Academy of the Fine Arts, Philadelphia, 1920; "Fifteen Paintings from the Collection of Randolph-Macon Woman's College," circulated by the Alumnae Association between Oct. 1949 and Jan. 1950 to its chapters in Nashville, Birmingham, Atlanta, and Asheville, #13.

Recorded: Jan Buys, "Exhibitions from the Art Collection," *Alumnae Bulletin* 43 (Feb. 1950): 37–38.

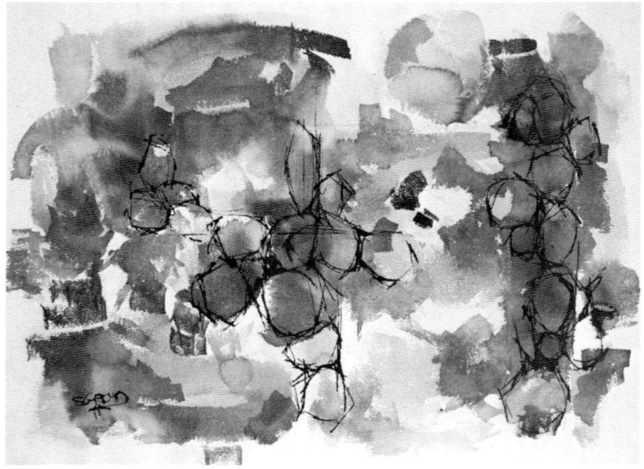

## DAVID SEBOLD
Born 1932

151. Rocks 1962

Watercolor: 21 × 29 in.; 53.3 × 73.6 cm.
Signed, lower left: Sebold
Gift of Harriet Fitzgerald '26, in 1968, through the Northern Delaware Chapter

*The concept of the "Rock Form" progressed from a desire to remove the surface beyond the idea of pure color and to centralize the color in a controlled manner.*

*Being concerned with color, but not with a variety of shapes, I chose the (to me) simplistic form (natural) of the rock. Movement without confusion was attained.*

David Sebold

Exhibited: See Appendix C.

152. Sea Pod 1965

Collage: 48 × 24 in.; 121.9 × 60.9 cm.
Signed, center right: Sebold
Gift of Mrs. Andrew A. Smith (Mary Virginia Barnes '35), 1966

## LEOPOLD SEYFFERT
1887–1956

153. PORTRAIT OF ALEXANDER W. TERRELL, M.D. 1932

Oil: 49 × 30 in.; 124.4 × 76.2 cm.
Signed and dated, lower right: Leopold Seyffert 1932
Gift of the Alumnae Association, 1932

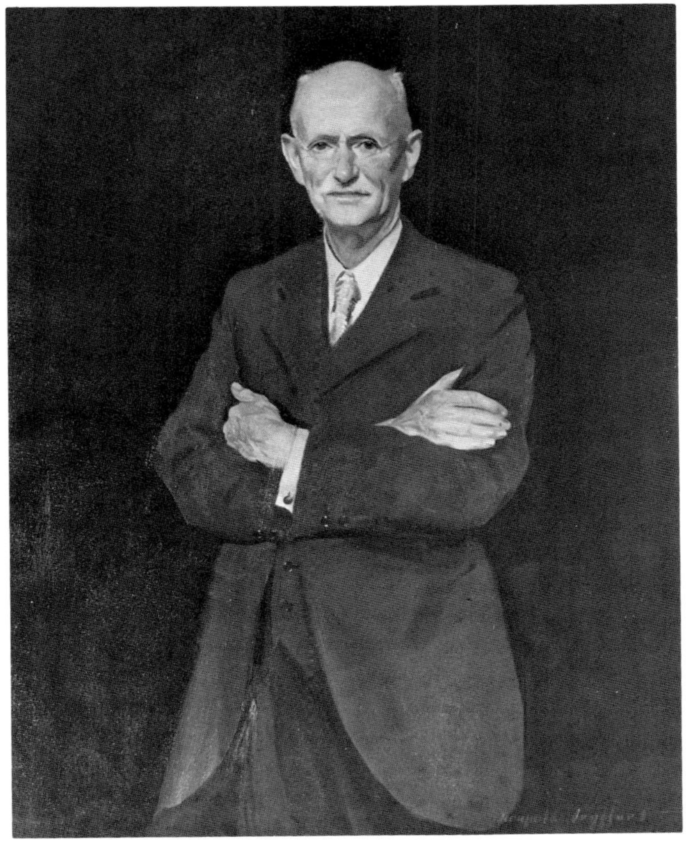

The statement below was written for this catalogue as a record of Dr. Terrell's forty-nine years of service to the College and because the entry lacks any comment from either the artist or the subject.

*Dr. Alexander Terrell served as college physician from the opening of Randolph-Macon Woman's College in 1893 until his death in 1942. The infirmary is named for him. He was a native of Lynchburg, a descendant of its Quaker founders.*

*Dr. Terrell's professional competence won him the respect of his fellow physicians and he had a large private practice, but his first responsibility was always to the College. His relations with his students, for whom he had a personal concern, were paternal rather than professional. There was so little formality in an office consultation, or a bedside visit, that the patient hardly realized with what professional skill she had been treated.*

*To the gift of healing, Dr. Terrell added the gift of friendship and gaiety, all salted with common sense and kindly humor. Lynchburg can remember few citizens who inspired so much love in the community or were so constantly sought for good companionship.*

Gillie A. Larew (1964)

Recorded: Roberta D. Cornelius, *The History of Randolph-Macon Woman's College*, repro. following p. 430; *Alumnae Bulletin* 26 (Feb. 1933), repro. p. 2.

154. Dahlias 1932

Oil: 29 × 25 in.; 73.6 × 63.5 cm.
Dedicated, dated, and signed, lower left: To Dr. and Mrs. Terrell 1932— Leopold Seyffert
Gift of Dr. and Mrs. Terrell, about 1937

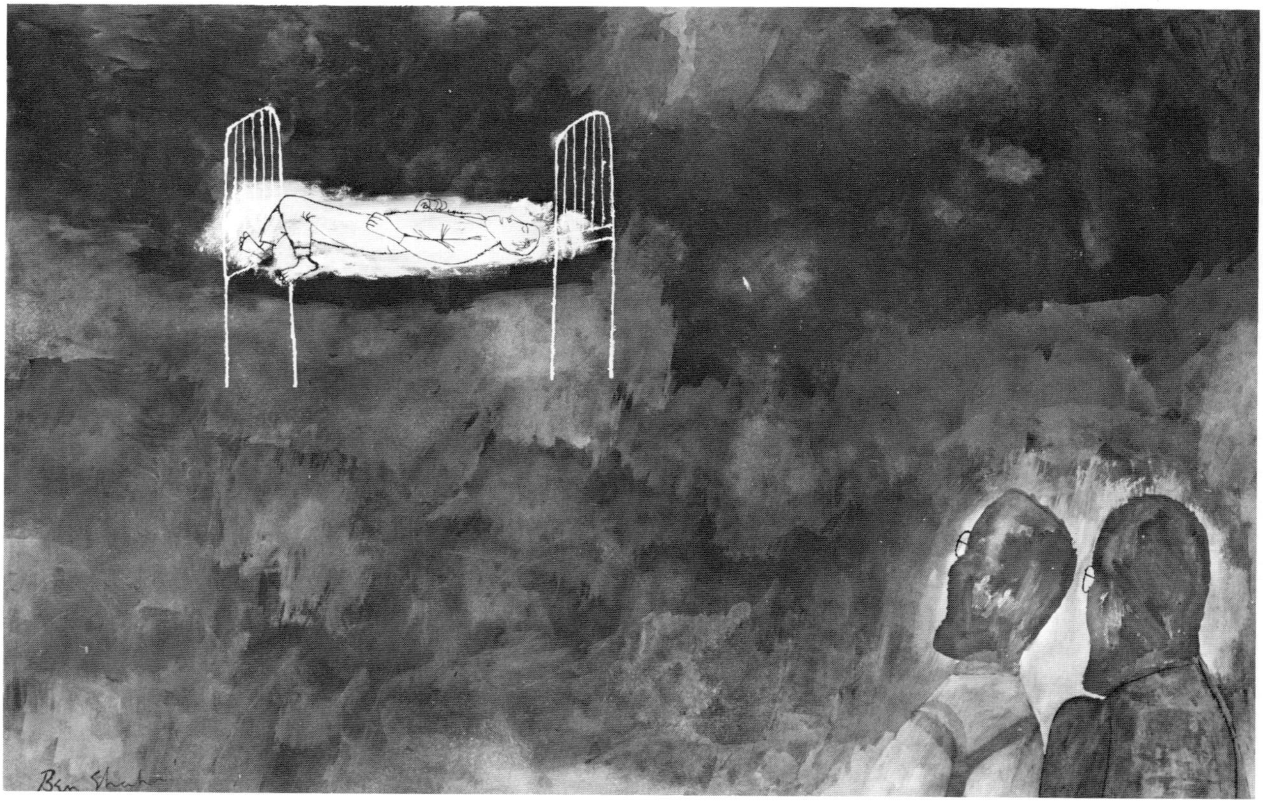

## BEN SHAHN

1898–1969

155. IT'S NO USE TO DO ANY MORE (Lucky Dragon Series) 1961–62

Tempera: 25½ × 39 in.; 64.7 × 99 cm.
Signed, lower left: Ben Shahn
Louise J. Smith Fund, 1966

The title is based on Kuboyama's remark, "It's no use any more," when he realized that he would die from the effects of radioactive ash that fell on the fishing boat *Lucky Dragon.*[1]

Exhibited: "Contemporary American Painting and Sculpture," University of Illinois, Urbana, Mar. 3–Apr. 7, 1963, #127, repro. p. 215; "Fifty-fifth Annual Exhibition," at the College, Mar. 12–29, 1966, #17; "Loan Exhibition" of 33 paintings from the College Collection circulated between Oct. 1966 and June 1967 to museums in Wilmington (Del.), Oxford (Pa.), Montclair (N.J.), Greensboro (N.C.), and Louisville (Ky.); "Ben Shahn Exhibition," circulated between July 1967 and Jan. 1968 to Santa Barbara Museum of Art, La Jolla Museum of Art, and John Herron Museum of Art, Indianapolis; "Ben Shahn, A Retrospective Exhibition," N.J. State Museum, Trenton, Sept. 20–Nov. 16, 1969, #83, with repro.; "Exhibition of Ben Shahn," National Museum of Art, Tokyo, May 21–July 5, 1970, #44, repro. p. 57; "Randolph-Macon at Reynolda House," Winston-Salem, N.C., Mar. 17–26, 1972, #7; "Ben Shahn: A Retrospective," circulated between Oct. 1976 and Jan. 1978 to the Jewish Museum in New York, University of Georgia at Athens, Amon Carter Museum at Fort Worth, University of Texas at Austin, Cincinnati Art Museum, and Spertus Museum, Chicago.

Recorded: Catalogues of the exhibitions; James Thrall Soby, *Ben Shahn* (New York, 1963), repro. #98; Richard Hudson and Ben Shahn, *Kuboyama and the Saga of the "Lucky Dragon"* (New York, 1965), p. 43 and color repro. #8; Allen S. Weller, *The Joys and Sorrows of Recent American Art* (University of Illinois, Urbana, 1968), repro. pl. 16; *Art Journal* 25 (Summer 1966), repro. p. 400, and 32 (Winter 72/73) p. 195, repro. p. 193.

1. Hudson and Shahn, *Kuboyama,* p. 43.

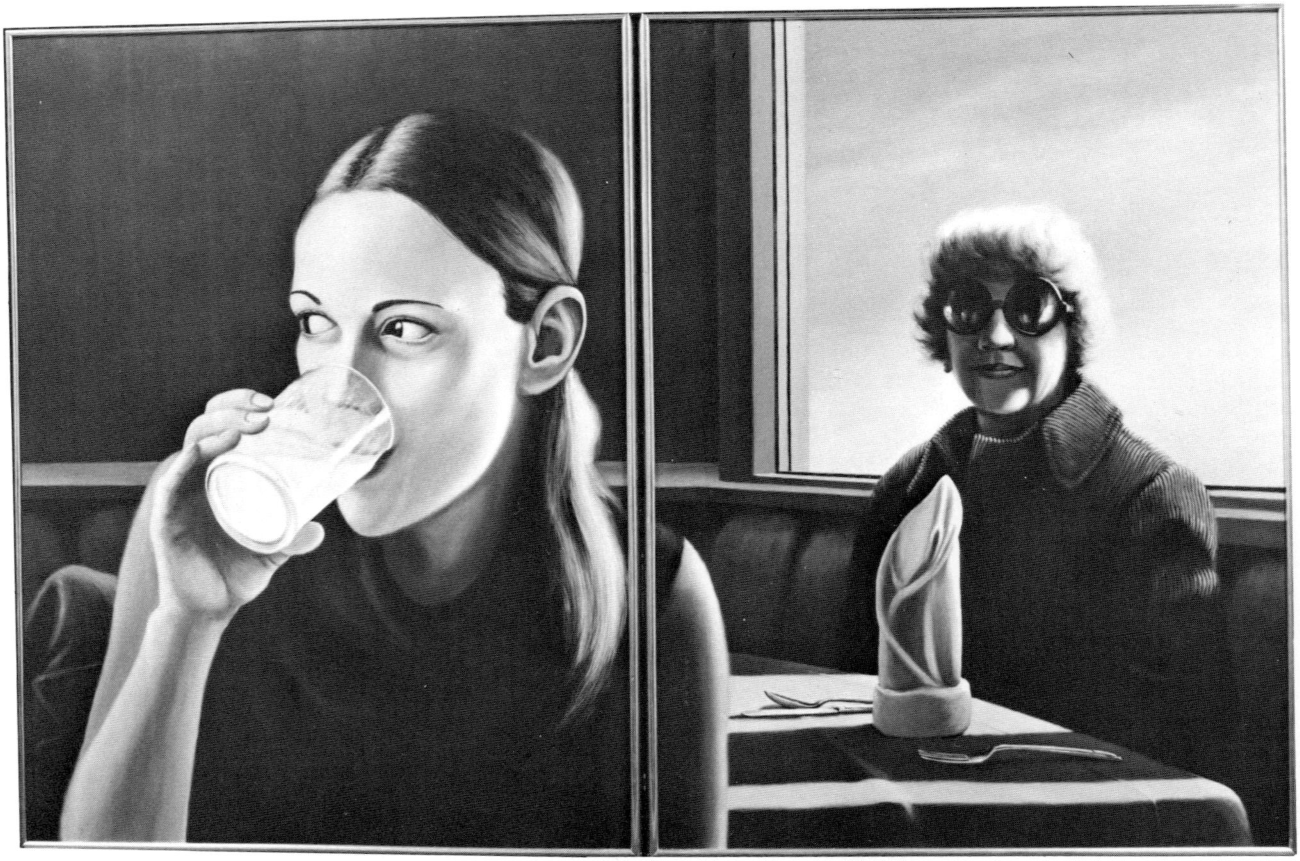

## BARCLAY SHEAKS

Born 1928

156. WATCHERS 1972

Acrylic on masonite: 48 × 72 in.; 121.9 × 182.8 cm.
Signed, lower right: Barclay Sheaks
Gift of alumnae of the Hampton Roads Chapter, 1976

*This picture is essentially two separate portraits combined in one painting. They represent my daughter-in-law, Marcia Trentor Sheaks (girl drinking milk), and my wife, Edna Daniel Sheaks (woman at the table). I decided to use the possibilities provided by the diptych with its two panels, enabling each subject to be self-contained and yet a part of the total picture. It took two years to find the "right" configuration for each subject. I discovered the one for my wife in a restaurant in Lexington, Va., and the one for my daughter-in-law two years later in a restaurant in Nags Head, N.C. It is difficult to write about the crystalization of images and ideas. It is a very personal experience. When the "right" combination of image and situation occurs, I am aware of it without any shadow of doubt. Both drawings and photographs were used as reference.*

Barclay Sheaks

Recorded: *Daily Press* (Newport News, Va.), Apr. 20, 1976, with repro.

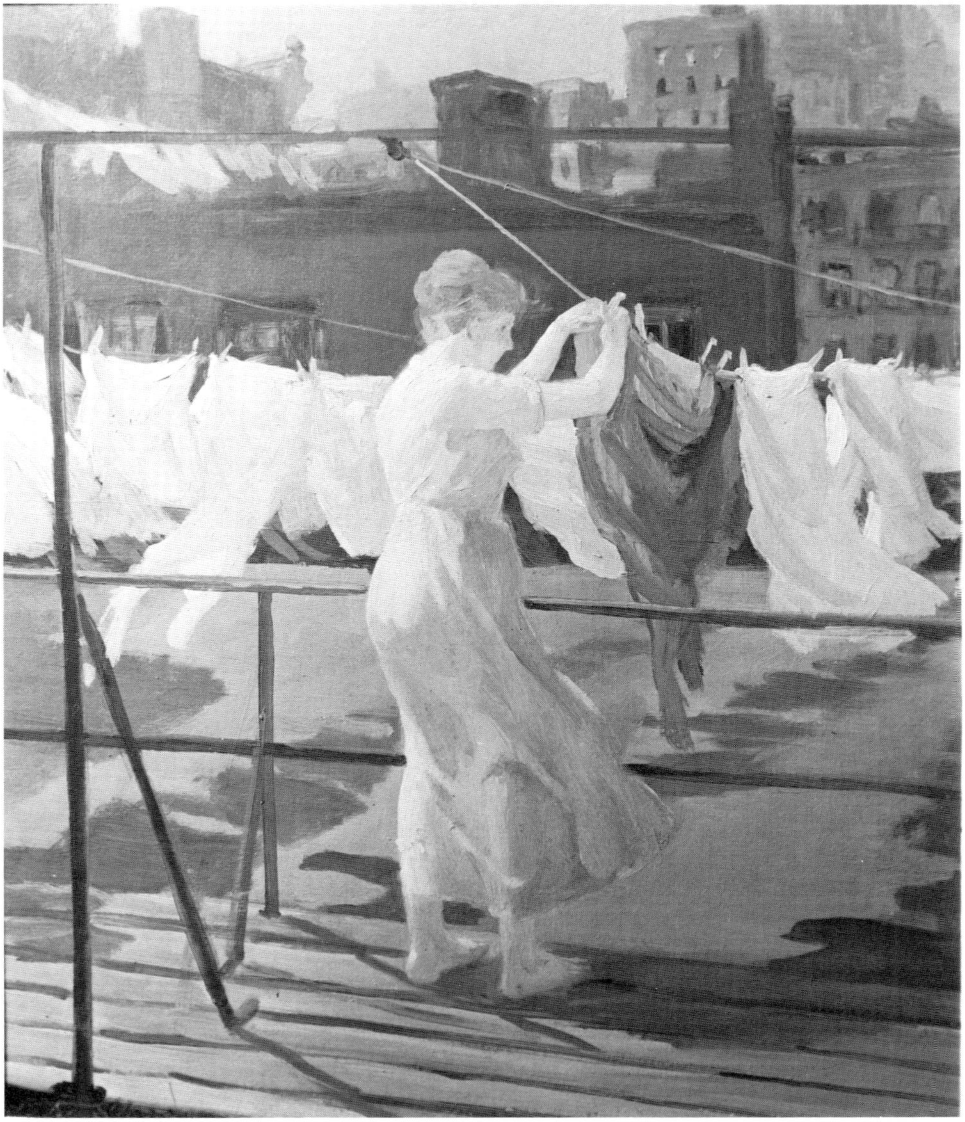

JOHN SLOAN
1871–1951

157. Sun and Wind on the Roof 1915

Oil: 24 × 20 in.; 60.9 × 50.8 cm.
Signed, lower left: John Sloan
Fine Arts Fund, 1947

*An urge to record my strong emotional response*

*to the city woman, any woman running up the colors of a clean fresh wash. Sun, wind, scant clothing, blowing hair, unconscious grace give me great joy. This is a try at handing it on.*

John Sloan[1]

Sloan also wrote, "The subject, a woman putting out her wash, is one that never loses its charm for me."

Provenance: Charles Whalen (1939); Mr. and Mrs. Paul Lamb of Cleveland (1947).

Exhibited: "The Life and Times of John Sloan," Wilmington (Del.) Society of the Fine Arts, Sept. 22–Oct. 29, 1961, #19; "Oil Paintings by John Sloan," Pennsylvania Academy of the Fine Arts, Philadelphia, Nov. 19–Dec. 23, 1961, #45; shown in five exhibitions of the College Collection listed in Appendix B: at Richmond and at Roanoke, 1964; Tampa, Orlando, Gainesville, and Jacksonville, 1965; in six Mid-Atlantic states, 1966–67; and in the Virginia Museum's Artmobile, 1969–70.

Recorded: *Arts Magazine* 11 (Apr. 1927), repro. p. 172; John Sloan, *Gist of Art* (New York, 1939), repro. with comment p. 244; *Arts in Virginia* 2 (Spring 1962), p. 26, repro.; *Nashville Tennessean*, June 25, 1967, with repro.; Bruce St. John, *John Sloan* (New York, 1971), p. 41.

1. This quote and the following one are from Sloan, *Gist of Art*, pp. 244, 299. Quoted by permission of Mrs. John Sloan.

## LOUISE JORDAN SMITH

1868–1928

158. SELF-PORTRAIT 1897

Pastel on canvas: 28¾ × 23½ in.; 73 × 59.6 cm.
Signed and dated, lower right: L. J. Smith
Paris '97
Bequest of the artist, 1928

Exhibited: Salon of 1897, Paris. In the catalogue (dated Apr. 20, 1897), the entry (p. 242) reads "Smith (Mlle. L.) née aux Etats-Unis; élève de M. Jules Lefebvre et Tony Robert-Fleury—Rue Mansart 11, 2554—Portrait de l'auteur; pastel." Other exhibitions: "Art Loan Exhibition," Lynchburg Art Club, Nov. 30–Dec. 8, 1899; lent by the artist to the College for permanent exhibition at the request of the Class of 1911; "Paintings by Miss Louise Jordan Smith," at the College, Apr. 14–May 6, 1929, #8; "Randolph-Macon Woman's College Collection," Virginia Museum, Richmond, Sept. 11–Oct. 18, 1964, #45.

Recorded: Elizabeth Nottingham, "Silhouette of Miss Louise," *Alumnae Bulletin* 32 (Nov. 1938), repro. p. 2; Roberta D. Cornelius, *The History of Randolph-Macon Woman's College*, p. 157, repro. after p. 428; Margaret Royce, "Art at Randolph-Macon Woman's College," *The Commonwealth* 20 (Sept. 1953), pp. 24–25, repro. p. 25; Ruth Homes Blunt, *The Lynchburg Art Club and Its Affiliates* (Lynchburg, 1962), p. 13, repro. p. 12.

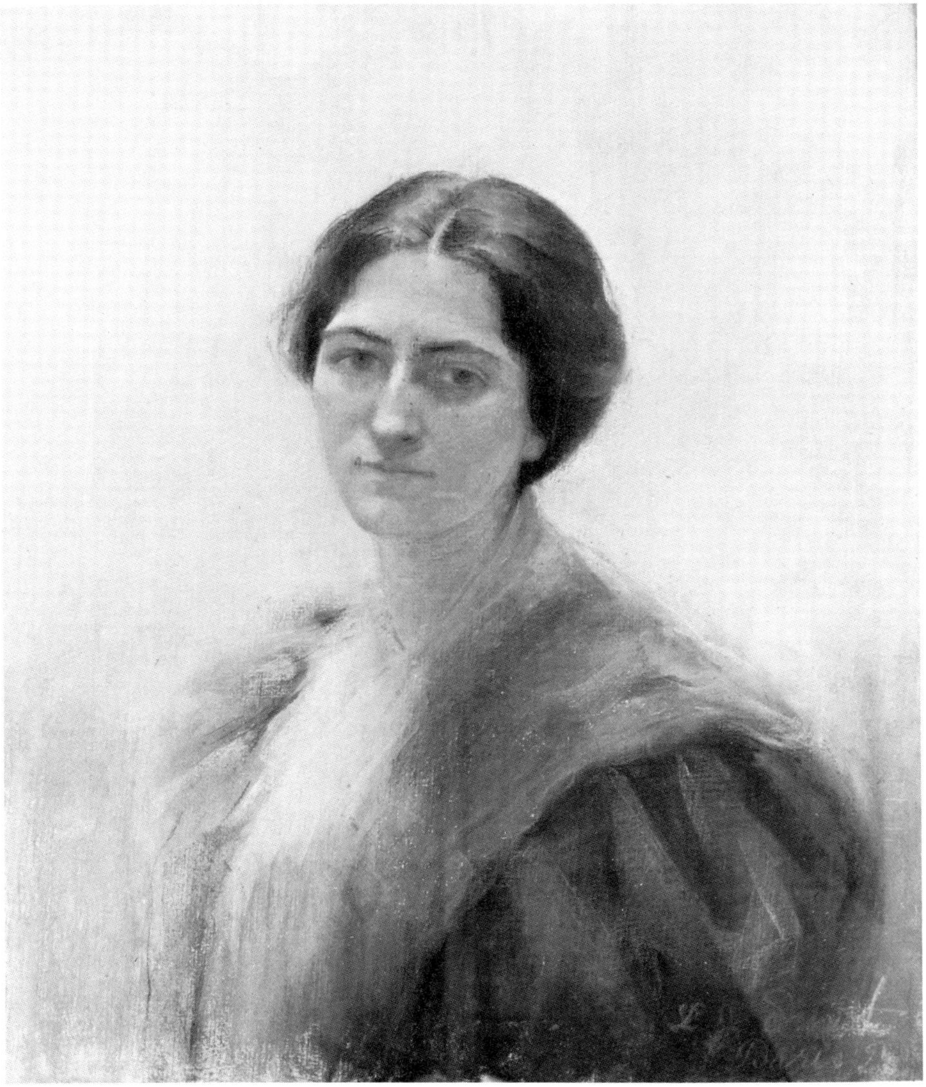

## LOUISE JORDAN SMITH (cont.)

### 159. A Campus Group About 1925

Oil: 20 × 16 in.; 50.8 × 40.6 cm.
Unsigned
Bequest of the artist, 1928

This was painted about eleven o'clock on an autumn morning, two-thirds of the way from the College gate to Main Hall, about 1925. The figure in front is the late Marjorie Harris, who became professor of philosophy. In 1964 she recalled that Miss Smith asked her to stop and pose for just a minute, which became half an hour or so.

Exhibited: "Exhibition of Paintings by Louise Jordan Smith," at the College, Dec. 5–10, 1927, #8, and Apr. 14–May 6, 1929, #13; "Randolph-Macon Woman's College Collection," Virginia Museum, Richmond, Sept. 11–Oct. 18, 1964, #43.

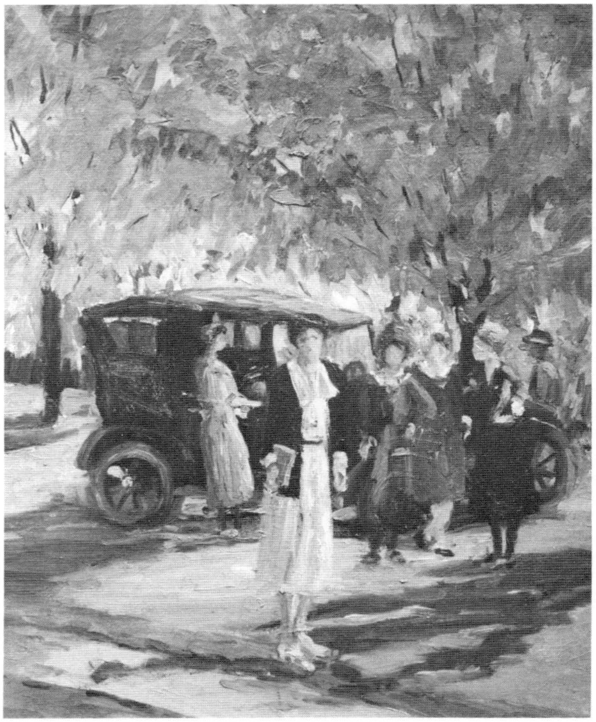

### 160. Our Wistaria (Wistaria Porch)

Oil: 29 × 36 in.; 73.6 × 91.4 cm.
Signed, lower right: L. Jordan Smith
Bequest of the artist, 1928

Exhibited: "Exhibition of Paintings by Louise Jordan Smith," at the College, Dec. 5–10, 1927, #23, and Apr. 14–May 6, 1929, #1; "Randolph-Macon Woman's College Collection," Virginia Museum, Richmond, Sept. 11–Oct. 18, 1964, #44.

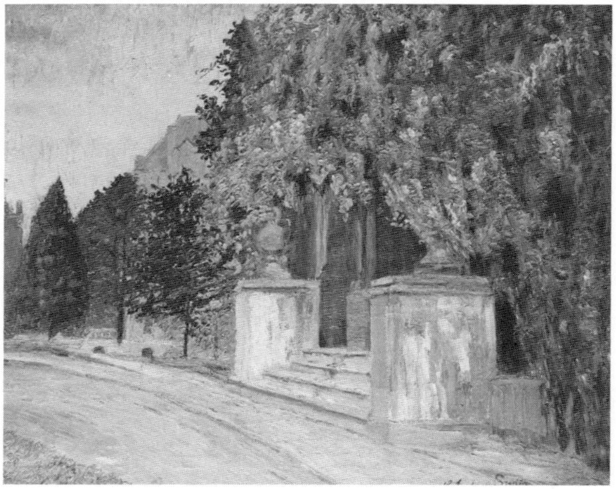

161. Old Street in Concarneau

Oil: 24 × 20 in.; 60.9 × 50.8 cm.
Signed, lower right: L. Jordan Smith
Bequest of the artist, 1928

Exhibited: "Sesquicentennial International Exhibition," Philadelphia, 1926, as "A Street in Concarneau"; "Exhibition of Paintings by Louise Jordan Smith," at the College, Dec. 5–10, 1927, #41, and Apr. 14–May 6, 1929, #6.

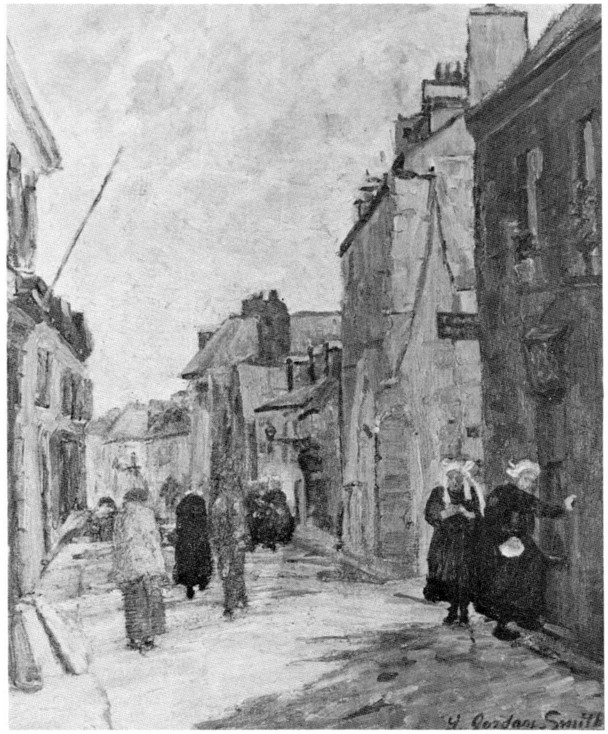

In addition to #158–61, listed above, the artist bequeathed the following fourteen paintings:
Natural Bridge
Front Royal (Chester Street)
Wheat Shocks
Virginia Mountains (Afton Valley?)
Althea in Bowl
Lady in Brown
View from my Living Room Window
Mountains from Blue Ridge National Park
Blue Ridge Mountains (National Park)
View from Front Royal Road
Looking East from Blue Ridge National Park
East Hall
The Farm Road
Fields and House

In her will, Louise Jordan Smith offered each friend on the faculty the choice of any painting not already designated as a bequest. The following sketches, chosen by Dr. Roberta D. Cornelius '09, were purchased from her in 1972 and given anonymously. The titles in parentheses were assigned by the curator.

Landscape (Misty Mountains)

Oil on cardboard: 10 × 14 in.; 25.4 × 35.5 cm.
Signed, lower left: L. Jordan Smith

Landscape (Mountains and Red Earth)

Oil on cardboard: 10 × 13½ in.; 25.4 × 34.2 cm.
Signed, lower right: L. Jordan Smith

## Henry B. Snell
1858–1943

162. Sunset on the Coast

Oil: 9½ × 13¼ in.; 24.1 × 33.6 cm.
Signed, lower left: Henry B. Snell
Gift of Mrs. John Page Jones (Miriam Moss '19), in memory of Mrs. L. Hill (Eva Drewry '07), 1968

## EUGENE SPEICHER
1883–1962

163. Portrait of Dr. Theodore H. Jack 1946

Oil: 50 × 40 in.; 127 × 101.6 cm.
Signed, lower right: Eugene Speicher '46
Gift of the Alumnae Association, 1947

*I think there were never more ideal circumstances under which to paint a portrait. Dr. and Mrs. Jack came up to Woodstock and gave me uninterrupted time daily. Mrs. Jack was present at all the sittings in my quiet studio, without even a telephone to disturb. It was all very restful and peaceful, with good conversation going on between us, whenever we felt like it. Dr. and Mrs. Jack took short naps on our closed porch after lunch each day, after which we would have the brief afternoon sittings. I sincerely hope that the portrait evidences some of my pleasure in meeting Dr. Jack and that I caught some of his fine qualities.*

Eugene Speicher (1958)

*It was decided that I should sit for the portrait at Mr. Speicher's home in the Artist Colony at Woodstock, New York, rather than to have him come to Lynchburg.*

*Almost instantly the Speichers and the Jacks decided that we were "close friends." I am not quite sure what information he had received about me,—and I am still uncertain in the face of one of his first remarks that I was just the sort of person he had expected to see. This remark is subject to various interpretations!*

*Mr. Speicher had arranged for two sittings a day, one in the morning and one in the afternoon, with ample time for rest and relaxation. Mrs. Speicher and Mrs. Jack often sat in on the sittings, with various comments on the sitter,—all of which served to make for a pleasant task. Mr. Speicher never spoke of his distinction as an artist, and to my delight, I found that he felt his chief claims to fame were his ability, when young, as a basketball player, and the fact that he once played a round of golf with the famous Bobby Jones in Augusta!*

*We were privileged to meet a number of well-known painters who lived in Woodstock, and, best of all, to have tea with Mrs. George Bellows, who pleased me very much when she said that Mr. Bellows always considered our "Men of the Docks" one of his finest paintings.*

*Mr. Speicher has a sense of humor, so he and I got along famously. When the painting was finished and we were standing before it, praising it and discussing various angles,—and I treasure this quip—Mr. Speicher calmly remarked: "Well, Mr. Jack, I think I did a very good job with what I had to work on!" And I think he did!*

Theodore H. Jack (1959)

Dr. Jack (1881–1964) was president of the College from 1933 until his retirement in 1952.

Exhibited: "Fifteen Paintings from the Collection of Randolph-Macon Woman's College," circulated by the Alumnae Association between Oct. 1949 and Jan. 1950 to its chapters in Nashville, Birmingham, Atlanta, and Asheville, #14; "Randolph-Macon Woman's College Collection," Virginia Museum, Richmond, Sept. 11–Oct. 18, 1964, #46.

Recorded: Harriet Fitzgerald, "The Problem of the Contemporary Portrait," *Alumnae Bulletin* 40 (June 1947), pp. 4–11, repro. p. 2, and 58 (Fall 1964), "Theodore Henly Jack, 1881–1964," (obituary) with repro. p. 3.

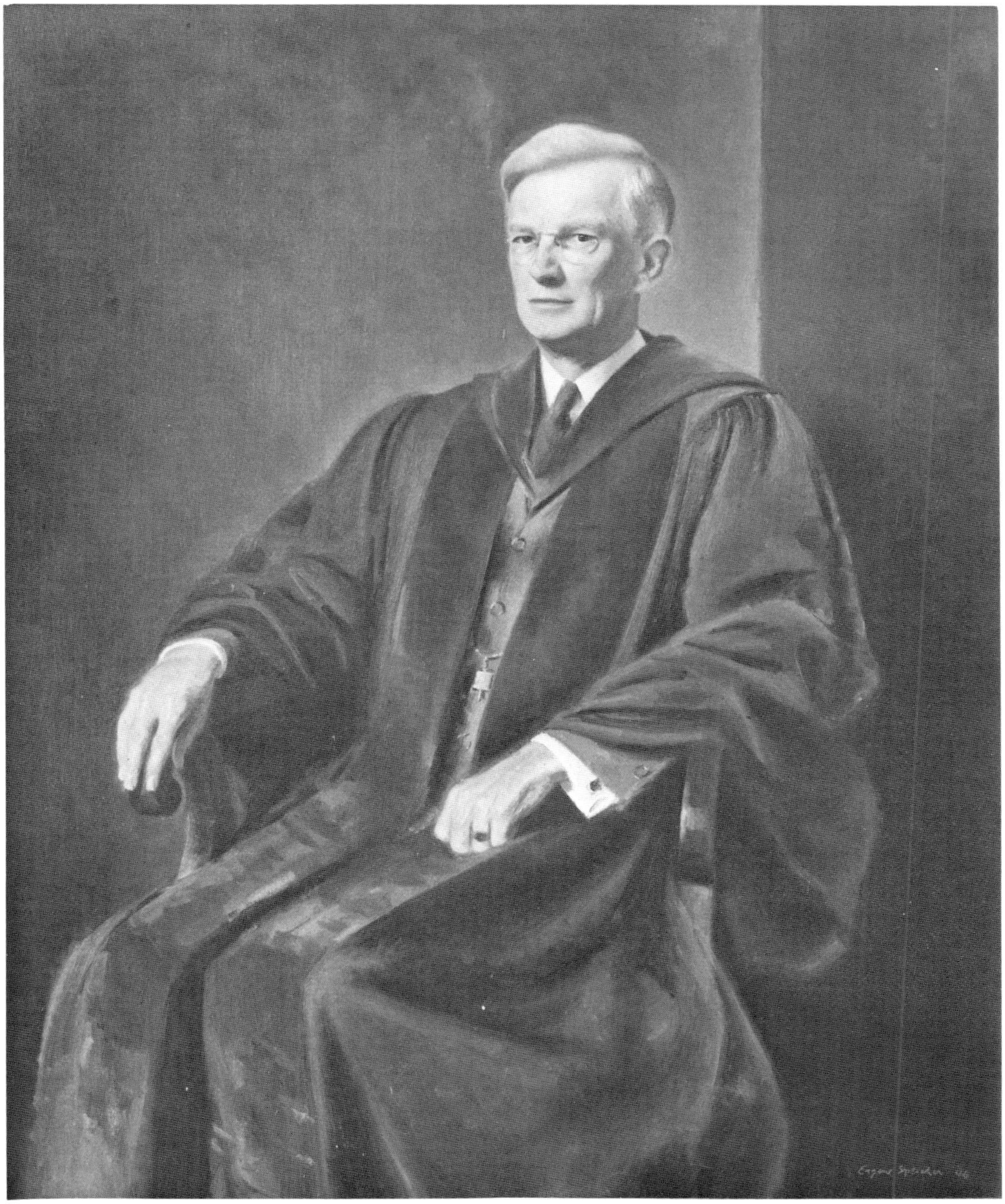

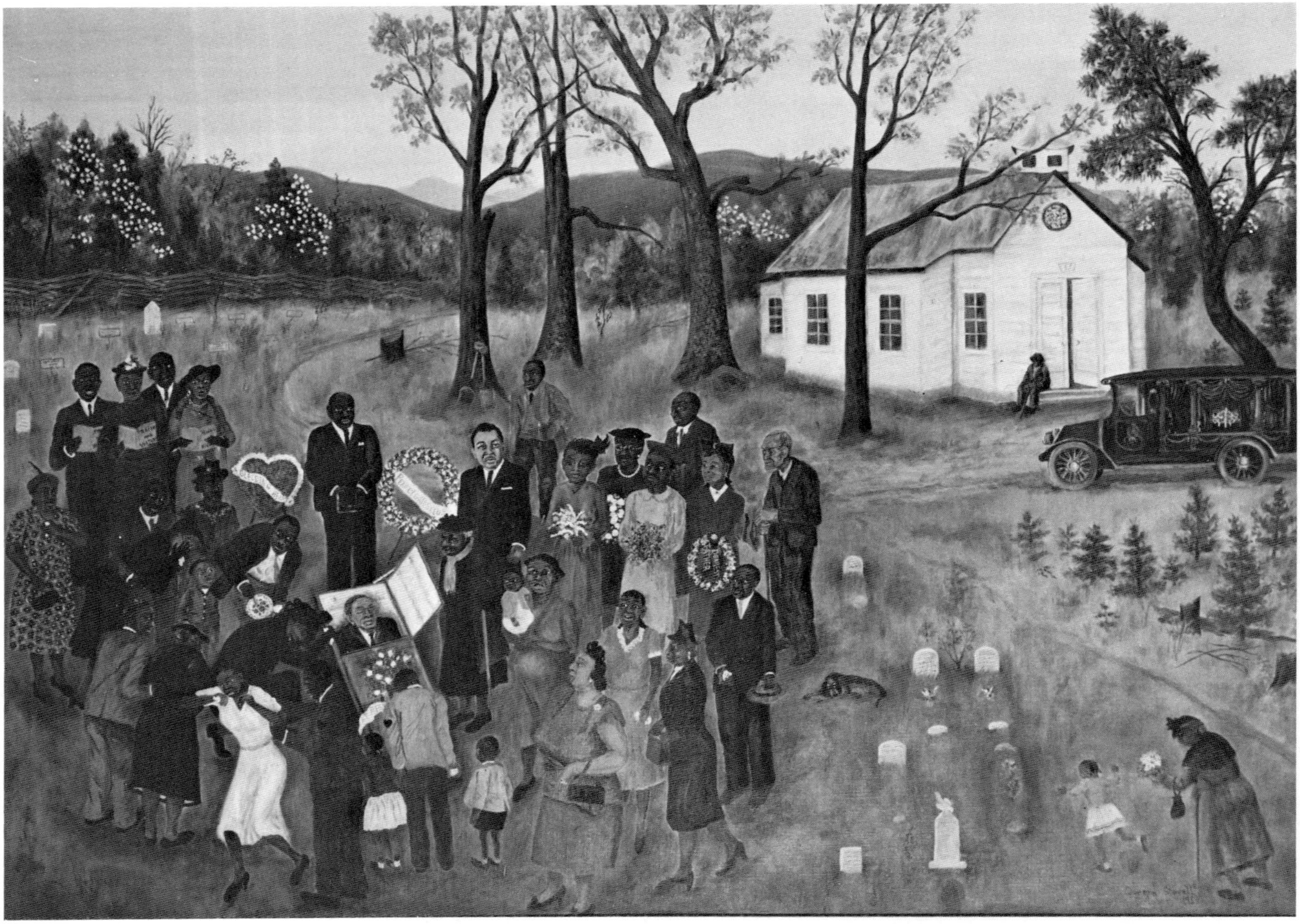

## QUEENA STOVALL (Mrs. J. B.)

Born 1888

164. Swing Low, Sweet Chariot 1953

Oil: 28 × 40 in.; 71.1 × 101.6 cm.
Signed and dated, lower right: Queena Stovall, October 1953
Purchased 1965

*"Swing Low" was painted from memory of the many Negro funerals that I went to. In the nineteen-twenties and thirties the Negroes did not have many cars and I had to go because I could provide some transportation. The setting is at Pleasant View (a rural community near Lynchburg). The church is Timothy Baptist right in the bend of the road. Etta Rose (in foreground with purse) would bring me a man's light colored coat and a heart to sew on the sleeve. Idell, who is wearing her white dress, always brought a man with her to help in case she would fall out with her grief. They are all people that I knew and loved, many of them worked for me at some time or another.*

Queena Stovall

Exhibited: "Presenting the Works of Queena Stovall," Lynchburg Art Center (1013 Church Street), Apr. 15–27,

1956, #13; "Virginia Artists 1957," Virginia Museum, Richmond, Mar. 8–Apr. 21, 1957; "17th Annual Spring Purchase Exhibition," Springfield (Mass.) Museum of Fine Arts, May 12–June 16, 1957; "1957 Virginia Artists," traveling exhibition circulated by the Virginia Museum, 1957–1959; "Paintings by Queena Stovall," at the College, Feb. 7–23, 1965, #5; "Randolph-Macon Paintings," circulated in six Mid-Atlantic states, 1966–67 (see Appendix B); "Queena Stovall," a loan exhibition supported by a grant from the National Endowment for the Arts, organized jointly by the three institutions at which it was shown: Lynchburg College, Oct. 6–25, 1974; Abbey Aldrich Rockefeller Folk Art Collection, Williamsburg, Va., Jan. 12–Mar. 15, 1975; New York State Historical Association, Cooperstown, N.Y., Apr. 27–Sept. 30, 1975, #40.

Recorded: "At the Art Center" (editorial), *The News* (Lynchburg), Apr. 17, 1956; "R.-M.W.C. Purchases Painting by Stovall," *Sun Dial* (Lynchburg), Feb. 18, 1965; Mary S. Ellett '71, "A Kind of Magic–The Paintings of Queena Stovall" (unpublished paper, 1971), pp. 11-12, 15-16, with repro. Two catalogues were published for the circulating exhibition of 1974–75. A preliminary one, "Queena Stovall: An Exhibition of her Work," listing forty-two unnumbered paintings (including "Swing Low, Sweet Chariot") was issued by Lynchburg College. The definitive one, "Queena Stovall, Artist of the Blue Ridge Piedmont: An Exhibition," listing forty-one entries, was published for use in 1975 at Williamsburg and Cooperstown, but it named Lynchburg as the first place in the itinerary of the exhibition. "Swing Low, Sweet Chariot" (#40) was reproduced in color on its cover. Louis C. Jones, "The Genre in American Folk Art," *Papers on American Art* (published for Friends of Independence National Historical Park, 1976), p. 58, repro. #9.

## GILBERT STUART

1755–1828

### 165. Portrait of Mrs. Polly Hooper 1811
(Color plate, page 31)

Oil on wood: 26 × 21 in.; 66 × 53.3 cm.
Unsigned
Fine Arts Fund and
Dr. and Mrs. Ben T. Bell
(Dorothy L. Fincke '26), 1961

Mary (Polly) Williams married Robert Hooper of Marblehead, Mass., and commissioned Gilbert Stuart to paint five family portraits, of which this is one. After marrying her second husband, Dr. R. G. Robbins, she bought from Gilbert Stuart the very same house (in Roxbury, now a suburb of Boston, Mass.) in which the portraits had been painted, for many years his home and studio. She hung her paintings in the long hall leading to the former studio.[1]

Provenance: Mrs. Polly Williams Hooper Robbins of Roxbury; Rev. Chandler Robbins of Boston, her son-in-law (1880); Samuel Robbins of Belmont, Mass.; Charles D. Childs (1944); Frances J. Eggleston (1946).

Exhibited: "Fiftieth Annual Loan Exhibition," at the College, Apr. 30–June 5, 1961, #2, repro. p. 6; included in four groups of paintings from Randolph-Macon Woman's College: loan exhibitions to Richmond and to Roanoke, 1964; circulating exhibitions to Florida, 1965, and to Mid-Atlantic states, 1966–67. For galleries and dates see Appendix B.

Recorded: Henry T. Tuckerman, *Book of the Artists* (New York, 1867), p. 110; George C. Mason, *Life and Works of Gilbert Stuart* (New York, 1879) pp. 200–201; Lawrence Park, *Gilbert Stuart* (4 vols.; New York, 1926), vol. 1, pp. 408–9; James Thomas Flexner, *A Great Life in Brief: Gilbert Stuart* (New York, 1955), p. 178; *Alumnae Bulletin* 54 (June 1961), repro. p. 20; Charles M. Mount, *Gilbert Stuart, A Biography* (New York, 1964), p. 369.

1. The books by Mason, Park, and Flexner (mentioned in *Recorded*) refer to these facts.

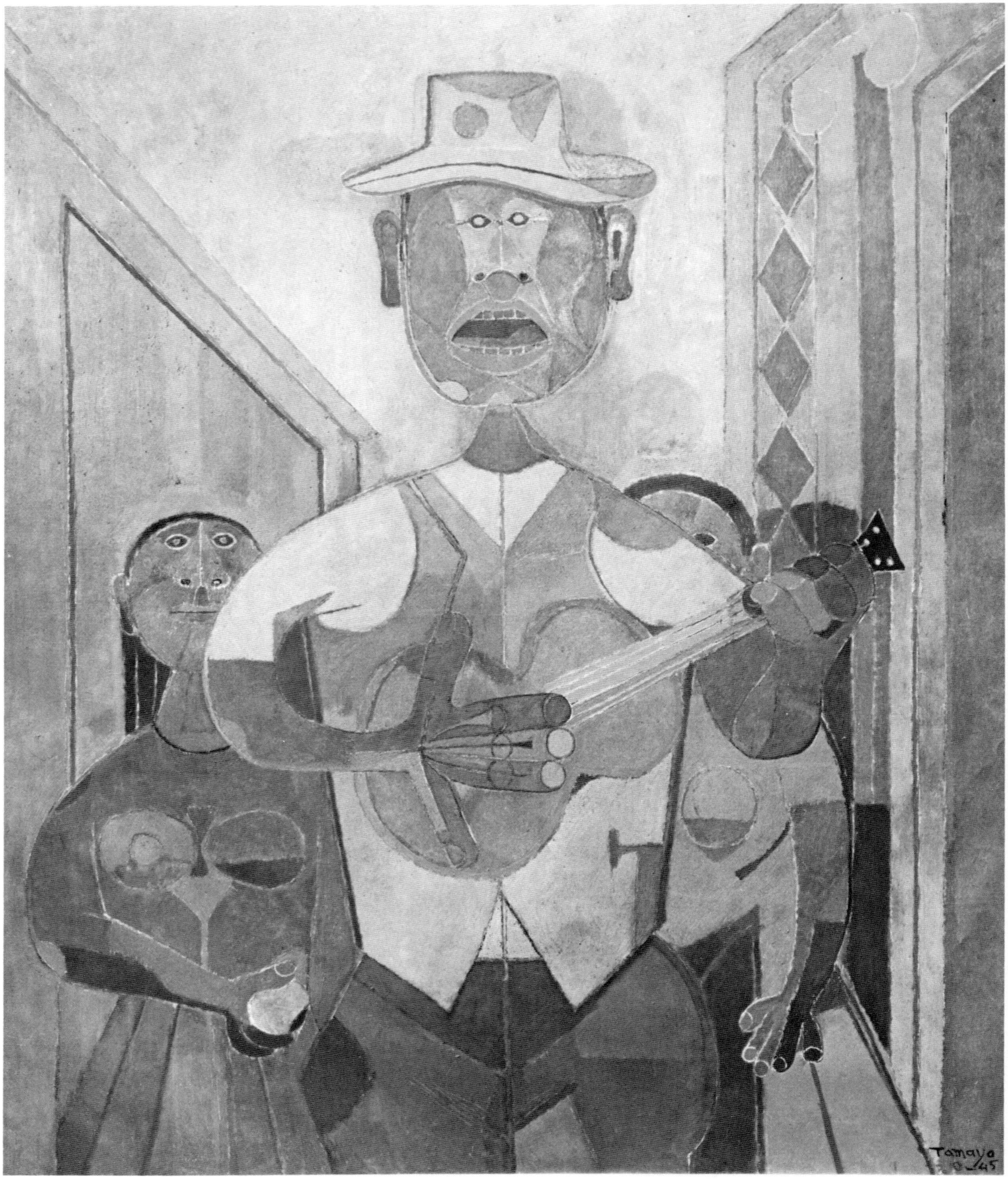
Tamayo

## RUFINO TAMAYO

Born 1899

166. TROUBADOUR 1945

Oil: 60½ × 50 in.; 153.6 × 127 cm.
Signed and dated, lower right: Tamayo—45
Gift of Stephen C. Clark, 1949

Exhibited: "Venticinquesimo (XXV) Biennale Internazionale d'Arte," Venice, June–Sept. 1950, #75; "Mexican Art from Pre-Columbian Times to the Present Day," a traveling exhibition sponsored by the government of Mexico, circulated to Musée Nationale d'Art Moderne, Paris, May–July 1952, #1072, to Liljevalches Konsthall, Stockholm, Sept. 1952, #1057, and to Tate Gallery, London, Mar. 4–Apr. 26, 1953, #1049; included in five groups of paintings from Randolph-Macon Woman's College: loan exhibitions to Richmond and to Roanoke, 1964; circulating exhibitions to Florida, 1965; and to six Mid-Atlantic states, 1966–67; and exhibition at Winston-Salem, N.C., 1972. For galleries and dates see Appendix B.

Recorded: Robert Goldwater, *Rufino Tamayo* (New York, 1947), pl. 66 on p. 106.

## SISTER M. THEOPHANE

167. STREET SCENE 1968

Collage: 30 × 20 in.; 76.2 × 50.8 cm.
Unsigned
Gift of alumnae of the Northern Delaware Chapter, 1968

*During the wonderful year that I spent in New York with the Abingdon Square Painters I became very interested in collage. This picture is my impression of the city of New York, which I love, in a medium that was then new to me.*

Sister M. Theophane

Exhibited: See Appendix C.

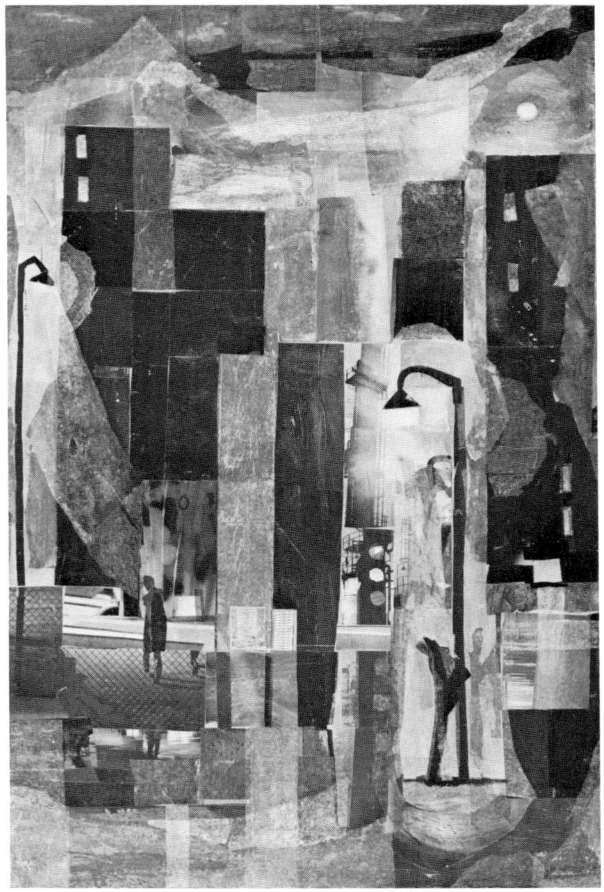

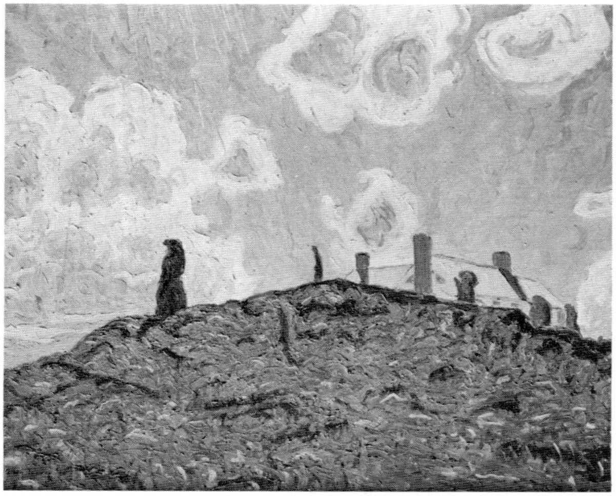

## ALLEN TUCKER
1866–1939

168. The House on the Hill

Oil: 40 × 50 in.; 101.6 × 127 cm.
Signed, lower left: Allen Tucker
Gift of the Allen Tucker Memorial Foundation, 1958

Painted between 1923 and 1931 at Bedford Hills, N.Y.

Exhibited: "Paintings by Allen Tucker," Century Association, New York, Apr. 3–30, 1931, #7.

169. The Gorge 1921

Oil: 25 × 30½ in.; 63.5 × 77.4 cm.
Signed and dated, lower right: Allen Tucker 1921
Gift of Mrs. Eleanor C. H. Winslow through the Macbeth Gallery, 1942

## JOHN H. TWACHTMAN
1853–1902

170. Azaleas *About 1898*
(Color plate, page 31)

Oil: 30 × 24 in.; 76.2 × 60.9 cm.
Signed, lower left: J. H. Twachtman
Gift of Mrs. Andrew C. Gleason, in honor of Mrs. Powell Glass, 1949

Provenance: Henry Smith of New York (1915); E. and A. Milch, Inc., New York (1922); J. K. Newman (1935); Leo Elwyn & Co. (1943); Milch Galleries.

Exhibited: "Panama-Pacific International Exposition," San Francisco, 1915, #4064; "American Landscape Painting Dating from 1750," M. Knoedler & Co., New York, May 17–June 11, 1943, #36; "Paintings by American Artists—Late 19th and Early 20th Centuries," Milch Galleries, New York, May 1945, #12; "Fifteen Paintings from the Collection of Randolph-Macon Woman's College," circulated by the Alumnae Association between Oct. 1949 and Jan. 1950 to its chapters in Nashville, Birmingham, Atlanta, and Asheville; "American Painting 1865–1905," organized by the Art Gallery of Toronto in collaboration with Lloyd Goodrich, Director of the Whitney Museum of American Art, New York, shown between Jan. 6 and June 18, 1961, in Toronto, Winnipeg, Vancouver, and New York, #68, repro. p. 28; "American Traditional Painters," a traveling exhibition of the American Federation of Arts circulated between Oct. 1, 1962, and May 19, 1963, to Louisville (Ky.), Allentown

(Pa.), Columbus (Ohio), Seattle, Peoria (Ill.), Des Moines, and Charlotte (N.C.), #32; "Randolph-Macon Woman's College Collection," Virginia Museum, Richmond, Sept. 11–Oct. 18, 1964, #49; "Impressionism in America," University Art Gallery, University of New Mexico, Albuquerque, and M. H. de Young Museum, San Francisco, Feb.–Apr. 1965, #60, repro. p. 55; "Art of the United States 1670–1966," Whitney Museum of American Art, New York, Sept. 28–Nov. 27, 1966, #279, color repro. p. 68.

Recorded: Catalogues of the exhibitions; *J. K. Newman Collection Sale* (American Art Association, Anderson Galleries, New York, 1935), #21, repro. p. 17; "Azaleas," *Alumnae Bulletin* 40 (Nov. 1946), pp. 10–12, with repro.; Roberta D. Cornelius, *The History of Randolph-Macon Woman's College*, repro. following p. 430; J. Douglas Hale, "John Henry Twachtman" (doctoral dissertation, Ohio State University, 1957), #32; Vincent Price, *The Vincent Price Treasury of American Art* (Waukesha, Wis., 1972), color repro. p. 174; *Art Journal* 32 (Winter 72/73), p. 195 with repro.

## ELLIOTT R. TWERY

Born 1923

### 171. Twilight in the Garden of Eden 1958

(Reproduced on page 160)

Acrylic on canvas: 72 × 48 in.; 182.8 × 121.9 cm.
Signed, lower right: Twery '58
Fine Arts Fund, 1960

*"Twilight in the Garden of Eden" is an effort to create a visual symbol of the immense grandeur, profusion, and mystery of our world.*

Elliott R. Twery (1964)

Exhibited: "Paintings by E. R. Twery," at the College, Dec. 7–31, 1958, #6; "Virginia Artists 1959," Virginia Museum, Richmond, Mar. 13–Apr. 19, 1959, awarded Certificate of Distinction; lent to the Art-in-Embassies program of the United States Department of State for exhibition in the embassy at Valletta, Malta, 1968–70; see Appendix B for exhibitions of the College Collection in Richmond, 1964, in six Mid-Atlantic states, 1966–67, and in Winston-Salem, N.C., 1972.

### 172. Randolph-Macon Woman's College 1959

(Reproduced on page 161)

Oil: 18 × 40 in.; 45.7 × 101.6 cm.
Signed and dated, lower right: Twery '59
Gift of Leonard Bocour, 1963

*I liked the eccentric skyline and the foliage of front campus from the moment I first saw them. Painting them was a challenge I didn't want to resist. This, the first version, was done with sharpness and contrast to emphasize the architecture of the scene. The second version, now at Reading University (see #173 below), was an attempt to capture the idyllic effect that springtime casts upon the area.*

Elliott R. Twery

Exhibited: "The Randolph-Macon Woman's College Collection," Virginia Museum, Richmond, Sept. 11–Oct. 18, 1964, #50.

### 173. Randolph-Macon in the Spring 1959

Oil: 18 × 40 in.; 45.7 × 101.6 cm.
Signed and dated, lower right: Twery 59
Anonymous gift for exhibition at Randolph-Macon at the University of Reading, England, 1972

Recorded: *The News* (Lynchburg), May 21, 1972, with repro.

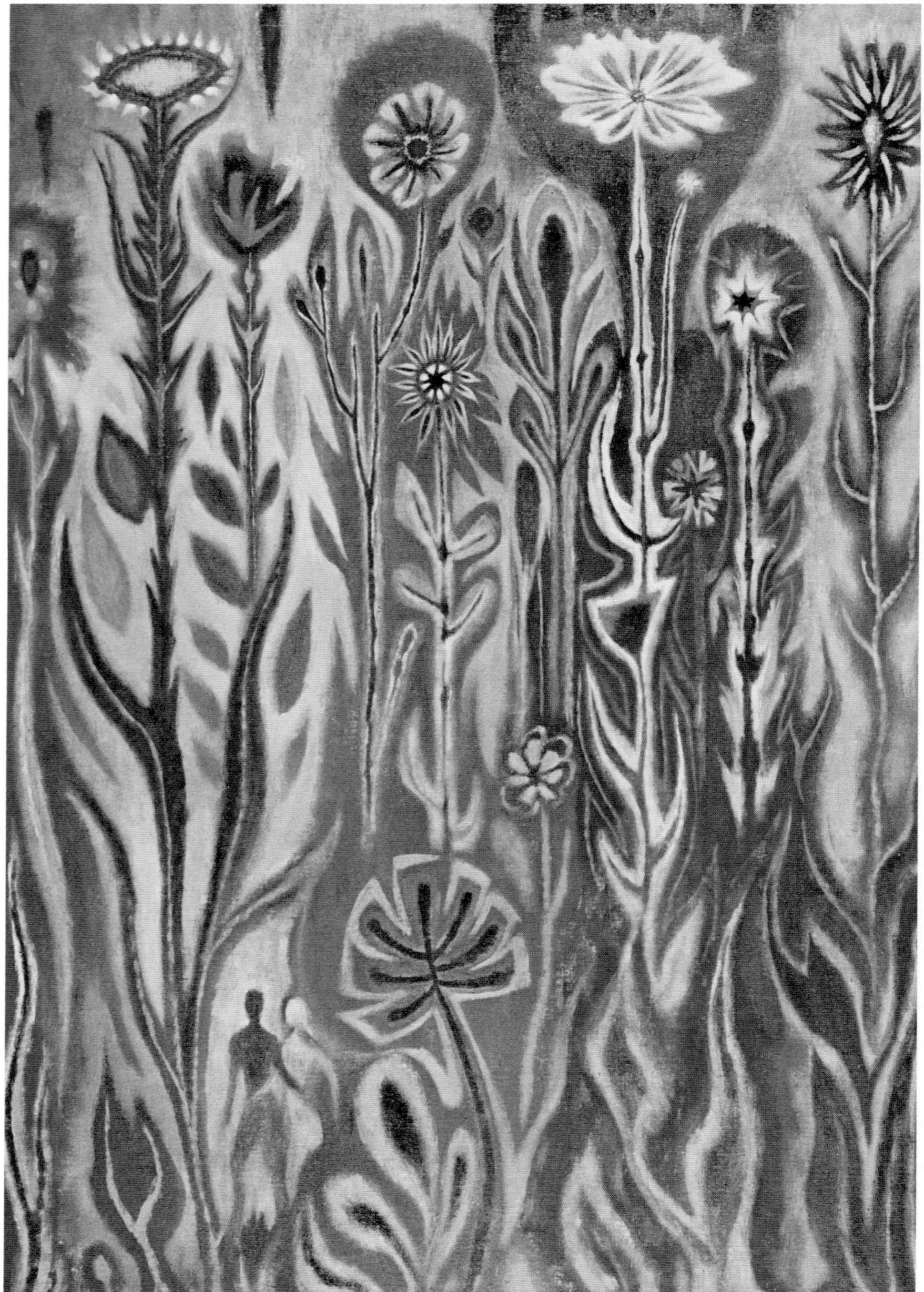

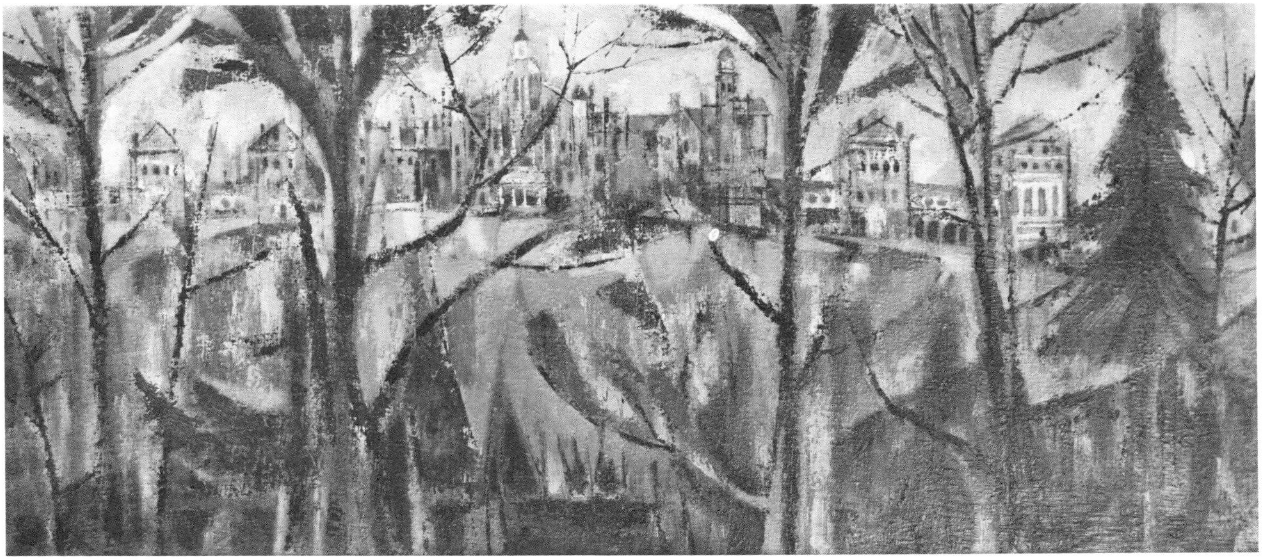

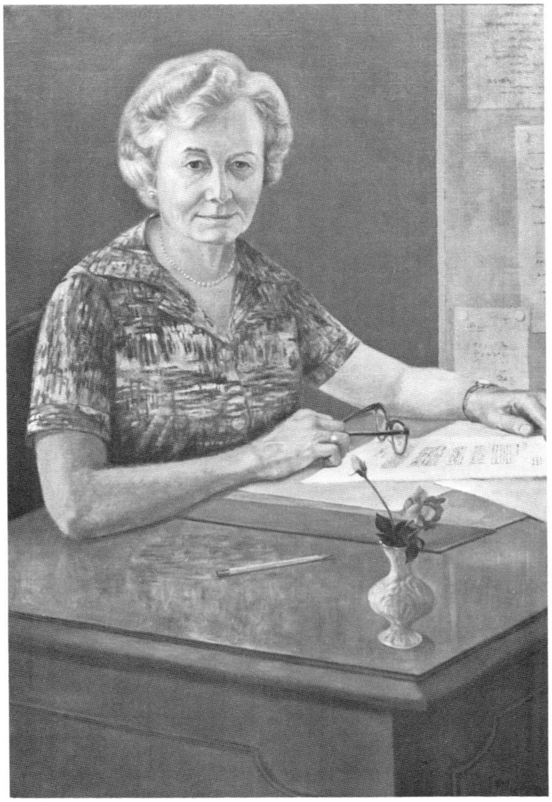

## ELLIOTT R. TWERY

174. PORTRAIT OF DEAN HARRIET D. HUDSON 1975

Oil: 36 × 24 in.; 91.4 × 60.9 cm.
Signed and dated, lower right: Twery '75
Gift of the Class of 1975

*Being commissioned by the Senior Class of 1975 to paint one of the people I admired most here at R-MWC was an assignment I relished. I had long wanted to paint Harriet and this was the perfect occasion.*

*The first session, in her office, was a photographic one in which I used a roll of 35mm film to try out various compositional angles. Back in the studio, I roughed out the composition I felt worked best. I made further ink studies in her office of her desk and numerous objects upon it. It was my feeling that the design should include this desk, since her office was the arena in which she met with students and faculty so much of the time. For the nineteen years I had been working with her, it was certainly a most familiar sight.*

*In July when the painting began, she came to pose in the newly opened air-conditioned Leggett Building and was thereby the very first subject to be painted in the new facilities. It was only fitting since she did so much to make the building become a reality.*

*The first painting session went very well, I thought. Until at the end of the morning, I stepped back and looked. What I warn my students about all the time had happened. The individual parts which seemed perfect just didn't fit together in the right relationship. . . . I wiped it out and started all over the next morning. Four morning sessions of posing were enough, along with another week of refining the color, editing materials on and off the desk . . . and it was finished.*

Elliott R. Twery

*Having been privileged to know Elliott Twery as a friend and a professional colleague at Randolph-Macon for nearly twenty years, I experienced a very special kind of pleasure in watching him work during the five mornings which I spent as the model for this portrait. (Each day, after the first, it was apparent that he had been working on the painting and thinking about it during the intervening hours also.) I was impressed to see that qualities I admire in Elliot Twery were so apparent in his approach to his work: creativity, keeness of intellect, kindliness, integrity of the relationship between the man and his work, intense concentration on the task, enjoyment of the process of painting, and full use of his large talent.*

*The fact that the portrait was commissioned by the Class of 1975 adds to the meaning of the picture for me.*

Harriet D. Hudson

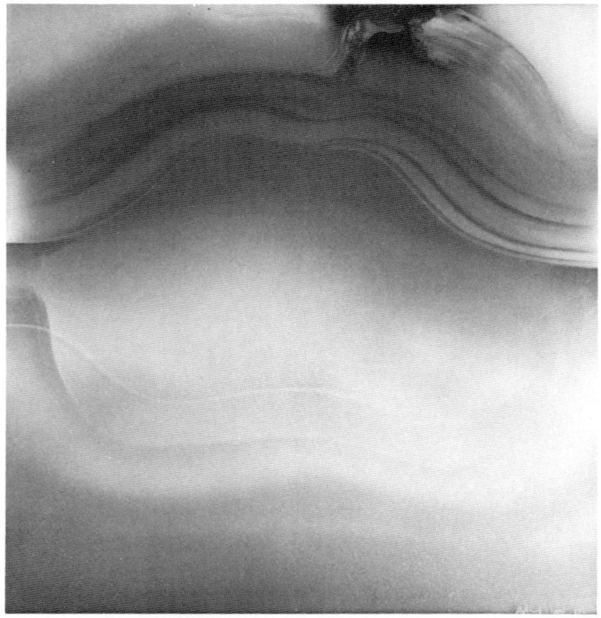

## RICHARD VAUX

Born 1940

175. SUSPENDED LIGHTSCAPE 1972

Acrylic on vinyl: 42 × 40¾ in.; 106.6 × 103.5 cm.
Signed and dated, lower right:
Richard Vaux 1972
Fine Arts Fund, 1974

*I think of myself as a Landscape Painter. All of my paintings deal with a formal synthesis of environmental phenomena. Organic form, both tangible and atmospheric, Light, and Architectural form merge and are formally coordinated in each Visual Poem. "Suspended Lightscape" is a recent work. My concerns for the use of incidental Light as an inherent part of my "Landscape Subject" is exploited by painting with acrylic glazes on transparent vinyl. The light passes through the layers and reflects off the ground, causing inner illumination (an old idea, but still useful).*

Richard Vaux

Exhibited: "Sixty-third Annual Exhibition: A Soho Sampler," at the College, Feb. 8–28, 1974, #21.

## ROBERT VICKREY
Born 1926

176. PULSE 1972
(Color plate, page 32)

Tempera: 30 × 40 in.; 76.2 × 101.6 cm.
Signed, lower right: Robert Vickrey
Louise J. Smith Fund, 1973

*"Pulse" is a picture of my son, Sean. He was posing for a different work when he suddenly discovered his own pulse. This new pose was much better than what I had in mind, and so I painted it. I feel it is one of my best pictures.*

Robert Vickrey

Exhibited: "Contemporary Realists," Cleveland Museum of Art, Oct. 8–Nov. 10, 1972; "Sixty-second Annual Exhibition: Contemporary American Painting," at the College, Feb. 8–27, 1973, #22.

Recorded: *The News* (Lynchburg), Feb. 13, 1973, with repro.; "'Pulse,' by Robert Vickrey," *Alumnae Bulletin* 60 (Summer 1973), p. 23, with repro.

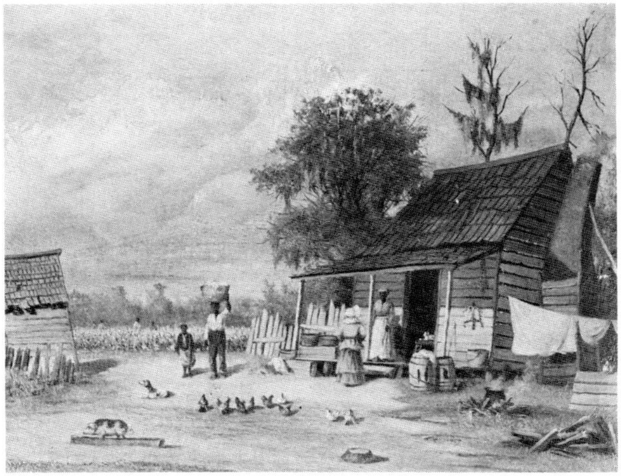

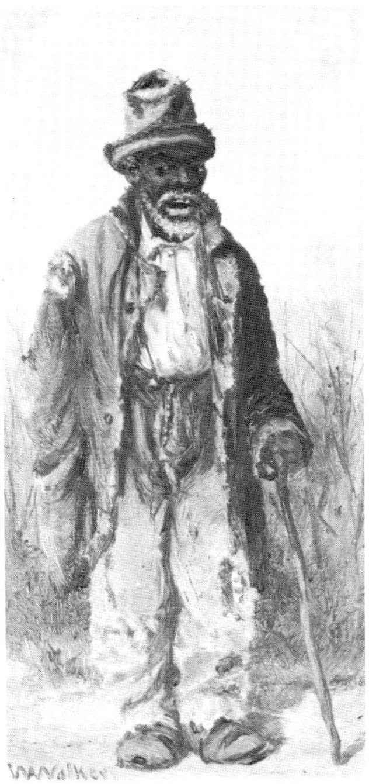

## WILLIAM AIKEN WALKER
1838–1921

177. LIFE ON THE PLANTATION

Oil on cardboard: 8⅞ × 11¾ in.; 22.5 × 29.8 cm.
Signed, lower left: W. A. Walker
(first three letters as monogram)
Gift of Mr. and Mrs. Max Guggenheimer (Mary E. Strickland '29), 1950

This cabin appears in many works by Walker, for example, "South Georgia Shanty," painted about 1897.[1]

Recorded: *The Daily Advance* (Lynchburg), Nov. 15, 1950, with repro.; *The News* (Lynchburg), Nov. 16, 1950.

178. AN OLD NEGRO MAN

Oil on cardboard: 8 × 3¾ in.; 20.3 × 9.5 cm.
Signed, lower left: W. A. Walker
(first three letters as monogram)
Gift of Mr. and Mrs. Max Guggenheimer (Mary E. Strickland '29), 1938

Recorded: *The News* (Lynchburg), Jan. 21, 1949, and Nov. 16, 1950.

1. A. P. Trovaioli and R. B. Toledano, *William Aiken Walker, Southern Genre Painter* (Baton Rouge, 1972), pl. 23.

## FRANKLIN WATKINS
1894–1972

179. NEGRO SPIRITUAL About 1933

Oil: 54 × 36 in.; 137.1 × 91.4 cm.
Signed, lower right: F.W.
Louise J. Smith Fund, 1942

*The sad thing is that I can give you little definite dating. I would guess that "Negro Spiritual" was painted in 1933 or started in that year. . . . I am working now on a picture that I abandoned many years ago—just when I do not know—but the question of "when started" will come up some day and I shall be unable to answer. It's sort of all one long process with me that changes in manner and intent, as I change myself, and I can't date these sequences, anymore than one dates grey hair—it kind of creeps up on you.*

*Now the motive—subjectwise—back of picture derived from that Negro Spiritual that goes "It ain't the Preacher, but it's me, Oh Lord, knocking at the gates of Heaven. It ain't the Preacher but it's me, Oh Lord—me, Oh Lord, me, Oh Lord," etc. Do you know it? You probably would if I could whistle it for you. I tried to paint the striving upward from the broad base (which I may have overdone) as an anchor or weight to the earth. All this, of course, just a subject motive for a movement of masses that I thought might interest me in paint and work integrally.*

Franklin Watkins (1958)

Some information from Mr. Watkins' letter of July 12, 1958, quoted above, was paraphrased in a study sheet prepared in 1963 for the use of students in front of the painting. Attention was called to the purposeful distortion and to the exaggeration of masses. When this sheet was submitted to Mr. Watkins for his approval, he replied on July 23, 1963:

*It was an illustration of a Religious Experience—self-induced as was, no doubt, St. Paul's. I painted the picture a life-time ago, but, if I remember correctly, the massive lower quarters were a device to add lift towards the top—AND my model did wear extremely baggy pants. I did not take great liberty in my exaggerations.*

Franklin Watkins (1963)

In a letter to Andrew Ritchie about this painting, Watkins wrote, "I heard a fine Negro choir at the Barnes Foundation sing. . . . It echoed in my head and the picture was the result."[1] For Ben Wolf he described his model: "A Negro just arrived from the South. . . . He was happy just being in the studio. . . . His hands were crusted with thick calluses produced by a lifetime of hard work."[2]

Preparatory drawings for "Negro Spiritual" are reproduced as #207.

Exhibited: "Thirty-first Annual International Exhibition of Paintings," Carnegie Institute of Technology, Pittsburgh, Oct. 19–Dec. 10, 1933, #54, pl. 42 (as "Illustration to a Negro Spiritual"); "Century of Progress," Art Institute of Chicago, June 1–Nov. 1, 1934, #712; "Franklin Watkins, First New England Exhibition," Smith College Museum of Art, Northampton, Mass., Apr. 11–25, 1938, #8; "Golden Gate International Exposition, Contemporary Art," San Francisco, Feb. 18–Oct. 29, 1939, #395 (awarded second prize in the unrestricted division open all European and American contemporary paintings); "Contemporary Painting in the United States," shown Jan.–Mar. 1939 in Ottawa, Toronto, Montreal, #52; "Paintings by Arthur B. Carles and Franklin C. Watkins," Philadelphia Museum of Art, Feb. 17–Mar. 17, 1946, #39; "American Painting from the Eighteenth Century to the Present Day," Tate Gallery, London, June–July 1946, #214; "Franklin C. Watkins," Museum of Modern Art, New York, Mar. 21–June 11, 1950, #8, repro. p. 18; "A Collector's Choice," a traveling exhibition selected by William H. Lane and circulated by the American Federation of Arts between Oct. 15, 1957, and May 22, 1958, to Carbondale (Ill.), New York (N.Y.), Savannah and Atlanta (Ga.), and Nashville (Tenn.); "Twenty-five Years of American Painting 1933–1958," a traveling exhibition of seventy-five paintings by twenty-five artists, organized by the United States Information Agency, shown from Oct. 31, 1959, through Sept. 15, 1960, in Naples, Florence, Rome, Berlin, Milan, Darmstadt, Gothenburg, and York, #79; "Franklin C. Watkins Retrospective Exhibition," Philadelphia Museum of Art, Mar. 6–Apr. 5, 1964, #6, repro.; included in five groups of paintings lent by Randolph-Macon Woman's College: loan exhibitions to Richmond

1. Quoted from Ritchie, *Franklin C. Watkins*, p. 8.

2. Wolf, *Franklin C. Watkins*, p. 76. Quoted by permission of the author.

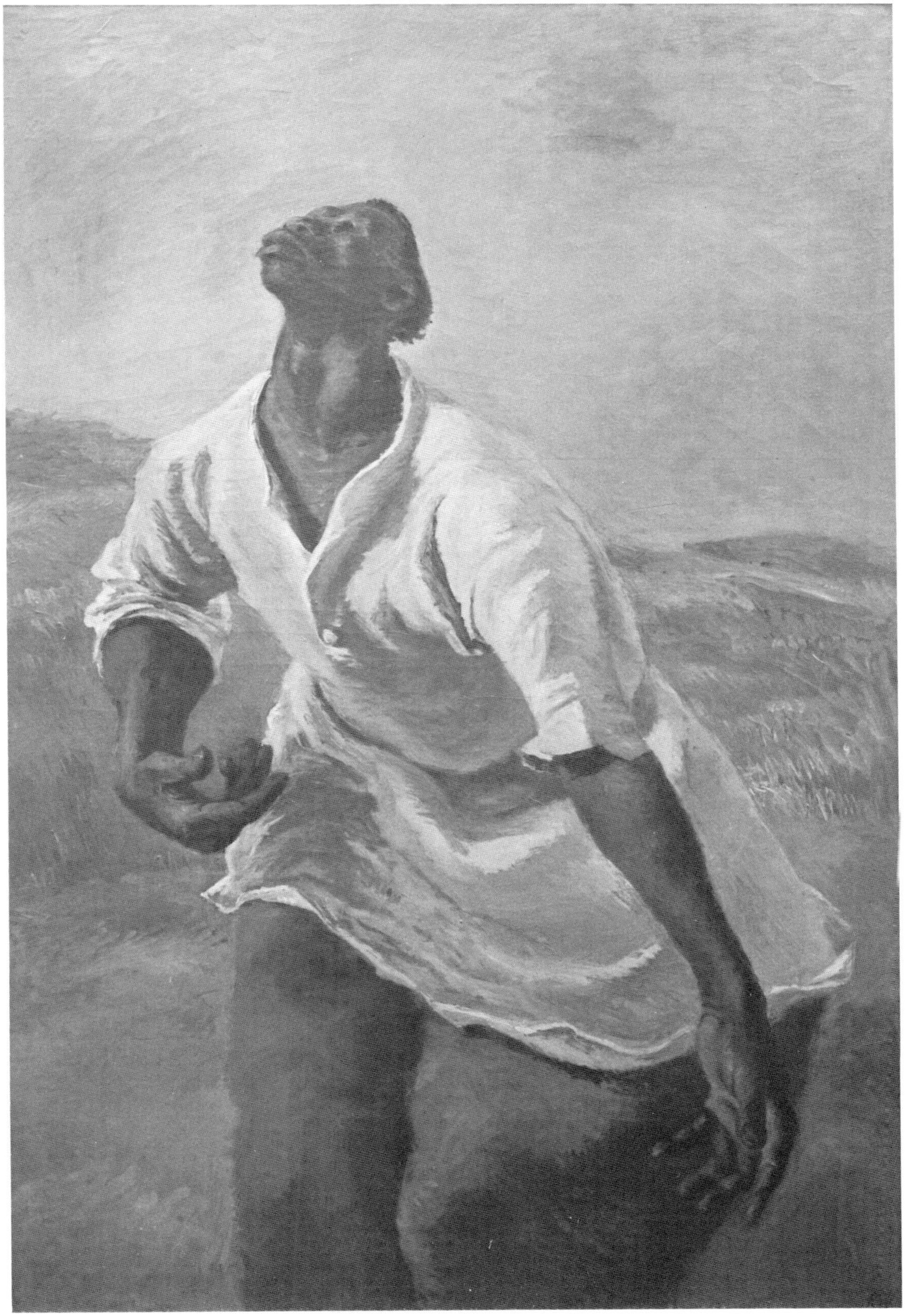

and to Roanoke, 1964; circulating exhibitions to Florida, 1965, and to six Mid-Atlantic states, 1966–67; and a loan exhibition to Winston-Salem, N.C., 1972. For galleries and dates see Appendix B.

Recorded: Catalogues of the exhibitions and Andrew Carnduff Ritchie, *Franklin C. Watkins* (Museum of Modern Art, New York, 1950), p. 18, repro.; *25 Anni Di Pittura Americana* (Rome, 1959), p. 42, repro.; *Modernt Amerikanskt Maleri* (Göteborg, 1959), #79, repro.; *Arts in Virginia* 2 (Spring 1962), p. 29, repro.; Ben Wolf, *Franklin C. Watkins* (Philadelphia, 1966), p. 76, #6, repro.

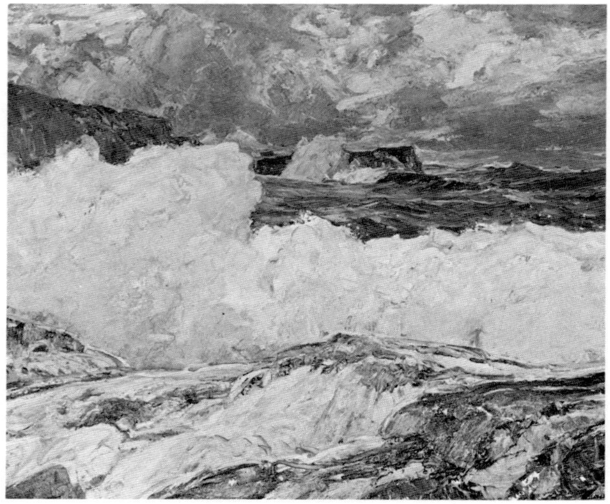

## FREDERICK JUDD WAUGH

1861–1940

180. KELP-COVERED ROCKS 1923

Oil: 22 × 26 in.; 55.8 × 66 cm.
Signed, lower right: Waugh
Purchased jointly by the College and the Art Association, 1924

This is not the Waugh painting that was originally bought. The late Herbert C. Lipscomb recalled that Louise Jordan Smith preferred this work to the first one and prevailed on the dealer to make the exchange. This canvas reflects the warmer colors that Waugh used after spending the fall and winter of 1921–22 in the Caribbean.

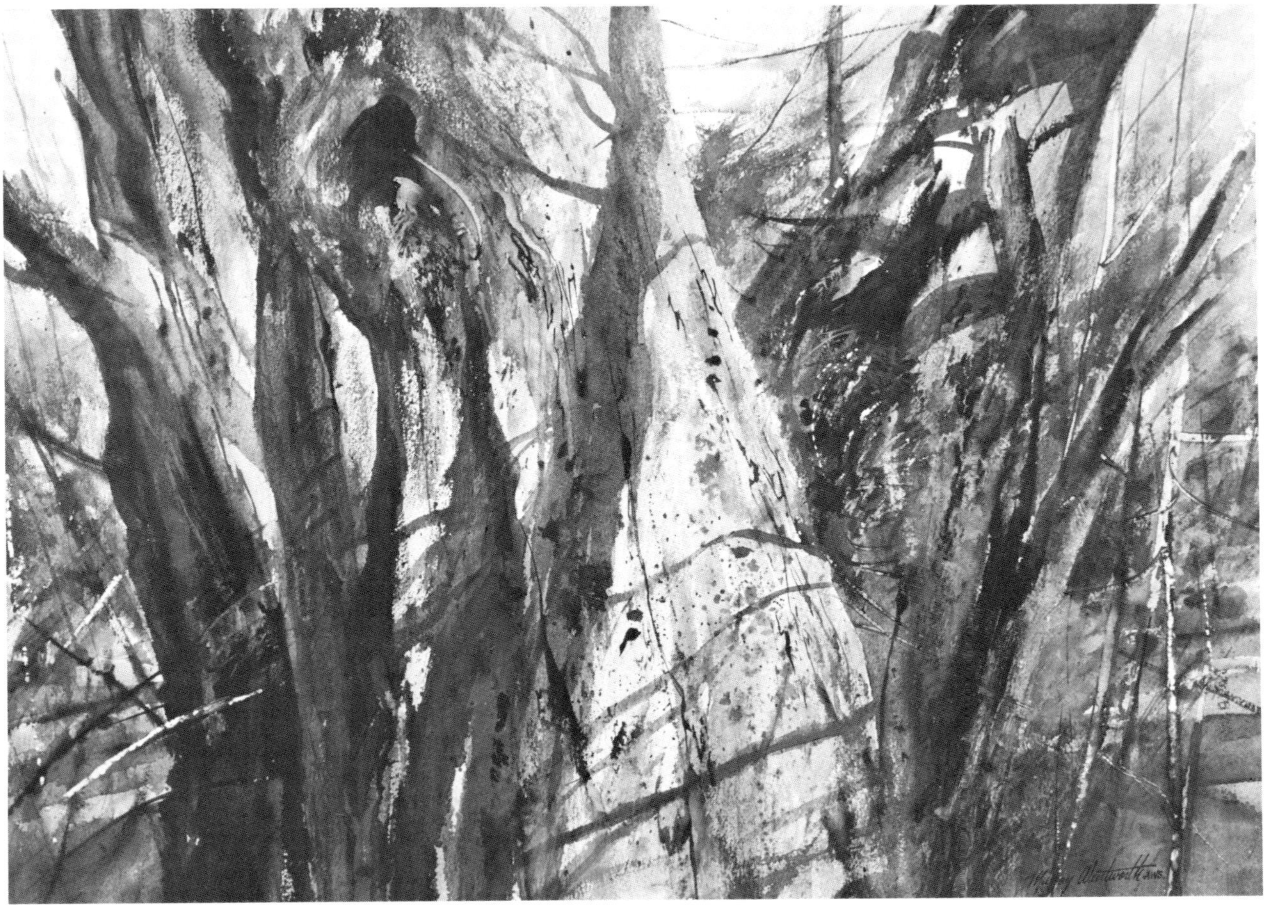

MURRAY WENTWORTH, A.N.A., A.W.S.
Born 1927

181. SHADOW PATTERNS 1965

Watercolor: 20½ × 28¾ in.; 52 × 73 cm.
Signed, lower right: Murray Wentworth AWS
Gift of the National Academy of Design
(Henry Ward Ranger Fund), 1967

*Painted in the wooded area of Southern Massachusetts near my studio, after observing the subject on the previous day. I became excited about the pattern of sunlight and shadows, the contrasts on the wood and the background, returned to the spot, prepared the composition at the same time of day, when shadows made the most interesting breakup of shapes. I usually work for two or three hours and return to the studio for final refinements and analysis of the work as a whole. I find this wooded subject matter about the most difficult, as it is so easy to lose sight of a value pattern. Most always work directly on location to capture the feeling of the moment, as in this painting.*

Murray Wentworth

Exhibited: "Traveling Exhibition of the American Watercolor Society," May 1965–June 1966, in Idaho, Iowa, Kentucky, Michigan, New York, Pennsylvania, S. Carolina, Texas, Virginia and Washington State.

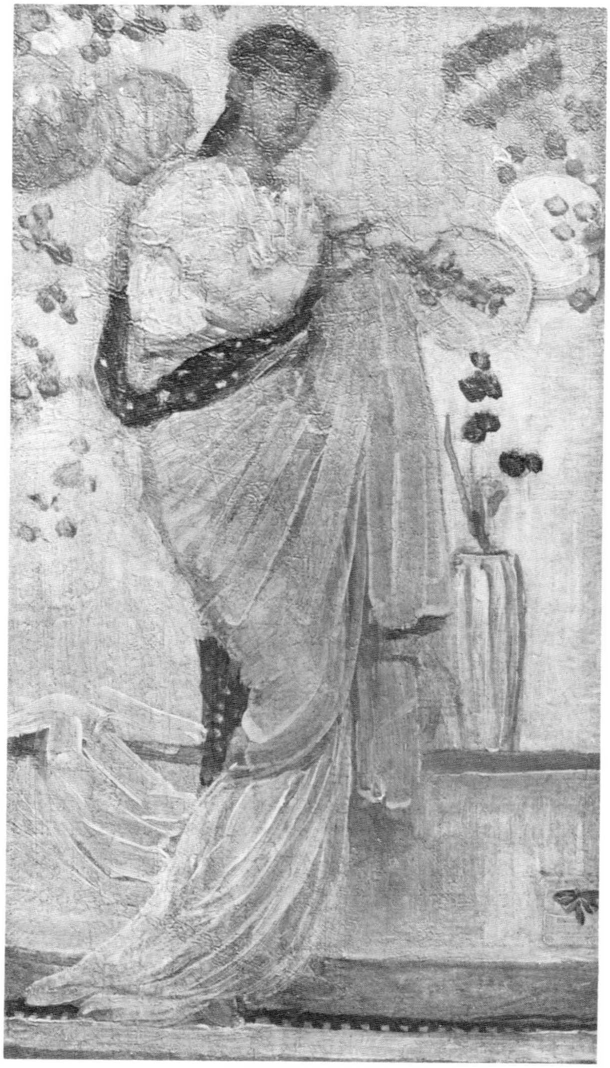

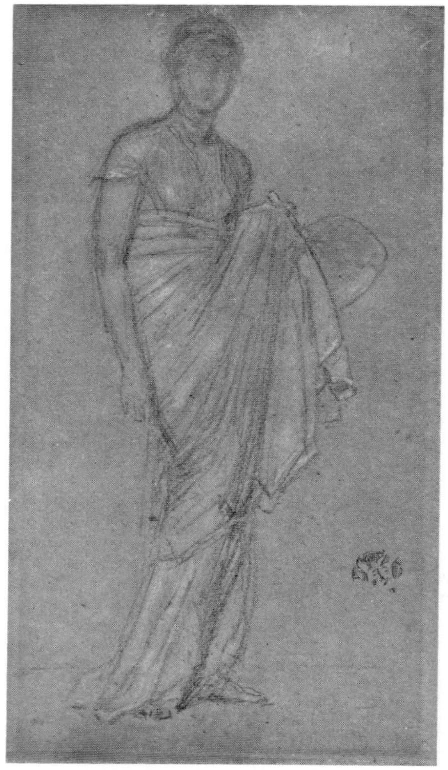

Figure 182a. "Tanagra," drawing by Whistler (10¾ × 6 in.; 27.3 × 15.2 cm.). Black crayon on brown paper, touched with blue, red, and purple. Reproduced courtesy of the University Art Collections of the University of Glasgow.

## JAMES McNEILL WHISTLER
1834–1903

### 182. TANAGRA About 1867–70

Oil: 12¼ × 6⅞ in.; 31.1 × 17.4 cm.
Signed, lower right, with the Whistler butterfly
Fine Arts Fund, 1953

When acquired, this painting bore only the descriptive title "Lady with a Japanese Fan." In 1960, A. McLaren Young, curator of Fine Art Collections at the University of Glasgow, Scotland, prepared the catalogue of the Whistler exhibition organized by the Arts Council of Great Britain and the English-Speaking Union of the

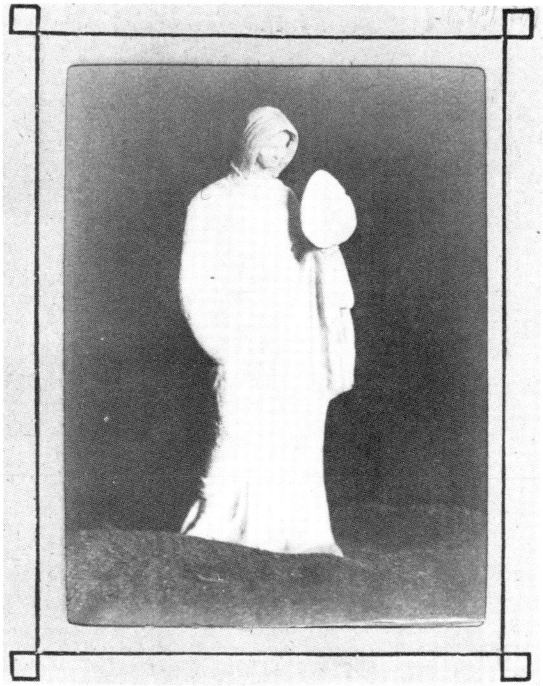

Figure 182b. Number 2 in Whistler's album of photographs of Greek terra cotta figurines from Tanagra. Reproduced courtesy of the University Art Collections of the University of Glasgow.

United States, incorporating in the catalogue the results of his study of the Whistler material at the University of Glasgow. Mr. Young related this painting to "Tanagra" (figure 182a), a crayon drawing made and also named by Whistler, and, further, to a photograph of a Greek terra cotta statuette in Whistler's album of photographs of Tanagra figurines. (See figure 182b.) In the exhibition catalogue Mr. Young listed the oil painting as "Tanagra." This is now the accepted name. He pointed out that Whistler's drawing has a rounded Japanese type of fan, although the effect seems still to be Greek. Mr. Young called our attention to a drawing by Whistler in Washington, D.C., that is related to both "Tanagras." It is a study made from a nude model with a Japanese vase and several fans. (See figure 182c.) In the oil, Whistler completed the transformation from Greek to Japanese by reclothing the figure and by using the pink and lavender tones of certain Japanese woodblock prints.

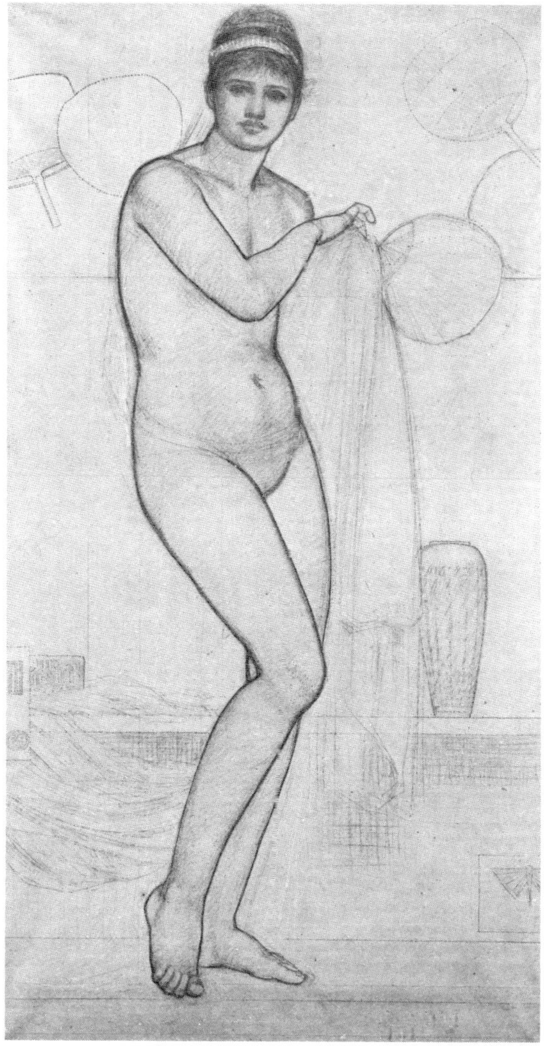

Figure 182c. "Drawing of a standing figure of a naked woman; a fan in her left hand," by Whistler. Reproduced courtesy of the Smithsonian Institution, Freer Gallery of Art, Washington, D.C.

## JAMES McNEILL WHISTLER (cont.)

Provenance: Collection of Robert Woods Bliss, Washington.

Exhibited: "James McNeill Whistler," The Arts Council Gallery, London, Sept. 1–24, 1960, and Knoedler Galleries, New York, Nov. 2–30, 1960, #22; included in four groups of paintings lent by Randolph-Macon Woman's College: loan exhibitions to Richmond and to Roanoke, 1964; circulating exhibitions to Florida, 1965; and to six Mid-Atlantic states, 1966–67 (for galleries and dates see Appendix B); "James McNeill Whistler," Art Institute of Chicago, Jan. 12–Feb. 25, 1968, and Munson-Williams-Proctor Institute, Utica, N.Y., Mar. 17–Apr. 28, 1968, #16; "The Classical Spirit in American Portraiture," Brown University, Feb. 6–29, 1976, #41, repro. p. 102.

Recorded: Catalogues of the exhibitions of 1960, 1968, and 1976, on pages noted above.

## WINSLOW WILLIAMS

Born 1917

183. Portrait of Dr. Herbert C. Lipscomb 1961

Oil: 50 × 40 in.; 127 × 101.6 cm.
Signed, lower left: Winslow Williams 1961
Gift of Dr. Lipscomb's students and friends, 1961

*Dr. Lipscomb's kindly and genial nature and his wide range of interests early established a fine relationship and provided many good conversations. He displayed much interest in the various stages of the portrait and his perceptive observations were most helpful as we went along. Upon completion, I felt I had not merely painted another portrait but had made a new friend as well.*

Winslow Williams (1963)

*Sitting for a portrait by Mr. Winslow Williams was a delightful and instructive experience. In periods of relaxation the artist, over a cup of tea, would support his theory of portraiture by citing passages from the lives of his favorite predecessors and by showing illustrations of their work. Or he would live over his happy days as a student in the School of Fine Arts at Yale University as evidenced by two of his treasured paintings depicting the excitement of the followers of the Blue on the day of the annual Harvard or Princeton game.*

Herbert C. Lipscomb (1962)

The earlier portrait of Dr. Lipscomb (1882–1973) is #19, painted by John Carroll in 1949.

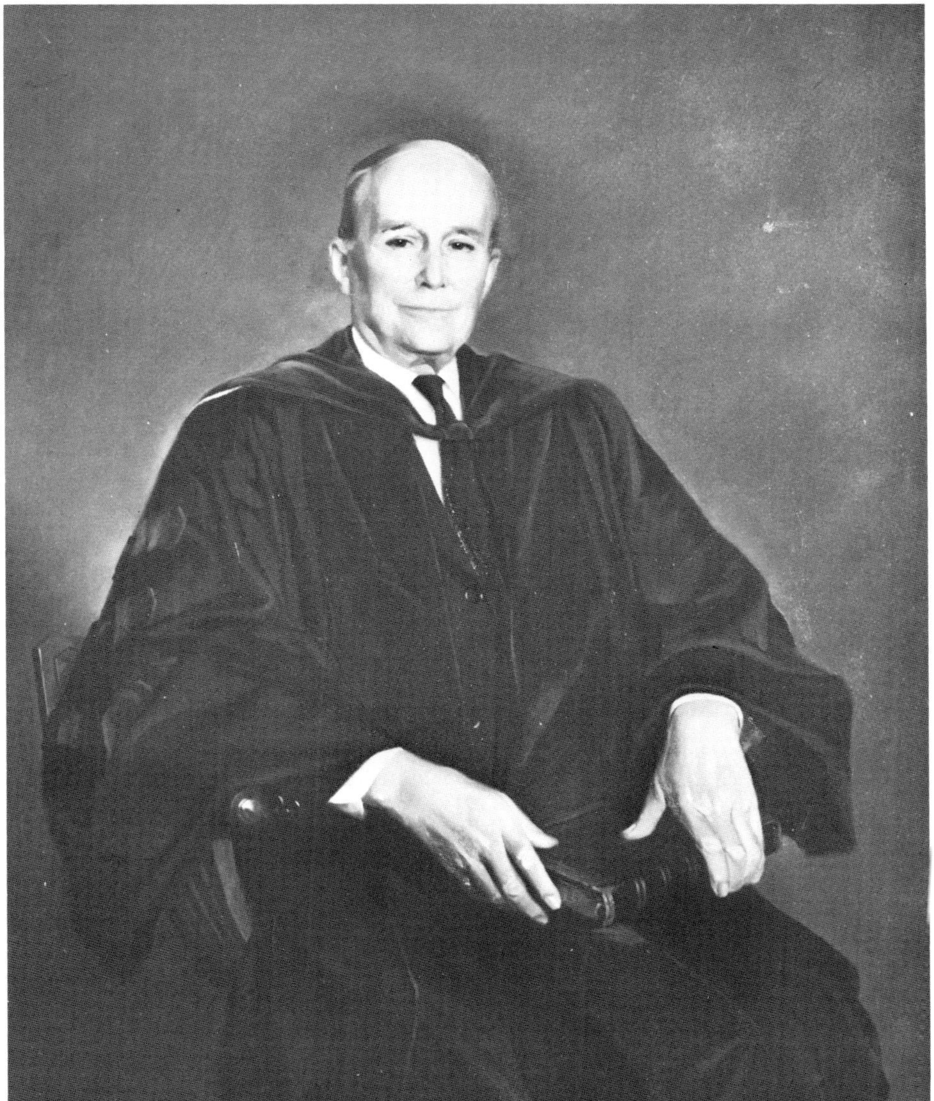

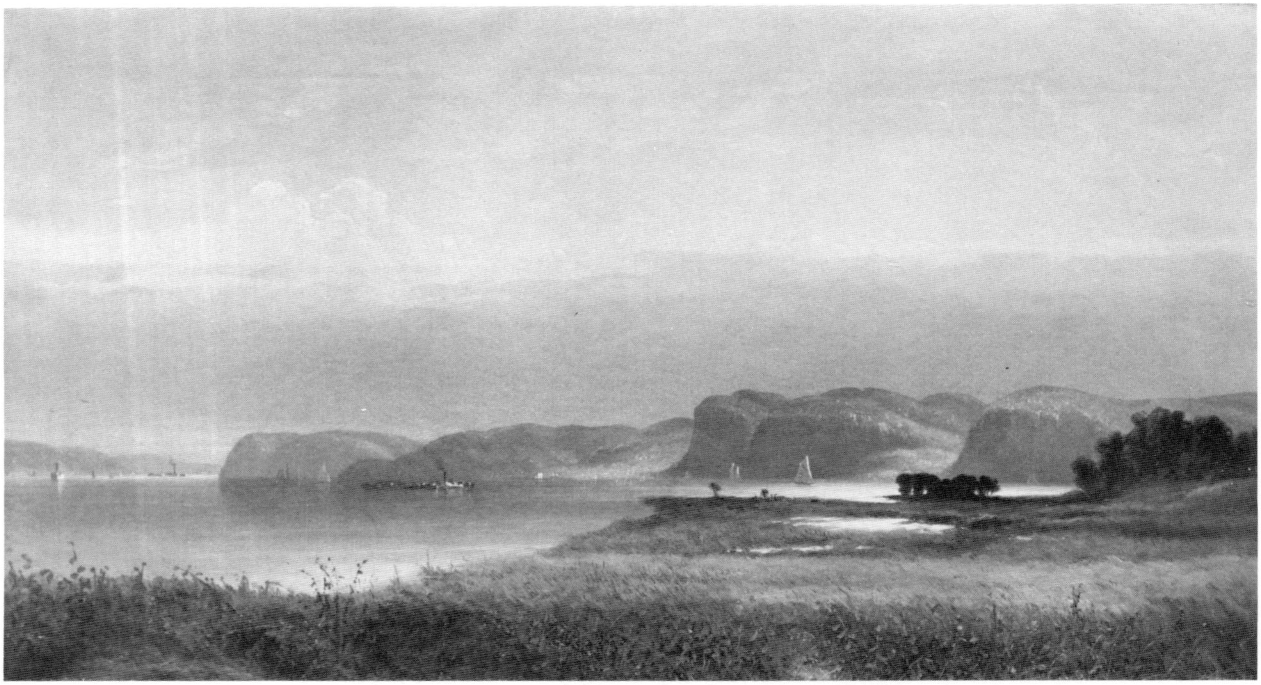

## JOHN WILLIAMSON
1826–85

184. AUTUMN, HUDSON RIVER 1871

Oil: 18 × 32¼ in.; 45.7 × 81.9 cm.
Signed and dated, lower right: JW 71
Signed and dated on the back, lower right:
Autumn, Hudson River By Jn° Williamson
N.Y. 1871
Gift of Thomas F. Torrey II, 1955

Exhibited: "The Randolph-Macon Woman's College Collection," Virginia Museum, Richmond, Sept. 11–Oct. 18, 1964, #54.

# Drawings

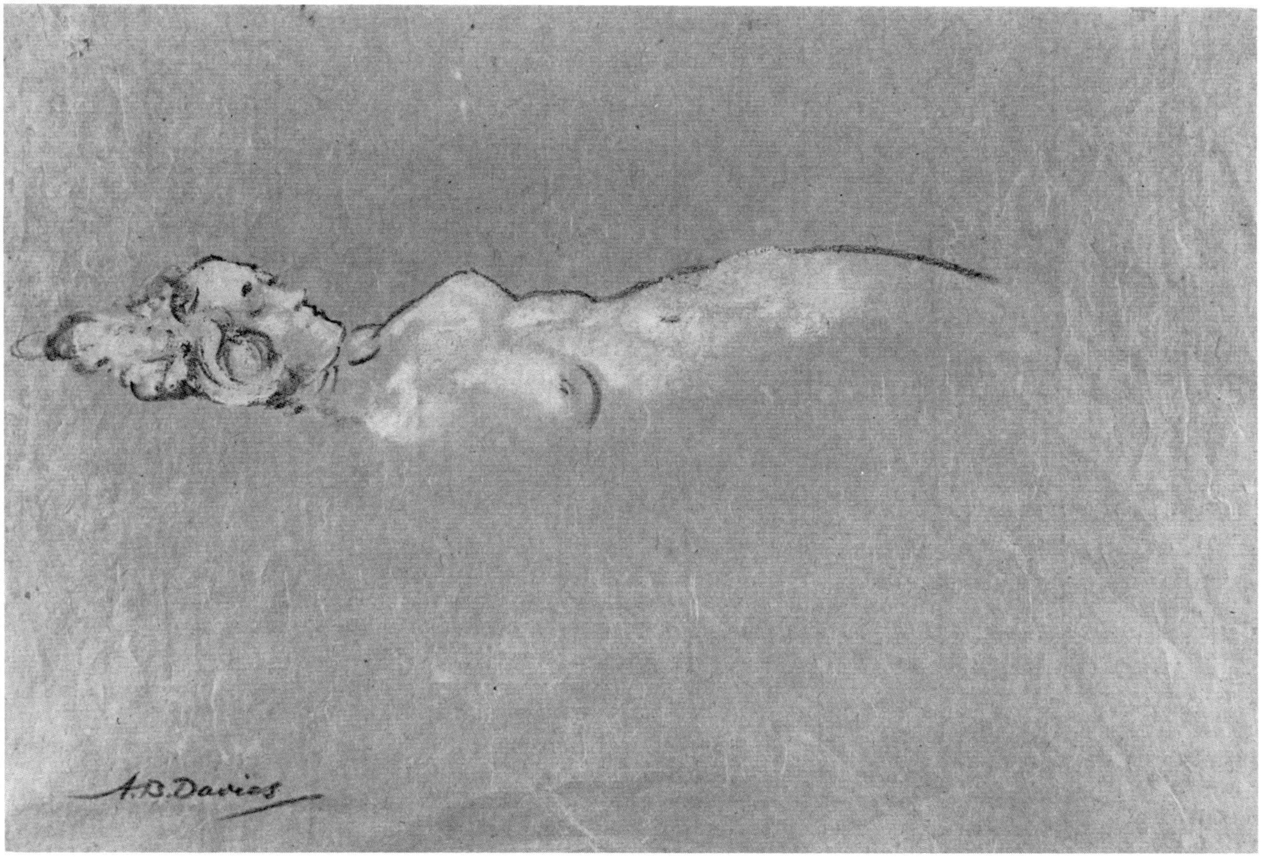

## ARTHUR B. DAVIES
1862–1928

The following seventeen drawings by Davies belonged to Lizzie P. Bliss. Except for the first, all were given by her sister-in-law, Mrs. C. N. Bliss, in 1949 or in 1953, when Mrs. Bliss had become Mrs. A. Conger Goodyear.

185. SLEEPING NUDE WOMAN About 1908

Formerly "Reclining Nude"
Pastel on gray paper: 9⅛ × 13⅝ in.; 23.1 × 34.6 cm.
Signed, lower left: A. B. Davies
Gift of C. N. Bliss through the Macbeth Gallery, 1942.

This may well be a preparatory sketch for figures in the oil painting "Sleep" (1908: 18 × 39⅞ in.; 45.7 × 101.2 cm.), given to the Worcester (Mass.) Art Museum by C. N. Bliss in 1941.

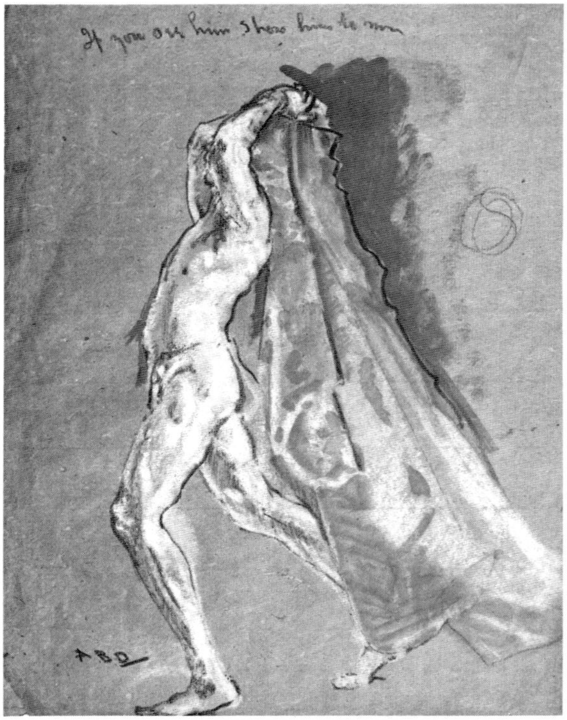

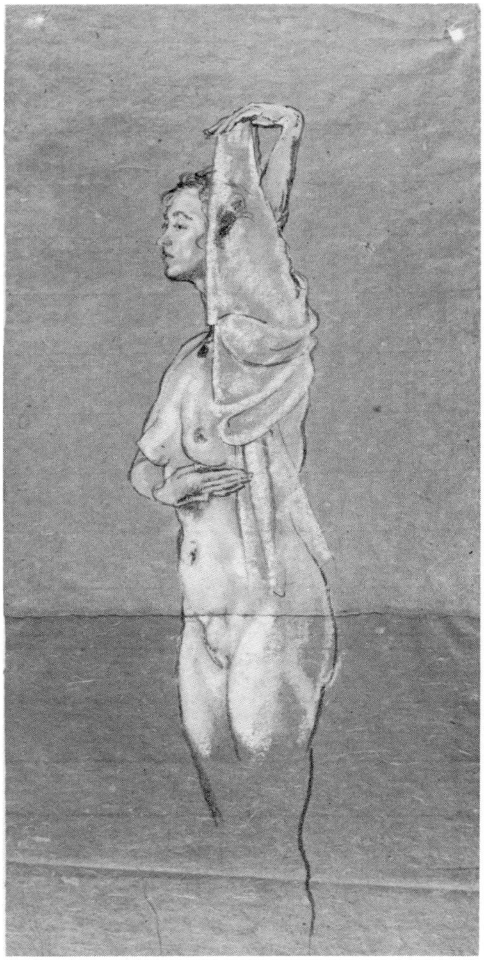

## ARTHUR B. DAVIES (cont.)

186. SKETCH FOR "TIPTOEING YOUTH" About 1910

Chalk and pastel; 14½ × 11 in.; 36.8 × 27.9 cm.
Signed, lower right: A.B.D.
Inscribed at the top: If you see him show him to me.

This drawing is for a figure at the far right in the oil painting "Tiptoeing Youth" (1910: 18 × 41 in.; 45.7 × 104.1 cm.) in the Whitney Museum of American Art, New York.

187. SKETCH FOR "DO REVERENCE" About 1912

Formerly "Nude with Drapery"
Pastel on two joined sheets of gray paper
Overall size: 22½ × 10¾ in.; 57.1 × 27.3 cm.
The upper sheet of light gray, with a height of 14½ inches, or 36.8 cm., overlaps the lower one, which is darker gray.
Unsigned

The oil painting "Do Reverence" (30 × 18 in.; 76.2 × 45.7 cm.), for which this drawing is a preparatory sketch, was #29 in the Davies exhibition of 1918 at the Macbeth Gallery. Its reproduction in the Macbeth Catalogue is accompanied by this unidentified statement: "Do Reverence—for I will breathe on thee with a favorable breeze, in love or on the bright-visaged sea." The oil, now owned by Herbert Baer Brill of New York, was painted in 1912, according to the list prepared by the artist's widow, Dr. Virginia M. Davies, and published in Cortissoz, p. 23 (see bibliography preceeding the catalogue of Davies paintings, #27–50). The painting was #19 in the Davies exhibition at Knoedler's in New York, March 11–April 15, 1975, and was reproduced in color on the cover of the catalogue.

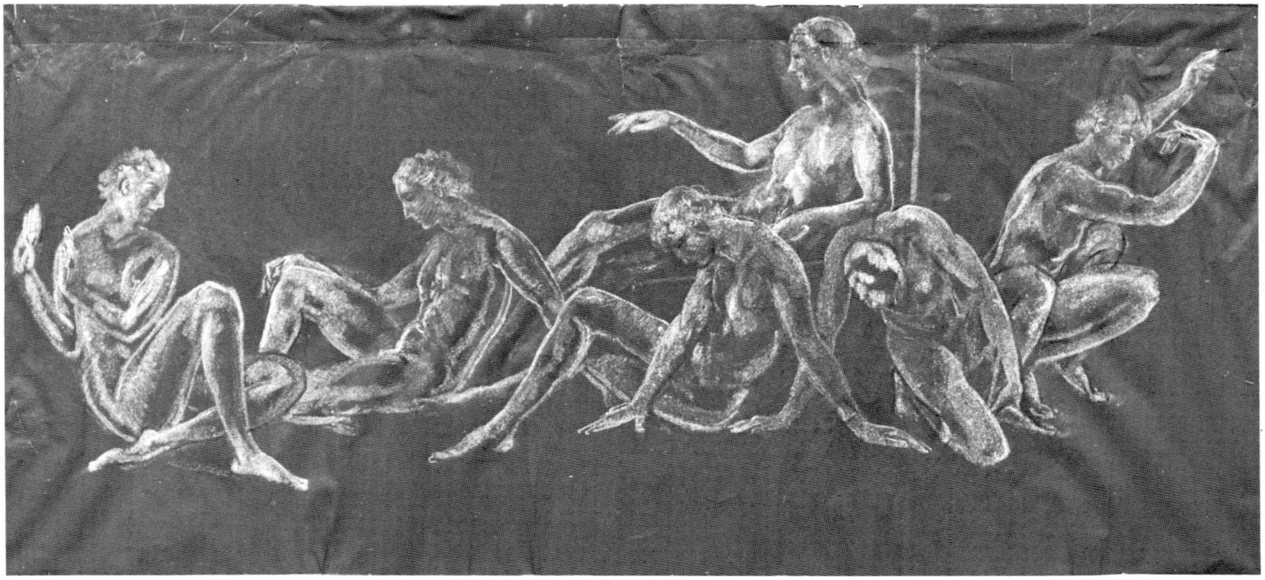

188. Constellations I

Six nude figures; stars in the sky
Chalk on black paper, damaged at upper corners
About 21¾ × 49¼ in.; 55.2 × 125.1 cm.
Signed, lower left: A. B. Davies

189. Constellations II

Six nude figures; no stars
Chalk on black paper with a strip added at the top, onto which the drawing extends
Overall size: about 21⅞ × 49 in.; 55.5 × 124.4 cm.
Unsigned

Exhibited: Brooklyn Museum, N.Y., June 1926, lent by "Miss L. P. Bliss"; 1930 Memorial Exhibition, #139, repro.

Recorded: Duncan Phillips, *Arthur B. Davies: Essays on the Man and His Art* (Washington, 1924), last repro.

190. Two Figures

Charcoal and chalk on green paper
11 × 9 in.; 27.9 × 22.8 cm.
Unsigned

191. Nude

Sketch in black and white (charcoal and chalk)
12 × 8 in.; 30.4 × 20.3 cm.
Unsigned

192. Head of a Woman

Chalk and crayon: 14 × 7½ in.; 35.5 × 19 cm.
Signed and dated: ABD 1920

193. Crouching Nude

Chalk and pastel: 8⅜ × 11⅝ in.; 21.2 × 29.5 cm.
Unsigned

194. Nudes

Pencil sketches: 16½ × 21½ in.; 41.9 × 54.6 cm.
Signed: Arthur B. Davies

195. Male Figures

Charcoal and chalk: 10 × 17 in.; 25.4 × 43.1 cm.
Signed: Arthur B. Davies

## ARTHUR B. DAVIES (cont.)

196, 197. Nude Dancing Figures

Two drawings framed together; seven nude females in each
Chalk on black paper
Each drawing: 22 × 42 in.; 55.8 × 106.6 cm.
Unsigned

198. Mars and Venus

Chalk on black paper, damaged at the top and extended at the bottom by a strip onto which the drawing spreads
Overall size about 23 × 45 in.; 58.4 × 114.3 cm.
Unsigned
Given in 1953

199, 200, 201. Floating Figures

Three drawings framed together with silver mat; blue, black, and white pastel on gray paper
Each drawing: 16⅞ × 11 in.; 42.8 × 27.9 cm.
All unsigned
Drawing on the right inscribed in two lines, lower right (if correctly read): "Putting us you / Round through House."
Given in 1953

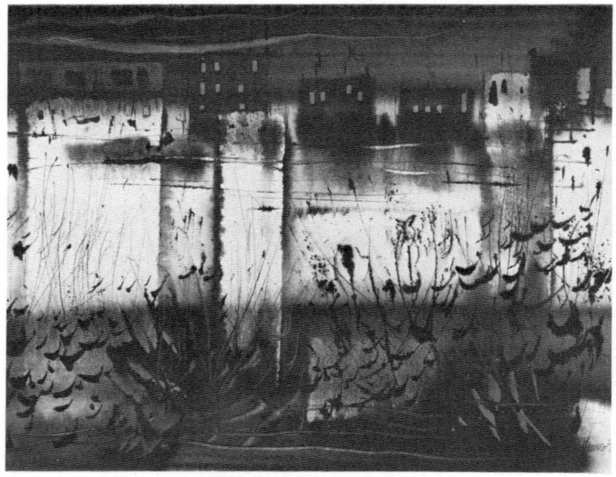

## FRED L. MESSERSMITH, A.W.S.

Born 1924

202. RIVER 1972

Wash drawing: 19 × 25½ in.; 48.2 × 64.7 cm.
Signed, lower right: Messersmith
Gift of alumnae of the Northern Delaware Chapter, 1968

*"River" is one of a series of works in ink that I have made since coming to Florida. I think one only has to look at Whistler's "Nocturne" paintings to see how I have been inspired to try and capture the quality of reflected lights upon the rivers of central Florida. Taking a cue from Whistler, I have used a limited and subdued palette and asked the viewer to let himself be drawn into the picture through a flattened perspective and use of receding tones.*

Fred L. Messersmith

Exhibited: See Appendix C.

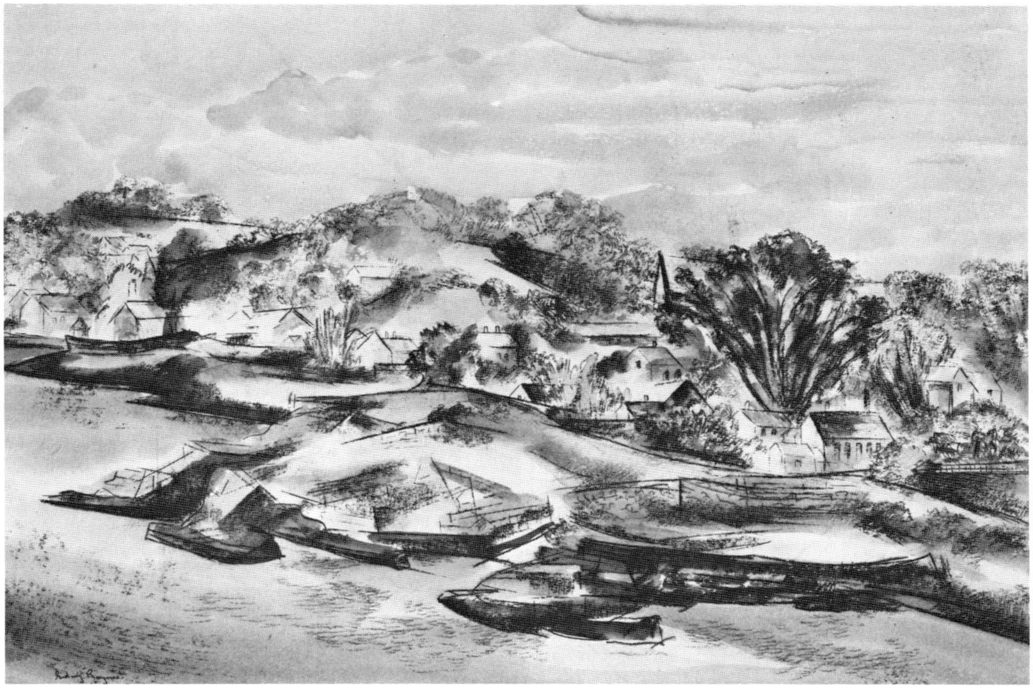

## SIDNEY RAYNES

Born 1907

203. LANDSCAPE, ROCKPORT

Wash drawing: 11½ × 16½ in.; 29.2 × 41.9 cm.
Signed, lower left: Sidney Raynes
Gift of the American Academy of Arts and Letters
(Childe Hassam Fund), 1953

*In this painting I have tried to capture the mood of all Cape Ann—the peace and simplicity of the town, the quarries—Pigeon Hill—as contrasted with the rugged coast and the feel of the rest of New England.*

Sidney Raynes (1960)

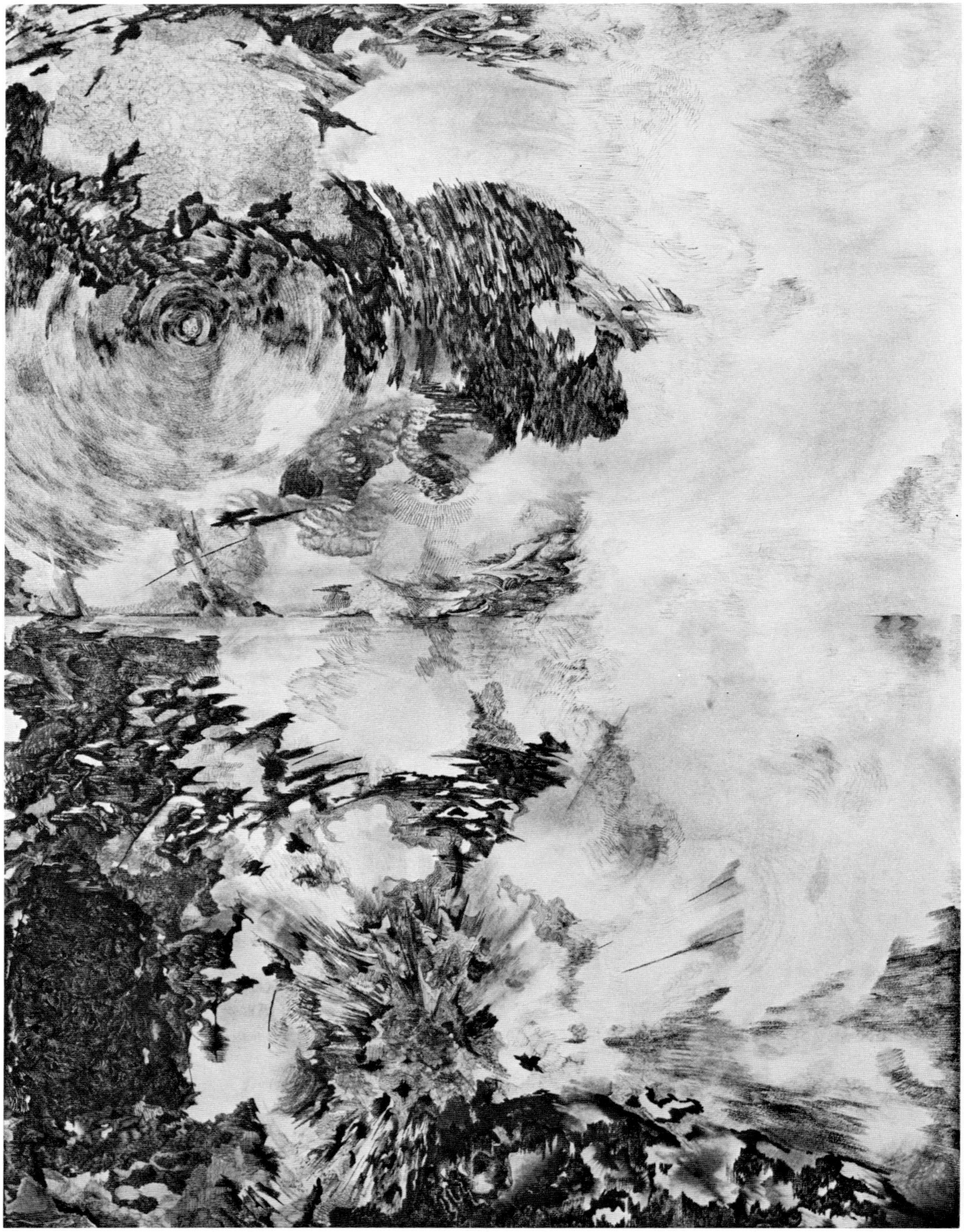

## DOROTHY RUDDICK

Born 1925

204. #9 1969

Ink: 40 × 30 in.; 101.6 × 76.2 cm.
Signed, center bottom: Dorothy Ruddick 1969
Fine Arts Fund, 1972

*The limits set by my medium, pen and ink, and by black and white, without color, have determined the course of my work itself. Two dangers would be delicacy (because of pen) and coldness (because of the absence of color). Therefore, my effort has always been to find as much strength and warmth as I can, with such beautifully limited means. As for the content, the less said, the better; I have an abiding prejudice against post facto explanations of that sort. I have always been preoccupied with outdoor space and "picture" space, sky (on the one hand) and white page (on the other), and this picture is merely a delineation of that preoccupation. I did not begin with a symbolic or literary notion of any kind.*

Dorothy Ruddick

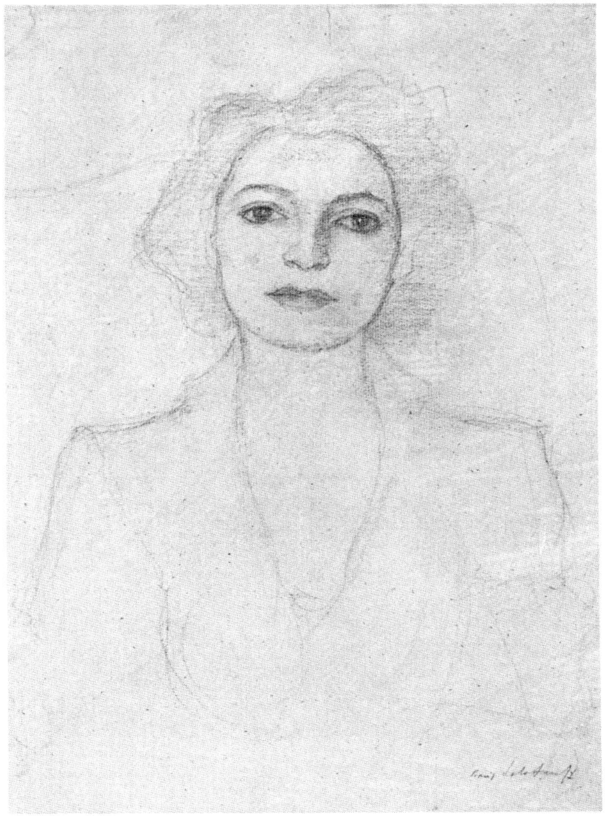

## BORIS SOLOTAREFF

1889–1966

205. Portrait Triste—Norma Chambers

Pencil on beige paper: 15½ × 11⅛ in.; 39.3 × 28.2 cm.
Signed, lower right: Boris Solotareff
Gift of Harriet Fitzgerald '26 in memory of Norma Chambers '27 (1906–52), in 1967

206. Portrait of Shirley

Pencil and crayon: 16½ × 15¼ in.; 141.9 × 38.7 cm.
Signed, lower right: B. Solotareff
Gift of Bess Barzansky (Mrs. Charles), 1966

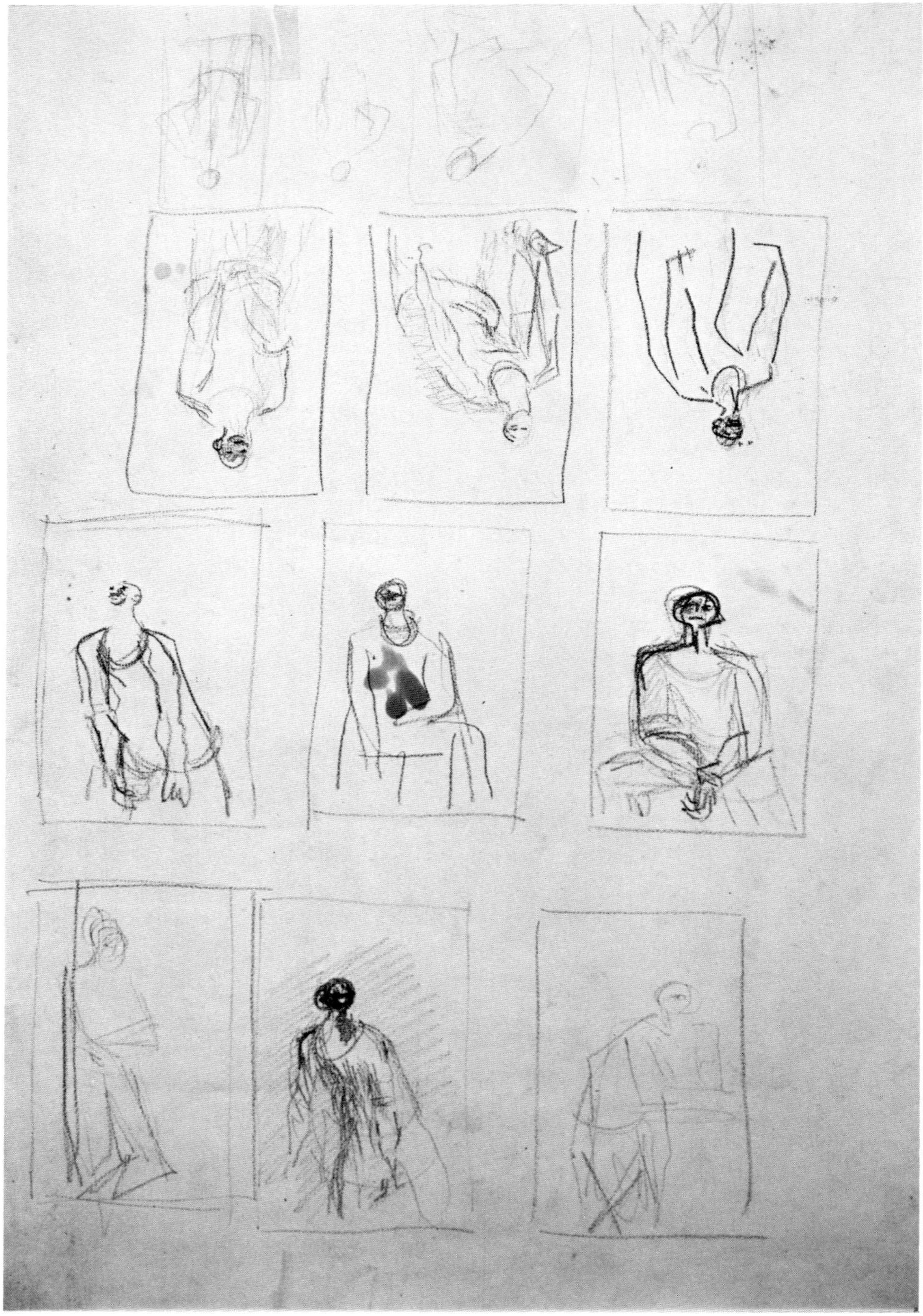

## FRANKLIN WATKINS
1894–1972

207. Sheet of Drawings for "Negro Spiritual"
About 1932

Pencil: 16¼ × 22½ in.; 41.2 × 57.1 cm.

Twelve vertical rectangular pencil-drawn frames, each containing one male figure, seated or standing, and one unframed male figure. On the other side of the sheet (not reproduced): three nude male figures looking and reaching up. The artist, many years later, suggested that these three figures "seem to apply to a painting called 'Crucifixion' owned by the Penna. Academy of the Fine Arts."[1]

Unsigned

Gift of the artist through Mrs. Stuart Saunders, 1967

See #179, the oil painting "Negro Spiritual."

1. Franklin Watkins to Mary F. Williams, January 29, 1970.

## JAMES McNEILL WHISTLER
1834–1903

208. Houses Along a Venetian Waterfront
About 1880–81

Pencil and crayon on dark brown paper: 7⅝ × 11⅜ in.; 19.3 × 28.8 cm.

Unsigned

Gift of Sterling Henkens through Robert G. McIntyre of the Macbeth Gallery, 1946

## ANDREW WYETH

Born 1917

209. ILLUSTRATED LETTER: TWO DRAWINGS OF A HEARSE 1956

a. HEARSE WITH WHEELS: 3 × 7½ in.; 7.6 × 19 cm. (drawing)

b. WINTER: 5¼ × 7½ in.; 13.3 × 19 cm. (drawing)

Ink (letter and drawings), dated July 16, 1956
Signed at the end: Andy
Gift of Mr. and Mrs. Andrew A. Smith
(Mary Virginia Barnes '35),
in honor of Dr. Herbert C. Lipscomb, 1968

The letter, addressed to Richard Layton from Cushing, Maine, refers to the two drawings thus:

*Went to a new island the other day called Louds. Walked up through a deep woods and found a half acre of clear ground filled with white grave stones with a stone wall and picket fence around it. Such a wood. On one corner of the lot was a small building and in it was this:*

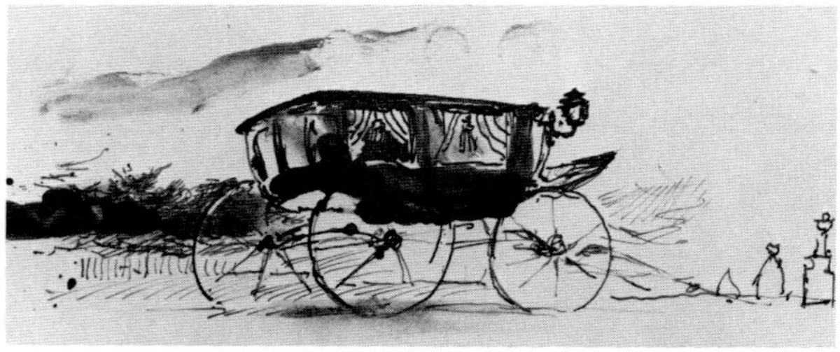

*It is interchangeable for both summer use or—*

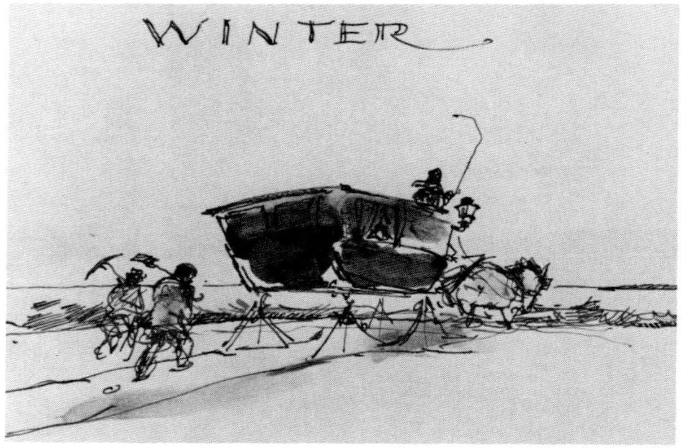


*There is a good chance I might be able to buy it, that is, if I can find a way to get it off the island.*[1]

1. Quoted with the writer's permission.

# Prints

## Major Gifts

1937 About thirty prints illustrating the history of the graphic arts, given by the Carnegie Corporation. See # 240 by Whistler.

1940 Twelve etchings and twelve lithographs by Childe Hassam, given by Mrs. Childe Hassam. See #233 by Hassam.

1949 Eighteen prints by Arthur B. Davies from the Collection of Lizzie P. Bliss, given by Mrs. C. N. Bliss. See # 211–229 by Davies.

1964 Twenty framed modern prints for a rental collection, given by Theodore J. H. Gusten, International Graphic Arts Society, in memory of Paul J. Sachs. See #235 by Koppelman.

1967 The Margaret H. Wright Collection of her etchings (with the cabinet made for them) and her collection of European and American prints, given by her son and his wife, Mr. and Mrs. James H. Wright (Mary C. Stigall '35). See #241 by Wright.

1973 Twenty contemporary prints, given by Mr. and Mrs. Samuel Dorsky. See #210 by Calder.

1976 Seven American and European prints, given by Francis R. Whitehouse, M.D. See #237 by Peterdi.

## Selected Prints

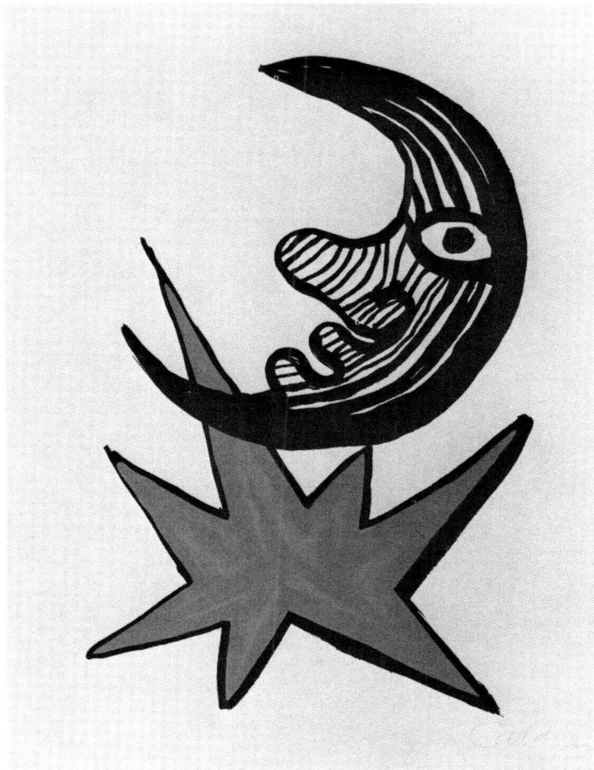

ALEXANDER CALDER
1898–1976

210. Black Moon 1971

Lithograph: 27½ × 21 in.; 69.8 × 53.3 cm. (the sheet)
Signed in pencil, left to right: IV/XXV Calder
Gift of Mr. and Mrs. Samuel Dorsky, 1973

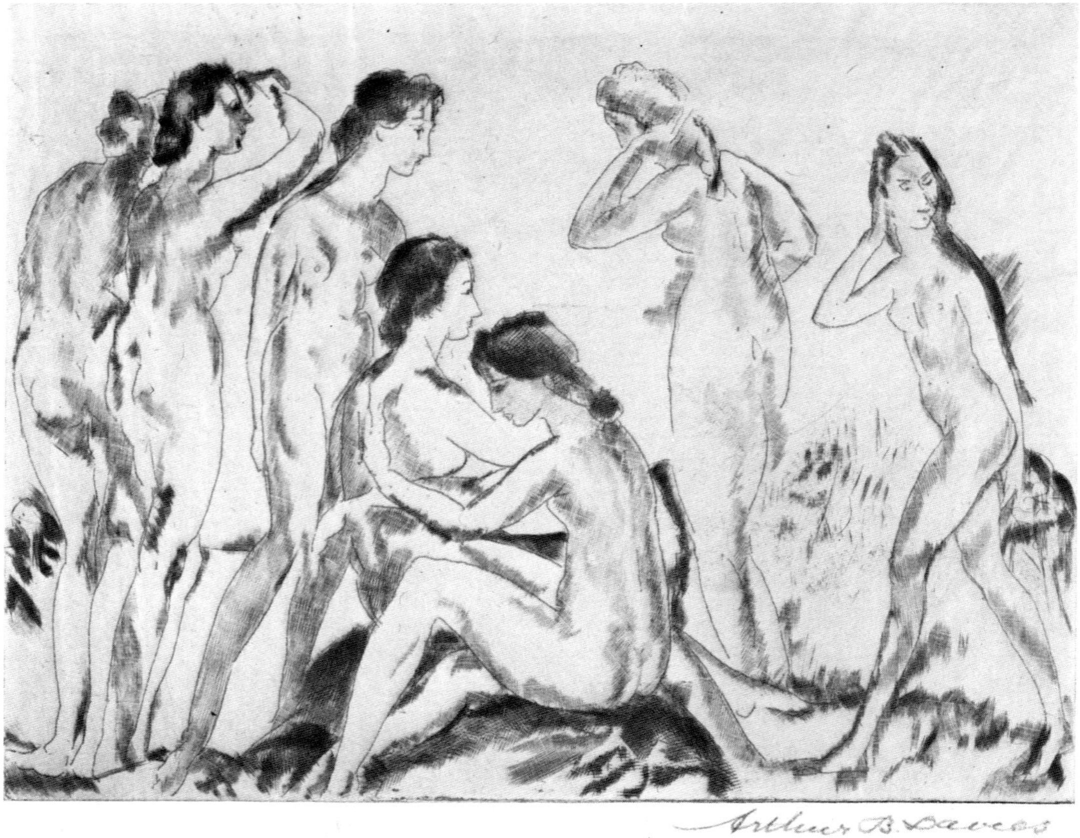

# ARTHUR B. DAVIES

1862–1928

211. PLEIADES 1919 (P172)[1]

Soft ground, aquatint & roulette, second of 5 states

6 × 7⅞ in.; 15.2 × 20 cm.

Signed in pencil, lower right: Arthur B. Davies

Gift of Mrs. C. N. Bliss, 1949

1. The letter *P* refers to Frederic Newlin Price, *The Etchings and Lithographs of Arthur B. Davies* (New York, 1929). The number is the one given by Price to this print. His numbers are used throughout the following entries, but his measurements (in which height and width are sometimes transposed) have been corrected.

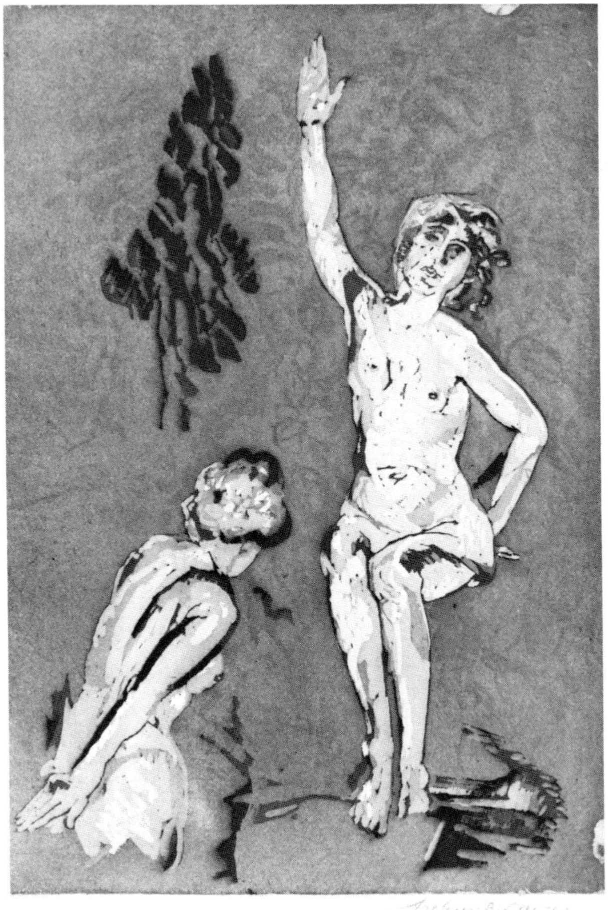

212. AMBER GARDEN 1920 (P50)

Aquatint, only state: 12 × 7⅞ in.; 30.4 × 20 cm.
Signed in pencil, lower right: Arthur B. Davies
Gift of Mrs. C. N. Bliss, 1949

The watercolor by Davies, #48, has the same design, only reversed.

213. THE TEMPLE (ANTIQUE WORKSHOP) 1922 (P12)

Aquatint, only state: 11⅞ × 7⅞ in.; 30.1 × 20 cm.
Signed in pencil, lower left: Arthur B. Davies
Gift of Mrs. C. N. Bliss, 1949

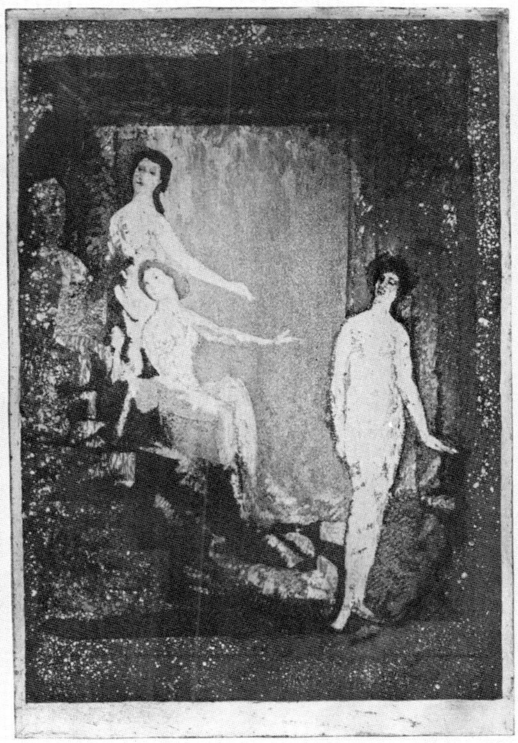

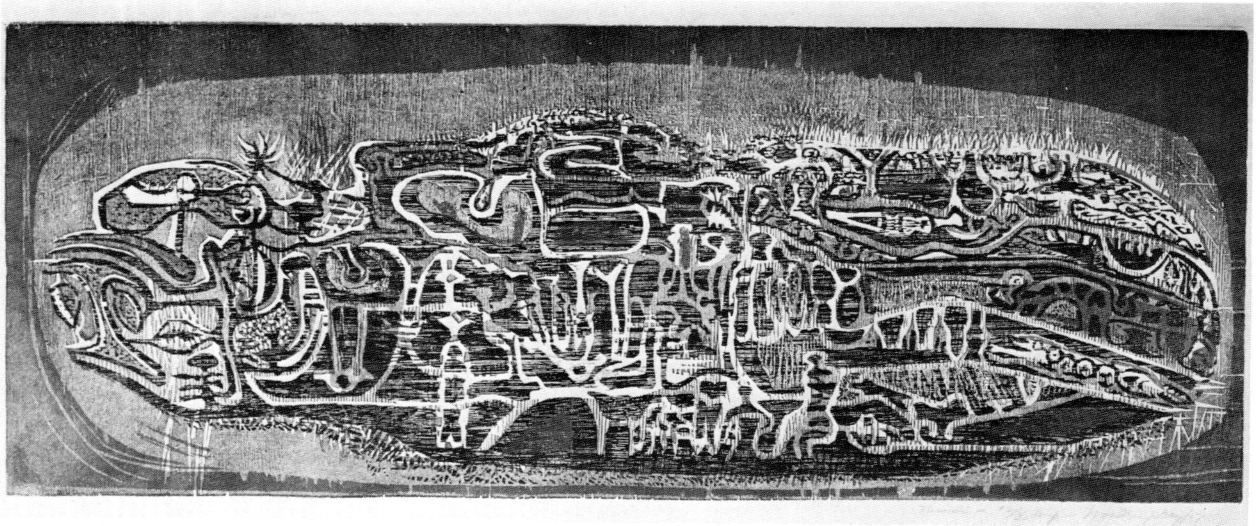

## ARTHUR B. DAVIES

All of the following prints by Arthur B. Davies (for which the identifying numbers assigned to them by Frederic Newlin Price are also listed) were given in 1949 by Mrs. C. N. Bliss, except "Toil of Three" (#228), which was given by Robert G. McIntyre in 1949.

214. Iris (P3)
215. The Brothers (P10)
216. Potentia (P16)
217. Sisters (P19)
218. Nocturne (P20)
219. Mirror of Illusion (P29)
220. Kingdom of the Sun (P42)
221. By the Caliban (P45)
222. By the Sea (P46)
223. Antique Mirror (P52)
224. Bacchantes (P66)
225. Lunette (P129)
226. Diane (P155)
227. Ecstasy (P165)
228. Toil of Three (P169)
229. Baptism (P201)

## WÖRDEN DAY '34

230. TUMULI 1951

Color woodcut: 8⅝ × 22⅛ in.; 21.9 × 56.2 cm.
Signed and dated in pencil, lower right:
Tumuli—12/30 Imp—Wörden Day / 51
Purchased 1956

*This print I did in Wyoming. It was inspired by images peculiar to the west—the Indian burial mounds called "tumuli" and wood patterned by termite feeding trails. One of the two main blocks is walnut, the other mahogany.*

Wörden Day

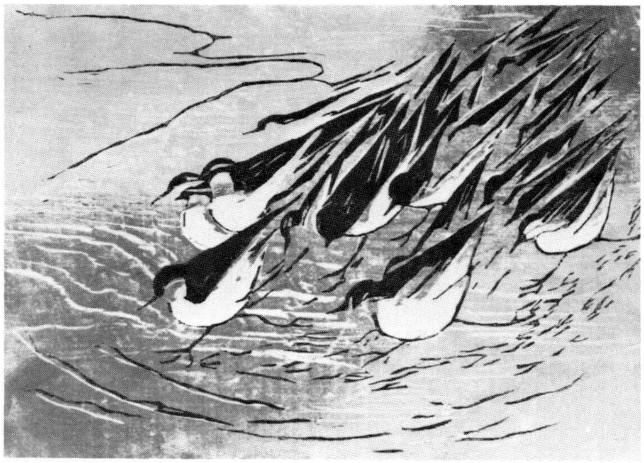

## EDYTHE FERRIS

Born 1897

231. Run, Run 1958

Color woodcut: 15 × 21 in.; 38.1 × 53.3 cm.
Signed and dated in pencil, from extreme left to extreme right: Run, Run 27/35 1958 Edythe Ferris

Purchased from a solo exhibition at the College, October 1–26, 1961.

*"Run, Run" comes from a vacation visit to Ocean City, N.J., in 1956. The plovers were so swift as they ran down the sand, always in a body. I have learned from them to make slim and hard pattern forms of lines in action. These give a vitality that detailed sketches lack. The freedom of motion of birds fascinates me. Plovers move as a group, always down-beach seeking, seeking, then the sudden burst into flight and individual freedom. Drawings made at the zoo never turn out; basic patterns of action are destroyed by confinement.*

Edythe Ferris

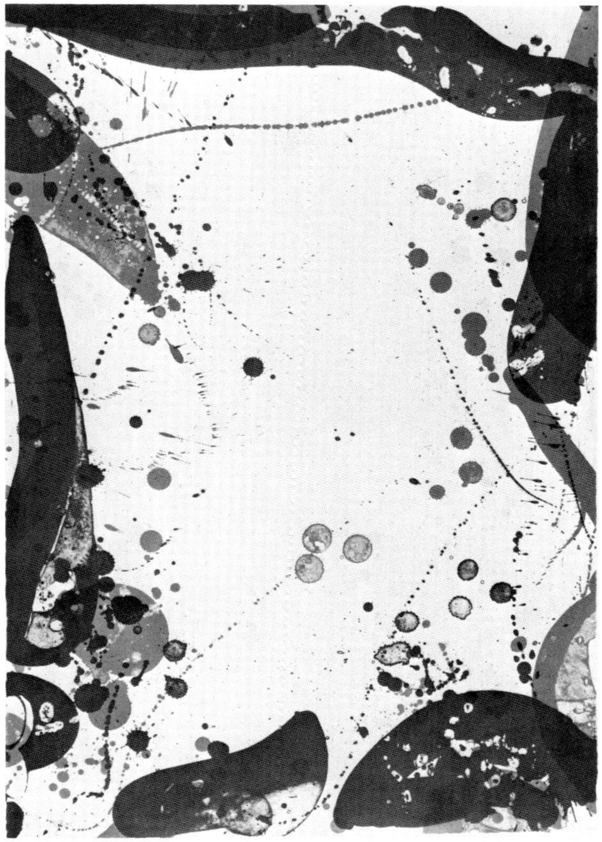

## SAM FRANCIS

Born 1923

232. Untitled 1967

Lithograph: 28 × 20 in.; 71.1 × 50.8 cm.
Signed in pencil, left to center: 50/50 Sam Francis
Lower right corner: the chop of the San Francisco Museum of Art (the Women's Board commissioned this print) and the chop of the printer, Joe Funk of Los Angeles.
Gift of Suzanne Foley '55, in honor of Mary F. Williams, 1973

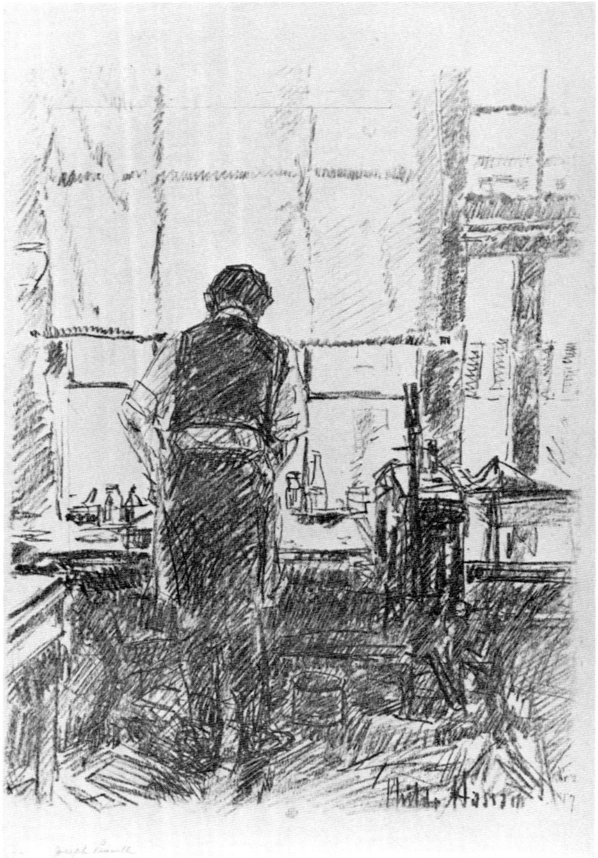

## CHILDE HASSAM

1859–1935

233. PORTRAIT OF JOSEPH PENNELL 1918 (K31) (G3)[1]

Lithograph: 15⅜ × 12⅛ in.; 39 × 30.8 cm. (the design)
Signed in pencil, lower left: Joseph Pennell; at center in pencil: cypher
Signed and dated on the plate, lower right: Childe Hassam Nov. 2, 1917
Gift of Mrs. Childe Hassam, 1940

1. The letter K indicates the number of this print in Kleeman Galleries, *The Lithographic Work of Childe Hassam* (New York, 1934). The letter G indicates the number of this print in Fuller Griffith, *The Lithographs of Childe Hassam*, Smithsonian Institution, United States National Museum, Bulletin 232 (Washington, 1962).

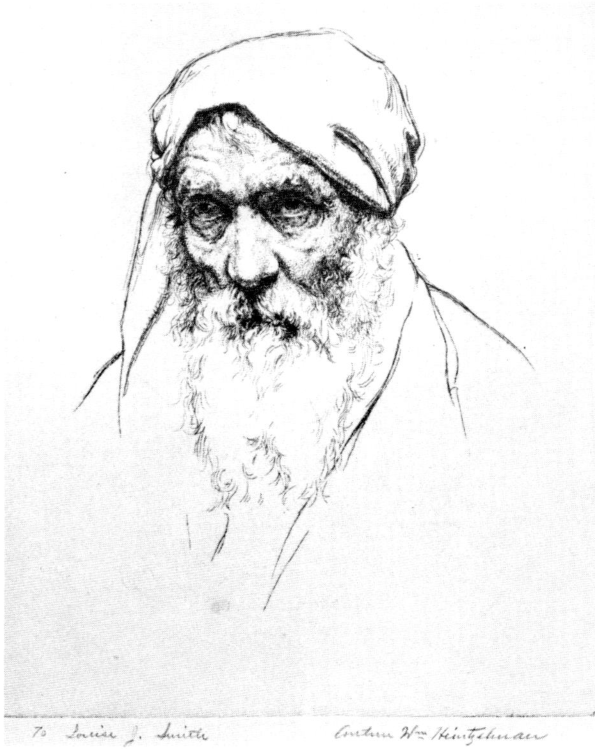

## ARTHUR WILLIAM HEINTZELMAN

1890–1965

234. PORTRAIT OF AN OLD MAN

Etching: 6 × 4⅞ in.; 15.2 × 12.3 cm.
Signed in pencil, left to right: To Louise J. Smith Arthur Wm. Heintzelman
Gift of the artist, about 1922, to Louise Jordan Smith, who gave it to the College

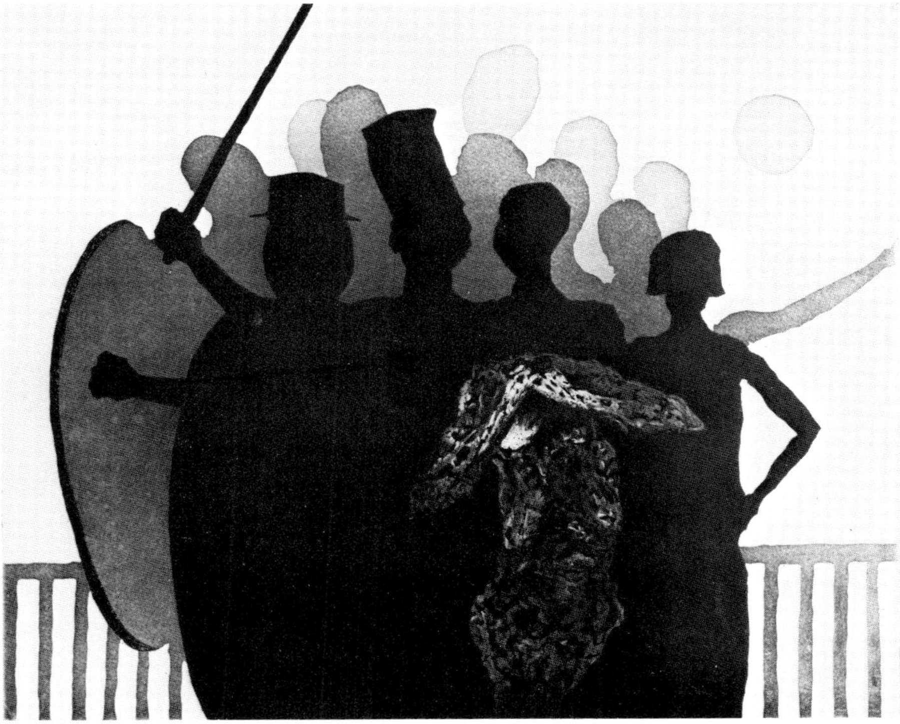

## CHAIM KOPPELMAN

Born 1920

235. ON MEETING BEAUTY 1958

Etching: 14½ × 18 in.; 36.8 × 45.7 cm.
Signed and dated in pencil, left to right: 93/200 On Meeting Beauty II Chaim Koppelman '58
Gift of the International Graphic Arts Society, 1964

*In this print I tried to express how people met the most beautiful way of seeing the world that I know, Aesthetic Realism, the philosophy founded and still taught by the American poet Eli Siegel. On meeting great beauty persons have been jealous, angry, grateful, glad, uncaring, possessive, deeply stirred, gushing, and more. All these responses to beauty have been mine and I wanted to compose them in one work, the good and the bad.*

Chaim Koppelman

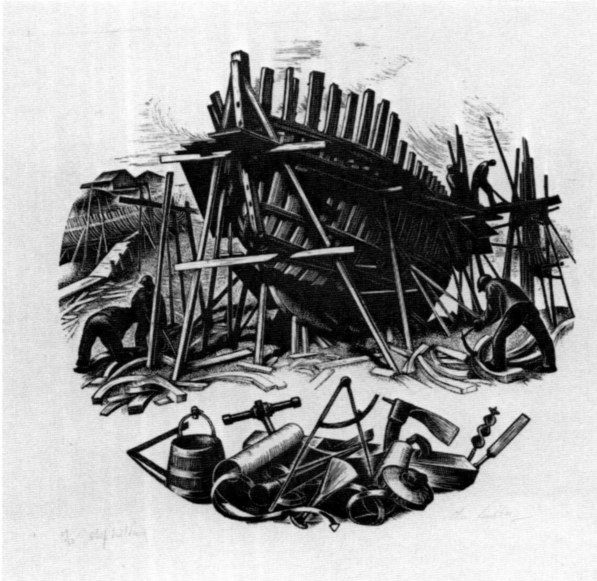

## CLARE LEIGHTON

Born 1901

236. Ship Building  Late 1940s

Wood engraving: 9½ inches round; 24.1 cm. round (design)
Signed in pencil, left: 24/50 Ship building
right: Clare Leighton
Gift of Mrs. Albert Coates (Gladys Hall '24), 1967

*This wood engraving (not wood cut) was designed and engraved by me for Josiah Wedgwood as one of twelve subjects for Wedgwood plates showing New England Industries such as Whaling, Maple Sugaring, Ice Cutting, and Quarrying Marble. I had difficulty finding authentic material for Ship Building, one of my favorites. I found a lot about the tools for wooden ships in Ipswich, Mass., and a great richness of material in the Mariners Museum, Newport News, Va. The set of plates, produced and marketed in 1954, is no longer available, but I still had the pleasure of printing (with Wedgwood's permission) a limited edition of my wood engravings.*

Clare Leighton

## GABOR PETERDI

Born 1915

237. Rolling Sea 1964

Etching: 16½ × 23¾ in.; 41.9 × 60.3 cm.
Signed and dated, extreme left to extreme right:
60–100 Rolling Sea Peterdi 64
Gift of Francis R. Whitehouse, M.D., 1976

*"Rolling Sea" is part of a print-and-painting cycle I am still working on. In all my work I am moved by the various aspects of nature. Obviously, my prints are not primarily descriptive. I am always hoping that I can succeed in translating a personal and subjective experience into a more universal, symbolic statement. "Rolling Sea" is force generated by wind clashing against the interruptions of rocks.*

Peterdi

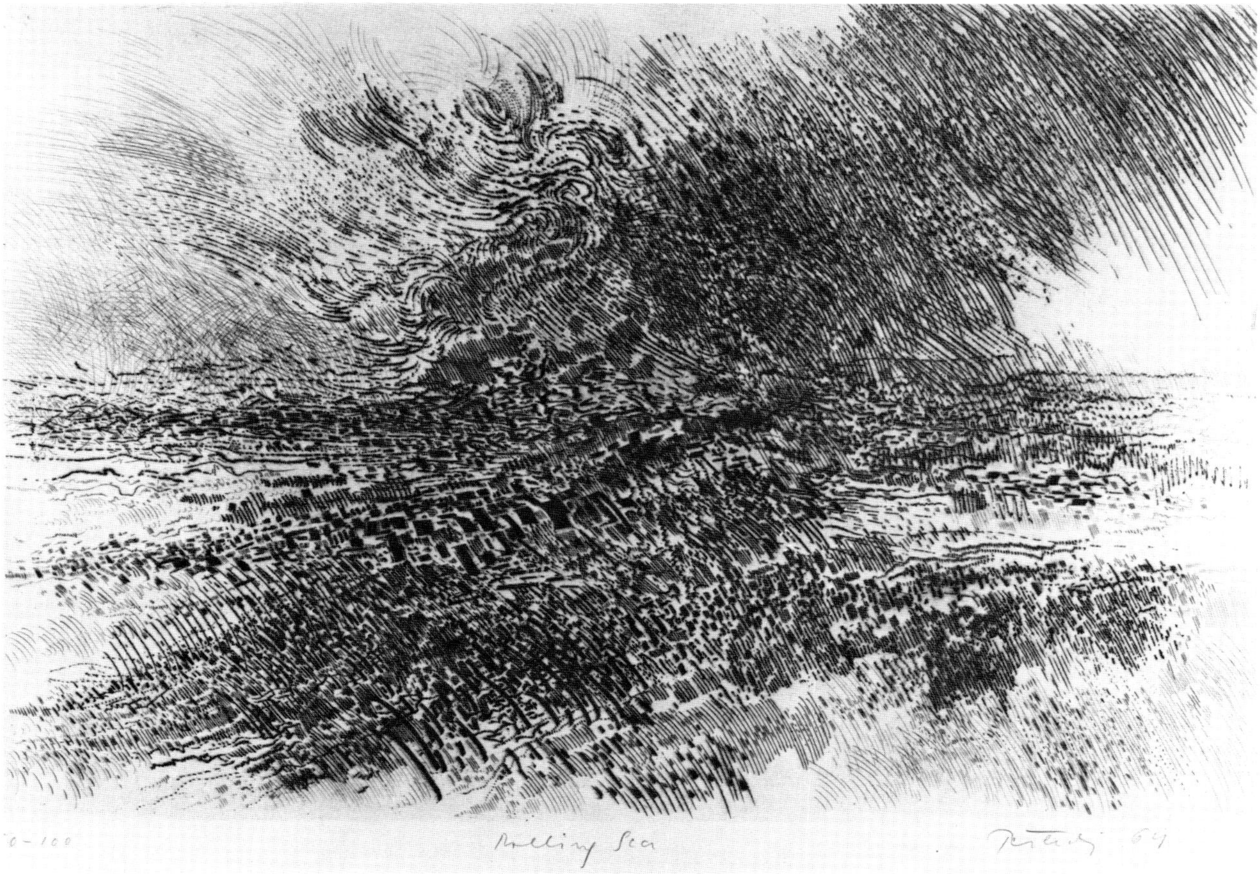
Rolling Sea

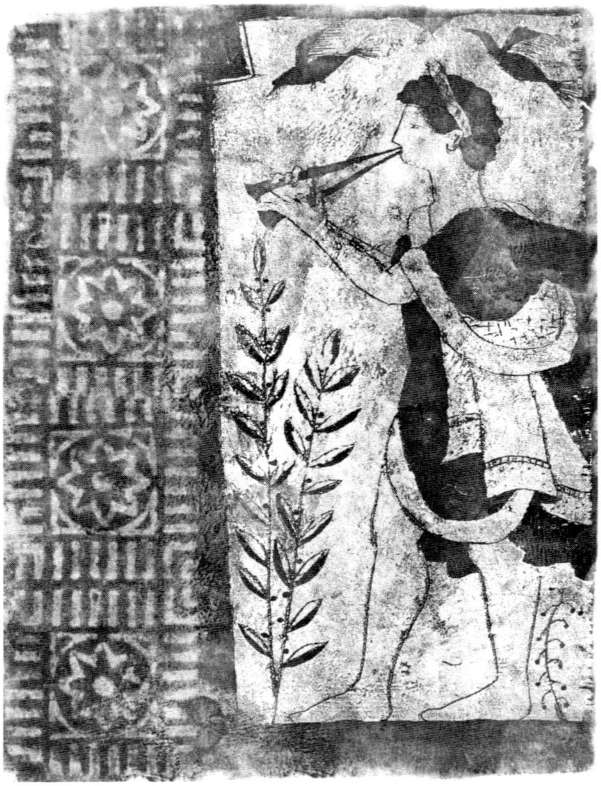

## FRANCES PHYSIOC ROWAN (Mrs. W.J.) ex-'32

Born 1908

238. THE MINSTREL 1968

Woodcut: 19½ × 14 in.; 49.5 × 35.5 cm.
Inscribed in pencil left to right: The Minstrel 3/50 Etruscan Series #IV imp. Frances Rowan
Gift of the artist, 1969

*Yes, indeed, the design at the left comes from those old bricks on the path in front of the English-Art building at Randolph-Macon. They fascinate me. When I returned for our 35th reunion, I was allowed to have one.*

*The print does look like a lithograph, but it really is a woodcut. It is so difficult to describe how I made it. The figure side was cut out of ¼″ pine plywood on which I rolled opaque white ink and printed that part. For the left side I made a rubbing of my brick with yellow and opaque white. When that was dry I rolled bright red, then sepia on the back of the print. I used a mouth atomizer to spray varnolene (mineral spirits) on the front after each color application, then blotted it. A light coat of sepia was also applied to the front, which was sprayed and blotted again.*

Frances P. Rowan

Exhibited: "Alumnae Achievement in the Arts," at the College, June 13–15, 1969.

## BEN SHAHN

1898–1969

239. GANDHI 1965

Serigraph in black:
Sheet, 40⅛ × 26 in.; 101.9 × 66 cm.
Design, 36¼ × 24⅛ in.; 92 × 61.2 cm.
Edition: unspecified; 29 known
Signed, lower right, in red-brown with brush:
Ben Shahn
Upper left: orange red chop
Fine Arts Fund, 1966

Exhibited: In the home of an alumna, Birmingham, Ala., Nov. 15, 1966; "Ben Shahn," Oct. 12-Nov. 2, 1968, Kennedy Galleries, New York, #44 with repro.; "Ben Shahn: A Retrospective," circulated from Oct. 1977 to Jan. 1978 to The Jewish Museum, New York, University of Georgia in Athens, Amon Carter Museum in Fort Worth, University of Texas in Austin, Cincinnati Art Museum, and the Spertus Museum in Chicago.

Recorded: In catalogues of the exhibitions; and Kneeland McNulty, *The Collected Prints of Ben Shahn* (Philadelphia, 1967), #20 with repro.; Kenneth W. Prescott, *The Complete Graphic Works of Ben Shahn* (New York, 1973), p. 59, with repro.

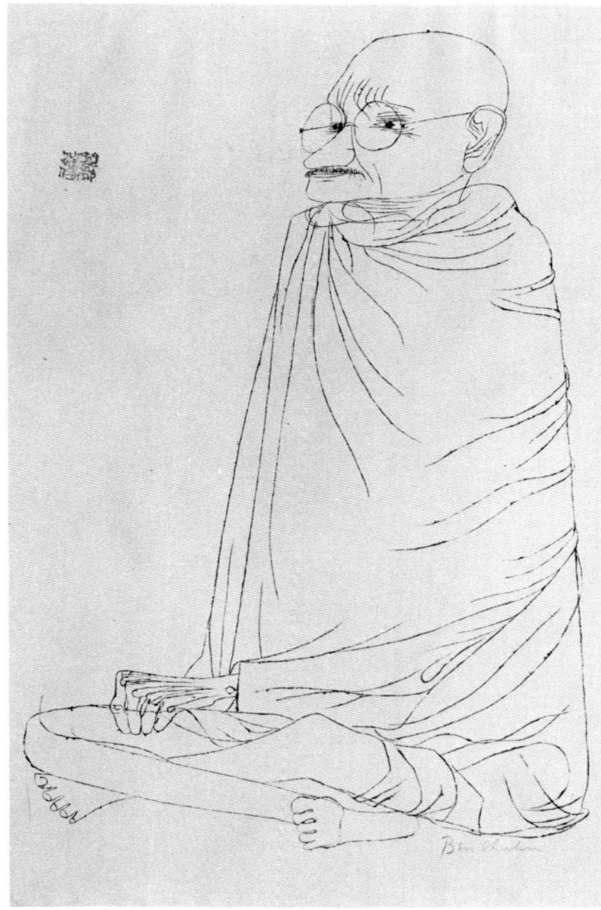

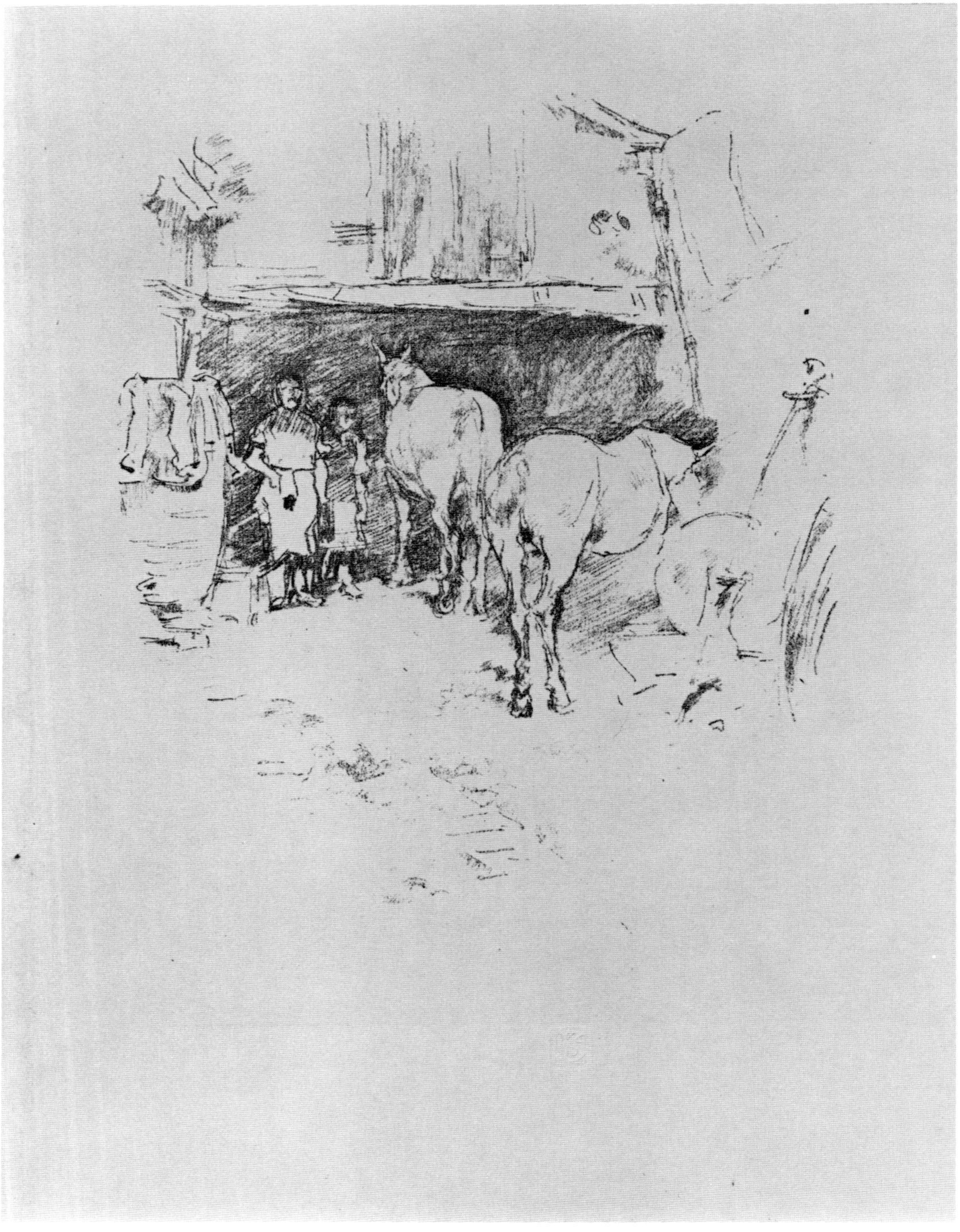

## JAMES McNEILL WHISTLER
1843–1903

240. THE SMITH'S YARD 1895 (W88)[1]

Lithograph,
Sheet: 11½ × 8½ in.; 29.2 × 21.5 cm.
Design: 7¼ × 6¼ in.; 18.4 × 15.8 cm.
Gift of the Carnegie Corporation, 1937

The date is 1895 because the proofs were pulled then, but the first actual publication occurred in two issues of *International Studio*, one dated February 1897 and the other March 1897. The blindstamp (embossed without ink) differs in the two editions. This one (bottom, right of center), *I S* in a square, identifies the second printing. The stained left edge of the print shows where it was tipped into the periodical.

1. The letter *W* indicates the number of this print in Thomas R. Way, *The Lithographs by Whistler* (New York, 1914).

## MARGARET H. WRIGHT (Mrs. J. H.)
1869–1936

241. CALVAIRE, ST. GUIMILIAU 1904

Etching: 7¾ × 10 in.; 19.6 × 25.4 cm.
Edition of 25
Signed in pencil, lower right: Margaret H. Wright
Edition recorded in pencil, lower left: ed 25
Gift of Mr. and Mrs. James H. Wright (Mary C. Stigall '35), 1967

Recorded: Mary Stigall Wright, "Conway Rang for Graphic Arts," *Alumnae Bulletin* 63 (Summer 1970), p. 2, repro. p. 4.

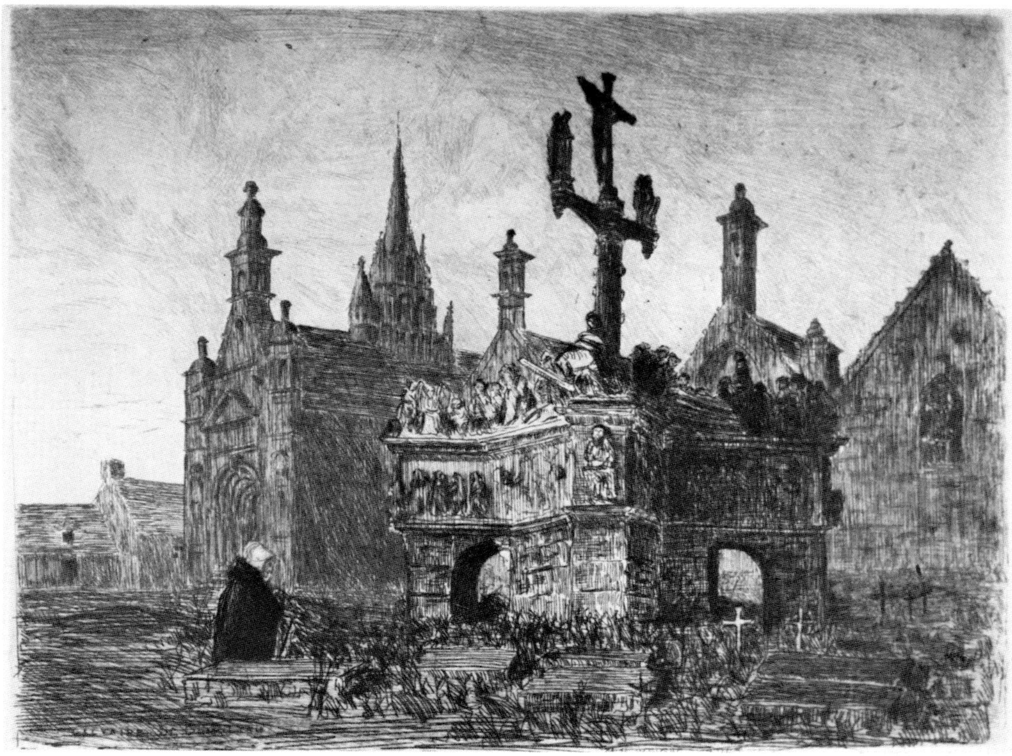

# Recent Acquisitions (through October 1976)

## Hazel Ladin

The Secret Place 1975

Oil: 30 × 34 in.; 76.2 × 86.3 cm.
Signed, lower right: Hazel Ladin
Gift of Mrs. Andrew A. Smith (Mary Virginia Barnes '35), 1976

## Grandma Moses (Anna Mary Robertson Moses)

1860–1961

Old Water Wheel

Oil on composition board: 12 × 16 in.; 30.4 × 40.6 cm.
Signed, lower right: Moses
Gift of Mr. and Mrs. Sam R. Shaw (Anne W. Dunn '44) in honor of their daughter Dorothy Cobbs Shaw ex-'71, 1976

## Henry Rodrick Newman

About 1833–1917/18

View of Santa Maria Novella 1879

Watercolor: 18¼ × 22¼ in.; 46.3 × 56.5 cm.
Signed and dated, lower left: H. Rodrick Newman 1879
Louise J. Smith Fund, 1976

## Doris Rosenthal

1895(?)–1971

The following were given by the Estate of Doris Rosenthal through Mrs. Alan Gruskin, 1976

Pantheon San Dionisio 1965

Oil: 28 × 36¼ in.; 71.1 × 92 cm.
Signed and dated, lower right: Doris Rosenthal 1965

Begonia Silvestre, Yolanda

Pastel: 18½ × 23¾ in.; 46.9 × 60.3 cm.
Signed, center: Doris Rosenthal

Domingo Pacajó calling the coffee pickers to come in for the accounting

Charcoal: 23¾ × 19 in.; 60.3 × 48.2 cm.
Titled, left; signed, lower right: Doris Rosenthal

Seated Boy

Charcoal: 23¾ × 18½ in.; 60.3 × 46.9 cm.
Signed, lower right: Doris Rosenthal

Night Train

Lithograph: 14 × 10 in.; 35.5 × 25.4 cm.
Titled, numbered, and signed in pencil, left to right: Night Train, 64/73 Doris Rosenthal

Bottoms Up

Lithograph: 10½ × 14 in.; 26.6 × 35.5 cm.
Titled, numbered, and signed in pencil, left to right: Bottoms Up 98/109 Doris Rosenthal

Dahlias

Lithograph: 15 × 12 in.; 38.1 × 30.4 cm.
Titled, numbered, and signed in pencil, left to right: Dahlias 22/30 Doris Rosenthal

Flowers and Fruit

Lithograph: 15 × 11½ in.; 38.1 × 29.2 cm.
Titled, numbered, and signed in pencil, left to right: Flowers and Fruit 51/95 Doris Rosenthal

## Henry Miller

Born 1909

Portrait of Howard Levinson (1921–43) 1937

Oil: 18 × 14 in.; 45.7 × 35.5 cm.
Signed with a pen name, lower right: S. Mlawa.
Bequest of the subject's mother, Mrs. Frank Levinson (Hortense Harrison '18), 1976

Appendixes

Bibliography

Index

# Appendix A: Donors (through October 1976)

## Groups

Allen Tucker Memorial Foundation
Alumnae Association
Alumnae of Atlanta, Georgia
Alumnae of the Hampton Roads Chapter
Alumnae of Massachusetts
Alumnae of New York, New York
Alumnae of the Northern Delaware Chapter
American Academy of Arts and Letters (Childe Hassam Fund)
Anonymous
Art Club of Randolph-Macon Woman's College

Class of 1907
Class of 1910
Class of 1912
Class of 1928
Classes of 1930 and 1931
Class of 1954
Class of 1975
Commercial Trust and Savings Bank, Lynchburg
Cooperative Building and Loan Association, Lynchburg

Depositors Bank, Lynchburg

Faculty Members
First Federal Savings and Loan Association, Lynchburg
First National Bank of Lynchburg
Friends of the College

German Club

Cynthia Hellman Memorial Fund

International Graphic Arts Society

Lynchburg Historical Society Members

Macbeth Gallery (William Macbeth, Inc.)

National Academy of Design (Henry Ward Ranger Fund)

People's National Bank and Trust Company, Lynchburg

Randolph-Macon Art Association (1920–26)
Rothschild Foundation

Salmagundi Club
Steptoe and Patteson, Inc.
Students and Friends of Herbert C. Lipscomb
Students of Pierre Daura in the Classes of 1947, 1948, 1949, and 1950

## Individual Donors

*The following list includes the maiden names of donors who are alumnae.*

G. Murrell Alexander
Susie Ames
Burch D. Arthur

Frederick Clay Bartlett
Bess Barzansky (Mrs. Charles)
Dr. and Mrs. Ben T. Bell (Dorothy L. Fincke)
W. J. Davis Bell
Mrs. Tyler Berry, Jr. (Sarah M. Roberts)
Mr. and Mrs. Chauncey J. Blair

Cornelius N. Bliss
Mrs. C. N. Bliss (later Mrs. A. Conger Goodyear)
Laura Bliss
Mrs. Paul Bliss
Louise A. Blunt
Ruth H. Blunt
Mr. and Mrs. Leonard Bocour
George E. Booker, III
Mrs. E. M. Bowman (Ellen O. Sheltman)
E. Thurman Boyd
E. R. Brumley

Evelyn Wiggin Casner (Mrs. Sidney)
Norma Chambers
Mrs. Walter B. Chandler (Georgia Harman)
William Merritt Chase
Owen R. Cheatham
Mrs. Donald Church
Imogene B. Claiborne
Stephen C. Clark
Merton Clivette
Susan P. Cobbs
Timothy Cole
Roberta D. Cornelius
John W. Craddock
Phyllis Crawford
Catherine Carter Critcher
Hélène Crooks

Susan H. Dabney
Pierre Daura
Mabel Davidson
Mrs. John H. Davis (Hilda L. Forsberg)
Dr. and Mrs. David H. Dawson
Mrs. Horace T. Day (Elizabeth Nottingham)
Mr. and Mrs. Samuel Dorsky
Mrs. E. Gorham Downing
Edward Dufner
Mrs. Middleton H. Dulaney

S. G. Fisher
Harriet Fitzgerald
Ida Fitzgerald
Mrs. M. A. Floyd
Robert S. Fuller

Annie Kate Gilbert
Mrs. Andrew C. Gleason
Mr. and Mrs. Sam Golden
Mrs. Claiborne W. Gooch
Mrs. A. Conger Goodyear
Mr. and Mrs. C. Wesley Goyer, Jr.
Mrs. Benjamin Guggenheim
Mr. and Mrs. Max Guggenheimer
(Mary E. Strickland)

Mrs. Simon Guggenheimer
Mrs. C. Bell Gurkin (Clara Bell)

Dorothy Harrison
Mrs. Childe Hassam
Hester Hastings
Margaret Helbig
Mr. and Mrs. W. B. Helferich
Lena Bondurant Henderson
Sterling Henkens
Mr. and Mrs. Edward L. Holsten
(Nancy Stinnett)
Jules Horelick
Dorothy Hughes
M. Gweneth Humphreys

Mrs. Paul Ingraham (Lulu Clark)

Theodore H. Jack
Eleanor Jennings
Mrs. Orville M. Johnson (Mary Ball)
Mrs. John Page Jones (Miriam D. Moss)

Mary Virginia Kagey
Thomas H. Kenny, Jr.
Mrs. Ben Witt Key
Mr. and Mrs. John P. Kirby
Margaret M. Kirkpatrick
Virginia Lee Kiser
Mrs. Eric T. H. Kjellstrom

Gillie A. Larew
Mrs. Harold G. Leggett
Bequest of Mrs. Frank Levinson
(Hortense Harrison)
Herbert C. Lipscomb

Mrs. Robert W. Macbeth
Mrs. William Macbeth
Lawrence R. McCoy
Robert G. McIntyre
Mrs. Robert McKey (Mattie Lee Toomer)
Marion V. Magruder
Julia Mahood
Mrs. William M. Maiden (Rachel Bell)
Mrs. Reginald Marsh
Julie Marshall
Paul Martel
Mrs. Gerhard Masur
Mrs. Fordyce Mitchel
Mrs. Clifford B. Moller (Mary S. Elkins)
Catherine Murphy

Mr. and Mrs. Roy R. Neuberger
Catherine Nicholson

Mrs. Laurent Oppenheim

Mrs. Ross E. Pearl (Louisa Dallis)
Mrs. Kirk Perrow, Jr.
Duncan Phillips
Althea Hill Platt
Mrs. John Garland Pollard, Jr.
Margaret Love Porter

William F. Quillian, Jr.

Mr. and Mrs. Alfredo Ramón
(Elizabeth J. Uelsmann)
Mrs. John Marshall Ribble (Anne Jeter)
Douglas A. Robertson
Estate of Doris Rosenthal
Mrs. Walter J. Rowan (Frances Physioc)

Mr. and Mrs. Edwin St. Vincent
Mrs. Stuart Saunders
Mr. and Mrs. Philip L. Scruggs
(Kathleen Morris)
Mr. and Mrs. Sam R. Shaw (Anne W. Dunn)
Dr. and Mrs. Andrew A. Smith
(Mary Virginia Barnes)
Louise Jordan Smith
Mr. and Mrs. Carl Stern
Eleanor Struppa

Mr. and Mrs. Alan H. Temple
Dr. and Mrs. Alexander H. Terrell
Mary Frances Thelen
Nan Thornton
Thomas F. Torrey II
Mrs. George Turner

Mrs. Matthew Walzer
(Katherine Bowman)
Franklin Watkins
Ethel Watson
Willie T. Weathers
Francis M. Weld
Mrs. Addison White (Carolyn C. Webb)
Dr. Francis R. Whitehouse
Annie C. Whiteside
Mabel K. Whiteside
Mary Frances Williams
Mrs. J. W. Wiltshire, Jr.
Mrs. Robert N. Winfree
H. Donald Winkler
Mrs. Eleanor C. H. Winslow
Elizabeth Eley Wright
Mr. and Mrs. James H. Wright
(Mary C. Stigall)

Mrs. Annie Henderson Young

# Appendix B: Loan and Circulating Exhibitions of the Collection

The paintings in each exhibition are identified in the table following this list.

I. 1949–50 *SOUTHERN STATES* "Fifteen Paintings from the Collection of Randolph-Macon Woman's College," circulated by the Alumnae Association.
Nashville, Tenn., Centennial Club, Oct. 10–21, 1949;
Birmingham , Ala., Birmingham Public Library, Nov. 1949;
Atlanta, Ga., High Museum, Dec. 4–18, 1949;
Asheville, N.C., Pack Memorial Library, Jan. 1–31, 1950.

II. 1964 *RICHMOND, VA.* "Randolph-Macon Woman's College Collection," Virginia Museum, Richmond, Sept. 11–Oct. 18, 1964 (fifty-four paintings).

III. 1964 *ROANOKE, VA.* "Selections from the Randolph-Macon Woman's College Collection," Roanoke Fine Arts Center, Dec. 6, 1964–Jan. 17, 1965 (twenty-one paintings).

IV. 1965 *FLORIDA* "Two Centuries of American Painting from the Collection of Randolph-Macon Woman's College" (twenty-one paintings), organized by the Tampa chapter of the Alumnae Association, and sponsored by local chapters to celebrate the seventy-fifth anniversary of the College in 1965–66.
Tampa Art Institute, Feb. 27–Apr. 25, 1965.
Loch Haven Art Center, Orlando, May 14–31, 1965.
University Gallery, Gainesville, June 6–27, 1965.
Cummer Gallery of Art, Jacksonville, June 29–Aug. 1, 1965.

V. 1966–67 *MID-ATLANTIC STATES* "Paintings from the Collection of American Painting at Randolph-Macon Woman's College" (thirty-three paintings).
Wilmington (Del.) Society of the Fine Arts, Oct. 10–Nov. 6, 1966.
Lincoln University, Oxford, Pa., Nov. 10–27, 1966.
Montclair (N.J.) Art Museum, Dec. 11, 1966–Jan. 22, 1967.
Weatherspoon Gallery, University of N.C., Greensboro, Feb. 11–Mar. 5, 1967.
J. B. Speed Art Museum, Louisville, Ky., May 9–July 30, 1967.
Tennessee Fine Arts Center, Cheekwood, Nashville, June 28–July 30, 1967.

VI. 1969–70 ARTMOBILE "The Randolph-Macon Woman's College Collection of American Art" (eighteen paintings), an exhibition organized by the Virginia Museum, Richmond. The Artmobile visited twenty-eight chapters and affiliates of the Virginia Museum and sixteen colleges and universities.

VII. 1972 *WINSTON-SALEM* "Randolph-Macon at Reynolda House," Winston-Salem, N.C., Mar. 17–26, 1972 (ten paintings).

## Paintings in Each Loan Exhibition of the Collection

| This Catalogue Number | Artist | Title of Painting | I (1949–50) | II (1964) | III (1964) | IV (1965) | V (1966–67) | VI (1969–70) | VII (1972) |
|---|---|---|---|---|---|---|---|---|---|
| | | | The numerals below the dates refer to the number of a painting in the list or catalogue of the loan exhibition. | | | | | | |
| 7 | Avery | "Child and Mother" | | 1 | 1 | 1 | 1 | 1 | 1 |
| 8 | Beal | "Launching the Boat" | 1 | | | | | | |
| 9 | Bellows | "Men of the Docks" | | 2 | 2 | 2 | 2 | | |
| 10 | Benton | "Preparing the Bill" | | 3 | | | | | |
| 11 | Blume | "Crucifixion" | | 4 | 3 | 3 | 3 | 2 | 2 |
| – | Carlson, J. F. | "Winter" | 2 | | | | | | |
| 19 | Carroll | "Portrait of Dr. H. C. Lipscomb" | | 5 | | | | | |
| 18 | Carroll | "Summer Afternoon" | 3 | 6 | 4 | 4 | 4 | | |
| 22 | Chase | "Portrait of Elbert Hubbard" | | 7 | | | 5 | | |
| 21 | Chase | "Portrait of Pres. W. W. Smith" | | 8 | | | | | |
| 25 | Cole | "Corway Peak, New Hampshire" | | 9 | 5 | 5 | 6 | 3 | |
| 26 | Daura | "Lozzi, Island of Corsica" | | 10 | | | | | |
| 29 | Davies | "Gypsy Encampment" | | 11 | | | | | |
| 44 | Davies | "Outskirts of Paris" | | 12 | | | | | |
| 42 | Davies | "Star in the North" | | 13 | | | | | |
| 34 | Davies | "Wild He-Goat Dance" | | 14 | 6 | 6 | 7 | | |
| 52 | Davis, S. | "The Fountain" | | 15 | | | 8 | | |
| 53 | Day, E. N. | "Edge of the Wood" | | 16 | | | | | |
| 57 | Day, W. | "Wilderness III" | | 17 | | | | | |
| 61 | Dove | "Cow #1" | | 18 | 7 | 7 | 9 | 5 | |
| 64 | Durand | "The Sketcher" | | 19 | | | | | |
| – | Dwight, Mabel | "Dusk" (litho.) | 4 | | | | | | |
| 66 | Eakins | "Portrait Sketch of W. H. Macdowell" | 5 | 20 | 8 | 8 | 10 | | |
| 72 | Fitzgerald | "1957 Forest Series #4" | | 21 | | | | | |
| 81 | Fowler | "Portrait of Lena E. Bondurant" | | 22 | | | 11 | | |
| 85 | Fuller, R. S. | "Round Table No. 1" | | 23 | | | | | |
| 84 | Fuller, R. S. | "Yellow Apples" | | 24 | | | | | |
| 87 | Graves | "In the Night" | | 25 | | | 12 | 6 | |
| 91 | Gwathmey | "Front Porch" | | | | | | | 3 |
| 92 | Hall | "Chestnut Woods in Fall" | | 26 | | | | | |
| 94 | Hartman | "Connecticut Highway" | 6 | | | | | | |
| 95 | Hassam | "Early Evening After Snowfall' | 7 | 27 | 9 | | 13 | | |
| 98 | Henri | "Tom" | | 28 | 10 | 9 | 14 | 7 | |
| 101 | Homer | "Paris Courtyard" | | 29 | 11 | 10 | 15 | 8 | |
| 102 | Hopper | "Mrs. Scott's House" | 8 | 30 | | 11 | 16 | 9 | |
| 104 | Inness | "Perugia and the Valley" | | 31 | | | 17 | 10 | |
| 116 | Köllner | "Lynchburg in 1845" | | 32 | | | | | |
| 117 | Kuhn | "Medicine" | | 33 | | | | | |

Paintings in Each Loan Exhibition of the Collection (contd.)

| *This Catalogue Number* | *Artist* | *Title of Painting* | The numerals below the dates refer to the number of a painting in the list or catalogue of the loan exhibition. I *(1949–50)* | II *(1964)* | III *(1964)* | IV *(1965)* | V *(1966–67)* | VI *(1969–70)* | VII *(1972)* |
|---|---|---|---|---|---|---|---|---|---|
| 122 | Lawson | "Moret-sur-Loing" | | 34 | | | | 11 | |
| 123 | Levine | "Café" | | 35 | 12 | 12 | 18 | 12 | 4 |
| 133 | McFee | "Golden Leaves" | | 36 | | | 20 | | |
| 130 | Marin | "Taos Mountain" | 9 | 37 | 13 | 13 | 19 | 13 | 5 |
| 138 | Morris | "Toward Yesterday" | | | | | 21 | 14 | |
| 141 | O'Keeffe | "Yellow Cactus" | 10 | 38 | 14 | 14 | 22 | 15 | 6 |
| 143 | Palmer | "End of a Holiday" | 11 | | | | | | |
| 145 | Prendergast | "The Idlers" | | 39 | 15 | 15 | 23 | 16 | |
| 147 | Robinson | "Valley of the Seine" | 12 | 40 | | | 24 | 17 | |
| 149 | Ryder, A. P. | "A Country Girl" | | 41 | 16 | 16 | 25 | | |
| 150 | Ryder, C. F. | "Vermont Hills" | 13 | | | | | | |
| 155 | Shahn | "It's No Use To Do Any More" | | | | | 26 | | 7 |
| 157 | Sloan | "Sun and Wind on the Roof" | | 42 | 17 | 17 | 27 | 18 | |
| 159 | Smith | "A Campus Group" | | 43 | | | | | |
| 160 | Smith | "Our Wistaria" | | 44 | | | | | |
| 158 | Smith | "Self-Portrait" | | 45 | | | | | |
| 163 | Speicher | "Portrait of Dr. T. H. Jack" | 14 | 46 | | | | | |
| 164 | Stovall | "Swing Low, Sweet Chariot" | | | | | 28 | | |
| 165 | Stuart | "Portrait of Mrs. Polly Hooper" | | 47 | 18 | 18 | 29 | | |
| 166 | Tamayo | "Troubadour" | | 48 | 19 | 19 | 30 | | 8 |
| 170 | Twachtman | "Azaleas" | 15 | 49 | | | | | |
| 172 | Twery | "Randolph-Macon Woman's College" | | 50 | | | | | |
| 171 | Twery | "Twilight in the Garden of Eden" | | 51 | | | 31 | | 9 |
| 179 | Watkins | "Negro Spiritual" | | 52 | 20 | 20 | 32 | | 10 |
| 182 | Whistler | "Tanagra" | | 53 | 21 | 21 | 33 | | |
| 184 | Williamson | "Autumn, Hudson River" | | 54 | | | | | |

# Appendix C: Exhibition Itinerary of the Abingdon Square Portfolio

Spring 1968

Michigan Technical University, Houghton, Mich.
College of St. Scholastica, Duluth, Minn.
Baker University, Baldwin, Kans.
Friends University, Wichita, Kans.
King College, Bristol, Tenn.
Methodist College, Fayetteville, N.C.
Oklahoma City University, Okla.
General Beadle State College, Madison, S. Dak.
Sullins College, Virginia Park (Bristol), Va.
Keystone Junior College, La Plume, Pa.

# Bibliography of the Collection

All of the following publications except item 9 are illustrated with reproductions of paintings.


1. Blunt, Ruth Homes. *The Lynchburg Art Club and Its Affiliates*. Lynchburg, 1962.
2. Buys, Jan. "Exhibitions from the Art Collection." *Alumnae Bulletin* 43 (February 1950):37–38.
3. Cornelius, Roberta D. *The History of Randolph-Macon Woman's College*. Chapel Hill, N.C., 1951.
4. Gilchrist, Agnes Addison. "The Growth of an Art Collection." *Alumnae Bulletin* 50 (November 1956):30–33.
5. Lipscomb, Herbert C. "Fiftieth Annual Exhibition: A Significant Anniversary." *Alumnae Bulletin* 54 (June 1961):19–20.
6. Nottingham, Elizabeth. "Silhouette of Miss Louise." *Alumnae Bulletin* 32 (November 1938):3–7.
7. Royce, Margaret. "Art at Randolph-Macon Woman's College." *Commonwealth* 20 (September 1953):24–25.
8. Von Keller, Beatrice. "Acquisition from the Bliss Collection." *Alumnae Bulletin* 43 (November 1949):3–4.
9. ______. "History of Randolph-Macon Woman's College Art Collection and Annual Exhibitions." In *Thirty Paintings: The Thirty-Eighth Annual Exhibition of American Art*. Lynchburg, 1949.
10. Williams, Mary Frances. "Paintings as Teachers." *Arts in Virginia* 2 (Spring 1962): 22–29.
11. ______. "The Randolph-Macon Woman's College Collection." *Alumnae Bulletin* 58 (Fall 1964):20–21.
12. ______. "The Painting Collection at Randolph-Macon," *Art Journal* 32 (Winter 72/73):192–95.
13. ______. "Time Makes Ancient Good Uncouth." *Alumnae Bulletin* 65 (Winter 1972):35–38.

# Index